The Battle for Palestine 1917

The Battle for Palestine 1917

JOHN D. GRAINGER

THE BOYDELL PRESS

First published 2006
The Boydell Press, Woodbridge

ISBN 1 84383 263 1

The Boydell Press is an imprint of Boydell & Brewer Ltd PO Box 9,
Woodbridge, Suffolk IP12 3DF, UK and of Boydell & Brewer Inc.
668 Mt Hope Avenue, Rochester, NY 14620, USA
website: www.boydellandbrewer.com

A CIP catalogue record of this publication is available
from the British Library
This publication is printed on acid-free paper

Typeset in Adobe Warnock Pro and Myriad Pro
by David Roberts, Pershore, Worcestershire
Printed in Great Britain by
Athenaeum Press Ltd, Gateshead, Tyne & Wear

Contents

List of Illustrations

List of Maps

A Note on Names

The combination of the erratic, more-or-less phonetic, spelling by the writers of the many British accounts of these events, the difficulty of transliterating Arabic into English, and the widespread replacement of the old Arabic place-names by Hebrew names, renders any attempt to devise an acceptable roster of place-names wholly impossible. I have therefore adopted a rule of thumb process by which the normal usage of 1917 is usually the name I have used. This is by no means a universal practice, and I have made no serious attempt at consistency – and in fact neither has anyone else. Despite the renaming of places in Hebrew it would only cause confusion to use modern names, and to discover any accepted general terms among the British forces is hopeless. In some cases names for features changed; in others the spelling changed (sometimes from page to page in the same book); and often a name was invented for a particular occasion – 'Sausage Ridge' more than once – and abandoned later.

A similar difficulty applies to the names taken by Turkish and Arab persons. Transliterating from Arabic to English is again unstandardized, and the replacement of the Ottoman Arabic script by the modern Turkish version of Western letters renders it only confusing when referring to or quoting contemporary (i.e. 1917) documents. For example, the Turkish Minister of Marine and governor of Syria is called Djemal in his book *Memories of a Turkish Statesman*, Jamal or Jemal in British accounts, and Cemal in modern Turkish. Hence I use a perhaps idiosyncratic set of names, but none is without precedent. For the rest I beg the reader's indulgence.

Introduction

T H E British campaign to conquer Palestine in 1917 is a founding event of the modern world. It brought about the definitive destruction of the Ottoman Empire and the creation of its successor states in the modern Middle East. The campaign therefore merits our attention.

Of recent years it has been studied with regard to the larger strategic and imperial problems, or from the point of view of the ordinary soldier. Here I hope to strike a balance between these two equally legitimate approaches, and to add in some consideration of the Turkish point of view, both the soldiers and the commanders.

Earlier studies have emphasized the role of the two main British commanders, Generals Murray and Allenby, and the contrast between them. I do not dissent from the emphasis and contrast, though I feel Murray deserves some sympathy. The dominant person is, however, Allenby, with no doubt at all. Yet the interpretation placed upon his actions, particularly at the third battle of Gaza and to some extent in the fighting in the Judaean Hills, is something I cannot accept. I feel that a new interpretation of his conduct of the fighting by no means diminishes his stature; rather it enhances it.

It is also necessary to bear in mind the outside pressures on the commanders, Murray's necessary partial preoccupation with events in and around Egypt, Allenby's constant difficulties with the War Office, and his need to pay attention, however intermittent, to the French. For one of the driving forces behind this campaign was an imperial competition between Britain and France. This was articulated in the various partition agreements made during and after the war, a process in which the British enlisted, with considerable diplomatic skill, both Arabs and Jews in furtherance of their own designs. And as a result of this diplomatic sleight of hand, the British Empire in the Middle East lurched from crisis to crisis for thirty years, and ended in chaos and the birth of the modern situation.

To the Border of Palestine

I N the first days of 1917 the British army in Egypt expelled the invaders, and moved right up to the boundary line which separated Egyptian territory from that ruled by the Ottoman Sultan. There was one final place to be captured, and then all Egypt would be free of the Turkish invaders. That place was Rafa, just a few hundred yards inside Egypt, and to attack it some of the British forces had to cross the border.

Rafa consisted of an unimportant village and, a little way off, a solid building in the form of the keep of a medieval castle on a hill called el-Magruntein. All around this central strongpoint was an open, almost flat area with well-sited Turkish trenches encircling it. To attack this position the British used a force of mounted infantry, British, Australians, and New Zealanders. The New Zealand Brigade rode right around the Turks' position to face it from the north, the Australian brigades faced it from the east and north-east; the British 5th Mounted Brigade blocked the west; between the 5th and the Australians was the Imperial Camel Corps Brigade.[1] To reach their assigned position the New Zealanders had to cross and recross the international border, which was also that between Africa and Asia. At the border Colonel Mackesy of the Auckland Mounted Regiment is said to have halted his men, ridden alone over the line, and thanked God he had been permitted to enter the Holy Land.[2]

The New Zealanders had two preliminary tasks: to capture Rafa village to prevent the people there from raising the alarm. The capture was made and the people corralled, but the alarm was nevertheless raised by the women, who set up an ululation which was clearly heard by the main Turkish force at el-Magruntein. The second task, which fell to the Wellington Regiment, was to put out a flank guard to the north-east to investigate the possible approach of Turkish forces from that direction.[3] At the actual attack, therefore, only the Auckland and Canterbury Regiments were at full strength. As they arrived at their assigned positions the New Zealanders found some incomplete trenches and captured several German and Turkish officers; 163 Turkish soldiers were also taken in the advance[4] – the surprise was thus almost complete. One of the captured German officers denied that it was possible for even the New

Zealanders to be able to take the fortified position. The New Zealand colonel is said to have replied: 'Huh, all right, we'll see – we're going to have a go – tell you later on'.[5]

Starting soon after dawn, the attack went on all day, and for a long time it looked as though the German officer was right, for it got nowhere. The British forces were pinned down in open country, facing a well-entrenched Turkish force that fought with determination. The defences in fact consisted of a circle of strong positions linked by communication trenches, the approach to which was a smooth open slope, a good mile wide. The one thing lacking was barbed wire, but, even so, attacking across the open land looked like suicide. It was impossible on horseback, for a man on a horse would present a huge target. The whole British force dismounted, the horses kept back out of range, and the men lay down. The only way to succeed was to use artillery, machine guns, and concentrated rifle fire to drive the Turks into their trenches and keep them there; for the men to crawl forward until the were within charging distance of the trenches; and then for the men to charge as fast as possible over the open ground. The most important of these was the artillery, for the British had an overwhelming superiority in that branch in the fight. The other weakness of the Turkish system was that it was in effect just a single circle of positions, so that once one part of it was taken, the line they were defending would break, and the rest would crumble. The Turks knew this, and knew too that if they could hold on long enough a relief column would arrive from the north which would attack their enemies and break their encircling line.

The initial conflict was at long range, consisting of artillery and machine-gun fire. There were few casualties, but gradually the Turkish fire slackened, perhaps due to a limited supply of ammunition. The dismounted troops advanced only slowly, but did so in a way which reminded observers of manoeuvres in training.[6] But the advance by short rushes was time-consuming, and expensive in ammunition.

By the late afternoon both machine-gun and artillery ammunition began to run short among the British attackers.[7] The machine-guns in the armoured cars were only kept going by their bandoliers being refilled by infantry riflemen from their own supplies.[8] The Inverness Battery of the Royal Horse Artillery had to be withdrawn from the fight when it ran out of ammunition.[9] Major Wilkie of the Wellington Regiment dumped a cart-load of cable on the road and used the cart itself to bring up extra ammunition for his regiment's machine-guns just in time for them to cover the final advance.[10]

The machine-gun squadron on a low ridge, which was able to give powerful support to the attack, was commanded by Lieutenant P. D. Russell of the Auckland Regiment. During the fight, it was recalled,

> The Squadron expended 40,000 rounds of ammunition, which exceeded the amount laid down to be carried by a Squadron. The ammunition pack animals could not be brought up to the gun positions to replenish supplies, which necessitated extra work for the ammunition carriers; had the ordinary regimental supplies also been brought up, the guns could have been used to greater advantage, as the fear of a shortage curtailed the volume of fire.[11]

The reserves of ammunition, and of food, had been left at Sheikh Zowaid, several miles back, in order that the night advance be swift and quiet.

In view of this Lieutenant-General Sir Philip Chetwode, in overall command of the attacking forces, apprised of the approach of the Turkish relief column by information extracted from the captured German officers and by reports from the detached Wellingtons and Australians, and afraid of being caught between the two Turkish forces, decided at about half past four that the fight was over, and orders were prepared for the retreat.[12]

This was, in fact, a most important moment in the whole campaign. A similar moment of decision had occurred in another fight two weeks before, at Magdhaba. There the problem had not been a shortage of ammunition, but of water. The general who decided to withdraw was Major-General Harry Chauvel, commander of the Anzac Mounted Division. He was in effect overruled by an impromptu charge by some of his troops, in which one of the Turkish redoubts was taken, leading to the progressive collapse of the whole position.[13]

Now the same situation had recurred. The commander this time was a newly arrived Englishman, who had only come to in Egypt in December, appointed to command all the mounted forces, as the Desert Mounted Column. When he ordered withdrawal from el-Magruntein it suggested that the worst weakness of the Egyptian Expeditionary Force lay in its commanders. But the order was actually more a sign of the commander's lack of confidence in his troops. Chauvel had learned that lesson, but he did not disagree with Chetwode, so far as we can see. Chetwode himself was also about to learn it.

The 5th Mounted Brigade, closest to the headquarters, got the orders first and began their retirement.[14] The New Zealanders were the most distant from headquarters and were the last to receive the order. Some New Zealand accounts suggest that it was not in fact received at all, and the war diaries of the

Wellington and Canterbury Regiments make no mention of it.[15] One account, however, by the author of the Official New Zealand history, is defiant: the 'instructions fell on deaf ears, for General Chaytor had just issued an order for the final charge'.[16] The men knew perfectly well that the withdrawal was about to happen and, presumably annoyed at all their work and losses would have been for nothing, the New Zealanders made a bayonet attack, machine guns covering the charging men, and broke into the Turkish line.[17] On the opposite side of the position the Australians and the Cameliers followed suit, and the Turks found themselves attacked from both sides.[18] At once they began to surrender. Suddenly the fight was over.

Nevertheless it had been an uncomfortably close thing. Chauvel had sent out a covering force to face the approaching Turkish relieving force, and it was in action by the time the Rafa defences were falling.[19] The whole British force was then so desperately short of ammunition, and Chauvel so apprehensive of the imminent counter-attack, that he ordered the immediate evacuation of almost all the troops, leaving one of the Light Horse Brigades as a rearguard to cover the removal of the wounded who were being cared for by a field ambulance.[20] The British had suffered 70 dead and over 400 wounded; the Turks had about 200 killed, and all the rest, over 1,600 men, were made prisoners.[21]

The charges of the New Zealanders and the Cameliers were the decisive actions, but in the longer view it was the British artillery which was the really vital arm. The charges could never have been launched had not the British artillery superiority forced the Turks to take shelter in their trenches. The Turks had only four light mountain guns with them; the British had four batteries of heavier guns, each of three or four guns, and they were positioned next to the units who charged.[22]

The German officer captured by the New Zealanders before the fight, and who had dismissed their chances of conquering, was very surprised at the result, and, according to the New Zealand version, 'his professional interest no doubt thoroughly aroused, began to ask all sorts of questions about these wonderful troops from the ends of the earth who had accomplished the impossible'.[23]

At the same time, their British colleagues were in no doubt of their accomplishment, and showed it when the victors returned to their camp, by turning out to cheer them home. 'Also, what was appreciated very much, they volunteered to man the pumps till all horses had been watered'.[24]

The main participants in this encounter were only a section of the British and Turkish forces in the wider area, but it was representative in many ways of the fighting which was to develop in the next year. The Turks were defending, the British attacking. The Turks held a fortified position, the British were in the open. The general gave up the fight before his men. The solid, unspectacular, basic fighting, the machine-gun and artillery fire, without which nothing could have been done, was carried out mainly by the troops from the British Isles; the decisive attack was carried out, informally and without orders, by a New Zealand battalion and by a brigade of Cameliers recruited from several countries. And most of the dead were Turkish soldiers, though the British suffered more if the dead and wounded – both of these were incapacitated, after all – are counted together. The defence was a very strong situation, and to attack required the attackers to outnumber the defenders strongly, and to be willing to accept a long list of casualties.

CHAPTER 1

The Decision to Invade

THE capture of Rafa concluded the first phase of that part of the Great War which was centred on Egypt. For the British the country was valuable above all because the Suez Canal ran through it, for this formed a vital part of the main route linking Britain and its eastern empire – India, Malaya, East Africa, Australia, New Zealand, and so on. In enemy hands it would provide just as easy an access to those lands. It was because the Turks had reached the east bank of the Canal, so closing it for a time, that the British forces had been fighting in the Sinai desert for the previous two years. During that time a series of other conflicts in the region had also developed, so that what had been a single area of fighting along the Canal had spread all over the Near East and nearby Africa. The fight at Rafa had marked the end of the two-year process of driving the Turks from the Canal, but the whole Near Eastern situation had changed in that time, and it now marked not just an end, but a point at which new decisions had to be made.

Egypt had been technically Turkish territory until 1914, though by then it had had for a century its own autonomous ruler, the Khedive. He in turn had gone into debt to greedy European money-lenders, and had been subjected to supervision by a Financial Commission whose purpose was to service those debts by managing the khedivial finances, and through them the whole Egyptian economy. Hardly surprisingly, this had not been to the liking of the Egyptians, for their welfare was low in the Commission's priorities, and in order to ensure that the Commission could operate, the British had occupied the country in 1882. The Khedive was retained in nominal authority, but a British High Commissioner was in charge of civil matters and a British Sirdar was in command of the Egyptian army; theoretical suzerainty still lay with the Ottoman Sultan.[1] The Ottoman layer of this curious situation was removed in 1914, when Egypt became a British protectorate, in the process of which the reigning Khedive, who was in exile, was replaced. This had been one of the justifications for the invasion by a Turkish army out of Palestine. The Turks had been stopped at the Suez Canal.[2]

In the Western Desert the Senussi tribe, which inhabited the desert and its oases west of the Nile and across the western border into Italian Libya, was roused to fight Islam's battle against the Christian British and Italians; in the south the Sultan of Darfur made a bid for independence from the British-controlled Sudan.[3] On the other hand, to the east, a complex series of intrigues in 1916 roused a rebellion against the Turkish government by the Sharif of Mecca in western Arabia,[4] while further south a Turkish force had invaded the country inland of Aden, a British-protected territory.[5] So during 1915 and 1916 Egypt, from the point of view of the British High Commissioner in Cairo, seemed to be besieged by enemies to the east, west and south, not to mention German submarine activity in the Mediterranean. But during that time the various enemies were gradually overcome. The action to capture Rafa had, in fact, been almost the last of these: the Senussi were overcome by November of 1916, and the rebellious Sultan of Darfur was defeated, though he did not fully admit it for some time; Aden could be ignored.[6]

Independently of all this, a British force had occupied part of southern Persia in 1914, and another had invaded Turkish Mesopotamia, at first to ensure access to the local oil supplies, but also to deter any Turkish attempt to attack India. The campaign was run mainly from India, and had resulted in a major British defeat during 1916. Though the southern part of the country around Basra was still held, the Persian oilfields were occupied, and revenge for the defeat was being planned.[7]

So at the beginning of 1917, with Egypt and the Suez Canal secured and the Turks expelled from Egypt, the question was what to do next. This was something the Commander-in-Chief in Egypt, General Sir Archibald Murray, had views about, but it was a matter in which he had to await the decision by the British Cabinet in London. And there the question was under debate.

General Murray had large responsibilities, not only for the defence of Egypt, but also for some aspects of the Allied forces in Slavonic. He had succeeded in defending his main base, in pushing back the Turkish invaders, and in beating down the Turkish-supported rebels, but the precise point at which to stop the advance east into Sinai had never been made clear. When the Turks were on the east bank of the Suez Canal he had made the valid point that to stand on one side of that 100-mile ditch and prevent the Turks from crossing was a very inefficient method of defending Egypt and the Canal, requiring five divisions of troops who simply occupied expensively constructed fortifications.

Murray argued that the best position at which to defend Egypt was well forward to the east, at the narrow point between the sea and the desert. The dryness of the Sinai desert would deter attacks by land, and the Royal

Navy would prevent any seaborne attack. A relatively small force, perhaps of Egyptian personnel, could be thus employed, and Murray identified el-Arish, a small village 30 miles west of the Palestinian border, as the most suitable place to locate it. He envisaged basing a mobile force there to intercept any attack which might come through the desert to the south, along the few tracks across Sinai. As a supplementary deterrent, the wells and water supplies in Sinai could be blocked up.[8]

So during 1916 the Egyptian Expeditionary Force under Murray's overall command advanced by stages across the northern edge of the desert of Sinai. The process was slow, because the Turks resisted with stubborn skill. They were reinforced by German and Austrian soldiers – specialists such as gunners, machine-gunners, and airmen: the whole group is referred to as 'Pasha I' (there was a later 'Pasha II'), and their importance led to the tactical command of the whole of the force being entrusted to the Bavarian Colonel Baron Friedrich Kress von Kressenstein. The Turks held on to a series of positions, each of which the British captured only after making considerable preparations.[9]

Apart from the fighting, which in each case was relatively brief, the main problem was supplies, particularly fodder for the many animals, and water for both animals and men. The solution, as befitted the country which still thought of itself as the Workshop of the World and had conquered the Sudan by means of a railway, was a railway for men and goods, and a pipeline which would carry water from the Nile to the troops at the fighting front. Neither of these could advance beyond secured territory, so the capture of each position was at once followed by the construction of a further section of railway and pipeline.

El-Arish was captured on 21 December 1916, after long preliminary work – and the Turks withdrew just before the attackers arrived.[10] This completed the project laid out by General Murray in March 1916, and was as far as he had intended to go. Perhaps it was what he still intended. He had accomplished a great deal in a year. The elimination of all threats to Egypt rendered the country a safe base for the British forces; the reopening of the Canal and its renewed safety removed most anxieties about the eastern empire, and it was now possible to reconsider the purpose of the British force in Egypt: was it to be a garrison, a reserve, or an offensive force? The Chief of the Imperial General Staff, General Sir William Robertson, whose job it was to lay out the strategic options for the Cabinet's consideration and decision, had always seen the forces in Egypt as an imperial reserve, available to be used in the Mediterranean or in the Indian Ocean as necessary. 'Egypt must be regarded as my general reserve', he wrote to Murray in March 1916, 'and of course the troops there must be ready for action.'[11] Robertson therefore disliked any offensive activity by Murray, other than that required to make Egypt and the Suez Canal safe. The need to look further east was much reduced once the Canal was secure, and the CIGS shifted his ground. 'All we want from you is to give the Turks a good hiding in the Sinai Peninsula', he wrote in August.[12]

A little later, in October 1916, Murray moved his headquarters from Ismailia on the Canal to the Savoy Hotel in Cairo. In his place a corps headquarters for the Sinai force, called the 'Eastern Force', was set up under the command of Major-General Sir Charles Dobell. The move and the change were made by agreement with London, and there were certainly some sensible reasons for them. The responsibilities of the C-in-C were much wider than the front in Sinai, and control of Egypt was his first priority; also the distance from the fighting front in eastern Sinai was physically not much more when in Cairo than it had been in Ismailia; but psychologically it was very much greater. For to the troops Cairo was rest, relaxation, women, drink, a place to go to on leave if possible. For the commander-in-chief to be there implied an uninterested attitude toward the campaign they were waging. Murray had excellent reasons for the move: with the end of the threat to the Canal, his presence was not needed; he was inevitably much involved in administration, a task he did very well, and Cairo was the best place to be for such work. And perhaps he really believed that the campaign in Sinai was finished, and that the defensive stance would be resumed once el-Arish was taken.[13]

Yet the troops in Sinai viewed this move in a very different light. Their conditions were most uncomfortable. They lived in tents, amid numerous unpleasant insects and reptiles; they ate boring food; they were in a land of sand and rock, with scarcely a chance to wash, never mind bathe; and periodically they had to be deloused. They suffered sores from the combination of all these unpleasantnesses, and, above all, most of them were civilians in uniform.[14] While their commander-in-chief was living in Ismailia, a dismal place on the Canal which many of them knew from their first arrival in Egypt, he was within reach of the fighting. The news that he had moved to Cairo, and to the Savoy Hotel there, brought out all the latent class hatred which existed particularly in the Australian troops, but also in the British soldiers from industrial and radical areas, such as South Wales, Glasgow, Norfolk, and parts of London. It was remarked by more than one diarist that at Rafa Generals Chetwode and Chauvel were close to the fighting. Many of them did not even know *who* Chetwode was,[15] for he had only recently arrived, but they knew *where* he was. Murray suffered badly by comparison. Yet if the aim of the campaign in Sinai was only defensive, the troops' opinion scarcely mattered.

There were still Turkish forces within reach of el-Arish: at Magdhaba in the desert to the south, and at Rafa, 30 miles further east. Both of these were dealt with in December and January. In doing so, and in using mounted forces, the British demonstrated the accuracy of Murray's estimate made before the advance began: the position at el-Arish was indeed ideal for mounting a mobile defence of Egypt. Robertson sent his congratulations, but added: 'Unofficially I think that you can do a great deal more with them yet, and give the Turks a real good shaking.'[16] He was no more specific, but it was clear that the issue of the future campaign was now open again.

The need to attack Rafa in particular had shown that el-Arish would have to be an active post, and that it had now been succeeded as the most advanced post by Rafa itself. But if Rafa was to be held instead of el-Arish, the situation was drastically altered, for Rafa was not a good point from which to defend Egypt. It was vulnerable to attack from Palestine, being much closer to the Turks' positions than to el-Arish, which was the nearest British post. And yet Rafa could hardly be given up or abandoned after its difficult and costly capture. It had had to be taken in order to defend el-Arish, which was needed to defend Egypt; now it was necessary to defend Rafa, and that meant the necessity of capturing Gaza. And Gaza was as much the entrance to Palestine as it was the defence-post for Egypt.

Thus the British found themselves dragged repeatedly eastwards, from the Canal to el-Arish to Rafa to Gaza. Yet it was not really necessary: el-Arish was far enough east for the purposes of defence. Further advances were needed only if the overall aims of Murray's command had changed. Murray's reasoning in 1915 was still valid. It would have been fairly easy to destroy the redoubt at Rafa, or even simply to ignore it if the Turks reoccupied it. But by the time the decision had to be made as to what to do next, the wider conditions of the area had changed radically, and it was no longer a matter of defending the Canal and Egypt.

Murray had arrived in Egypt in January 1916, just at the time when, across the Mediterranean, the allies were evacuating Gallipoli. His first priority had been to ensure the security of Egypt, and then to receive and succour the Gallipoli evacuees. This was fully in keeping with Robertson's definition of the place as an imperial base, but in the meantime a new commitment had been made to the Sharif of Mecca, and in Europe the conquest of Serbia and Romania by the Germans and Austrians during 1916 opened up the enemy route by land from industrial Europe to Constantinople. Russia's army had been badly damaged by defeats in 1916, and in France and Belgium the armies were still entrenched on much the same line all though the year and the casualties seemed horrific. (1916 was the year of Verdun and the Somme.)

Also during 1916 Britain had become the lynch-pin of the Alliance, the one power with a reserve of men and material and resources to maintain the fight. The main conflict was with Germany, but the Allies were also at war with Austria, Bulgaria, and the Ottoman Empire, and these could not be ignored. (Just as Germany could not ignore Italy and Serbia.) The Turks in particular had shown an extraordinary resilience for a country which for nearly a century had been commonly referred to as 'The Sick Man of Europe'. Turkish armies had defeated the British invasions of the Straits at Gallipoli and of Mesopotamia at Kut el-Amara, and had invaded Aden and Egypt. They had suffered defeat in the Caucasus and a Russian invasion of their eastern lands, but Russia showed no ability to advance further. They had been removed from the vicinity of the Canal, but if the British in Egypt remained on the defensive at el-Arish, the Turks could thin out their defences in southern Palestine, and use those troops, stiffened no doubt by a German detachment, perhaps in Mesopotamia, or against Russia. For the sake of the alliance, it was simply no longer possible to stay on the defensive in Sinai.

And then there was the new political situation in London. Early in December 1916 the Liberal-dominated coalition government of H. H. Asquith had fallen, and a new coalition had been put in place under David Lloyd George. The process had been messy, and a large part of the Liberal Party followed Asquith into opposition. Lloyd George, a Liberal, therefore headed a government whose main support came from the Conservatives. His position was necessarily weak, and it was essential that he stamp his authority on all sources of power. He strengthened government authority at the centre by using a small War Cabinet, and formed a Cabinet Secretariat that made him less dependent on other ministers to carry out Cabinet decisions.

Another node of power was the army, notably in the persons of General Sir Douglas Haig, the commander of the British Expeditionary Force in France, and General Robertson, the Chief of the Imperial General Staff in London. These two believed that it was their duty to fight the war in the most efficient way, which they interpreted as meaning that they should concentrate on the main enemy, Germany, in France. The new Prime Minister had a better strategic insight than the generals. Recoiling from the casualties in France, and seeking an early victory to help consolidate his own position, he wanted to explore alternatives. The result was the Egyptian Expeditionary Force saw the Rafa front converted from the defensive to the offensive. And that, again, meant Gaza. Robertson, who at first had been incredulous about Lloyd George's ideas, was reluctantly brought to accept that it could be worth trying.[17]

Yet his and Haig's argument, from which neither man ever wavered, that the decisive theatre of the war was the Western Front, was persuasive, and the War Cabinet agreed that a major attack should be launched in France in the spring of 1917. This required the greatest possible concentration of forces in France, and Murray was told in January that any offensive out of Egypt would

1 *Gurkhas in the trenches.* A Lewis gun post of the 3/3rd Gurkhas in front of Gaza. Unlike many official photographs, this shows a trench as it was in use, not cleaned up and tidied for the photographer. It is perhaps 5 feet deep, and built up higher by a sandbag parapet and by excavated spoil, with a fire step allowing the machine gunner to see through a gap in in the parapet. All around is the accumulated clutter collected by men who have used this position for some time. (Crown Copyright: Imperial War Museum Q 12937b)

not be possible before the autumn. Meanwhile one of his divisions would be withdrawn to fight in France.[18]

The force available to Murray had changed repeatedly during his time in command. The evacuated troops from Gallipoli were largely brought to Egypt to recover; most of them were moved on fairly quickly to France, but some remained in the east, and one division was sent on to Mesopotamia. Then the ending of the Senussi uprising released both the troops who had been protecting the Nile valley towns from Bedouin raids and the forces being used against the Senussi themselves, while the retreat of the Turks towards Rafa and Gaza meant that the Canal did not need to be so heavily protected. The division which Murray sent to France in February, the 42nd East Lancashire, had been a major force in Egypt since it had paraded through Cairo in November 1914 as a show of force to intimidate any rebellious-minded Egyptians.[19] Its departure, the various changes, and the need to plan for the autumn offensive, all required the army in Egypt to take stock.

What was available was a collection of units from all parts of the British Empire.[20] The Australian and New Zealand Mounted Division (already being called 'Anzac' for short), which had fought at Rafa, consisted of two brigades of Australian Light Horse, the 1st and 2nd, the New Zealand Brigade, which had broken the Turkish line at Rafa, and the British 22nd Mounted Brigade. Each brigade consisted of three battalions and a machine gun company, a total of about 1,000 men per brigade, so that, including attached units and headquarters staff, each division had a total of about 5,000 men, though usually fewer were available, due to sickness, leave, casualties, and so on.

A new unit, the Imperial Mounted Division, was formed with two more Australian Light Horse Brigades – the 3rd, transferred from the Anzac Division, and the 4th, formed from three light horse regiments which had been unbrigaded since arriving from Gallipoli – plus the 5th and 6th Mounted Brigades, which comprised battalions of British yeomanry from various counties. These two four-brigade divisions were the mounted part of the army, a very much greater proportion of the whole than had become customary since the development of the machine-gun. They were put under the command of Chetwode, as the 'Desert Column'.

In addition there were two independent mounted brigades. The Imperial Camel Corps Brigade had been active at Rafa; it was composed of volunteers from other units trained to move on camels but fight as infantry (as were the mounted brigades, of course). This was a substantial unit, of about 2,000 men, aggressive and self-confident, for its men had chosen to transfer to it largely in order to see more action. The second was similarly exotic, the Imperial Service Cavalry Brigade, formed of three regiments contributed by Indian Princes to the common Imperial effort. It consisted of the Jodhpur Lancers, the Mysore Lancers, the Hyderabad Lancers, a signal troop, and a field ambulance, about 1,000 men. As yet it was still small, but unlike the other Indian units in Egypt it was included in the force available for action.

The ending of the threat to Egypt released the infantry divisions and other units within the country from garrison duties. There were three divisions of infantry in Egypt after the 42nd was sent to France. The 52nd Lowland Division was composed of twelve Scottish battalions in three brigades; it had been in garrison on the Canal, and had moved east in the wake of the advance, essentially in garrison at each step. The 53rd Welsh Division was composed of three British infantry brigades, each of four battalions (five Welsh and seven English); it had been in garrison in Upper Egypt. The 54th East Anglian Division, which had also been garrisoning the Canal, was made up of three brigades of four battalions of infantry, mainly from East Anglia, London, and the East Midlands. In theory each of these three divisions was about 12,000 strong. A varied collection of other units, including several British dismounted yeomanry battalions and a number of infantry battalions, was then organized as the 74th Yeomanry Division, but this remained badly under-equipped for some time – it had no artillery, for example – and was under strength as well, for most of the units had fought and suffered serious casualties at Gallipoli. Each division had attached to it a variety of other units, artillery batteries, signals and engineer units, and headquarters staff, and each brigade had a machine gun squadron included in its establishment.

In garrison in Egypt, in the Nile valley, and along the Canal were a series of other units. A large number were stationed alongside the Canal: three Indian infantry brigades, two West Indian regiments, and several British garrison battalions. Others were also visibly present in the cities and the valley. The way these rearward troops were spread out was a vivid reminder that Murray had to pay particular attention to controlling Egypt, as well as fighting the Turks. It was the essential base for everything else, central to any Allied moves anywhere in the Near East: Murray sent units to Salonica, Arabia, and Mesopotamia, and had to watch Aden, the Western Desert, and Sudan as well.

As a result, a great part of the army in Egypt was effectively immobile, or otherwise unavailable to any attack on Gaza or beyond. When he was told not to attack before the autumn, Murray pointed out that he would need more troops when he did attack, and his present forces needed more and better equipment. Further, it was clear that most of the troops he did have needed extra training. For merely enumerating the units and counting the numbers is only the first part of organizing an army. Few of the units in Sinai had seen serious fighting on any scale – even the fight at Rafa had lasted only one day and was against a Turkish force of fewer than 2,000 men. The troops who had been in garrison were undoubtedly slack; all needed to be retrained in the latest fighting techniques; above all the defensive mentality which had affected everyone in Egypt since 1914 had to be replaced by an offensive one.

General Murray set to. He accomplished the reorganization during January and February, and, no doubt encouraged by Robertson's comment that he could do something with his army, he planned his next move, which was technically a preparation for the attack which was intended to invade Palestine. The Prime Minister had made it clear that, despite the need to concentrate on the war in France, the Egyptian Expeditionary Force was expected to get busy. Murray, in his sensible, careful, preparatory fashion, promoted the construction of the railway and the pipeline as far as Rafa, and planned an attack to capture Gaza, which was intended to give him a starting point for the invasion of Palestine.

CHAPTER 2

Defeat at Gaza

T HE Turkish army which had invaded Sinai in 1915 and had been slowly driven back to Gaza since then was usually commanded in the field by Colonel Kress von Kressenstein, but in overall command of the whole region and its armies was Jamal Pasha. He was governor of Syria, which included Palestine, and as such he was also commander of the armies in his province. He was one of the conspirators who had carried out the coup in 1908 which had seized power in the name of the Young Turks.[1] An able man, but one whose ambition was suspect, he was still a conspirator at heart, with plenty of his own plans for the future. At times he and von Kressenstein were in conflict, both because of their differing priorities and differing loyalties.

Von Kressenstein, whose official position was as Jamal's Chief of Staff, was an able and intelligent officer. He had gained substantial experience on this front over the past year, and had inspired considerable respect among his opponents. He was, however, hampered by an inability always to get the Turks to do what he wanted, and, of course, his loyalties were divided between Germany and his army. He was somewhat bull-headed and tactless, despising everyone on his side and on the enemy's; his ancestry was among the patrician class of Nuremberg, and his appearance was almost a caricature of the block-headed, thick-necked, pale-eyed, monocled German officer. He and Jamal shared a mutual personal contempt; this did not help their joint enterprise.[2]

The problem Jamal and von Kressenstein faced in defending Palestine was that they could not be certain what the British would do until they began to move. The obvious magnet was Gaza, but it was just possible that something different might be done. So at the beginning of 1917 Gaza was held by a small garrison of no more than two battalions of infantry and an Austrian mountain battery. The other obvious target for the British was Beersheba, a village with a substantial supply of water about 30 miles to the south-east of Gaza, all the more tempting because it was on the railway which the Turks were using to bring up supplies: this place was held by an infantry battalion and a cavalry regiment. Neither of these garrisons was intended to do more than be in occupation of their respective places. The real strength of the Turks lay in carefully located forces at prepared positions elsewhere, forces which were designed to cover the main targets. They were located at el-Kossaima, el-Auja, Shellal, and Khan Yunis, a series of mutually supportive posts along the border.[3]

Jamal also feared that the British would use their command of the sea to land a force somewhere on the Palestinian coast north of Gaza, so he held his 53rd Division well back at Jaffa, located so as to be able to meet such an incursion anywhere in southern Palestine, where the coast of dunes and beaches was ideal for a landing. Von Kressenstein himself was at Khirbet Jemmame, a day's march east of Gaza, with the 16th Division, and 4 miles away, at Tell esh-Sheria on the Beersheba railway, was the 3rd Cavalry Division. These two places were more or less equidistant from Gaza and Beersheba, but were actually facing the middle of the line between them. The two divisions were therefore ready to be moved to the danger spot, whenever it was revealed.[4]

The strength of the Turkish army in Syria was in theory nearly 60,000 men, but, as with the British forces, a good proportion had to be held back in the interior, both for internal security duties and because supply was difficult. In February 1917 the advanced posts along the border were abandoned, again just before the British were about to attack. The line between Gaza and Beersheba was now more densely occupied.[5]

This was a geographically well-chosen series of positions. Gaza was almost on the coast, a city of about 40,000 inhabitants, and so it became a substantial fortress; Beersheba was close to the Judaean hills, difficult land in which to move; it was on the railway and had a large and reliable water supply; the land between the two centres was rolling countryside, with a connecting road running along a slight ridge – a useful situation on which to develop defences. For the present, however, the Turks used a mixture of fortified centres – Gaza and Beersheba – and mobile forces located conveniently between them as a flexible defence.[6] This was essentially the same sort of defence as, on a much smaller scale, they had mounted at Rafa.

Both sides had air forces whose most useful role for the present was in reconnaissance, though the British had also used them as spotter planes to note the fall of artillery shells at Rafa,[7] and both sides indulged in bombing. The Turkish aircraft – in fact German, with German personnel – were based at Ramleh, in central Palestine, with an advanced base at Beersheba. This base was bombed several times by British craft, whose advanced base was at Sheikh Zowaiid, until the Germans pulled out.[8] The German airmen were also adept at bombing the British camps – large targets – and the railway and the pipeline were popular targets as well. The German bombs were aimed especially at the British engineers working to extend the railway along the northern Sinai coast. The Egyptian labourers sensibly ran away to escape the bombs, and this caused serious disruption to the construction programme. Construction never entirely stopped, and repairs were relatively easy to accomplish. The Germans had the edge in air power at this time, but the British were able to maintain themselves in contention. Shortage of aircraft prevented either side from maintaining anything like a permanent patrolling presence; both sides were a long way down the list when it came to receiving the latest planes.[9]

The Turkish retreat from Khan Yunis and Shellal and the other border posts unbalanced the British forces, which had to delay their next move until the railway and the pipeline reached Rafa; this came about late in March. The British had also now arrived in more benign country, and active measures were taken to locate and develop water supplies.[10] But to reach the troops the water still had to be carried. Camel trains were used, each camel carrying two small metal tanks, called 'fanatis', each of of which held 12 gallons. In the rear of the army there was a constant traffic of these animals, herded by Egyptian labourers, who often reached right to the front line with their supplies. Even so, until the army reached well into Palestine, water was the main constraint on activity, after the enemy.

As preparatory moves for the eventual invasion of Palestine, General Murray laid down that the army should achieve certain objectives: it should gain control of the Wadi Ghazze, a deep and difficult desert valley several miles in front of Gaza; inflict damage on the Turkish forces, that is, not permitting them to withdraw as they had at el-Arish and Khan Yunis; and make a swift capture of Gaza city.[11] The responsibility for this lay with General Dobell, the new army commander. He had been in command of the Western Desert Force for the last three months, having previously commanded the British forces who had conquered the German Cameroons. He was competent at commanding small forces, but it became clear that he was out of his depth at Gaza.

The British plan was that the Welsh Division and the 161st Brigade of the East Anglian Division would march directly against the city, while the Desert Column of the Anzac and Imperial Mounted Divisions would sweep round the city to the east, cutting it off from reinforcement by the troops known to be positioned at Beersheba and Tell esh-Sheria to the north and east. This move was to be commanded by General Chetwode, while Dobell commanded the infantry attack itself as well as exercising overall command. Dobell therefore sited his headquarters close to those of General Dallas, in command of the

Welsh Division – not a comfortable arrangement. The city was expected to fall easily, since it was believed to be lightly held. What the generals did not realize was that their plan had been anticipated by von Kressenstein's staff well before it went into operation, as is evident from the disposition of the Turkish forces.

Given the long process of preparation for the next phase of the British advance, it was unlikely that strategic surprise would be achieved, for neither side was able to establish a sufficient air superiority to deny its own air space to the enemy. Air reconnaissance therefore meant that both sides were fairly well acquainted with the position of each other's forces, though only in general terms. The accumulation of British forces in the first half of March was known to von Kressenstein and his staff, and the difference between the concentrations of infantry on the coastal side and the masses of horses on the inland side showed quite clearly that the British were aiming for a repeat of Rafa on a much bigger scale. Von Kressenstein responded by pushing reinforcements, including artillery, into Gaza itself. This was not clear to the British, for estimating the size of a garrison in a city was much more difficult than in open camps.[12] Nor did the British appreciate that the Turkish 53rd Division was about to move south from the Jaffa area.

The British had a distinct problem in their estimations of the enemy's position and strength. The first paragraph of Dobell's operation order for the battle, dated 24 March, is replete with uncertainties:

> The enemy's main body is in Tell en-Nejile-Huj area, south of the Wadi el-Hesi, covered by detachments about Gaza, Tell esh-Sheria, Abu Hureira, and Beersheba. He appears to dispose of two weak divisions, and fragments of two other divisions – the equivalent in all of between 2 1/2 and 3 divisions. One of these divisions appears not to number more than 6,000 rifles.[13]

Chetwode in his own operation order for the Desert Column, of the next date, estimated the number of Turks in Gaza at 2,000.[14] Later accounts silently increase this to 4,000, but this may still be an underestimate. It is clear that no reliable intelligence about Turkish strength had reached the British commanders. In fact, the city was now held by seven battalions of infantry and fourteen guns, together with a squadron of cavalry and some camel troops, all under the command of the German Major Tiller. Jamal was persuaded to start moving his 53rd Division towards the city, but they had quite a way to go, and Jamal did not accept the full urgency of the situation. Von Kressenstein himself moved his headquarters forward to Tell esh-Sheria, closer to the two divisions he was intending to use as a relieving force.

General Dobell, the commander of the attacking forces, was rightly apprehensive about his landward flank in view of the Turkish dispositions. The inclusion of the remaining two infantry brigades of the East Anglian Division in the Desert Column reassured him; they were designed especially to block such interference, but Chetwode also had to detach mounted forces to watch that flank. The British attack therefore was to be made by two infantry and two mounted divisions, but only part of the infantry could be used in the direct attack; the rest, plus a good many of the mounted men, had to be deployed to watch for the Turks outside the city.

The Wadi Ghazze was the first of Murray's preliminary objectives; it had been reachable ever since the Turks had withdrawn from Khan Yunis. It ran right across the front of the advancing forces, and this became the British jumping-off point. It was deep, sandy, and dry, and the high, steep sides provided good cover for both an attacking and a defending force, but it also presented a difficult obstacle. From the wadi the landscape as far as Gaza could be clearly seen.

The road from Rafa crossed the Wadi Ghazze about 4 miles from the city, and ran along a low ridge, the first of three. The ridge was quite straight, between the coastal sand-dunes on the left, and a second ridge, called the es-Sire Ridge, on the right. This second ridge culminated a little to the east of Gaza in a hill called Ali el-Muntar, which overlooked the city. Spread between Ali el-Muntar and the sand-dunes, across the road and in front of the city, were the gardens, olive groves, and fields around the city, divided into small sections bounded by cactus hedges. The cactus was man-high, up to 5 feet thick, and extremely tough and clinging – a natural barbed-wire, and much more difficult to penetrate. Parallel to the es-Sire Ridge was the third, higher ridge called Burjabye Ridge, which was interrupted about half-way to the city by a sudden rise at Khirbet Mansur. These three ridges were to be the lines of advance of the British infantry. They could be seen clearly from the city, and, once the troops were on the move, would be swept by fire from the shelter of the city itself, and from the cultivated, cactus-ringed land to its south. The whole Gaza position had been made into a position very like a huge Western Front fortress.

To the east of the Burjabye Ridge the land was less regular and less steep. Most of it was rolling downland, open and clear, cut by occasional dry wadis which were not as deep as the Wadi Ghazze. This was the terrain over which the cavalry would advance. It was good land for horsemen to gallop across, with few places, if any, where defenders could make a stand without extensive trenching. About 4 or 5 miles from the Wadi Ghazze, and running parallel to it in a south-easterly direction, was the road from Gaza to Beersheba, along a slight ridge. Though not yet an obstacle, this was the route along which the Turkish relieving force from Beersheba would advance.

The British plan was that the main infantry attack would be along the es-Sire and Burjabye Ridges, by the 160th and 158th Brigades of the Welsh Division respectively. The 159th Brigade was to be held in reserve to support either of these. The initial objectives of the infantry were about half-way

2 *Cactus hedges.* Every town and village in southern Palestine was surrounded by cactus hedges, which also often surrounded individual fields. They were several feet thick and provided a very difficult obstacle to an attacker and excellent cover for defenders, even more effective than barbed wire, with which they were often reinforced. The British soldiers found that only by cutting gaps in the hedges, at first using their bayonets, could they make progress, but once through one hedge, they usually faced another. The photograph shows a hedge near Deir el-Belah. (Crown Copyright: Imperial War Museum Q 13175)

from the Wadi Ghazze to the city, Khirbet el Sheluf for the 160th Brigade, Khirbet Mansura for the 158th. The Anzac Division would sweep out to the east and round to cut the city off from the north, while the Imperial Mounted Division would ride out farther to the east to provide mounted cover and to reconnoitre; Anzac detachments were to be sent out to the north similarly. Two brigades of the East Anglian Division, the 162nd and the 163rd, would follow the mounted advance to provide a firm basis to backstop the riders; they were to take up defensive positions at Sheikh Abbas. The Imperial Mounted Division would reach as far as the Beersheba road and send out patrols beyond.[15]

The first thing to note about this plan is its failure to use the numerical superiority of the British forces. Only two infantry brigades, a total of six battalions, were to attack the city, which by this time was defended by several Turkish battalions, so that the defenders may well have outnumbered the attackers. The mounted force was more concerned to watch for possible interference from the east than to attack the city, so that only three of its brigades would move against the city itself. These men were actually infantry, using their horses to reach their attacking positions, but they were only being used to mask the city when they could have been more usefully employed in providing a bigger force to attack from its vulnerable northern side. Much of the British infantry, including most of the Lowland Division, was held in reserve, and was never used in the battle.

The attack was set for dawn on March 26. For almost a week units had been moving up to their start line along the Wadi Ghazze, marching mainly at night in an attempt to conceal their moves from observation by the Turkish aircraft. The main problem, as ever, was water supply, which meant that troops had to arrive at their start lines at the last minute, but also that all units had to use the same watering points. The Welsh Division, commanded by Major General A. E. Dallas, at the tail of the line, had a march of almost 12 miles during the night of the 25th/26th – hardly a good preparation for a dawn attack.

Trooper Ion Idriess of the 5th Light Horse Regiment, part of the Anzac Division, had been keeping a diary since his arrival in the army. It eventually became so bulky that he threw out his emergency rations to make room for the successive volumes. The diary was eventually published in 1932, more or less as it was written, with only minimal editing, but it is one of the best accounts of life in the Australian forces in Palestine in 1917. He watched the British infantry moving up to the attack, and was suitably impressed. Here is part of his entry for 25 March:

It is black night now. The army has come, is coming, we can hear them marching by. All the Desert Column swarmed to the little crescent hills that line the great plain. Ragged men we are, a little weary, burnt almost black by the fierce suns of Sinai. We gazed into the dust-clouds that floated up between us and sun-set. A big cloud, spreading as it lazily rolled nearer was all crimson from the rays. I caught my breath.

We listened amazed, for there floated to us music – Bands! Masses of horsemen took shape. Then infantry! Brigade upon brigade, battalion upon battalion, column upon column, growing rapidly, spreading all over the plain, crushing wide lanes through the barley – the vanguard of the British Army.

... We gazed down on the closely packed ranks – they looked so well, so fit, so clear, altogether splendid. The rumble of their guns was a hoarse muttering – clink of chains – gleam of wheels – guns guns, guns! Splendid horses, shiny harness, polished chains, rumble, rumble, rumble, and ammunition columns coming, coming coming! ...

Then from all the little hills, the Desert Column called down joyful greetings to this splendid army. What boyish-faced, cheerful lads they are! ... And so on, right until after the sun dimmed down, tramp, tramp, tramp. It is late now, we feel that Constantinople is ours.[16]

The attackers crossed the wadi before dawn. Behind them the engineers began work at once in the wadi bottom to locate water. Before them, as the light grew, the attackers saw fog. Visibility was reduced to about 20 yards over much of the land they were to cross. The rising sun burned it off by about 9.30 a.m., but it hampered reconnaissance, especially by the staffs. The two brigades of the Welsh Division, the 158th (three battalions of Royal Welch Fusiliers and one of Herefordshire Light Infantry, under Brigadier-General S. F. Mott) and the 160th (one battalion each of Royal Sussex, Royal West Kent – the Buffs – Royal West Surrey, and Middlesex Regiments, under Brigadier-General W. J. C. Butler), advanced through the fog along the Burjabye and es-Sire Ridges respectively, and reached their half-way stages towards the city by 9.30. There they all waited as the brigade commanders conferred and objectives were allocated.

To their right the cavalry ride went exuberantly, the Australian Light Horse driving along at the gallop through the open country, cutting the telegraph on the Beersheba road, and riding right round to the northern side of the city. At Sheikh Abbas, south of the Gaza–Beersheba road, they chased after some

German aircraft which were parked on level ground; the planes escaped by superior taxiing speed.[17]

> At dawn [we] found ourselves in fine undulating grassy country. It was beautiful. Thousands of light horse and infantry marching across open country practically bare of trees with grass about a foot high, with here and there patches of poppies, daisies and buttercups.[18]

For men out of the Sinai desert this was a feast for the eyes, and many of the Australians surely saw it as a land very like their own.

By 10.30 the road out of the city to the north was cut, and in the process the Australians of the 7th Light Horse Regiment captured the commanding general of the Turkish 53rd Division, who was driving to Gaza in advance of his troops to prepare for their arrival. His escort fled, leaving him spluttering with fury – but he was in a carriage, not on a horse, so he could not flee.[19]

> The Turkish general refusing to pull up and surrender, Sergeant Holmes, in charge of a section of the screen, drew his revolver and shot one of the horses, taking the general and his staff prisoner subsequently.[20]

The general spent the rest of the day alternately demanding to surrender to an officer of his own rank, and complaining about Australian manners, a matter in which he would have found himself in full agreement with most British officers. An hour later some of the Australian horsemen reached the sea.

Behind them a great fan of horsemen spread out from the Beersheba road round to the northern road, a distance of 10 miles, with detachments thrown out towards the north and east to intercept any counter-attackers. In the process many small parties of Turks and Germans had been ridden down and captured, and there were still numbers of these enemy troops scattered about. Within that great fan of cavalry, the East Anglian Division, commanded by Major-General S. W. Hare, had moved forward to provide a more solid flank guard for the attack on the city by the two brigades of the Welsh Division. By 10.30, when the northern road was being cut, troops of the 163rd and 162nd Brigades of the East Anglian Division were entrenching themselves near Sheikh Abbas, thus prolonging the line held at that time by the Welsh brigades; the other brigade of the East Anglian Division, the 161st (four Essex battalions, under Brigadier-General Marriott Doddington), was at the Wadi Ghazze to act as a reserve for either the East Anglian or the Welsh Divisions. To the left, in the sand-dunes beside the sea, a detachment of one yeomanry and one infantry battalion (the Royal West Kent Regiment and the Royal Gloucestershire

Hussars Yeomanry) and two guns of the 15th Heavy Battery were to guard the flank. These troops were under the command of Lieutenant-Colonel N. Money of the West Kents, and the whole was referred to as 'Money's Detachment'. Its purpose was to block any possible Turkish moves through the dunes, but it was also prepared to attack if opportunity arose.

The fog had not really delayed by any appreciable extent any of the planned movements, which had gone ahead with precision almost to the minute. This is, however, a disputed matter. The cavalry tended to suggest that the infantry blamed the fog for the subsequent defeat; the infantry do not seem to have been seriously delayed. That there were delays is certain, but they were generally accounted for by other problems, like getting lost. The 158th Brigade's guide became lost, and then found that the tapes he had laid down had been removed by some officious officer; the brigade was led to its assigned position on a compass course by the Brigadier (Mott) on his horse, and were in position only a little late.[20] They then had to wait for others to arrive and for the Staff to confer; it was this which was the main reason for the delay. On the cavalry side, the Worcestershire's Medical Officer, Captain Oskar Teichman, became separated from the battalion when he attended to a man who had been hurt. Just as he was feeling lost, the battalion reappeared, having ridden in a circle by mistake.[21] The fog is mentioned in every account, but it seems to have played only a minor part in the problems of the battle – though it was a handy excuse later.

The fog did have one important effect, for it delayed the appreciation of the situation as a whole by the generals. As a result General Dobell, in command both of the whole attack and of the infantry assault directed at the central point of Ali el-Muntar, did not order it to begin until 11 a.m., and it did not actually get under way for another hour or so. Meanwhile, another brigade of the Welsh Division, the 159th (the Welch and Cheshire Regiments, under Brigadier-General Travers), was brought up to take part in the assault as well, and placed between the original two brigades. The 161st was also ordered forward to cover the right flank of the 160th, and took with it the rest of the East Anglians under Doddington. So when the attack began, it was made by four brigades of infantry. By that time the division had only one battalion in reserve, the Cheshires, and that was soon involved as well.[22]

Meanwhile the Turks and Germans were beginning to react. The capture of the hapless commander of the 53rd Division by the Australians was a sign that the Turks were already alert and moving. At Tell esh-Sheria von Kressenstein was informed of the British attack by 8 a.m. by an air patrol, and that it was developing as expected. His troops could not interfere with the British attack immediately, but he set them in motion to trap the attackers. He ordered Major Tiller, the commander in Gaza, to hold on to the last man – not an encouraging suggestion. He hoped to use the city as the magnet upon which the British would fasten while the Turks enveloped them from the east. One regiment of the 53rd Division was already on the march from Jaffa towards Gaza, and it was ordered to keep on marching after only a short rest. The 3rd Cavalry Division was set moving from the Jemmame area towards the village of Huj, and from there it was aimed directly at Ali el-Muntar, which was identified as the key to the whole Gaza position.[23]

These were moves which the British planners had anticipated, just as von Kressenstein had anticipated the British plan. But von Kressenstein had his own plan. The 16th Division at Tell esh-Sheria was sent to march to cut the British communications to the south of Gaza; since these troops were under von Kressenstein's own eye, no doubt they got moving first and quickly. The concentration of the British on the attack on Gaza meant that the Turkish troops at Beersheba were not required to stand on the defensive. They were accordingly directed to march on Khan Yunis, to cut the British communications, to harass any reinforcements and to trap those who might retreat from the potential débâcle at the city. Von Kressenstein had thus set a huge trap, a reverse of that of the British, and into it the British had obligingly walked. His aim was to destroy the whole British force.[24]

General Dobell had seen the danger of this move when the British plan was first made, which was why the mounted troops had been spread out so extravagantly. Von Kressenstein's numbers were somewhat fewer than the British, but he had certain advantages. The British were certainly not expecting such a huge envelopment; if it had actually come about, the Lowland Division at Khan Yunis might have foiled it, though not necessarily very quickly. Von Kressenstein could rely on a stout defence of Gaza, which would draw in the British infantry, who could then be caught in rear by his 3rd and 16th Divisions, if these formations could drive the British cavalry out of the way. The efficiency of the British mounted troops would rapidly decline the longer their horses went without water. The Turkish infantry, with machine-guns and artillery attached, would then be more than a match for the cavalry in the open. So, with the British infantry pinned to Gaza, and the degeneration of their cavalry, the Turks had a good chance of defeating the whole British force. The garrison of Gaza, over 4,000 strong since its recent reinforcement, was now being attacked by about three times that number of British infantry, and later by some of the cavalry as well. The bulk of von Kressenstein's force, 12,000 infantry and 1,500 horse, remained available for the envelopment movement. It was essential that Gaza hold out to allow the main force to operate.

So the delay of several hours by the British in launching the infantry attack towards the city along the two ridges was crucial. When it finally got under way, about noon, it went steadily, if slowly. The troops had to cope with artillery fire from the city, machine-gun and rifle fire from the gardens and olive groves, and with the hideous cactus hedges which lay across their path.

The British artillery was less effective than at Rafa, partly because Gaza was a much larger target. It was difficult to bring up sufficient supplies of shells to keep the guns working, and this time the Turks had more guns of their own, almost an equality in numbers. Observing the fall of shot was difficult, and communications with the infantry was poor. This was a legitimate complaint by the infantry, one they made much of later, but it did not seriously affect the outcome of the battle, which was decided by other factors altogether. Better artillery work would have certainly helped, however.

The Royal Welch Fusiliers and the Herefordshires of the 158th Brigade, advancing along the Burjabye Ridge towards Ali el-Muntar, reached the cactus first, and there halted to wait for the arrival of the other brigades on their left and right. It was then necessary to capture two preliminary hills before the assault on Ali el-Muntar itself could be made. Green Hill, south-west of Ali el-Muntar, from which machine-gun fire was blocking any advance by both the 158th Brigade and its left-hand neighbour, the 160th, had to be shelled severely before being partly captured by the Herefordshire men. 160 Brigade slowly cleared its way through the gardens south of the city, an area designated the 'Labyrinth' due to the complexity of the trenches there. The other hill, Clay Hill, south-east of Ali el-Muntar, was attacked by 159 Brigade, but not until the arrival of the artillery of the 161st Brigade could it be dominated and battered enough for an assault to be launched on the central objective, Ali el-Muntar itself.[25]

About 4 p.m. three Essex battalions of 161 Brigade began an attempt to complete the capture of Green Hill, but the task took until 5.30. Meanwhile a sudden attack by small parties of men of the Welch Regiment of 159 Brigade and the Welch Fusiliers from 158 Brigade had begun the difficult process of conquering Ali el-Muntar. They faced determined resistance from the Turkish infantry, but more British reinforcements came in, and the whole hill was captured by about the time the rest of Green Hill was taken. Clay Hill, shelled constantly, was captured by the battalions of the Welch and Cheshire

Regiments of 159 Brigade soon after 5 p.m. After rooting out the final resisters, all three hills, and the gardens around them, were in British hands by the time darkness fell. One author even comments that the troops were 'firmly established in the key position', that is, Ali el-Muntar.[26] In effect, the battle of Gaza had been won at this point, for these hills were the key to the whole Gaza position; the city was at the mercy of the British forces, had their commanders but known it.

All this had been too slow for the commander of the Desert Column, General Chetwode. After complaining several times in the morning about the slowness of the infantry attack, he had determined that his own men could take the city.[27] Dobell gave him permission to try, but it took several hours to organize, since to gather men for the attack Chetwode had to shuffle his forces, and it took a long time to communicate with them. By about 4 p.m. three of his brigades had been made available: the 2nd Australian Light Horse Brigade (commanded by Brigadier-General Ryrie) attacked the city from the north, the New Zealand Brigade (under Brigadier-General Chaytor) along the main road from the north, and the 22nd Mounted Brigade (Lincolnshire, Staffordshire, and East Riding Yeomanry under Brigadier-General Fryer) came in from the north-east.

The New Zealanders moved south along the Jaffa road about 4 p.m. The war diary of the Wellington Regiment gives the following account:

> Turkish ambulance station taken at 1625. The enemy shelled the advancing troops and a good deal of rifle fire was met with. But both were ill-directed and the advance went on rapidly up to the cactus hedges. Through these a way was cut with the bayonet and the advance continued. On the left … a Turkish trench with shallow narrow lagoon in front temporarily checked the advance but two troops under Lts Allison and Foley charged with the bayonet across the lagoon and bayoneted all the 32 occupants. In the centre the advance continued to the cemetery where strong posts were encountered and defensive positions taken up by us. On right a Turkish gun position was captured at bayonet point.[28]

These guns were later turned on a building from which rifle fire was coming. Trooper Harold Judge enjoyed himself very much in this advance:

> We had to gallop some distance across a flat intersected with ditches and low mud walls, and we jumped these in great style and as far as I know no one came to grief. It was very hard work for all concerned but

before night 'Samson's Hill' had been taken and a good foothold gained in the town ...[29]

The New Zealanders, by moving on horseback part of the way, got ahead of the Australians on their right (towards the sea), but all were slowed to a snail's pace by the cactus hedges and the sniping from the close country near the city. Each hedge had to be cut through, using only bayonets. Then there was another, only a few yards ahead. Progress was so slow that darkness fell before they were at the city itself. So far few shots had been fired at them, but that was ominous too: the Turks were apparently waiting until they could fire all at once. The 7th Light Horse Regiment reached a narrow lane, still some hundreds of yards from the buildings of the city, and stopped.[30]

To the south of the Australians the 22nd Mounted Brigade had much the same experience – a rapid approach and then a difficult struggle through the cactus, hindered by sniper fire. Both the 22nd and the New Zealanders made contact with men of the Welsh Division on Ali el-Muntar: 'patrols of [the 22nd] had already made contact in the streets of Gaza with patrols of the 53rd Infantry Division advancing from the south,'[31] and 'Such good progress was made that at 6.40 p.m. the 10th Squadron [of the Canterbury Regiment] closed in to the top of Ali Muntar simultaneously with the 53rd Division'[32] – though it was the soldiers of the Welch Regiment and the Royal Welch Fusiliers who took the hill.

This attack by the Welsh Division soldiers had been made several hours after the Turkish forces from the east had begun to exert pressure on the screen of mounted infantry put out by the Anzacs and the Imperial Mounted Division. The Worcestershire Yeomanry were in contact with the first Turks early in the afternoon, and spent several hours attempting to prevent their progress, by firing at the Turks from the flanks, so forcing the column to deploy, then disappearing. It was, on a small scale, the method used by the Turks themselves during the slow British advance across Sinai. It was an admirable use of cavalry against a less mobile opponent, and it stopped the Turks in at least one area.[33]

Lieutenant McConnan of one of the Anzac regiments which were sent out to delay the Turkish relieving forces had much the same experience, though not so successful militarily:

Things got very interesting that evening when it became our job to engage a large force advancing. My crowd was in support and did not get in touch with the enemy although there were plenty of bullets hopping about us.

Mounted work is good fun. You go for your life to a position with our guns behind tossing shells over your head. From the new position you look across a stretch of rolling country to a curtain of fire behind which are our friends coming. On ridges between you and them (on your side of the slopes) you see here and there a neat brown line and a little below the ridge a thicker brown line. The first is men and the latter the led horses. Then spreading out right up to the enemy go the armoured cars, which is wonderful work.[34]

In other words, the pressure was fairly constant from every direction from the north round to the south-east, and the British cavalry screen was compelled to draw back, if slowly. As darkness fell, not long after 6 p.m., therefore, the city of Gaza, still garrisoned by Turks and some Germans, with Austrian gunners, and somewhat battered by intermittent British shelling, was encircled from the north gate round to the south by Australian, New Zealand, and Welsh troops who were established at the edges of the city and in control of Ali el-Muntar. The mounted troops, however, had been driven back from their own most advanced positions in the open country, but were still some distance from the city. Beyond them the Turkish relieving forces had made some progress, and were clearly capable of more next day.

On the seaward side Money's Detachment in the sand hills had made some small advances, much hindered by sniper fire and by the sand, but had made no real progress. Their presence, however, proved essential as they dissuaded any Turkish attempt to reach the crossing of the Wadi Ghazze behind them, and they occupied the attentions of the nearby entrenched Turkish garrison. They may not have done much, but the action in this area was not to be forgotten.[35]

As the troops of the Anzac Division and the Welsh Division arrived at the edges of the city, darkness fell. This was decisive. The Turkish forces which were attempting to interfere with the British attack were threatening; the British forces were close to taking the city but had not yet penetrated into the built-up area. The situation was in a sort of balance, and either side might feel that it was on the verge of victory. Certainly the British troops felt so. But none of the commanders on either side was prepared to go on fighting into the night. Von Kressenstein agreed that all his troops should halt where they were until the morning. Major Tiller in the city had already given up, and was prepared to surrender, having blown up his wireless station; this attitude was common. The British soldiers understood that 'the Turks were completely disorganized and that they could be heard rushing about in Gaza in the greatest confusion'.[36] Tiller found that the expected assault on the city did not materialize, nor did anyone demand his surrender. The British infantry dug in for the night, and their commanders began to think about the problem of the approaching Turkish relieving force.

The decisive factor was the condition of the mounted troops, or rather their horses. There were no sources of water in the land they were occupying, and it was not possible to get supplies to them, scattered as they all were. Chetwode believed that if they were to survive he could do nothing but order them to withdraw. So as night fell the British mounted troops were all ordered to withdraw: this included the New Zealanders, the Australians, and the men of the 22nd Mounted Brigade who were on the edge of the city, as well as all the Imperial Mounted Division and Anzac men covering them.[37]

This was the decisive event, for it meant that the Turkish relieving forces could reach the city in the morning and reinforce it without hindrance. They had no more than 5 miles to march, and would arrive soon after dawn. And this is what happened. The British cavalry, of course, had to be brought back south of the city for water, for the only adequate supply was in the Wadi Ghazze, from where they had started. General Chetwode sent the order to retire just after darkness fell, and did not rescind it when he heard that Ali el-Muntar had been taken. It took all night to extricate the mounted troops, some of whom had to be used to cover the rest even at dawn, when the Turks attacked along the Beersheba road. The quickest way to recover the mounted troops would have been to take Gaza during the night, but it seems that Chetwode had fixed his mind on the recovery of his own troops, to the detriment of the overall intention of the attack.

There was another decision, by General Dobell this time, which was as crucial. The infantry forces could still have made good the campaign next day without the cavalry if they had had the chance. The capture of Ali el-Muntar was the key, since it dominated the city. If it had been held through the night, the Turks in the city would have had little choice but to surrender in the morning. But the staff messed it up. General Dallas, commanding the Welsh Division, and so in immediate command of the assault, was ordered to align his right, 158th Brigade, on the left wing of the 163rd. In turn the East Anglian Division, of which the 163rd was part, had been told to pull back from their advanced position at Sheikh Abbas to cover the Burjabye Ridge from the east.

But no one had told Dallas this, and he thought the order meant that he had to extend his right as far as Sheikh Abbas. Doing this would so thin out his line that he could not hold his advanced positions. His protest was dismissed, in part because he did not make it clear that he thought the East Anglians were so far off, in part because Chetwode, in whose command the East Anglians were, thought Dallas had been told of the East Anglians' new position. So Dallas pulled his advanced troops back from Ali el-Muntar, and only discovered the truth about midnight. Chetwode did not realize the misunderstanding until 5 a.m.[38]

Dobell had decided that if Gaza did not fall before dark he would have to pull back all his troops, but various items of information which reached him late at night changed his view. He finally became aware that Dallas's forces had actually captured Ali el-Muntar the previous day. It is unclear why he did not know earlier that they had been on that hill since 4 p.m., but this is of a piece with the communications difficulties the British had experienced all day. Dobell also received a delayed message from Cairo with the decryption of a desperate signal sent by Major Tiller to Kress the previous evening, making it clear that he was on the verge of surrender. Dobell did not get this message for several hours.[39]

Meanwhile Dallas had withdrawn his advanced troops from Ali el-Muntar and also from Green and Clay Hills, pulling back 3 miles along Burjabye Ridge and a mile or so back along es-Sire Ridge. He actually told Chetwode's staff that he was intending to link up with the East Anglian Division at Sheikh Abbas, but no one noticed the implications. When Dallas finally realized that the East Anglians were much closer to him than that, at Khirbet Mansura, it was too late to countermand the withdrawal; it was almost dawn before the advanced troops were all accounted for.

So the morning began with an attempt to recover this lost ground. Most of the troops had not slept during the night – for many of them their second night without sleep: they had fought hard against a determined enemy all day, under the command of men who scarcely knew what they were doing. Even so, all was not yet finally lost. The early morning patrol from 161 Brigade, a company of the Essex Regiment, found that the hills were still unoccupied. They therefore re-established themselves on Ali el-Muntar; two other Essex companies reoccupied Green Hill. On their left, patrols sent out by the Herefordshire and Middlesex Regiments to retake Clay Hill and es-Sire respectively were much slower in starting, so the Essex men were left exposed, and a counter-attack by the Turks from the city retook both their hills. The sight of the retirement of these men further delayed the attack on Clay Hill. The Essex men returned to the attack and regained their two hills, but they were then attacked by a much more powerful Turkish force from the east. The Turkish relieving troops from the east had at last arrived.[40]

Colonel Kress von Kressenstein had as great a dislike as the British commanders for night attacks. His marching columns had halted where they were at dusk, and had therefore had a night's rest, and food. Before dawn the column marching along the Beersheba road, the 16th Division from Tell esh-Sheria, was already in action against the covering force of Australian 3rd Light Horse Brigade, who were assisted by the 7th Light Car patrol. Since they were merely covering the withdrawal of the other mounted forces, the Australians put up little serious resistance, merely withdrawing steadily so that the Turks had a clear march along the road as far as Gaza city. The two brigades of the East Anglian Division which had been at Sheikh Abbas, and could have interfered with this Turkish morning stroll, had they still been there, had been withdrawn to a useless position parallel with the Burjabye Ridge, where it was completely out of touch with the enemy. It was this virtually fresh Turkish force which encountered the Essex companies on Ali el-Muntar and Green Hills when they returned to those hills for the second time.

The British forces had been placed in such positions that few of them could actually be used. They occupied parts of the two ridges, es-Sire and Burjabye, but little else, so their position was a long narrow salient. The cover provided during the previous day by the mounted troops on the east had gone, and the whole of their position was within reach of the Turkish and German artillery. The rear areas of Dallas's forces, the ammunition dumps, the wounded, the food supplies, came under intermittent bombardment from Turkish artillery near Sheikh Abbas by 8 a.m. as the first of the guns of the Turkish relieving force arrived. So now, in order to be able to maintain the Essex's position on Ali el-Muntar, it was necessary first to take Sheikh Abbas, the position abandoned during the night. This was seriously considered, but before anything could be done, the Essex companies on Ali el-Muntar and Green Hill were swamped by the strong Turkish attack. The first hill was taken quickly, the second, where there were more troops, resisted longer, but by 10 a.m. that had been lost as well. The British were thus driven back to the line to which they had been withdrawn during the night.[41]

The British deployment was now unenviable. The Turks contented themselves for the next few hours with a leisurely but steady bombardment of their positions. The shelling could even interfere with men and supplies crossing the Wadi Ghazze. The situation was obvious to everyone, and the only solution was for the British to withdraw, but it took all afternoon for the various generals to be consulted and to agree that there was no point in resuming the attack. The withdrawal began soon after dark. It took nearly all night to complete: another night without sleep for the infantry.

Von Kressenstein was triumphant. He had defeated a major British attack, the first really large-scale assault his forces had had to face; and he had employed only a portion of them to do so. He now wanted to put his original plan into motion, to drive into the British rear areas at Shellal, the Wadi Ghazze, and Khan Yunis. But Jamal Pasha forbade it. When he had calmed down, von Kressenstein agreed. He had in fact already used most of his available troops in forcing the British withdrawal. Had he sent the intended force – one infantry battalion and one cavalry battalion – against Shellal and Khan Yunis, they would have run right into the withdrawn Anzac and Imperial Mounted Divisions, with the fresh Lowland Division nearby, and would have been annihilated.

The British called the attack an attempted *coup de main*, and so could delude themselves into the belief that it was a minor operation which just did not work. General Murray, in his report to London, did indeed describe it as a partial victory: 'We have advanced our troops a distance of 15 miles from Rafa to the Wadi Ghuzze', he telegraphed, omitting to note that the wadi had been the start line for the attack. He wholly failed to mention Gaza.[42] In truth it was a defeat brought about by a bad plan concocted by generals who managed to be out of touch with their fighting forces for much of the battle. The plan had been only too obvious to the enemy, who had made sensible and effective preparations to deal with it. No provision was made for the failure of the plan. Neither of the commanders with the power of decision – Dobell and Chetwode – knew that the crucial position, Ali el-Muntar, had actually been captured until after they had ordered the withdrawal, which meant its abandonment.

This battle showed up some serious faults in the British side. Communications were slow and delayed all day. The artillery was well served when it was in action but slow to operate and unresponsive to the tactical needs of the infantry; also its ammunition supply was inadequate. None of the commanders seem to have understood the vital part artillery played in capturing well-fortified positions; the fact that the commanders had to confer about their next moves when the attacking troops were half-way to the city had demonstrated a lack of serious planning. This was the antithesis of intelligent generalship. The arrival of darkness seems to have paralysed the generals' powers of thought, and the only thing they could think of was to pull back. Von Kressenstein at least ordered his men to stay where they were during the night, so as to be ready to march in the morning. By ordering a withdrawal, and one taking place at night, the British commanders got the worst of both worlds – their men were exhausted after a second night without sleep, and their advanced positions were abandoned.

For controlling the battle it was clear that the British command system needed drastic improvement, both in the planning and in the accuracy of information transmitted. The plan had been far too obvious, and the staff work during it had been slow, partly because of a shortage of properly qualified officers, and partly because none of the generals seems to have understood the situation.

If there was any doubt about the result, the casualty figures clearly showed it. The British lost almost 4,000 men, the Turks and Germans fewer than 2,500. The British were back in the positions from which they had started the battle; their enemies were still in possession of the object of the battle, the city of Gaza.

CHAPTER 3

Defeated Again

G ENERAL Murray's report to the War Office implied a greater success on 25 March than had actually occurred. For some days the War Office believed him, but, prodded by the War Cabinet, Robertson eventually asked for full details, and on 1 April Murray replied with a long telegram which gave fuller information. It was written in a way which suggested that his original claim for a victory was justified; yet a close reading showed clearly that his forces had attacked Gaza and been repulsed. His estimate of Turkish casualties had climbed to over 8,000, and he understated his own losses.[1]

This was a mistake. He might fool Robertson, who tended to take such reports as truth, but the War Cabinet included some of the sharpest political minds in Britain, men who were well used to seeing through the spin. Robertson replied to Murray on 2 April without censuring him, but taking it for granted that Murray was now able to advance to capture Jerusalem. Robertson stated that he had intelligence that the Turks had no more than 30,000 rifles in Palestine, pointed out that the Canal was now in no real danger, and promised supplies and, perhaps, reinforcements.

Murray's report emphasized the ability of the mounted troops to tackle any opposition in open country, but he also noted that when the Turks were encountered in prepared positions – in other words, in trenches and other fortifications – they were 'very tenacious'. Elaborating from that, it could be assumed that any attack on Gaza city would have been extremely difficult and costly, and would have taken a considerable time. This was a disguised excuse for failure, since his forces clearly did not have much time and the original plan called for the city to be seized by a *coup de main*. Both sides, in fact, took due note of these points. Murray pointed to 'the fog and waterless nature of the country' as the ultimate reasons for the failure of the attack, but these were only partial explanations. Nobody was seriously inconvenienced by the fog, no matter what they said afterwards, and the lack of water was fully understood beforehand: it was the basic reason for the attempt to seize the city swiftly.

Had Murray been honest from the start, his problems would have been much reduced. All he needed to do was to emphasize the time element, that the attack was intended to be a swift seizure of the city, and that the mounted troops were never intended to operate in the field for more than a day and a night. By claiming success and then being exposed as wrong, he distorted the perception of the whole battle. This distortion exists to this day, and is reflected in complaints in the regimental histories, notably those of the New Zealand and Australian regiments, that the withdrawal was somehow unfair, or a puzzle. These units knew the plan, or at least their commanders did; they knew their water problem; and later experience showed them the hideous cost of sending light horsemen against fortified positions. The withdrawal was a correct military decision which saved several hundred lives.

The essential problem lay with the system of command, its inadequate manning, its uncertainty, slowness, and bad planning. There should never have been a conference of generals between the advance of the infantry and the central assault: that it took place shows that no real thought had been given to assigning objectives beforehand. Chetwode with the Desert Column did not need to do this, though he did have to wait until the conference was over before advancing. So the fault lies with Dobell, and beyond him, with Murray. It is presumably because he realized this that Murray submitted his misleading reports.

As a result of his presentational errors, his over-optimistic estimates of success, and his deliberate obfuscations, Murray found he was expected to do in the spring that which he had originally been told would only be allowed in the autumn: he was to conquer Palestine at least as far as Jerusalem, and his railway would be extended to Jaffa. He would receive supplies, but it was now reckoned that he would not need much in the way of new troops: a comb-out in Egypt and along the Canal would provide most of the forces he would need.[2]

This perhaps surprised Murray, but it did not change things in any serious way. It was still necessary to capture Gaza first, since it blocked the way north. Nor can he have expected to be sent more troops, given the overpowering need for men for France. He appears to have made no plans for anything beyond Gaza – no plans for exploitation after the battle, that is – and it was the capture of the city which remained the one target he aimed at.

Accordingly the railway was extended to Deir el-Belah, only 5 miles from the Wadi Ghazze, which was now the British base line. Units which had been left behind in March were moved forward to join their parent divisions: two Australian Light Horse Brigades, and the whole of the Yeomanry Division (though it was still lacking its artillery component). The artillery batteries, which had left part of their components behind in March, were brought up to strength, and ammunition supplies were replenished and increased. A supply of gas shells arrived from Britain. Eight rather elderly and worn tanks were sent out.[3] Supplies of the Hotchkiss machine gun, which the soldiers liked, partly because it was lighter than the Lewis and Vickers they also used, were also delivered.

3 *Tank.* A Mark II tank on the move somewhere in Palestine. Supposedly going into action, it is in fact probably not near the front line at all, judging by the casual attitudes of the spectators. (One does not stand in full view on the skyline anywhere near an enemy who has snipers and good rifles.) The first tanks sent to Palestine were old and in poor condition, and so they broke down even more frequently than usual, and when one appeared in an attack they became immediate targets for any enemy guns within range. That any of them actually reached the enemy trenches was due to the sheer persistence and bravery of their crews, most of whom were killed. (Crown Copyright: Imperial War Museum Q 13213C)

As a result, when the next fighting began the British had 7,000 more troops available for combat than in March, and double the number of guns. The Royal Flying Corps, however, received no new aircraft, and the numerically inferior but technologically superior Germans were able to reconnoitre almost at will. They had the faster machines, but only ten of them – eight Rumplers, which arrived in March, and two Halberstadts. The Royal Flying Corps Fifth Wing, which consisted of two Australian squadrons, had, on 22 March, 21 serviceable aircraft, twelve B.E.2cs and nine Martinsydes (and as many more which were unserviceable). The German craft were faster and more manoeuvrable than the British. The Halberstadts attacked where possible, slowly reducing the RFC strength, but with only two aircraft they were unable to interfere with British reconnaissance. The Rumplers evaded combat in order to conserve their numbers; both sides were still able to carry out regular reconnaissance of their enemy's dispositions.[4]

The Turks knew that another attack would come, both from general likelihood and from their reconnaissance. The repulse of the British in March had not been decisive enough to discourage them from a new attempt, and they had been close enough to success to encourage them to try again as soon as possible. The Turks, however, could gather only a few more troops – they were to be outnumbered two-to-one – but they did bring up extra guns. Above all they carefully noted the elements of the British failure in March. From the Turkish point of view, it was obvious that the mounted troops were formidable at first encounter, but very vulnerable when deprived of water. They were also less effective in the face of the 'tenacious' Turkish foot soldiers in their trenches than the British infantry, not least because their numbers were fewer and their artillery was lighter, because it had to be mobile. The lesson for the outnumbered Turks was to dig in, so they put their full energies into intensifying and extending their fortifications, and attended carefully to the registering and control of their artillery. It had been the city itself which had foiled the first British attacks, enabling the flanking forces to intervene, but this would not necessarily work a second time. The next British attack would likely be launched directly at the city, and the great mounted manoeuvre would not be repeated on the same scale. Therefore, fortifications and guns. The Turkish army was set to digging.

The city was ringed all around, except on the north, by redoubts. To prevent its being wholly surrounded and hence besieged, a line of fortified positions were constructed along the Beersheba road. This lay more or less along a low ridge, which was the approximate watershed between wadi-systems to north and south, so that the positions had a good field of fire before them, and their rearward areas were hidden from easy view. Beginning about 2 miles from Ali el-Muntar, the first positions were relatively weak, but they could be dominated and protected by artillery fire from the city; there was a single strongpoint, a small redoubt, not far from Khirbet Sihan, with almost continuous trench works to either side; this system stretched to almost 3 miles from the city. Further east along the road the line was not as densely occupied; instead there were three major systems, named by the British the Atawine, Hairpin, and Hureyra Redoubts, from their locations or map-appearances. Each of these was a separate redoubt, rather on the pattern of el-Magruntein near Rafa, without the keep, but with barbed wire. They were spaced close enough to provide mutual support, had good communications with their supporting guns, and were strong enough to stand a major attack. The whole line stretched from Ali el-Muntar to Hureyra for a little over 10 miles, Beersheba being another 15 miles to the south-east.

By concentrating in this line of redoubts the Turks had less need to hold forces in reserve, or to prepare for an outflanking movement. The size and strength of the fortifications were such that they would absorb the great majority of available Turkish soldiers, but they would also require just about the full British manpower to make a serious assault feasible. The failure of the British to use their naval power to assist their attempted *coup de main* in March made it even less likely that their next attack would use it. The 53rd Division could therefore be brought forward and placed to occupy the trenches immediately east of Gaza. Beyond it, in the major redoubts, was the 16th Division, brought forward from Khirbet Jemmame. The 3rd (infantry) Division was concentrated in the various fortifications in and around the city. The only reserve was the 3rd Cavalry Division, which was concentrated behind the line at Tell esh-Sheria, as before, where it covered the open flank beyond the Hureyra Redoubt. This weak cavalry division – probably not more than 1,500 soldiers – was the only intercepting force, a clear indication that no outflanking move was expected; Beersheba was only lightly held by a division in process of formation, the 54th.[5]

All this fortification rapidly became obvious to the British planners, whose first scheme for the next attack had to be abandoned. The Turks worked quickly, for the British plan was made by 10 April, by which time the new Gaza defences were sufficiently advanced and powerful to compel its revision.[6] British planning was therefore being shaped by the enemy dispositions. In other words, even though they were on the defensive and outnumbered, Colonel

Kress von Kressenstein and the Turks were effectively dictating where and how the coming battle would be fought.

One of the major constraints on the deployment of the British troops was still that of supplies. Without control of Gaza itself they had to camp out in the desert, where water had to be brought forward along the pipeline from the Nile. The main pipe, of 12–inch bore, had now reached el-Arish, and from there onwards a variety of small-bore pipes had been laid as far as Deir el-Belah. This place was also the current railhead, and it was also a port of sorts, to which supplies could be brought by sea and landed from lighters. All supplies had then to be carried forward from Deir el-Belah for the last 5 miles to the Wadi Ghazze. With the increase of numbers at the front all this supply effort had almost reached the stage where it was collapsing under its own weight. The pipeline, for instance, pumped 600,000 gallons of water a day from Qantara on the Canal; at the other end, no more than 36,500 gallons reached the troops, all the rest having gone to supply the railway, the labourers, the supply troops, and the animals along the supply route. In the same way, half the trains on the railway were either hospital trains or trains required for railway maintenance; any increase in numbers of men to be supplied would strain the capacity of the system beyond its limits.[7]

Water supplies were located in the Wadi Ghazze, at Shellal, and at Khan Yunis, and developed by the Royal Engineers. They produced a substantial quantity of water, but no one knew just how fully these local wells would produce in the summer heat. Two solutions were proposed to the general problem: to double the pipeline from the existing 12–inch pipe all the way from Qantara, and to double-track the railway as well. This would more than double the capacity of the trains to supply the troops. An alternative solution was to capture Gaza, where water and food could be obtained, and where southern Palestine – the land flowing with milk and honey, of course – should be able to provide at least some supplies, especially water, and whose ports could be opened to relieve the railway. The difficulty with the first solution was that it was reckoned that it would take eight months to double the railway, though perhaps rather less to double the pipeline – once the pipe had been obtained. It was clearly a better option to attempt the capture of Gaza first since that would obviate the need to make the great effort of construction. But the number of troops who could be brought into battle was limited by the size of the railway and by the capacity of the pipeline. Given the new strength of the defences, with the entrenchments, artillery, long-range rifles, and machine-guns, it might not be possible to bring sufficient British forces to ensure victory. That is, sufficient troops could be supported only by enlarging the capacity of the railway and the pipeline, but these enlargements would take so long that the Turkish defences might be impregnable by the time the work was done; yet an immediate attack might fail because of a shortage of supplies caused by the inadequacy of the railway and the pipeline. Being soldiers, Murray, Robertson, and Dobell opted for an immediate military solution. After all, the first attempt had almost succeeded. It was now a distinct gamble, more of one than the first attempt had been. Murray had a problem which could only be solved by the battle troops under his command.

The first plan of attack using just two infantry divisions was quickly produced, but the Turkish fortifications were constructed so rapidly that it was soon seen to be inadequate. There was some discussion about an advance along the shore, in the sand-dunes between the city and the sea – the area where Money's Detachment had operated – but this was abandoned because it gave no opportunity for the use of the horsemen.[8] This made sense, for the mounted force was one of the main strengths of the British force, but once the Turkish defence line had been constructed, the power of the mounted force was blunted.

The plan which was ultimately adopted shifted the emphasis in the attack from the cavalry to the infantry. The cavalry was now to act as no more than a flank guard for the infantry, which was to make a direct assault on the fortified city. Three infantry divisions – the Welsh (53rd), the Lowland (52nd), and the East Anglian (54th) – were to advance across the former battleground, but on a much wider front than before, the Welsh between the coast and the Rafa road, the Lowland directed at Ali el-Muntar, and the East Anglian towards the first part of the Beersheba road line. Each division put two brigades into the attack, with the third in reserve. The Yeomanry Division was put into the line on the British right, facing east to protect the flank, but was not intended to take part in the assault.

The mounted forces, the Anzac and Imperial Mounted Divisions, were still called the Desert Column and still commanded by Chetwode. They were to ride out eastwards beyond the Yeomanry Division, to confront the three Turkish redoubts along the road. The Imperial Camel Corps Brigade was to link the East Anglian Division with the Imperial Mounted Division opposite the strongpoint in the Turkish line near Khirbet Sihan. The Imperial Mounted Division was to confront the Atawine Redoubt; the Anzac Division was to go further east and south-east, as a flank guard for the whole force. It would be spread over a wide front, and was also to confront the Hureyra Redoubt. Both divisions were to go against the Hairpin Redoubt. They were not intended to do more than threaten the redoubts.

The purpose of this disposition was to do two things, first to provide a screen out to the east to prevent any Turkish interference from that direction, by the troops at Beersheba perhaps, or by the 3rd Cavalry Division from Tell esh-Sheria. The second aim was to provide a credible threat to the redoubts so that the troops in the trenches there should be pinned down and be unable to go to the assistance of those in the city. Just how far to go with this threat was a problem for the division commanders, Major-General I. W. Hodgson of the Imperial Division and Major-General Harry Chauvel of the Anzac. A good deal of latitude would also lie with the brigadiers. These several men came up with differing answers.

All units except the Yeomanry Division were up to strength in artillery, and assistance had been sought and provided by warships, the old French coast-defence ship *Requin*, a powerfully gunned vessel referred to at times, by landsmen, as a battleship, which had been particularly useful in the defence of the Canal, and two British monitors. These floating batteries were to supplement the bombardment of the city's fortifications by the land-based guns. All the divisional headquarters were sited well back, behind or close to the Wadi Ghazze, and General Dobell's headquarters were at Deir el-Belah. Behind him, General Murray had travelled to Khan Yunis in his command train. He could contact Dobell, and Dobell could contact the divisional headquarters, but, as usual, the real difficulty lay in transmitting information and orders between brigades, battalions, and divisions.

The attack was to take place in two stages, the first a general advance to a line a mile or two in front of the Turkish positions, stretching from the sea to Sheikh Abbas, to be made by the infantry; beyond Sheikh Abbas were the mounted forces. The second stage, after a day devoted to digging in and the collection of supplies, was to be the assault. The plan had the merit of simplicity, and gave the troops a break in the advance in which to rest and prepare, but it was all too similar to what had actually happened in March, when there had been the break for the staff conference. There did not seem to be a great deal of tactical imagination among the planners.

The first stage of the attack came on 17 April. The three infantry divisions moved forward at dawn, and by 7.30 a.m. were at their chosen positions, where they entrenched. The Turks did little to interfere, though one of the British tanks exposed itself unnecessarily and was put out of action by accurate Turkish artillery fire. Clearly one of the tasks which had been successfully accomplished on the Turkish side during the three weeks since the first battle had been accurate artillery registry of all the visible places in the area where the attack would necessarily come. Otherwise the only Turkish reaction was desultory artillery fire on the new British positions.

On the cavalry wing, everything was equally quiet. The Imperial Mounted Division threw out an outpost line to within 2 miles or so of the redoubts at Atawine and Hairpin. This move was supposed to provide a threat to these positions and so prevent the Turks from moving troops along the road to reinforce Gaza. The Turks showed no inclination to do anything of the sort, but sat tight in their bunkers and watched, just as at the city. A patrol of the Worcester Yeomanry, part of the 5th Mounted Brigade, reached and cut the telegraph wire near the Hairpin Redoubt before dawn and came back safely.[9] Further west, the New Zealand Brigade of the Anzac Division rode out towards Beersheba, and observed troops marching along the road from that town. Once they had seen where the British were committed, and in what strength, the Turks understood that there was no threat to Beersheba, and the soldiers of the 54th Division there could be called west. It had been hoped that the threat to the Atawine Redoubt might persuade the Turks to reinforce from Hureyra, and so open up a gap which the horsemen could exploit; instead all were being reinforced from Beersheba. At the end of the day the mounted troops were recalled to the Wadi Ghazze to water and rest, only outpost lines being maintained.[10]

The second stage of the attack, after a day's work on trenches and dugouts, went as might be expected, considering it was made by soldiers walking over open ground towards well-entrenched and protected men armed with rifles and machine guns. An artillery bombardment of an hour or so, including the gas shells, and including fire from the ships at sea off Gaza, seems to have woken up the Turks rather than intimidated them – there was still insufficient British artillery to provide a really serious bombardment. The Turks did not actually notice the gas shells: the higher air temperature appears to have encouraged rapid evaporation. At 6.30 the Imperial and Anzac Mounted Divisions rode out on their long journey towards the Turkish redoubts once more. An hour later the infantry advanced. The Welsh Division moved to attack the Turkish trenches among the sand-dunes between the Rafa road and the coast. The Lowland Division went to attack the central Turkish position at Ali el-Muntar. To their right the East Anglian Division marched to attack the entrenchments of the Turkish 53rd Division along the Beersheba road.

The Scots of the Lowland Division had the most important task, and their target was the most unpleasant. Their ultimate objective, Ali el-Muntar, itself a redoubt, was only the last of a series of interlocking fortified areas, each of which was entrenched, wired, and manned by determined defenders – 'very tenacious' was a mild term for them. These redoubts had been located and named by the British patrols and air reconnaissance in the previous three weeks. This was also the area which had been fought over by the Welsh Division in March, when the objectives had been Clay Hill and Green Hill, in front of Ali el-Muntar. These were, of course, still fortified – though the name Clay Hill was now abandoned – but in front of them were two areas evocatively called the Warren and the Labyrinth, from the dense networks of trenches; two hills in front of them were also fortified and were now termed Outpost Hill and Middlesex Hill. Off to the left was Samson's Ridge, a dune across which the Rafa road passed, which was to be attacked by the Welsh Division, but from which it was possible to fire at the Scots as they moved towards Ali el-Muntar and its preliminary satellites.

The attack fell to two battalions of the King's Own Scottish Borderers, whose target was Outpost Hill, and two battalions of the Royal Scots Fusiliers, who were to attack Middlesex Hill. It was Outpost Hill which proved to be the real problem, since it commanded the approach to Middlesex. It was attacked by the 5th KOSB, which advanced in eight waves, and was met by withering fire from two sides.[11] Two tanks were to lead; one fell into a nullah and was lost; the second, in which all the crew were seriously wounded, reached the semi-circular position (called, technically, a 'lunette') on the hill, and was there disabled.[12] This hill was not an especially useful position to hold, but it became the position both sides felt had to be controlled. The 5th KOSB were reinforced by the 4th KOSB, and both were led into the attack by Major W. T. Forrest, a well-known rugby player. He strolled about in the open organizing and encouraging the mixed force of KOSB and some of the Royal Scots Fusiliers. Then he led them in a charge which gained the lunette, driving out of force of 'about 50 Turks'.[13]

A tank and three battalions had been used, and used up, to take this hill, which in the end had been defended by 'about fifty Turks'. The Turks certainly took casualties, but the power of the defence had been clearly shown. Not only that, but the hill at once became a trap for the conquerors. It was captured at last in the early afternoon, but then it was bombarded for the next several hours while the Turks crept closer on all sides, while the approaches were swept by fire from both flanks. A lieutenant recalled the situation:

We were now under direct fire from a number of machine guns, rifles, minenwerfers, and a battery of artillery. Nearly every man had been killed or wounded, and, in spite of the additional danger of being rushed by the Turks, we were thankful as darkness fell when a few men crawled down a ditch to us and helped to hold the left of the hillside.[14]

The arrival of darkness enabled the men trapped on the hill to get away, though this was no easier than any other task that day:

Towards 6 p.m. Lieut R. B. Anderson of the 4th was the senior officer in charge of the 70–strong garrison of the lunette. He noticed parties of Turks dangerously far forward between himself and the 4th R.S.F., and wisely decided to evacuate the lunette after seeing to the removal of the wounded. This of course, could only be managed after dark. It was successfully accomplished, but the gallant young Anderson was shot dead.[15]

The detail of the withdrawal is even worse, as the account by the last officer to leave, Second Lieutenant Broomfield, makes clear:

When darkness came we realized that it was impossible to hold the redoubt in the absence of reinforcements, which were sorely needed, and we therefore decided to retire across the open. The trench we were in was very shallow, and only by lying down was it possible to obtain cover from the hail of bullets which passed over the trench. The men left the trench by ones and twos, and after Lieut. Dickson had gone I was just about to follow him when I heard a man shouting for help. Going along the trench I found one of our men pinned under the dead body of a comrade who had fallen on top of him. I managed to extricate the man with the help of another soldier. These men left, and I was about to follow them when I recognized the voice of Major Forrest, who was calling for water ... his condition was such that he could not be moved. I was obliged to leave the trench, especially as the Turks were practically upon me.[16]

The 155th Brigade had suffered over 1,000 casualties in this attack, almost half its strength.[17] It had not even penetrated to the first Turkish line.

This failure had repercussions both to the left and to the right of the Ali el-Muntar positions. The Scots of 156 Brigade, to the right, two battalions each of the Royal Scots and the Scottish Rifles (the Cameronians), could not advance because fire from Outpost and Middlesex Hills prevented it; they tried to move forward as their fellow Scots reached these hills, only to be fired at from Green Hill as well. It did not help that the brigade's right flank was uncovered by the advance of the East Anglian Division.[18] The third brigade, the 157th (Highland Light Infantry and Argyll and Sutherland Highlanders) were at one point ordered to support the attack on Outpost Hill, but by the time they could get into position it was too late and the order was cancelled.[19]

To the left the Welsh Division could not make a serious attack on its two objectives, Samson's Ridge and the post at Sheikh Ajlin on the shore, until Outpost Hill was secured. As a result the ridge was not taken until well after noon (when Outpost Hill was precariously held by the Scots), at which point the Turks withdrew from Sheikh Ajlin.[20] The division had been given a second set of objectives, but the resistance to its right, at Outpost and Middlesex, again made it impossible to make any further advances. This division had had a very bad time three weeks earlier, and its commander, General Dallas, had resigned after the first battle, to be replaced by the promoted General Mott, the former commander of the 158th Brigade.[21] The division's morale was clearly somewhat fragile, and its attacks this time were very cautious.[22] Again, the division had the use of two tanks, only one of which reached the Turkish lines, separated from the infantry. The adventures of the tank are a lesson in the difficulties of using these early versions.[23] As a result of its caution the division actually achieved more than the Scots, and with fewer casualties.[24]

At one point the Official Historian of the Royal Flying Corps contrasts the German policy of sending some of their best aircraft to each theatre with the British policy of sending a lot of inferior machines to Egypt; he remarks that 'numbers and courage may never fully compensate, in the air, for inferiority of equipment'.[25] This applied equally on the ground. In this case the superior equipment was the Turkish defence system, and the numbers and courage those of the dead Scotsmen. The Welsh Division was accused, by the Official Historian of the land fighting, of sloth and an unwillingness to attack; the Scots' charge was, on the other hand, 'splendid'. In effect the Scots were being praised for being killed in a reckless attack, and the Welsh Division soldiers condemned for a sensible caution. It bears repeating that the Lowland Division achieved none of its objectives, whereas the Welsh Division achieved some of its. A higher casualty rate is hardly an intelligent measure to judge success.

To the east of the attack on the city, the aim of the East Anglian Division's attack was to break through the Turkish fortified line along the Beersheba road and then take the city itself from the north-east. It was possible that this might succeed even if the Lowland Division's attack on Ali el-Muntar failed – but again, it was all too reminiscent of the events in the first attack in March. In the result the events on this front were much the same as with the Lowland Division's attack. The 162nd Brigade advanced towards the apparent gap between the city and the first of the fortified positions along the road. The 4th Northamptonshire Battalion, on the right, was halted by heavy fire from the Turkish positions;[26] the left battalion, the 10th London, faced both the fortified line and the unfortified section closer to the city. The left half of the battalion was able to move into the gap, and so became separated from the right as the latter endeavoured to keep in touch with the Northamptons. After some time the whole attack inevitably stopped, with the left half of the Londoners high and dry.[27] The 11th London was sent in from the reserve, but had no effect.

To the right of this stalled attack, the 163rd Brigade faced the same problem as the Northamptons. The two attacking battalions, the 4th and 5th Norfolk, had differing objectives; the 4th, on the left, faced a line of trenches, the 5th, on the right, had to tackle the strongpoint near Khirbet Sihan. At the same time, farther to their right, the Imperial Camel Corps became involved in the same attack. It was towards this strongpoint, and a couple of small hills called Jack and Jill, that the two tanks which had been assigned to the division were directed.

One of the tanks was hit and stopped early on. The second got lost at first, then manoeuvred on a ridge, where it drew concentrated fire from the Turkish artillery, which was as accurate as usual. It had become mixed in with some of the Camel Corps, who suffered from that barrage as well as from shrapnel and machine-gun fire as they advanced. Even so, the tank kept going until it drove over the redoubt's wire and into the very centre of the position.[28] Once in the strongpoint it became the immediate target of all the nearby Turkish artillery. When the tank was destroyed, the Norfolks and the Cameliers who had managed to get into the redoubt along with it were driven out or captured. The reserve battalion, the 8th Hampshire, was sent in as support, but had no effect.

The fighting at the strongpoint was largely invisible to the rest of the brigade, for it took place beyond a small ridge. From brigade headquarters Lieutenant Buxton was sent to find out what had happened, and gives a description of the results of a failed attack:

> The advance had been held up just below the Turkish line, and one could see our men lying out in lines, killed or wounded. The 1/5th Norfolk 'B' Company, under Captain Blyth, had captured Tank redoubt and had

held it for some time, till the ammunition was spent. No support came up, and so those who did not get away, sixty in all, were captured in the Turkish counter-attack. My second tank, under Captain Carr had done very well in getting into the redoubt. The first tank had had a direct hit and was burning. It was obvious that our attack here had failed, and that most of our men had been killed. So I waited a bit longer, and when things were a shade quieter, got out of my shell-hole and ran back over the rise. There I came on about forty men of our brigade of all regiments. Major Marsh, who was O.C. 8th Hants, was there too, and Lieutenant Wharton of the 4th Norfolk. These men were just stragglers and all collected there. We decided it was no good going on then, so we started to dig ourselves in. This was all quite early in the morning – about 9. Marsh had a telephone line so I phoned back to Brigade H.Q. and gave them all the news.

4 *In the Front Line.* The fighting before Gaza was the closest approximation to Western Front-style warfare in the war against the Ottoman Empire. The combination of sand and rock made it necessary to use huge quantities of sandbags, filled on the spot. The British army's experience of Indian warfare on the North-West Frontier meant that their defensive posts, as here, tended to look like sangars from the Indian hills. This photograph was clearly taken as a souvenir long after the fighting was over. It took a long time for these trench systems to be removed, and many simply faded away, filled by windblown sand. Note the almost flat landscape, where a hole in the ground gave the best protection. (Crown Copyright: Imperial War Museum Q61496).

There were a lot of dead men and wounded all round us. Some of the latter we got behind our lines, in case the Turks tried a counter-attack. We were about forty men and one Lewis gun, and no one on our left or right for several hundred yards. The place we were holding was the top of a rounded hillock. The Turks kept us under pretty good machine-gun fire all day. Marsh and I lay in a rifle pit and ate dates and biscuits for a bit. We allowed no firing, as we wished to keep all our ammunition in case of a counter attack.

About 4 in the afternoon the 5th Suffolk were sent up to support us and to consolidate the position we had held. This was really a great relief. About seven the Brigadier came out after dusk and saw the place. He ordered us to retire during the night right back to our starting point, for it would not have been possible to hold this advanced position as long as there was no one on our flanks at all.[29]

The strongpoint was from now on called Tank Redoubt.

This was an attack on a single strongpoint and a stretch of trenches a little over a mile long, by four battalions. It had made no progress after being expelled from the strongpoint, and it had only reached so far because of the bravery of the tank crew (three men). The last reserve of the 163rd Brigade was a single battalion, the 5th Suffolk, which was at last sent forward, as Buxton noted with relief, late in the afternoon. With no more troops available, the brigadier had no option but to pull all the survivors back.

To the left, the 10th London were driven out of their isolated post in the afternoon, and the 162nd Brigade was thus also finished. Indeed, to Brigadier-General Hare of the 163rd it was clear by soon after 2 p.m. that the attack had failed. He at first ordered another attempt, then stopped it, and ordered the whole of the 163rd Brigade to stand fast.[30] His visit to the Buxton-Marsh foxhole after dark was clearly to rescue the men, rather than to plan a new assault.

The mounted attacks by the Imperial and Anzac Mounted Divisions went much the same way. Two Australian Light Horse Brigades, the 4th and the 3rd, were put to attack the Atawine Redoubt, advancing well spaced through the barley, sprinkled with shrapnel and soon the target for machine guns. To their left they watched the British tank attacking the strongpoint in which it was destroyed, and this assisted their own attack because all the enemy artillery concentrated on the destruction of the tank, but as soon as that was accomplished 'the guns swung back on to the Light Horsemen and we suffered many casualties.' They halted a while in the cover of a wadi, and then resumed the attack in combination with some men of the Camel Corps, though that is rather too formal a way of putting it. The front line was a confused place, with units becoming mixed together. This mixed group succeeded in reaching the ridge and the road, and began to dig in. They did this in the unfortified gap between the Atawine and Tank Redoubts, which was also the unit boundary between the Turkish defending divisions. The mixed group were also involved in the attack on Jack and Jill in the wake of the momentary setback for the Turks caused by the tank attack. A sudden reinforcement and a charge fuelled by desperation and determination brought them into the two small redoubts, but only briefly. The Turks retreated, and this marked the deepest penetration of the Turkish lines made all day. The position they reached was never less than precarious, and in the end the whole force was pulled back, where they were reinforced by the Dorset Yeomanry.

It is evident, particularly from the episode of the tank with the 5th Norfolk and the Cameliers, that the Turkish artillery was under clear and intelligent command. The historian of the Ottoman air force notes that the system the British had used at Rafa, of aircraft spotting for the artillery in radio communication with the gunners, was being used by the Turks – or rather by the Germans and Austrians, who were the artillerymen and the pilots: 'Excellent artillery direction by the wireless-equipped Rumplers halted the attackers, wrecked the armoured cars and turned the assault into a complete failure.'[32]

The co-operation between British artillery and aircraft was less successful, according to the Official Historian, because 'on the 18th and 19th observation was impeded by haze and cloud, and by the dust thrown up by the bombardment',[33] though this was not apparently a problem for the other side. The Germans sent over bombing raids, opportunistically, it seems, and several accounts mention being attacked from the air by bombs and machine guns. The men of the 11th Light Horse witnessed one of the few direct conflicts between opposing airmen – usually they failed to meet, being tasked above all with reconnaissance and artillery spotting:

> While here we witnessed a thrilling air duel between a British and a German pilot directly to our front but over no man's land. The German zoomed high in the air and dived suddenly at the British plane, but the pilot slipped his machine aside, and as the Hun went past swooped after him at a terrific pace. Straight as a plummet, with engines roaring the British machine roared down upon his adversary, but the terrific strain

was too much for his craft, and one of the wings snapped off close to
the body of the machine and was whisked into the slip stream like a
pocket handkerchief. Losing balance the plane twisted into a spin and
with engines still roaring, dropped like a stone between the opposing
lines, sending up a great cloud of smoke and dust.[34]

The roving aircraft were hated by the ground troops. The rear areas were
crowded and busy, providing plenty of targets. Driver Thomas Marshall of
the King's Shropshire Light Infantry, in charge of the section of the Egyptian
Labour Corps for his unit, wrote a brief description in a letter home:

> [L]ong columns of infantry were always moving to and fro, thousands of
> camels carrying water, powerful tractors, and endless transport wagons,
> aeroplanes ever hovering around, and the horsemen from distant out-
> posts come gallopping in from all sides; really it is impossible to realize
> at home the work the troops are doing under great difficulties in this far
> away land.[35]

Trooper Idriess's regiment, also behind the lines, was attacked from the
air, and his diary comment gives a good indication of the feelings of people
everywhere subjected to air attack – 'taubes' was the term used for German
aircraft:

> Again came the taubes; they roared as the swerved viciously down. We
> dismounted and blazed back hatefully while their machine guns spat
> down as they roared and rocked above. And with all their noise and hate
> they only got one man.[36]

The Anzac Division faced the Hairpin Redoubt as well as the Hureyra; the
New Zealand Brigade's attacks on it were as ineffective as every other attack
that day. They had pushed back the Turkish outpost, but were then held up at
some distance from the redoubt itself. The Wellington Regiment went in as
reinforcement. Trooper Judge described the situation:

> Moved further on at Midday, and went into action about 2 p.m. under
> very heavy fire. Shrapnel and high explosives. We were holding a ridge
> which had been taken from the Turks earlier in the day, and Jacko
> advanced to try and retake it, but his heart failed him before he reached
> us. Nevertheless things looked pretty ugly at one stage of the proceed-
> ings, and the Aussies made a bolt for it, and soon the Yeomanry would

have followed but our CO ran out and cajoled and entreated them, and in the end stopped what promised to be a bad stampede. Never thought so much of Major Hurst as I did on that occasion. I took a message to Col. Findlay and returned unhurt under heavy fire. Withdrew across the Wadi about dark.[37]

The Anzac Division was spread even thinner than the Imperial Division, and came under attack from the east by a regiment of the Turkish 3rd Cavalry Division, which, like the troops from the Beersheba garrison, endeavoured to take the British attack in the flank. This was an obvious move for the Turks to make, and they had sensibly waited until the British attacks on the redoubts had been blunted. It seems to have been intended to attack with both infantry from the redoubts and cavalry south of the road, but the co-ordination was ineffective. The Tasmanians of the 3rd Light Horse Regiment saw this move first, as they met about 'a thousand' Turkish cavalry moving west on both sides of the Wadi Imlieh. They had, that is, already swung round the eastern end of the Turkish positions on the road and were almost in the rear of the attackers of the Hureyra Redoubt. The Tasmanians met their advance by concentrating on their centre, so that the Turks divided into two parts, one veering to the north, the other south-west.[38] The southern group encountered the 7th Light Horse, where they received similar treatment from a small group of the Australians who were armed with machine-guns, and who stopped their advance for a time, but were then forced to retire when bombarded by Turkish light artillery.[39]

The accounts of both these encounters are described in the Australian regimental histories as though they were devil-may-care victories-against-the-odds. Yet the original engagement, with the Tasmanians, simply sent the two halves off in new attacking directions, which seems to have been the Turks' intention anyway; the second encounter, with the 7th Light Horse, clearly stopped the Turks for a short time, but then a few shells forced the Australians to retire. Neither of these encounters can be considered a victory. At best, the Turks had been discovered somewhat earlier than they expected to be, which is what the Australian outposts were for.

For once we have a description of some of this from the Turkish side, by the Turkish commander. This was Rafael de Nogales, 'Nogales Bey', a Venezuelan adventurer who had travelled to Europe at the beginning of the war to offer his services to the Belgian army. He was rejected, and suffered the same rebuff from five other Allied countries; in the end he was accepted by the

Turks: clearly he simply wanted to fight. He was by 1917 a staff officer with the 3rd Cavalry Division, and organized the flanking attack which the Australians faced. His account is somewhat at variance with those of the Australians, who overestimated the numbers involved. But they were right that many of the Turkish troops were Bedouin; and Nogales was very impressed by the work of the Australian machine-gunners.[40]

The troopers of the Lincolnshire Yeomanry may have became involved in this episode. They were part of the Anzac Division's 22nd Mounted Brigade, which was on the ultimate right flank of the whole army, north of the Wadi Ghazze. This was an unlikely area to be attacked, but the Turkish force at Beersheba was known to be moving west, and the 3rd Cavalry Division was a hovering threat. The Lincolnshires found themselves involved because of the appearance of scattered groups of what they called irregulars. Scouting parties had been sent out by one of the Australian brigades, and these met the Turks in greater numbers and closer to them than they could deal with. Or perhaps it was part of Nogales Bey's mixed force of Turkish regular cavalry and his Bedouins, who had driven the 7th Light Horse back. The fleeing Australians came towards the Lincolnshires, a scatter of small parties who were closely pursued by the Turks, who are described as 'a horde', and 'probably Circassian Irregulars', though in fact they were the regulars of the 3rd Division mixed with locally recruited Bedouin. 'We felt that we ought to help the Aussies by stopping their pursuers', remarks the Lincolnshires' biographer. They brought out four guns, whose firing persuaded the Turks to withdraw – just as the Turks' firing had compelled the Australians to retreat.[41]

It is worth noting, and emphasizing, how the same events are seen so differently by different participants. The whole affair was clearly fast-moving, distant, and confusing, and writing it up later involved attempting to impose some sort of a pattern on it. Numbers in particular were exaggerated, and this may be taken as an inflexible rule – all numbers estimated of enemy forces are wrong, and all numbers of enemy casualties are wildly exaggerated.

This attempt to attack the British rear areas was thus unsuccessful, but so was every part of the British attack on the main Turkish positions. By the end of the day no ground of any significance had been taken. The Turks remained in possession of every position they had occupied at the start. The British troops had pulled back to the line they had occupied the day before, which had been partially prepared with trenches and dugouts. The question for the British was then, again, what to do the next day. Murray, in his command train at Khan Yunis, ordered that no ground should be given up during the night.[42] This was ignored when inconvenient, and obeyed – in so far as the forward troops knew of it – in the spirit, but not the letter. On the front of the East Anglians, the forward troops near the Tank Redoubt were hideously exposed to Turkish fire and were withdrawn under cover of activity by the Imperial Camel Brigade, who also withdrew from their advanced post at Khirbet Sihan.[49] Elsewhere the expectation was not so much of an early resumption of the attack, which some British generals suggested, as of an enemy counter-attack in the morning. So the ground was not given up; instead it was burrowed into, and the temporary line of the previous night solidified into a trench system.

Dobell dutifully began to compose orders for the resumption of the attack, but was rescued from actually giving the orders by reports from the divisional commanders that they had suffered heavy casualties, and that they were very short of ammunition.[44] So he postponed the new attack for a day, and reported back to Murray, saying that the renewal of the advance was not possible, and that other generals agreed with this. Murray had to accept this, but still hoped to try again for several days. The Royal Flying Corps located a Turkish force near Huj, claimed to be 2,000 infantry and 800 cavalry, who looked as though they were about to mount an attack; they were assailed by four bombers, and scattered. It is assumed – and claimed – that this prevented the attack.[45] It may be assumed, on the contrary, that both the numbers and the effects of the air attack are exaggerated.

General Murray still hoped to attack again on the 22nd, but then decided that the Turks had been reinforced, though this does not seem to have been the case. However, the idea did enable him to abandon any intention of a new attack. It seems doubtful that he could have persuaded his generals to carry one out. Several of these men had accepted defeat by the early afternoon of the 19th; resuming the attack was not possible for them.

The British casualties were not altogether clear to Murray, or to Dobell, until reports came in from the brigades and divisions on the morning of the 19th, but when they did arrive, it was finally clear that no attack could be mounted for some time. The British had suffered almost 6,500 killed, wounded and missing, two thirds of them in the East Anglian and Lowland Divisions.[46] It was not clear what the cost had been to the Turks, but it was obviously less than for the British. In fact, their casualties were 'only' 2,000,[47] so the British attacks had resulted in virtually cancelling out the numerical advantage they had started with.

What none of the British generals were prepared to do was admit that they had been defeated yet again, even though this was obviously the case. The forward line to which the troops had retreated was now 'consolidated', enabling them to believe that British control had been extended once more, by the distance between the Wadi Ghazze and the new line, just as Murray had claimed to have extended his control as far as the wadi in the first battle. But the new line in effect meant that the British troops were now fastened into fixed positions close to the enemy line, movement out of which was very difficult. They were also within reach of a constant Turkish artillery bombardment, which meant a constant dribble of casualties for the foreseeable future. This was precisely what the Turks and Germans would have wanted. The British were bound to renew the attack sooner or later, and would give plenty of notice of doing so; they would have to come out of their trenches across open ground, swept by machine-gun fire and artillery. They had already demonstrated that it was impossible to reach the Turkish lines without much greater quantities of artillery than they had, and which they showed no sign of getting. The Turks were safe enough for the time being.

CHAPTER 4

The Wider Context

Two British defeats at the same place within three weeks required changes. Dobell was the first to go, and Murray's position was obviously much weakened. Explanations were also needed. Dobell might prove a useful scapegoat, but there were necessarily deeper issues to be considered. These defeats would have to be avenged, but first the real reasons for them had to be discovered, and lessons learned.

In some ways the reasons were obvious. They had been seen, at least by some commanders, on the Western Front in France already: the futility of infantry advancing across open land in the face of artillery and machine-gun fire, the wastefulness of employing tanks singly, the absolute necessity of proper artillery power and preparation. In one counter-factual scenario one could imagine all eight of the tanks at Dobell's disposal being used as a group, perhaps to break the line for the East Anglian Division, which would then get through to take the city from the east, as intended. Two of the tanks on their own did indeed break into their target redoubts – suppose all had been used, against a softer target?

There was also the insistence on attacking the strongest points of the enemy line, Ali el-Muntar and its preliminary hills, and the redoubts along the road. This might be unavoidable in France, where the whole line was strong, but hardly so in Palestine. The advance of the battalion of the 10th London into the space between the city and the fortified road was certainly foolhardy and ultimately futile, but it gave a clear idea of the possibilities inherent in attacking the less well-defended parts of the line; the other 'farthest advance' took place between the Tank and Atawine Redoubts, but here the penetration was no further than the road. (The claim was disbelieved, but in November three Australian skeletons found there were held to prove it – but the dead cannot conquer.)[1] To men who had fought in France these ideas might have been obvious, but few men in the British forces in Palestine or Egypt had seen action there; Chetwode was one, but he was a cavalryman and had commanded only cavalry in France, which was not a good preparation for assaulting trenches. His command of the Desert Column had so far been competent, if unadventurous, and he had sent his horsemen to attack the redoubts, just as the infantry attacked Gaza's trenches.

There was no attempt to blame the troops, for it was all too clear that they had obeyed their orders with their customary stoic bravery. The vicious fighting in the Turkish trenches and redoubts bore witness to that, but above all it was proved by the dreadful casualty lists. The tools they had to use were also satisfactory, though there was clearly a need for a lot more artillery, and of heavier calibre, and a greater supply of ammunition. No commander in the Great War ever had enough artillery, but the quantity available in these two battles was clearly inadequate.

So neither the fighting qualities of the troops, nor their equipment had been at fault, rather the defeat had been caused by the use to which these men and their equipment had been put.[2] In both battles the basic problem was one of command and planning. This had been clear after the first battle, and improvements in the system had been made by the time of the second. Dobell did not command the assault directly this time, and was physically separated from the divisional headquarters, which in turn were situated where they could be reached from Dobell's headquarters and from their brigades. But this was offset by the arrival of Murray in his command train, to sit, metaphorically, at Dobell's shoulder. This certainly inhibited Dobell, who by the end was simply referring problems to Murray for a decision.[3] It is clear that Murray had not expected Dobell to conduct the battle well.

On the other hand, the preparation had been an improvement on the first battle. A clear plan of attack had been made, one which did not need the objectives for the battalions to be pointed out in the midst of the fighting, as had been the case with the Welsh Division attack in March. But the planners were too willing to accept that the enemy dispositions would dictate the fighting pattern; and the basic plan was too similar to that of the first battle, except that the mounted arm was scarcely used as it should have been; sending divisions of mounted infantry to attack fortified redoubts was a waste of the men, whose usefulness was, after all, primarily in their mobility. The Anzac and Imperial Mounted Divisions were used much less sensibly in the second battle than in the first.

These were all fairly obvious conclusions which any trained officer would see. Applying them to future operations was less easy, and it would require the use of a great deal more imagination and strategic and tactical insight than anyone in Egypt had so far displayed. Dobell certainly did not have it; Chetwode might, and so might some of the divisional and brigade commanders.

Murray had a good strategic sense, but did not choose good general commanders. He was mired in the administrative problems of the army in both Egypt and Sinai, which distorted his view, and he rather too obviously avoided becoming involved in the tactical situation.

Meanwhile, on the ground, the battlefield solidified. The British forces found themselves on a new line, closer to the Turks', but having to use shallow trenches. The first thing to do was dig down, but conditions were difficult and increasingly unpleasant. The closeness of the enemy meant that much of the work had to be done in the dark hours, while during the day the temperature rose inexorably. Water was short, cleanliness was difficult to achieve, sores developed, and the food was poorer than ever. Disease spread.[4] The historian of the Royal Scots shuddered at the insect life:

> The soil was infested with insects of every description and in the numerous trenches and hollows the troops found unpleasant companions in snakes, flies, tarantulas, scorpions, and centipedes. During the hot and dry weather the atmosphere was thick with dust so that even the tiniest scratch tended to become a septic sore.[5]

The Turks were well satisfied with their success, but made their defences stronger and larger. The two armies now occupied fortified lines only a mile or so apart, stretching from the sea to just behind the hill called Sheikh Abbas, a distance of about 7 miles; at that point the British line turned sharply away at right angles, and ran for the same distance in a line as far as the Wadi Ghazze. This had been done at the instance of General Chetwode, who succeeded to the command in the field. He pointed to the cost in manpower of continuing the line any further. This refused flank was therefore left open, and the cavalry was used to patrol the whole area east of Sheikh Abbas.[6] The Turkish line remained in its original position along the Beersheba road, anchored on the coast by the city of Gaza.

The battlefield had to be tidied up. On the British side this involved locating and evacuating the wounded, moving their guns to better locations, organizing supplies and the rotation of units in the line – all the basic administrative chores any competent army staff could do with minimum effort. On the Turkish side such things were hardly organized at all, and the men existed on poor food and not much of it. And among some of the Turks, there was another element involved. On the night after the battle Nogales Bey made his way to a meeting, in a shell hole, with other commanders. His journey, as described in his gothic prose, was nightmarish:

After the roar of day the silence now seemed complete. It was broken only by the wind rustling through dry shrubs, the weird howls of jackals, and the cries of the wounded, which, vibrating mysteriously from rock to rock to die out in sighs, sent a shudder through us from time to time and made us feel as if only ourselves and the Angel of Death were riding across those dark Wadis.

At every step we risked stumbling and falling headlong, or being picked off by the bullets of our own Arab volunteers who were scouring the desert in search of corpses to despoil or of wounded English to despatch – scenting them out like wild beasts. I glimpsed these vandals on every side, slipping about, silent as vampires through the nocturnal shadows and carefully avoiding close encounter with us through fear lest we be a Christian patrol. … [T]o kill and mutilate Christians even when they are ill or wounded is, for the Mussulman, a pious act which opens the door of paradise. Repeatedly I distinguished vaguely some heaps on the dark ground which on closer examination I recognized, with a sickening sense of horror, as the nude, mutilated bodies of English soldiers.[7]

It is noticeable that even Nogales, brought up a Christian, did not feel it necessary to give assistance to the wounded, or to organize such assistance. This was not every Turk's attitude. One British soldier was rescued from a heap of dead by a Turkish officer and sent to hospital in Gaza. He might have been rescued, but his experience was hardly reassuring:

[A] Turkish officer … ordered two of his men to take me back from the heaps of dead which ringed the redoubt, put me on a stretcher and took me behind the Turkish lines … [Taken to Gaza] I joined up with a band of other prisoners who aided me through the Gaza streets among the extremely hostile citizens …[8]

Nogales Bey's comments on the local *jihadi* feelings of the Bedouin were clearly shared by the Muslim inhabitants of the city, and equally clearly not by the Turkish officer. They were not usually shared by the front-line troops either, who were fairly compassionate towards men who might shoot at them but at least shared their privations.

The men in the trenches, digging and dirty, 'shirtless and septic',[9] scarcely heard anything but rumours about the changes which took place at the top. Murray sacked Dobell promptly on 21 April (just as Dobell had in effect sacked

Dallas in March). But no new blood was brought in to the command system; instead generals were all moved up a step: Chetwode moved from command of the Desert Column to command of the whole army; he was replaced at the Desert Column by General Chauvel from the Anzac Division, whose place there was taken by General E. W. C. Chaytor from the New Zealand Brigade.[10] And yet these moves signalled something new, even though they might have been familiar faces. All three men had more experience in the Egyptian and Palestinian theatre than Dobell, and Chetwode had commanded in France. A certain military diplomacy is also evident: Chauvel was Australian, Chaytor a New Zealander, Chetwode English.

Chauvel had hoped for his new command, but he was well aware that being an Australian was not a recommendation in the War Office or in the British officer corps generally. He wrote to his wife: 'I was very doubtful whether they would give it to me as the command is more than half British and no overseas officer has yet had a command of this size or one that included anything but a few details of British troops.'[11]

The background was Australia's rejection of conscription in the referendum of October 1916, held because the willingness of young Australian men to volunteer had declined. The same problem had bedevilled politics in Britain, where the issue was dealt with in Parliament. The Australian Prime Minister, Billy Hughes, put party first, unlike Lloyd George, and took refuge in the referendum.[12] In the process he left a nasty political and social legacy which poisoned Australian society for the next generation. In addition there were complaints in Australia that the British would not let an Australian take command where British troops were involved. Chauvel was fully aware of these nuances, and three weeks after his appointment he referred to them in another letter to his wife:

> My present appointment should stop all cavilling by Australia about their troops being commanded by British officers as ... I believe I have at the present moment more British troops under my command than any British general has Australians.[13]

Murray remained in place for the present, even though Robertson in London had recommended his dismissal on 23 April in an appreciation for the War Cabinet.[14] Perhaps Murray's speedy dismissal of Dobell pre-empted his own removal, but it is clear that his position was now shaky. At the same time, Robertson's comment could be seen as another sign of his dislike of Murray, which was not concealed. The two men had known each other for decades, having attended the Staff College together (Allenby and Haig were on the same course), and in France in 1914 they were both on the staff of Sir John French, the commander-in-chief of the Expeditionary Force, Murray as Chief of Staff, and Robertson as Quartermaster-General. Whereas Robertson was a great success in his post, Murray, burdened with far too much work by French, had fallen ill at the end of the year. On his recovery he was appointed to train the New Army by Kitchener, and in September 1915 was appointed Chief of the Imperial General Staff. But when French was replaced as Commander-in-Chief in France by Haig in December, Murray was sacked and Robertson took his place. On the insistence of the Prime Minister, Asquith, Murray was sent to Egypt early in 1916, but he must have regarded it as a demotion, and when Asquith himself resigned at the end of 1916, he lost his political protection.[15]

The relationship between Murray and Robertson, already unpleasant, was poisoned by these manoeuvres, in which Murray had consistently come out worst. It was not helped by Robertson's manner, inarticulate in speech, but very clear and sometimes all too blunt in writing. The tone of several of his communications to Murray during 1916 was distinctly unpleasant and at times patronizing: 'What we want from you ...', he began one sentence. This may have been the origin of Murray's disastrous claim of victory at the first battle of Gaza, where he may have been attempting to score over Robertson, who never did command an army in the field. The claim, when it was detected as wrong, clearly prejudiced the War Cabinet against him; and since it was the Cabinet which saw through the subterfuge rather than Robertson, Robertson's attitude to him was not improved. Murray did not make the same mistake after the second battle, but, having placed himself so close to Dobell with the intention of overseeing his decisions, he could hardly avoid blame for a second defeat. The removal of Dobell, with its implication that he alone had been responsible, only deflected part of that blame.

These command considerations have also to be seen in other, wider, contexts. It was quite possible that the British might once more reconsider their aims in the Near East, and if they decided not to pursue conquest in Palestine, Murray could be left where he was, diminished and ignored, simply the administrator and defender of the reduced Egyptian base, a role he had fulfilled well until the attacks on Gaza. A standstill was a most unlikely outcome, of course, not simply for reasons of prestige, but also because of a complex set of political considerations.

Between the capture of Rafa in January and the second repulse from Gaza in April the war went through a decisive change. The 'February' revolution in

Russia in mid-March had at first encouraged and then increasingly worried the Allies, as the initial promise of improved Russian warlike efforts failed to appear, and the prospect of a democratic regime to replace the tsarist autocracy seemed to mean that the Russian state would disintegrate. Then early in April the United States finally came to the decision that, with the fate of the world at issue, she could only be involved in the outcome and affect the conclusions if she were to participate in the fighting. Germany's decision to resume all-out submarine warfare in February contributed to this, giving the United States a morally superior excuse for joining in, and the removal of Russian tsarism assisted that process. It was, however, essentially a *realpolitik* decision, and an exertion of American power. It was nonetheless welcome to the Allies, as a replacement for Russia, but its effects would take a long time to appear, and the new German submarine campaign was a more immediate threat to the Allies' lifeline across the Atlantic.

The Allies in France mounted their major spring offensive, as intended, just as these more distant events were taking place. The British Third Army attacked at Arras on 9 April, with subordinate participations by the Canadian Army at Vimy Ridge and the Australian Division at Bullecourt. By the standards of the fighting on the Western Front this was a major success: Vimy Ridge was taken, and the German line before Arras pushed back several miles, though the attempt to take Bullecourt was a failure. (A second attack a month later succeeded.) Most notably the casualties in these attacks were relatively light, and it was clear that the decisive difference lay in the quality of the planning and preparation, and in the generalship – at Vimy and at Arras Byng and Allenby were outstanding, at Bullecourt Gough and Birdwood were much wanting.[16] In London the Prime Minister took due note. The French half of the offensive, planned by General Nivelle to capture the Chemin des Dames, went in a week later, and was a disastrous failure. The French pillar of the Alliance began to look much weakened, and there were several mutinies in the French army a month later.

Perhaps partly as a result of this weakening, the French government moved to assert itself in the Near East. French forces had been involved in the fighting against the Ottoman Empire from the beginning. The coastal-defence ship *Requin* had been of much assistance in the defence of the Canal, and had bombarded Gaza in the second battle; French ships and men had fought at Gallipoli, and it was at French insistence that some of the troops evacuated from that peninsula had been landed at Salonica to provide a continuing threat to Constantinople and Bulgaria.

The basic reason for French participation was a wish to acquire a French empire in the Near East, an ambition which dated from Napoleon's time, but which French propagandists linked with the Crusades, which they depicted as a French enterprise. So the French government had been foremost in Allied discussions on the fate of the Ottoman Empire after its prospective defeat. These discussions had produced a succession of agreements, whereby Britain and France proposed to take over various sections of the Ottoman Arab lands. Russia was soon involved in these agreements as well.[17] The arrival of Italy as an Ally had added another hungry mouth at the table, and British negotiations and agreements with the Sharif Husayn of Mecca had overlain these inter-Allied agreements with a contradictory Anglo-Arab layer.

The net result had been the proposed allocation of a large section of south-western Anatolia to Italy, adjacent to its islands in the Aegean, of the Straits and Armenia to Russia, and a division of the Arab lands between Britain and France. France was to acquire control over Lebanon, a longstanding and particular French interest, and the area of Syria east and north of that country; Britain claimed Mesopotamia, where its armies were fighting. This was close to the Persian oilfields, whose protection and control had been the object of the Mesopotamian expedition in the first place, and oil was known to be recoverable in northern Mesopotamia;[18] the possibility of settling surplus Indian peasants in the area was contemplated as well. The British also laid claim to Palestine. The status of Jerusalem was to be subject to an international regime of some sort, but Britain would predominate, given its proposed control of surrounding Palestine. All these agreements were necessarily tentative, not to say speculative, and the boundaries between the claims and around them were sketches only, and were repeatedly changed as new schemes were produced, but the intention was clearly to dismember and destroy the Ottoman Empire for the benefit of the European victors.[19] The Anglo-Arab agreements promised, in the same vague way, an Arab state in the interior, a concept which cut right across much of the Allies' notions.[20]

Before any of these agreements could be implemented, the war against Turkey had to be won. So far only in one area had there been any success, for General Maude had at last captured Baghdad in Mesopotamia in March, just before Murray and Dobell failed at Gaza. He issued a proclamation claiming that the British came to Baghdad as liberators, and, as evidence of Britain's good will, pointed to the independence of the King of the Hejaz, the former Sharif of Mecca. The implication, which was not spelt out, was that Mesopotamia would be independent, perhaps as part of Husayn's kingdom.[21] It was a

remarkably cunning document which would permit almost any political interpretation later. For the present, however, it was the conquest which counted.
Success in Mesopotamia, an area which the British had reserved for themselves in every inter-Allied agreement, could seem suspicious to Britain's allies
when it was not repeated in Palestine, whose conquest was necessary before
the French-claimed areas of Lebanon and northern Syria could be reached.

The French were very suspicious of British intentions – quite correctly
– and had made attempts to exert influence in the Arab Revolt in competition
with the British. They were eclipsed in their relationship with King Husayn
and his son Faysal by the charisma of Major T. E. Lawrence, but they had the
dubious satisfaction of noting that the rebellion had little success for several
months, so that the British had to send forces from Egypt to assist the Arabs.
This was not what the British had intended, for the Arab rebellion had been
induced so as to assist the British in Egypt by distracting the Turks; assisting
the rebellion was the wrong way to look at it.[22] But there were deeper waters
to negotiate than this. For the Arabs who were in revolt defined Arabia as all
that land inhabited by Arabs, reasonably enough. This included Palestine and
Syria and Mesopotamia, but these were the lands which the principal Allies,
France and Britain, had marked out as their spoils from the Ottoman Empire
after the war ended. Politically it would be most unfortunate to find that the
Arabs – their allies, now – had conquered those lands for themselves, though
all the professional soldiers regarded this as militarily impossible. Unless the
Allies actually occupied the lands they claimed, then their claim to them would
scarcely stand at the end-of-war conference.

All this had made several imperialistic interest groups in France very
excited, and wild claims had been voiced within these groups and to the French
government.[23] Any large-scale military involvement by the French army was
blocked by the French high command, who did not want to send troops overseas when parts of France was occupied by the enemy, but the government was
not deaf to the issue. So after the second Gaza battle, and in view of the British assistance to the Arab Revolt, the French now insisted on sending a small
force to take part in the Palestinian fighting, giving it the grandiloquent title
of Détachement Français de Palestine. The Italians followed suit. The French
contingent seemed a useful three battalions: one of French territorials and two
of Algerian *tirailleurs*, almost 3,000 soldiers. These troops arrived late in May,
and the Italian troops, 500 infantry, followed in June.[24]

To the troops on the ground, intermittently shot at and shelled in their
trenches, sent out on dangerous patrols, uncomfortable in their tented camps,

subject to unpleasant insects and nasty diseases, and disdainful of the locals on their very occasional leaves in Cairo or Alexandria, the land they were in and fighting for scarcely seemed worth the effort. Many of them hated the conditions they faced, and many detested the Palestinians they met. Mostly, until after the invasion north of Gaza, these were Bedouin, whose unpleasant habits Rafael de Nogales described; they were suspected of passing information to the Turks, and widely regarded as thieves and murderers; they were also feared and hated by the pilots, since if they were brought down the Bedouin routinely killed them for any possessions they had.[25] On the other hand, many of the Bedouin also worked for the British as intelligence agents,[26] and were quite unrepresentative of the people of Palestine, though the troops would only discover this when they penetrated past Gaza. For the moment disillusionment was general.

Yet Palestine was not just the people, and a land which was a welcome green and fertile after the brown sand and grey rock and extreme weather the troops had experienced in Sinai. It was the Holy Land. *The* Holy Land. It was the land where Jesus had lived when on earth. It was a land which every western Christian had heard about all his life. Jerusalem, Bethlehem, Joppa (now Jaffa), Caesarea Philippi, the Jordan, the Dead Sea, and so on, were places as familiar to every Englishman as London, or to every Scot as Edinburgh – for most Englishmen and Scots had seen neither London or Edinburgh, any more than they had seen Jerusalem. Almost every man in the Allied armies was Christian at least in name, many of them were active and practising Christians, and every one of them had received an education which included a Christian indoctrination. The Bedouin, as Nogales noted, called the British 'Christians', and in this they were quite accurate. To invade Palestine and wrest it from the grip of the Muslim Turk was to many of the British troops no more than a Christian duty. Repeatedly in the accounts written at the time or soon after, the participants invoke the medieval Crusaders, just as many of the men on the opposing side invoked the notion of *jihad*, holy war against the infidel, the unbeliever. For both sides this was at one level a holy war. In the circumstances, it is remarkable that it was so essentially gentlemanly. Mutual massacres would not have been surprising.

The chaplains of the British forces were repeatedly called on to relate the stories associated with such places as Gaza: Samson was often invoked. And yet many of the men who preached knew their audiences, and that to speak of fire and brimstone to men who faced such things daily, or even of a holy duty, when to many men 'duty' meant a chore, or the loss of a night's sleep, would be inappropriate, and might invite soldierly derision. One chaplain in the Australian forces became a keen archaeologist when a Roman mosaic pavement was found at Shellal. It had been damaged by Turkish trenching; the chaplain organized its excavation and removal. The exploit was commented on throughout the army almost in terms of a military victory. He would not have gained anything like the same attention if he had begun preaching wildly.[27]

The area, as everyone realized, was steeped in past events, but it was disappointingly unpleasant to live in the present. Remarkably few, however, paid any serious attention to the military past of the area. There are no references, for example, to the great battle of Raphia (now Rafa) in 217 BC, which involved 150,000 men. Gaza was, however, fulfilling its historic role before their very gaze, had they but realized it: it was Palestine's gateway to Egypt, and that was how the Turks had used it in their invasion of Sinai; it was also the Palestinian guardpost against an attack from Egypt, and this was how it had now come to be used since the British arrival at Rafa. It was, though it did not look it to eyes more than likely to disparage anything local, a fortress. It had been acting in that role for well over 3,000 years, in the time of Solomon, of Alexander, and of the Crusaders, to name only those whom the soldiers on both sides might have heard of. And though it might not look like a fortress, every Allied soldier in the Welsh and Lowland Divisions who had attempted to penetrate the modern Turkish trenches south of the city knew full well that it was one.

There is no sense of any understanding of this historical perspective in either side's appreciations, but both had stumbled on its essential truth in the fighting in March and April. The Turks, under the tactical direction of Colonel Kress von Kressenstein, an engineer officer by training, now deepened and expanded the defences they had already built around the city and along the Beersheba road as far as Hureyra; Beersheba itself was now also developed as a fortified town, and the redoubts along the road were extended. For it remained clear to both sides that only by a British attack which broke into and through the Turkish line could any change be accomplished in the stalemate established by the earlier battles. The Turks were not strong enough to launch a serious attack on the British, and yet they had every reason to believe that their defensive positions were fully capable of denying the British their breakthrough.

General Murray would have agreed. He knew that to break the Turkish line he would need more troops and guns and tanks and aeroplanes; and he would need a plan which gave some hope of using these troops to advantage.

In particular it was clear that just breaking the Turkish line was not enough; he would need a good reserve of troops who could then pursue the enemy vigorously enough to prevent any serious rally.

Murray believed that the Turks were strongly reinforcing their forces in southern Palestine, and a degree of intelligence supported this.[28] In fact, the Turks were concentrating their efforts on extending their fortifications, rather than bringing forward new troops. Their transportation system into the south of Palestine imposed serious limitations on the number of troops they could supply. The British had faced the same problem earlier because of the difficulty of advancing across Sinai, and had solved it with their railway and their water pipeline. The Turks had also developed a railway to help supply their forces in Sinai, and it had been extended through Beersheba and as far as the Egyptian border at Auja. This was well inland, since a coastal line would be in danger of disruption by naval bombardment, and the withdrawal of the Turkish defences to their line from Gaza to Beersheba left the extension beyond that town barely used.

The governor, Jamal Pasha, had in fact anticipated the British in their use of railways as a means of waging war. Before the war, when governor of Iraq, Jamal had been associated with Heinrich August Meissner, the German engineer who had built both the Hejaz Railway and the Baghdad Railway. When the war with Britain broke out Jamal's early attack aimed at cutting the Suez Canal failed, for which one of the identifiable reasons had been the difficulty of moving a sufficiently large army across Sinai to mount a substantial attack on the Canal. Jamal then conceived the idea of building a railway right through central Sinai to Bir Gifgafa, only about 60 miles from the Canal, which would let him deploy and supply troops relatively close to the Canal itself. Meissner was recruited to engineer the work.[29]

Meissner faced enormous problems. He had no means of buying or manufacturing rails; wood for sleepers was extremely scarce; nor had he any qualified engineers. Yet by improvisation, by collecting all the rails already accumulated for the unbuilt sections of the Hejaz Railway, by tearing up unused sections of railway, and by ruthlessly cutting trees down all over Syria, he built the new railway from central Palestine as far south as Beersheba by October 1915, a distance of over 100 miles. It was clearly a wartime project, not intended to be permanent, built away from the coast to avoid shelling by the Royal Navy; the shortage of coal required the use of wood as fuel, which was already in short supply. Labour was provided by conscripted Syrians, a thoroughly unpopular move.

Meissner wished to stop construction at Beersheba, but Jamal insisted on extending the line into Sinai, with the intention of supplying the forces he hoped to send to attack the Canal again. This section went more slowly, and by mid–1916 it had only reached el-Kossaima, more than 60 miles beyond Beersheba – but he was half-way to his goal, Bir Gifgafa. The rate of construction had slowed drastically when the line pushed out into the desert. It was not simply a shortage of rails, though this was a factor. The main difficulty was getting labourers forward to do the job, and keeping them alive. In other words, the Turks faced much the same sort of problems of construction as the British, in that they had to use the railway simply to keep the workers going, and that supplies for the troops were therefore used up. In addition, the Turks had chosen a route which left them with a railhead in the middle of the desert. Construction stopped when the Turkish outposts in the desert were driven back into Palestine, and when the British arrived, they attacked at Gaza, which was not on the line Meissner had built. So the Turks ended up with their supply problems doubled. Construction of Jamal's line stopped from late 1916, but the threat to Gaza then stimulated new thinking after the repulse of the first British attack in March 1917.

This new development was at last realized by the British in May, as a result of a patrol by the Imperial Camel Corps Brigade: the Turks were still using the railway. Reconnaissance by airmen had identified what seemed to be gaps in the line; believing the line was no longer in operation, they assumed that parts of it had been covered by wind-blown sand. But at the last station on the line, el-Auja, close to the Egyptian border, the Camel Corps patrol discovered that there were barracks, a hospital, and a large reservoir. The patrol attacked a moving train, but failed to stop it: a small group of Armenian railwaymen were captured, and, on being questioned, proved to be loquaciously informative. It emerged that the Turks were planning to dismantle the line beyond el-Auja and use the rails to build a new branch line which would serve Gaza from the north. The gaps attributed to drifted sand had in fact been a sign of the dismantling.[30]

This was more of Meissner's work. Following the fighting at Gaza he had begun the construction of a new branch line, taking off from the Beersheba railway at et-Tine, 7 miles or so south of its junction with the Jaffa–Jerusalem line. It was laid, at a prudent distance from the vulnerable coast, as far as Deir Sneid, 7 miles north of Gaza; then an extension was put in to Beit Hanun, 2 miles closer to the city. This line was finished and operating by the end of May.[31] It made up in part of materials from the railway south of Beersheba;

in other words the British had completely missed the dismantling of that line, which had been going on for months.

It had been Murray himself who had alerted the forward commanders to the problem, for he was also convinced that the Turks had received reinforcements. The dangers presented by a prepared base such as el-Auja, well to the south of the Turkish main positions, but in constant contact with them by the railway, were obvious, and those supposed reinforcements might well be the troops to be used in a desert raid, or an outflanking move. The Turks had, after all, reached the Canal in 1915 by the inland Sinai route. The danger was further highlighted by the exploits of a Turkish raiding party, led by the Venezuelan adventurer Nogales Bey. He was sent in early May on a raid deep into Sinai, and for the next month wandered about the peninsula almost at will.[32] He provoked several British units from the Canal garrison and from the railway and pipeline patrols into long exasperating chases in vain attempts to catch him. If Nogales could do that from a base as far back as Tell esh-Sheria, a fully prepared Turkish base as far forward as el-Auja seemed a much more serious threat. Attached to the main Turkish base by workable railway, it could be activated rapidly to house a substantial force which could raid the British communications at a critical moment.

The British railway and pipeline would be prime targets for a large raid. The vulnerability of the pipeline had been demonstrated during the second Gaza battle, when a German aeroplane landed beside it in an unpatrolled section. The two-man crew laid charges, and blew up a section of the main pipe. They waited around long enough to collect part of the pipe as a souvenir, then took off again.[33] This was one of the reasons why the Royal Engineers were so diligent in searching out new sources of water in the lands close to the British line. It was at this time that revealing calculations were made, showing that no more than 6 per cent of water pumped into the pipeline in Egypt actually reached the Palestinian end, the rest being used up on the way. Similar calculations showed that the British railway also required expansion. The only way to provide greater capacity was to double both lines.[34] It was estimated that this would take eight months. On 4 May another German aircraft carried out a raid on the pipeline, with similarly brief effects.[35]

The Ottoman Empire had been proving to be a surprisingly resilient political organism. Long assumed to be in imminent danger of collapse, it had fought off the Anglo-French assault at Gallipoli, and had attacked the British in Sinai and Aden. When the British replied, the Turks had fought successful defensive battles twice at Gaza. In Mesopotamia the loss of Baghdad was the second British attempt at conquest, the first having been blocked by a Turkish victory at Kut el-Amara. These are familiar events to any student of the Great War, but they bear being repeated, to emphasize just how powerful an existing state could be when on the defensive. The Young Turks in control in Constantinople were successfully mobilizing support for their government.

The Turks were faced by two offensives from the south: through Gaza and through Mesopotamia. The defeat of the attack on Gaza contrasted with the victory of the British in Mesopotamia. The loss of Baghdad, though not unexpected, was sensational, the name of the city being one of those with powerful resonance. It had resulted in an immediate Turkish appeal to Germany for help, and a plan was made to form a new army with which to recover Baghdad. The help from Germany came in the expert form of General Erich von Falkenhayn, and the promise of the despatch of a specialized force of German troops. This was to be small in number but extravagantly equipped with artillery and machine-guns; it was to be formed in Silesia under the name of the Asienkorps. Falkenhayn was created a Marshal in the Turkish army for the occasion and in May made a quick inspection of the situation in both Mesopotamia and Palestine.[36]

This visit coincided with a large patrol by two Australian Light Horse Regiments, one of a series of patrols designed to establish British domination of the area east of their lines and south of the Turks' lines. The regiment spread out in a line 3 miles long to the south of Karm; the 3rd Light Horse extended the line further south. Rather to their surprise, they found 'two regiments of Turkish cavalry and a battery' when they reached Karm. They were spotted soon after by the Turkish patrols and set out in pursuit, but were unable to concentrate sufficiently to be able to attack the main Turkish body. 'It was months after that we found that, under cover of that force, German and Turkish Generals had made a reconnaissance of our position with the object of attacking us.'[37]

Falkenhayn went back to Constantinople with the suggestion of an offensive in Palestine, an idea which horrified the Turks, in particular Jamal Pasha. The plan for the use of the Asienkorps was meanwhile fully worked out on the blackboard at the camp in Silesia. It was to thrust this force at great speed from Silesia right to Mesopotamia, travelling by train along the Baghdad railway and then by its own motor transport along the line of the Euphrates River to act as the spearhead of a joint German-Turkish counter-attack on the British force in Mesopotamia. The plan, good on paper, tended to ignore the friction of war, and the particular conditions of the Turkish war. These inimical conditions included popular disaffection, bureaucratic inefficiency, war weariness, shortage of food, heat, drought, the limited capacity of the Turkish railway system, Turkish resentment at the arrogantly patronizing tone of the Germans, and above all the disputes and disagreements within the Turkish governing group.[38]

The Turks intended to use forces which had become available as a result of the growing collapse of the Russian front. They would transfer forces from eastern Anatolia and Armenia, and others from Europe, but, again, it would take much effort and time to move them and organize the new army, which was to be called the Seventh Army. The Turks referred to the German contingent as 'Pasha II'; the Germans called it 'Army Group F'. The mixture of names is suggestive of the general confusion.

This whole plan was code-named 'Yildirim', a Turkish word meaning 'lightning', or perhaps 'thunderbolt'. It was selected to remind the Turks of the hero-Sultan Bajazet I in the fourteenth century, who was also nicknamed Yildirim, a commander noted for his speed of movement and his victorious wars in both Europe and Asia. Yet it was an unfortunate choice since he was eventually defeated and captured by the armies of Timur, who attacked from the east after the capture of Baghdad, just as the British were doing. Nor would it appeal to any non-Turks in the empire.

The Turks began assembling the Yildirim army in the region of Aleppo. From there it could be used either against the British in Mesopotamia, or against the attack which was expected at Gaza, and it was also a useful deterrent against a possible British landing at Alexandretta, which had been suggested several times in British planning circles, but which had always been abandoned. The Turks had evidently heard about it: the leakage of intelligence in both directions was always substantial. The British knew of the Yildirim force almost as soon as it had been set up, partly from gossip among Ottoman soldiers convalescing in Switzerland, partly from intercepted radio messages.[39] The Turks could be certain that the British would learn of the Aleppo army soon enough so that it would act as a useful deterrent. The main question for them was, however, how to use it actively.

The troops came from various sources. There had been seven Turkish divisions employed in Europe, two facing the immobile Allied force based at Salonica, two helping to protect Austria-Hungary against a Russian invasion in Galicia, and three others were part occupation force, part strategic reserve in Romania. With the lessening of the Russian menace in both the Caucasus and Galicia, and the increasing menace of the British in Palestine and Mesopotamia, it made sense to bring some of these far-flung Turkish troops back to defend their own empire. In June a conference assembled at Aleppo to decide what to do with it, and who was to command it.

Present at the conference were the leading men of the Ottoman military government. In the chair was Enver Pasha. He was the effective ruler of the Ottoman Empire, but a man whose position depended more on political and personal manoeuvre than either his strength of character or on his formal political position. By this time Enver's political ideas had become largely absorbed into the concept of Pan-Turkism, a super-Turkish nationalism, which envisaged the inclusion in a single state of all Turkish-speaking peoples, a state which would stretch from Istanbul to the borders of China.[40] From the Caucasus came two generals, Izzet Pasha, who had been winning small victories against the disintegrating Russian army, and Mustafa Kemal Pasha, whose reputation had been made in the vicious fighting at Gallipoli, and who now commanded the forces in the Lake Van area. From Mesopotamia came Khalil Pasha, the commander of the Sixth Army there, who was desperate to get his hands on the new force to shore up his crumbling front. Falkenhayn was there, as was the German Chief of the Turkish General Staff, General Bronsart von Schellendorf. In addition, Jamal Pasha, the viceroy of Syria, wanted to use the new force to shore up his Gaza defences, which he and Kress von Kressenstein insisted were much weaker than their successful defensive exploits tended to suggest.[41]

Jamal Pasha had gained increased, quasi-viceregal powers over Syria during 1915. He had ruled since then as a virtually independent sovereign, and had at one time contemplated formalizing this into actual independence. He had made contact with the British government through Armenian intermediaries in Copenhagen and Stockholm, and put forward the idea of himself as an independent king of Syria leading a revolt against the Ottoman Sultan. This was a promising idea, not because anyone liked Jamal very much, or thought the Syrians would benefit, but because of the disruption it would cause the Turks. The scheme did not get much beyond talk, however, because when the French heard about it they objected strongly; and the Russians and the British, on whom Jamal would have to rely to accomplish his aim, were as unwilling as the French to forgo possible imperial gains in the area. Even the prospect of knocking the Ottoman Empire out of the war – for its war effort could scarcely have survived such a rebellion in the midst of the fighting at Gallipoli and in the Caucasus, if Jamal had organized the thing properly – was not enough to persuade the Allies to give up their ambitions to gain control over Syria for themselves.[42]

Jamal was therefore compelled to continue operating as a loyal Ottoman agent. His intervention in the Aleppo conference, arguing strongly for the Yildirim army to be used in Palestine, was seriously disruptive, though he was not the only member to be doubtful of its success. Mustafa Kemal is said to have subjected Falkenhayn to a vigorous critique of the plan, leaving the German uncomfortably angry (though we may wonder whether this was an example of Turkish hero-worship of Kemal). As a result the conference did not decide the destination of the Seventh Army, though its accumulation at Aleppo was to continue. Jamal had made several telling points in his favour: in particular the possibility of a local rising taking place in Syria and the prospect of an Allied landing on the coast behind his front.[43]

The revolt in Arabia had certainly had repercussions in Syria. Jamal kept a firm grip there, but by resorting to regular executions of opponents – thirty-four of them in 1915 and 1916 – he produced a roll-call of martyrs; exiling and imprisoning others only spread the discontent. This was in addition to the severing of trade links with Europe, the subsequent economic depression, and the Turkish requisitions and conscriptions. The net effect was, as in Egypt under the British-imposed martial law, to produce a nationalist reaction directed mainly against Turkish rule.[44]

The Turkish politicians who disputed at the Aleppo conference exhibited all the signs of a polity in terminal crisis, squabbling over the fragments which remained, taking exception to each other's needs, advancing their own personal and political agendas. The appointment of Falkenhayn had not really helped this political situation. He had made a swift tour of inspection, going first to Khalil in Mesopotamia and then to Jamal in Syria, during which he ventured as far as Karm, where the Australian patrols met his escort. He reported that it was quite possible to defeat the British in Mesopotamia, but that the Palestine front should be made secure as well. So Khalil could call for the Seventh Army for himself, while Jamal was also able to demand part of it for Syria. Enver refused the latter request, but did not accede to Khalil's either. The decision on how to use Yildirim was thus deferred.

The Seventh Army gathered at Aleppo only slowly, and the Asienkorps took far longer to move than the Germans had expected, though much of its equipment and ammunition was collected at Haidar Pasha station across the Bosporos from Constantinople, ready to be picked up when the men arrived. All this was known to the British. The code name Yildirim was becoming less and less appropriate as time passed, giving plenty of scope for irony by all concerned.

One of the apparent threats from outside was a proposed landing in the Tripoli area. This was put forward in Paris by French imperialists who argued that it would gather support in the Lebanon, where the abolition of local autonomy, and the requisitions of the military authorities had created widespread resentment. This was particularly so among the large Christian population.[45] This was one of Jamal's considerations, for the communal tensions in Syria were clearly rising. Muslim–Christian tensions were constant, but there were also developing tensions between Arabs and Turks. The Young Turk revolution had taken to emphasizing Turkish nationalism, with the result that the Arab population of the empire was increasingly alienated.[46] The alienation of the Syrian Muslim population was not at the stage of near-revolt, any more than that of any faith group in the Lebanon. There were, however, significant stirrings among intellectual and bourgeois groups. Some Syrians had fled to exile in Cairo, where they angled for support, and secret nationalist societies existed inside Syria. However, there was little as yet in the way of a general feeling for independence. The most prevalent emotion appears to have been detestation for the Ottoman government.[47]

The Arab Revolt in Arabia added to the difficulties of the Ottomans in Syria, and in Palestine also it received some support. The Mufti of Gaza and his son set out to join the revolt, but were caught and hanged at the north gate of the city.[48] They were not the only Palestinians to join, or attempt to join, the revolt, nor were they the first or the last to suffer from arbitrary Ottoman, or Young Turk, justice. The Jews of Palestine, particularly those who had settled in the previous generation under the influence of the Zionist movement, were regarded with particular suspicion by the Turks, for many of them had retained their original nationality. This had safeguarded them in Palestine because they came under the protection of the various consuls, who had that responsibility under the Capitulations in the Ottoman system, which transferred jurisdiction over foreign groups to their own national representatives. But the Capitulations were abolished when the war began, and, since many of the Zionist settlers were originally Russian, their status changed overnight from that of a protected group to being enemy aliens. They inevitably suffered, and some responded by acting for the Allies; it was from among them that the British recruited an effective spy network.[49]

Intelligence of Turkish strength came to the British from a considerable variety of sources: their agents in Palestine, Jews, Bedouin, and Syrians, the flights and photographs of the Royal Flying Corps reconnaissance aircraft, radio intercepts, contacts, particularly in Berne in Switzerland, between

Ottoman diplomats and various Allied agents, including tentative negotiations with Talaat, a near-equal with Enver Pasha in the Turkish regime,[50]
consular reports from ostensibly neutral missions, that of the United States
consul in Damascus, for example. When the United States and the Ottoman
Empire broke off diplomatic relations in mid-1917, the departing United States
officials were free with information, including items concerning the Yildirim
plan. Yet all this was not well co-ordinated, some of the information going to
London, some collected in Cairo, or at headquarters in the field. Also, as with
all such work, conclusions drawn from the data were sometimes wrong, and
were always subject to interpretation through the preconceptions of the interpreters.[51]

Murray was convinced that the number of Ottoman troops in Palestine had
increased during May; Robertson in London had the same impression, working from different sources. So Murray would not allow another attack to be
mounted – not that anyone showed any willingness to do so. He reported to
London that in order to make any further attempt to defeat the Turks he would
need at least two more divisions,[52] a requirement he had repeatedly stated
before both Gaza battles. The forces he already had amounted to three infantry and two mounted divisions, plus the Yeomanry (infantry) Division, and
some other assorted units which he began to assemble to form another division, the 75th, but neither of the latter two was battle-ready or fully equipped.
All his present formations needed to be brought up to strength, and to become
equipped to the requirements of modern warfare, which meant above all artillery.

Murray was obviously correct in his appreciation, though wrong in his
understanding of the enemy's available manpower.[53] But he had fewer troops
after the second battle than before, and the new units which he was given
were from various distant theatres, under strength, and in some cases badly
infected with illness. A by no means untypical case is that of a battalion of the
Duke of Cornwall's Light Infantry, which had been in Aden for some time, and
now moved up to the line. The regimental historian describes the result:

> The health of the battalion was bad: cold nights with heavy dews affected
> the men considerably. Malaria and dysentery were rife and the numbers
> evacuated to hospital reduced the strength of the battalion considerably.
> By the end of May the health of officers and men was so poor that the
> 1/4th were sent back to El Arish to recuperate.[54]

This was all in addition to the slump in the army's morale as a result of two defeats. So Murray was quite incapable of attacking with any hope of success. His demands for more troops, and above all for more equipment, were hardly unreasonable in the circumstances, but he does seem to have made defeat and his shortage of manpower an excuse for general inaction, and it was difficult for the War Office to justify sending him more troops when he did not show any signs of being able to use them victoriously.

Not that he was not busy. The railway was extended to Deir el-Belah, and the construction of a branch line was begun from Rafa towards Tell el-Fara, 15 miles inland on the Wadi Ghazze, in order to ease the transport of supplies to the entrenched forces. The older recommendation to double the main line was agreed to and work began in June. Water sources were searched for and developed, and here pre-war archaeological researches proved useful. The fighting units were reorganized. A new mounted division was formed. The two existing mounted divisions each gave up one of their English brigades to the new unit, and two more brigades were transferred from Salonica; the result was three smaller divisions of three brigades each, in place of the earlier two. They were now named the Australian and New Zealand Mounted Division, commonly called Anzac, with two Australian and one New Zealand brigades, the Australian Mounted Division, with two more Australian brigades and the British 5th Mounted Brigade, and the Yeomanry Mounted Division, with three British brigades; each division also had a Royal Horse Artillery battery attached; one mounted brigade, the 7th, was kept under Army control along with the Imperial Camel Corps Brigade and the Imperial Service Cavalry Brigade.

The new infantry division which was being formed, the 75th, was a harbinger of what was to come in the next year. It had the usual three brigades, but each of these was formed from a varied set of battalions, two English and one Indian, which had been stationed along the Canal, or was brought in from Aden, East Africa, and India.[55] Indian troops had been used in garrisons so far, though one artillery battery, the Hong Kong and Singapore Mountain Battery, manned mainly by Sikhs, was highly regarded by all sides, and operated usually with the Imperial Camel Corps; it had the nickname of the 'Bing Boys'. But next year, after many troops were taken to France after the March crisis, the British forces in Palestine were to be very largely Indian in personnel, and the embodiment of some in the 75th Division was the first stage. There was also, of course, the Imperial Service Cavalry Brigade, directly under Army command, but not yet used.

For a month after the second battle Murray's forces did little but lick their wounds, rest, and patrol. Impatient messages began to arrive from London, contrasting Murray's inactivity with the success of Maude in Mesopotamia.[56] The comparison was rather unfair, as it was two months since the capture of Baghdad and Murray's army had fought two lost battles since then. Also the beginning of the formation of the Yildirim army had become known and its destination and potential were unclear. The revelation that the Turkish railway beyond Beersheba was still in use came just when Murray was under pressure to take action. Nogales's raid into Sinai had suggested how the railway might be a threat, while a major raid which could be conducted with relative safety would simultaneously resonate well in Britain, give the participating troops good on-the-job training, achieve the satisfying destruction of an enemy asset, and eliminate a perceived threat.

The Turkish railway system seemed to the British to be a worthwhile target. It was decided that most of the railway south of Beersheba should be destroyed. A large operation was laid on to do so, using almost all the mounted troops, horse and camel. There were to be two simultaneous distractions: a powerful artillery bombardment of the trenches at Gaza, and a demonstration by the Imperial Mounted Division against Beersheba. The latter would threaten the Turks there and prevent them from emerging to interfere with the work of destruction. The actual raid was to be carried out by two full mounted brigades: the 1st Australian Light Horse Brigade was to march from Shellal to cut the railway at Asluj, where there was a station and a bridge over the Wadi Ghazze; the Imperial Camel Corps was to march from Rafa against the station at el-Auja. Both brigades were to be accompanied by their own engineers and by extra engineers culled from other brigades and regiments who were to carry out the work of destruction.

The Australians' raid on Asluj arrived at 7 a.m., and by 10 a.m. had cut the line over a length of 7 miles, and had blown out every second arch of the bridge at Asluj. The Camel Corps took longer to reach el-Auja; by the time they did so their colleagues had cut the line, so they could carry out their work at leisure. The procedure of destruction was to blow a gap in every second rail on alternate sides. By the time they had finished the Turkish railway was unusable except for a few miles south of Beersheba, and it had no terminus other than the last complete rail.[57] The raid could be regarded as a success, in the sense that considerable destruction had been accomplished. Certain other benefits emerged also: knowledge of the country was much improved, as was the information on water resources in the area. As a large operation in a dry area, it proved that it was possible to move many animals and men through the desert terrain without the Turks' knowledge, and that the horses and camels could manage without noticeable distress. This in turn meant that locating water was a less critical problem than had been thought. It began to dawn on the British that with proper training, the men and animals' endurance could be significantly increased.

In terms of damaging the enemy, however, the raid was of little use. It appears that the Turkish command scarcely noticed it.[58] They had never really seen the extension of the railway beyond Beersheba as a useful resource since being driven out of Sinai, except for its sleepers and its rails. It was found, indeed, that the Turks themselves had already prepared the bridge of Asluj for demolition, and 'the Turks dropped messages from their aircraft a few days later, thanking the troops for doing what they themselves had intended to do and saving them trouble'.[59] The destruction of every other rail might render the railway useless as a railway, but it still left a good quantity of rails which could be reused. The Turks went on collecting them. More important, given the acute shortage of wood in Palestine, they collected the sleepers, which the British had ignored. The Turks were thus able to build their Huj branch line.[60]

A less tangible result was that Chetwode had his attention drawn to Beersheba. He noted that the Turks appeared nervous about this area, as was evidenced by their preparation of the bridge for demolition, and the raid demonstrated the ability of large mounted units to move through the region south of Beersheba. He began to take due notice of the whole area, which the British had consistently ignored and neglected since their arrival before Gaza.[61] At the same time the Turks' dismantling of the line was clear evidence of their defensive mentality: the British need not fear a major attack.

Welcome as the news of the raid may have been to the British government, it did not reconcile the Prime Minister to General Murray as commander. The earlier defeats at Gaza, the reported demoralization of the Egyptian Expeditionary Force, the need as he perceived it to seize physical control of Palestine to forestall the French and the Arabs, his old sympathy for the downtrodden peoples of the world, and the latent evangelism of nonconformist Wales, all pressured David Lloyd George to press for an early victory in Palestine, and the establishment of Christian rule in Jerusalem. It was clear that Murray could not provide that victory. By the end of May the search was on for a replacement, and he had been found by early the next month.

CHAPTER 5

The Allenby Effect

Replacing Murray had been under consideration since his defeat at the second Gaza battle. Robertson had suggested it to the War Cabinet as early as 23 April, and the Cabinet had agreed.[1] But finding the right man to succeed him was not easy. All the really competent generals were already fully employed. Further, the Egyptian post required a man who was in rank a general, who could command troops in battle, but who was also a diplomat, a courtier, and an administrator of ability. Murray had performed extremely well in the last three roles, while failing as a commander through being too cautious. Inducing the Arabs to revolt had been a very ticklish matter, and they had to be kept in the fight as well; the internal situation in Egypt was never easy, and it was always necessary to keep the khedivial court sweet; he had performed prodigies of organization and administration in sorting out the messy situation among the British forces who washed up into Egypt after the Gallipoli failure, and in organizing the expeditionary force into Palestine. He had been just as successful in pushing that force across the Sinai desert, with its attached railway and pipeline. His failures were as a commander of troops in active warfare and in his choice of subordinate commanders.

The new commander would need to be a vigorous fighting soldier, a man to inspire the dispirited troops to victory. The Prime Minister thought he found the right man in General Jan Christiaan Smuts, the former South African guerrilla leader who had commanded the imperial forces in German East Africa. He was, like Lloyd George, a lawyer, a politician, and a Christian, and the two men became friends; but the army command was by no means happy about him, for these were not the qualities required of a modern general. The campaign in German East had been only partially successful – the German commander there remained an active enemy until November 1918 – and Smuts's command there had been badly organized and appallingly expensive in men.

Smuts was offered the post on 1 May, and took the whole of the month to consider it. This in itself was a poor sign, for the matter clearly had a degree of urgency. He went to see Robertson at the War Office. There he realized that Robertson was wholly antipathetic to the Palestine adventure, and would provide little support.[2]

Smuts had clearly thought about the issue of levering the Turks out of Gaza, and put the suggestion of a landing from the sea to Robertson, who wrote to the First Sea Lord, Admiral Jellicoe, in terms which almost required a negative answer:

> Smuts does not wish to go unless it is going to be a real thing, and he doubts the feasibility of this. Smuts's idea is that the only way of doing the trick properly is to land a force of some hundred thousand men at Haifa. This I imagine you could not look at. But in any case Smuts would want to use some of the Syrian ports. I have told him you would look at nothing of the kind. Will you please be prepared to give your views on the question when it comes up. Smuts is by no means an advocate of the Palestine Campaign, but at the same time if they insist upon taking it on he wishes to make quite clear to them what they are in for. In this he is of course quite right.[3]

The suggestion was too much for the shipping resources available. But the impression one gets is that Smuts was pitching his demands so high that they had to be refused; he was also not keen to be marooned in Palestine, when, as Robertson made quite clear, the place was a 'side-show'. Robertson did an effective job of dissuasion, thus thwarting the Prime Minister. But someone who could be dissuaded by Robertson so relatively easily, as Smuts was, was not the man for this particular job. The Prime Minister finally received a definite refusal from him on 31 May.[4]

Robertson now came up with the name of General Sir Edmund Allenby, the commander of the Third Army in France, who had recently been successful at Arras. Lloyd George had already heard praise of him, for he had been mentioned to the Prime Minister as a suitable man to replace Haig as the commander-in-chief on the Western Front, if Haig could ever be levered out of the post. On the other hand, the whisperer was Colonel Repington, war correspondent of *The Times*, an obsessive meddler.[5] Allenby had recently been privately and distressingly outspoken in his dislike of Haig's latest plans for further assaults on the German positions in France, and Haig, who could never understand or abide opposition, feared that Allenby's near insubordination would spread. Allenby was by nature a duty-first man, one who would normally accept his superior's assessments and orders without question. If he was driven so far as to argue with his commander-in-chief, he had clearly become deeply disturbed by the Western Front fighting.[6]

Robertson, knowing that Haig was unhappy about Allenby's recent conduct, and concerned to support Haig, put Allenby's name to the Prime Minister when Smuts refused. Allenby, of course, unlike Smuts, would not have to be persuaded since, as a serving soldier, he could not refuse the post. He was not pleased, however, since it seemed to be a demotion, or at least a move sideways, and he cannot have been ignorant of Haig's attitude.[7] Robertson also knew that Allenby was convinced, as were all the Western Front commanders, that the decision in the war would have to come in France. The CIGS assumed that this conviction would continue to operate when Allenby went east. This, as it turned out, was a mistake.

For Robertson in this instance was easily outmanoeuvred by that master of politics and human manipulation, David Lloyd George. Allenby went to London thoroughly depressed, and was interviewed by Robertson and Lloyd George together. He had presumably already been seen by Robertson alone, who no doubt impressed on him the need to bear in mind the necessary priority of the Western Front, and how difficult it was to provide further troops for the Palestine area; this was exactly what he had said to Smuts. But in the interview with Lloyd George, Robertson found all these aces effortlessly trumped. The Prime Minister talked about the need for a victory, any victory, but especially for a victory which would inspire the ordinary people of the country. And he suggested that Allenby take 'Jerusalem before Christmas', 'as a Christmas present for the British people'.

Allenby had already discovered, if he did not already know, that there were great strains evident in British society by this stage in the war. He had seen the German bombers over London. There were great strikes in the industrial areas of South Wales and Scotland. He was already familiar with the manpower problem, which is to say, the difficulty of finding more men to put into the army. The Prime Minister was clearly convincing in this talk of the need for an inspiring victory. As Allenby left he gave him a copy of George Adam Smith's *Historical Geography of the Holy Land*. He claimed, perhaps as no more than a side-swipe at Robertson, that the book

> was a better guide to a military leader whose task was to reach Jerusalem than any survey to be found in the pigeon-holes of the War Office. Allenby afterwards acknowledged that it was invaluable to him for the accuracy of its information about the contour of the country.[8]

It is not clear just how much Lloyd George knew of Allenby before the meeting, other than his mediocre reputation as a Western Front commander, but his gift of the book was an inspired move. For Allenby was man of rather wider culture than most British generals. He was an amateur botanist and naturalist of some note, with a particular expertise in ornithology, a knowledge of French, though he spoke it only inaccurately, some knowledge of German, and an ability to translate Greek into English at sight. He was in the habit of reading extensively about any new country he was to visit, and one of his biographers suggests that he had already acquired a copy of Smith's book before the Prime Minister's gift. If so, the second copy only demonstrated Lloyd George's good sense and imagination. Allenby also had a deep knowledge of the Bible, at least in reference to the military topography of Palestine.[9]

It would seem that the general and the Prime Minister reached an accord which Robertson did not share. General officers of the British army in the Great War were usually strongly antipathetic towards Lloyd George, because of the latter's political radicalism before the war, but Allenby appears to have been an exception. Many years afterwards he refused to join in a collective criticism of Lloyd George which was mooted by a group of other generals. This is a mark of his independence of judgment, for his background as the son of a country squire, as a cavalryman, and as a soldier, would have suggested an instinctive dislike for the politician.

The presence of Robertson at the meeting was a deliberate ploy by the Prime Minister. He will have known of the CIGS's message to both Smuts and Allenby that, compared with the Western Front, Palestine was unimportant, and that nothing could be spared to increase the forces there. But now Lloyd George trumped that ace also. He told Allenby that the matter was so important that he could have whatever men and materials he considered he needed to achieve the conquest. When Allenby's appointment was agreed by the War Cabinet, he had already got it to adopt a form of words which loosened Robertson's grip. Lloyd George repeats them verbatim (but not as a quotation) in his War Memoirs: 'The policy to be adopted in that theatre of war would not be settled until General Allenby had assumed control.'[10] Thus it was that Robertson's careful plans fell apart. He had heard with his own ears this promise, and it was one which he could not, in the end, evade, though he did his best to do so. It was a lesson in the political arts which the CIGS could not forget. The evidence is that the whole performance inspired Allenby as much as it distressed and annoyed Robertson.

Robertson did not give up. He remained convinced that the Western Front was the only decisive theatre, and went on resisting diversions. By July, just as Allenby was arriving in Egypt, he was clear that the collapse of Russia meant a German reinforcement for the west, at a time when most politicians in the west were pleased at the potential reinvigoration of the Russian effort: 'By next year Russia may have dropped out of the war and the enemy forces on the Western Front be correspondingly increased', he wrote in an appreciation for the War Cabinet, and added, 'it is my present opinion that the purely military advantage to be gained' by the conquest of southern Palestine 'would not justify the expenditure of force required'[11] – but it was not, of course, a 'purely military' question.

Allenby flowered in the Egyptian post as a general and as a politician. This was unexpected, but not inexplicable. All his life he had been a subordinate. Even as a full general in France, he had been under Haig's command. Survival in such a situation, especially in the army, lay in obedience. Some could not manage it. One of Allenby's own subordinate generals, Major-General James Shea, had gone too far in his arguments with Allenby himself, and had been dismissed and sent back to England.[12] In circumstances which demanded initiative, however, Allenby had displayed it, in South Africa above all, but also on the few occasions he could on the Western Front. This, and his wider-than-usual interests, marked him out, for those with eyes to see, as one to whom subordination was also a restriction. Like one of his beloved birds, to free him was to let him fly.

He had a reputation among his own subordinates for harshness and bad temper. Yet his displays of anger were invariably directed at those who were not performing their duties diligently or properly. In the trenches he insisted that all troops within range of the enemy, himself included, should wear a tin-hat, and this was an oblique comment also on his toughness with his subordinates, officers, and soldiers alike. He was referred to as 'the Bull', which was partly a response to his powerful physical presence – 6 feet 4 inches, and burly – and partly to that propensity to rudeness and outbursts of bad temper, but it was also a comment on his manner and way of fighting. One perceptive contemporary thought he was mentally lazy when in France. But to be mentally active on the Western Front was to be in danger of either insanity or insubordination, or both. It did not mean he was stupid. No doubt a memory full of Greek and English poetry helped him survive.[13]

Allenby had the example before him of the conduct of command on the Western Front, both by Sir John French and by Sir Douglas Haig – and for that matter by the French generals as well. He had been unable to persuade Haig to accept criticism, and it may be that he had taken that lesson to heart. Once free of subordination, and in a position of independent command, he could be allowed to think for himself. A man who had attempted to argue with Haig should be able to accept argument from his subordinates and to accept their good ideas and suggestions. It is significant that when Robertson pointed out that Shea was still in England, and unemployed, Allenby agreed at once to take him to Egypt,[14] where he became a successful divisional commander, and was eventually singled out by Allenby for especial praise. This can be seen as an act of forgiveness, of Allenby not bearing a grudge, but it can also be seen as a recognition that a commander-in-chief needs men around him who will argue with him. He cannot do it all himself. In Egypt 'the Bull' was, as it soon appeared, open to argument and new ideas. Shea himself said later that Allenby was capable of listening to others' advice.[15]

Allenby's impact on Murray's Cairo headquarters has gone into legend, but the impression of a revolution is exaggerated. He arrived on 28 June, spent a week becoming familiar with the situation in the headquarters, going around the whole place asking each man what he did,[16] and then spent another two weeks on a swift tour of his command. He certainly changed the operating procedures at headquarters, but this was as much due to the changed political and military situation as it was to his replacement of Murray. He used the opportunity provided by his arrival to dramatize the change. He insisted on delegating as much paperwork as possible, and removing time-expired and incompetent officers from his headquarters – an episode which grew in the telling, but one which he surely knew would have instant appeal in the camps and the trenches.[17]

His arrival in the front line was widely noted and commented on. Captain C. J. Ratcliff noted in his diary:

> July 10 The new C-in-C breakfasted with us today. ... He is a smart looking man and looks as if he would stand no nonsense.[18]

But he went further than simply visiting and inspecting; he also rode out to have a look at the land and view, from a certain distance, the Turkish positions. The first of these 'stunts' was on 4 July, only a week after taking over the command. Trooper Harold Judge of the New Zealand Brigade, despite getting the new general's name wrong, noted the essentials:

> [4] July. Left camp last night on a stunt towards Beersheba, the idea being to drive the Turkish outposts in to enable General Allanbury, who has now taken charge, to see the country. Very long tiring ride and we only got back to camp about midnight. Hear very good accounts of General A. He seems to be shaking things up a bit in Cairo. Already a lot of 'backsheesh' officers have been shunted.[19]

The headquarters was moved out of Cairo to the desert, or rather to Umm el-Kelab, near Rafa.[20] It should not be imagined that after making this move, the general shared the troops' privations: Allenby did not live in a trench or a dugout on bully beef. One of his actions before leaving Cairo had been to recover the services of Murray's French chef, whom Murray had spitefully dismissed.[21] Allenby intended to be comfortable in his desert headquarters.

The proclaimed reason for Allenby's move was that the general should be with his troops; this was reasonable enough, but it was also a fact that several of Murray's responsibilities had now ended. The Darfur, Senussi, and Aden situations were no longer active problems; the Arab Revolt was now moving north, so Sinai was as good a place to keep in touch with it as Cairo. In fact, in July Lawrence and Prince Faysal carried out several raids in the Wadi Araba area, including the capture of Akaba. This cut yet another of the Turks' means of entry into Sinai, and opened up direct land communications with the new GHQ only 100 miles away.

Allenby's whirlwind tour was always remembered as dramatic in its impact. He tended to arrive surrounded by clouds of dust, carry out a swift inspection, and make some sharp comments on conditions of horses or the morale of troops, before vanishing amid more dust. He might arrive on horseback – he was a cavalryman, after all. His visit to the Imperial Camel Brigade was made that way, surely quite deliberately, for he must have known that relations between horses and camels are not of the best, and he was able to exploit this. He arrived at full gallop, with a flock of followers, accompanied by the usual cloud of dust. The followers were dropped off at some distance, and, alone on his charger, 'a gigantic man on a gigantic horse', he rode directly towards the Camel Brigade, drawn up in neat lines to be inspected. At 50 yards he stopped, no doubt amid another swirling dust cloud. The camels realized that this was a horse, and the whole line took several steps backward, noisily complaining. After savouring the moment – general alone defeats a full brigade – Allenby called forward the officers, on foot and individually, pierced each with his gaze from his position on horseback, which enhanced his already formidable physical presence, and uttered a terse comment. Then he rode off, at full gallop, naturally. The officers and men never forgot this exhibition, something surely thought out in advance.[22]

This was a fully theatrical performance. Allenby was a man of the calculated gesture, and it was surely done as a deliberate contrast with Murray's practice. At headquarters he acted in the same way. When he first sat in his office a large pile of papers was presented to him. After a short time, and the inspection of two or three of the papers, he threw them into a corner, commenting that these were decisions a junior officer should be making.[23] He made it clear to all at the front and in the headquarters that he would command the fighting. Everything else was secondary.

His visits to the army units had the purpose of showing himself to the men – he clearly understood the effect of his size and presence – to persuade them of his interest and determination. His arrival at XX Corps was always remembered: he was in the front passenger seat of a battered truck – his car was late – being driven by an Australian soldier wearing the usual Australian dress of singlet and short shorts.[24] That he took it all in good part seemed surprising, given his reputation as a stickler for detail. But there is a difference between insisting on wearing a helmet in the front line and ignoring dress regulations drawn up in London when in the desert. And he already knew about the Australians' habits, for he had commanded a battalion in South Africa.[25] Again, it

5 *The Camel Brigade.* One of the more exotic formations developed by the British in Palestine was the Imperial Camel Corps Brigade, a force comprised of volunteers from other units, men who were therefore selected for their adventurousness and willingness to try new things. It thus developed quickly into an elite unit, particularly in the opinion of its men. Its usefulness declined as the supply problems experienced by the horsemen were relieved in the better watered areas of central and northern Palestine, but in the Sinai desert and in southern Palestine the camels were invaluable. The photograph shows the brigade marching through Beersheba shortly after its capture early in November 1917. (Crown Copyright: Imperial War Museum Q 13157)

was a deliberately calculated performance, and it had its immediate effect. His unexpected visits produced a conspiracy among the units, whereby signals would be exchanged, by radio or even semaphore: 'BBA' meant 'Bloody Bull's about'.[26] But he moved fast, and he knew that these messages were flying. It was all grist to his mill, and provided him with the disguise of a commander as a character. No one had ever had to beware of Murray, or had told stories about him – most of the troops had never seen him.

Allenby had not behaved in this way in France, though there are indications that in South Africa he was liable to do so. In France he had to command in a style imposed by Haig, and by French before him. And, as he soon discovered, the style of warfare in Palestine was different than on the Western Front. His behaviour in Palestine may be described as theatrical – as I have done – but it was only so in comparison with Murray (or Haig). It is more likely that it was Allenby's own personal style made visible for the first time. He left Haig's command on 6 June, and took over in Cairo on 28 June. During those three weeks he was personally invigorated by the Prime Minister's talk, and he had time to think out his own approach to the new command. The whirlwind three weeks' inspection was the result.

The purpose of all this was partly to impose himself on the army, partly to distance himself from Murray and his methods, and partly to invigorate the army. This last was the most important, but the most difficult. His swift and sudden visits could only have a momentary effect. To make it permanent it would be necessary to develop a plan and to institute the necessary preliminary measures: training his forces, gathering supplies, description of the enemy, reconnaissance, patrols, and so on.

He found that General Chetwode, an old colleague for many years, was again his immediate subordinate. They were both cavalrymen, and their careers had intersected more than once already. Chetwode had been commander of the 10th Hussars under Allenby as brigade commander in 1908; before that they had both been in besieged Ladysmith during the South African War. Since then they had both been peripherally involved in the Curragh Incident in 1914, one of the politically most difficult episodes in British military history.

This had been a serious crisis among senior officers in Ireland, who objected to the Liberal government's intention to use the army to impose Irish Home Rule on Ulster. This measure had been passed by Parliament only after a long constitutional struggle, having been opposed tooth and nail by the Conservative opposition; it was rejected by the Protestant population of Ulster, who had organized themselves into a self-defence force, with the intention of defying the British Parliament and government. Many of the officers of the army which would have to deal with Ulster were in fact Ulstermen – a fact the government should have taken into account – and would therefore be ordered to attack their own neighbours and families. But they had also been covertly encouraged in their defiance by the Conservatives. The central figure at the Curragh (the army's headquarters in Ireland) was General Sir Hugh Gough, and it was he who urged the disaffected officers to resign their commissions rather than do their duty. This was then portrayed by the government as a 'mutiny'.[27]

Allenby, as Inspector-General of Cavalry, was on a visit of inspection at the Curragh when Gough spoke in his disastrous way to his officers. Allenby removed himself rapidly from Ireland to London, where he was carefully neutral in his comments, but reported to the CIGS, Sir John French. Chetwode, on the other hand, had been nominated as the new commander of the Third Cavalry Brigade, if Gough and his officers had persisted with their resignations. This was held against him by Gough among others, but Chetwode was in a very difficult position, and he surely discussed the matter with his superior, Allenby, at the time, for both were in London.[28]

In other words, these two men were old colleagues, and Chetwode had no hesitation in presenting Allenby with an appreciation of the situation which he had prepared for Murray. This paper, entitled 'Notes on the Campaign in Palestine', was dated 6 June and may well have been given to Murray before his supersession. If Chetwode gave Allenby a copy, this supposes that Murray had not done so. The paper was a strategic and tactical appreciation of the situation on the front, laying stress on the strength of the Turkish positions, and it presented an outline plan for future operations. Much stress was laid on the need to ensure water supplies at all stages of any attack. The Gaza position he considered too strong and extensive to be worth assaulting. The only identifiable weak point Chetwode could see in the line was a gap in the fortifications between the Hureyra Redoubt (which was now somewhat enlarged) and Beersheba (now also extensively fortified) – the gap which the Turks had used in April to try and take the British in the rear. The ploy he suggested was to leave Gaza and the redoubts as far along the road as Atawine menaced by infantry, while the cavalry would drive into the Hureyra–Beersheba gap. The result, he thought, would be a collapse of the Beersheba position, and the assaulting force could then swing left, pivoted on the Hureyra Redoubt, to cut Turkish communications in the rear and so encircle the whole Turkish force. He considered, and rejected, the idea of assaults on Gaza or on the central redoubts, and he warned that the Turks were in the process of preparing a series of fall-back positions, as far as the Jaffa–Jerusalem line, each of which might have to be assaulted in turn.

Chetwode's paper laid stress on the ground over which the fighting would need to take place, pointing out the unsuitability of the approaches to the main Turkish positions because of the lack of any sort of cover. Only on the British right, on the approaches to Hureyra and Beersheba, did the ground provide decent cover to allow troops to get close to the enemy positions. He had clearly inspected the whole line in some detail and personally, and he had a considerable reputation among his fellow officers for his keen eye for ground.[29]

What Murray's reaction had been to this paper was is unknown, but he may well have liked it. In essence it was Rafa and first Gaza writ large (and the Turkish riposte at the second Gaza in reverse), and Chetwode included a paragraph on manpower requirements, stressing the need to bring divisions up to establishment in both men and guns, and noting that the plan would require at least seven infantry divisions and three of cavalry. This was precisely what Murray had been asking for since before Chetwode arrived. Much of the 'Notes' was written by Chetwode's chief of staff, Brigadier-General Guy Dawnay, but there is no doubt that it faithfully reflected Chetwode's ideas and, more distantly, those of Murray. Allenby, like Chetwode a cavalryman, no doubt appreciated the general idea, though he reserved judgment. Unlike Murray, he went to have a look for himself, riding out with Chetwode to inspect the position at Beersheba.

Allenby spent three weeks on this familiarization process, and then, on 12 July, wrote to Robertson with his requirements, a formidable list, but one which echoed the views of both Murray and Chetwode. When his appointment was discussed in the War Cabinet, it had been agreed that his precise policy would only be formulated when he had had a chance to see the situation for himself. So his list was based partly on the need to be prepared to meet a Turkish attack (the Yildirim army) and partly on an outline plan to attack through the Turkish line and advance north as far as Jerusalem and Jaffa. For this he wanted the infantry force to be enlarged by two more divisions, and the existing divisions to be completed in both infantry and artillery to the regulation standard – they were short of 7,000 infantrymen to start with; a further contingent of artillery should be added to each corps – he was asking for an extra 142 guns in addition to a further 68 already promised; three more squadrons of aircraft for bombing and reconnaissance were required, and they should be of a sufficiently advanced technical standard to wrest control of the air over southern Palestine from the small German air contingent with its Halberstadts; he also wanted more engineer, signal, and medical units, and administrative personnel for his General Headquarters.

In order that these troops should be properly supplied it would be necessary to double the railway across Sinai, and double and extend the 12–inch pipeline to the full distance: a branch railway from Rafa to Shellal and then on towards Beersheba was also necessary (some of this was already in train). It was a formidable and expensive list, partly based on Murray's and Chetwode's experiences, but also partly on what Allenby knew of the fighting on the Western Front. Given the short commons on which the Egyptian Expeditionary Force had existed so far, in terms of reinforcements and equipment, the list was not unreasonable.[30]

Allenby did not get all he thought he required, even with the backing of the Prime Minister. He did receive another infantry division, the 10th Irish, which, like the London Division, was to be transferred from Salonica. For his second division he had to make do with the partially formed 75th, the new and under-strength division Murray had been forming before he was replaced. Nor did Allenby get the full quantities of artillery he listed, though his demands for aircraft were largely met, and it was agreed that the railway and pipeline should be doubled. It took a month to get Robertson's agreement to all this, and another month to bring the men and material to Egypt – shipping was always short – but from mid-August onwards Allenby was able to start planning seriously.

One of the shortcomings Allenby quickly identified was the Staff. It was not just that it seemed to be colonized by idle officers, which was the impression held by those facing Gaza, but that, paradoxically, there were not enough officers on the staff. That is, Murray's staff was not doing the work which Allenby intended it to do. And this applied at all levels, not just at Cairo, so that even at company level, where he ensured that the headquarters became better staffed with such essential personnel as runners and signallers.

Allenby's own staff was increased in proportion, and set to work researching the area where the fighting would take place, mapping the land, plotting the routes to the front, estimating timings and so on. Murray's Chief of Staff, Brigadier-General Lynden-Bell, was soon diagnosed unfit and was replaced by another of Allenby's former subordinates in France, Major-General L. J. Bols, and soon Chetwode's own Chief of Staff, the highly competent Brigadier-General Guy Dawnay, was transferred to Allenby's.

The forces who were to do the fighting were also reorganized into three corps: the three cavalry divisions plus the 7th Mounted Brigade and the Imperial Camel Brigade became the Desert Mounted Corps, commanded by

Chauvel; Chetwode became commander of XX Corps, having four infantry divisions, the Welsh, London, Yeomanry, and Irish (when it came); XXI Corps was placed under Lieutenant-General Sir Edward Bulfin, whom Allenby had known in France, and who had originally arrived as commander of the London Division; his replacement there was Shea, by Allenby's request. Bulfin's corps had three infantry divisions, the Lowland, East Anglian, and the new 75th. It was thus considerably weaker than Chetwode's corps, but in the event it was given a large proportion of the army's artillery.

This all took time, of course. The doubling of the railway was easier than the original laying, but it had still only reached half-way to Rafa by the time the attack took place. The London Division had arrived from Salonica in June, but it was rather the worse for wear medically: many of the men suffering from malaria. The Irish Division, however, did not arrive until September, nor did the artillery and aircraft materialize instantly. September was the time when the attack was intended, after the summer heat and before the winter rains, and the time until then was occupied also by the Staff in elaborating, altering, and developing the plan of attack. Chetwode's original paper did not go into any detail, and much work had to be done to define the precise objectives, timings, and the forces required. The original timetable, such as it was, slipped because of the late arrival of the Irish Division; an attack in October became the new aim.

Robertson was still reluctant to agree to Allenby's requests, but he was constrained by Cabinet authority. He had at least managed to avoid sending any divisions from France. He sent out a very bright officer, Lieutenant Colonel Archibald Wavell, to join Allenby. Wavell was to be his eyes and ears with Allenby. He made a point of explaining that Wavell was not there to spy on Allenby, which, of course, is exactly what he was doing. Allenby, perhaps remembering Lloyd George's tactics with him, went out of his own way to charm Wavell, with total success. Allenby, grieving for his son, killed in France at the end of July, quoted, in full, a Rupert Brooke sonnet to Wavell; nothing could have endeared him more quickly to the younger man, a lover of poetry and the compiler of the best poetry anthology of the twentieth century, *Other Men's Flowers* (1944). Whether this display was deliberate or not, its effect was to bind Wavell to Allenby for the rest of his life. Allenby's display of fortitude in his reception of and reaction to his son's death – his only child – endeared him also to the other officers. Suppressing personal feelings, and continuing with the everyday grind, was the sort of behaviour they all admired.[31]

The reply Robertson sent to Allenby's list of requirements was not particularly encouraging; he was clearly doing his best to fail to comply. But the Prime Minister, with the full weight of the War Cabinet with him, over-rode Robertson's misgivings, and on 10 August sent a special message that Allenby was 'to strike the Turk as hard as possible in the coming autumn or winter'.[32] Robertson did manage to restrict Allenby's reinforcements to troops already in the Eastern Mediterranean and India, and by conducting a parallel private and secret correspondence with Allenby, the CIGS hoped to persuade him of this view. Wavell's presence was clearly intended to reinforce it.

Chetwode's paper was in no sense a plan of operations. It was a description of the Turkish positions, emphasizing the difficulty of assaulting them, with a particularly pointed series of comments about the problems of water supply. His main suggestion was that the line was vulnerable between the Hureyra Redoubt and the fortifications around Beersheba. If the Turks in Gaza could be prevented from intervening, a breakthrough west of Beersheba would, he suggested, force Beersheba itself to submit and the mounted troops could push through and take the rest of the Turkish line in rear.

This was certainly the plan expounded by Wavell to Robertson in mid-August.[33] Robertson spent the interview staring at a map of France, indicating his major preoccupation, but he did provide most of what Allenby requested. The plan went through some changes between August and October, though these have been disguised by the repeated claim – by Wavell more than once, and by others, from Allenby down – that the plan of operations succeeded in all respects, and that it was based on Chetwode's 'Notes'. This claim is not wholly incorrect, for all Chetwode had done was to describe the situation and make a recommendation. He had not made a plan. Further, when the final plan was actually made, Chetwode's crucial point, that the Turkish line was vulner-able at the Hureyra–Beersheba gap, was ignored, and in the event the plan as laid out in Allenby's orders in late October was not actually adhered to. In the fighting numerous alterations had to be made in response to the conduct of the battle, so that it is only by imposing on events a pattern which cannot be sustained in detail that it can be claimed that the plan was carried out.

The Turkish conference at Aleppo on the target for Yildirim had taken place just as Allenby was travelling to Egypt. It had, of course, been indecisive, except that the new Seventh Army should be formed. This was not easy. Divisions had to come from a long distance, and by rail. The railways in Anatolia and Pales-tine were all single-track, as were most of those which had to be used in the Balkan countries. There was a massive bottleneck at Constantinople, where all passengers and goods had to detrain, be transported across the Bosporos, and then be repacked into other trains at the Haidar Pasha depot on the Asian side. The same process had to be repeated at the Cilician Gates, the pass through the Taurus Mountains, where a tunnel had been under construction all through the war, only to be finished in October 1918, the month the Turks surrendered. There had been another interruption at the Amanus Mountains, but this tunnel was completed early in 1917. The difficulties of shifting whole divisions, even the smaller Turkish divisions, from Galicia and Macedonia to southern Palestine were thus enormous, and enormously time-consuming, for the railway system had also to be permitted to continue its regular services, in particular in supplying the existing armies in Asia. (The difficulties continued in Syria, where there was a break of gauge at Damascus.)

Rayak

The result was that the divisions allocated to Yildirim which were in Europe could only be moved one at a time, and even then each took a long time to arrive. The 19th Division left Galicia on 11 June, and the 50th left Macedonia on the 20th, but the 24th did not leave the Dardanelles until early in July, and the second Galician division, the 20th, did not start its journey until 8 August. Yildirim was scarcely the most suitable name for this new army. The head-quarters of the new formation was established at Aleppo in August, but the last of its formations, the 42nd Division, did not leave the Dardanelles until September.[34]

In these circumstances, it did not matter too much that the ultimate employment of this army remained undecided. Marshal von Falkenhayn at a council of war in early August suggested launching a pre-emptive surprise attack on the Gaza front, then, having disorganized the British forces there, he would switch the Yildirim force to Mesopotamia and drive the British out of Baghdad, and perhaps all the way to the Persian Gulf. His proposed method in Palestine, interestingly enough, was a great wheel round the open flank and a march across the British rear to the sea, a bigger version of the plan designed by Colonel von Kressenstein in the aftermath of First Gaza, and, of course, a mirror-image of the suggestion in Chetwode's paper.[35]

This was all very well on paper, but it paid no heed to the problems of the Turkish transport system. The railways of northern Syria were of stand-ard gauge, but those south of Damascus were narrow gauge, and this change therefore imposed another bottleneck. Shortage of rolling stock and fuel in Palestine meant that the system could not cope with traffic on the scale required, nor, if the Yildirim army actually reached the Gaza line, could the railways provide the supplies needed to maintain the army there. Jamal poured scorn on Falkenhayn's plan. He was totally opposed to fighting in the desert, especially in view of the powerful defences the British had been constructing. He also could speak with some authority on the subject, having tried such an expedition himself. Enver tried to focus Falkenhayn's attention on Baghdad. Faced with the opposition Falkenhayn agreed to inspect the position in Palestine. Jamal was given an invitation to visit Germany, and eagerly accepted.

Falkenhayn left Constantinople on 4 September, knowing that the German component of the Yildirim force had reached that city or was about to. In fact, this had caused even more congestion on the Balkan and Anatolian railways, which was made worse by the quantities of equipment the German troops required. It was stored at the Haidar Pasha railway station, on the Asian side, where two days later there was a great explosion. The rumour spread that a moment's carelessness led to an ammunition box being dropped, followed by a chain reaction of explosions; it was also claimed as a deliberate plot by British intelligence agents. In fact, it seems that it had no effect on the Turks' transportation problems, which could scarcely have been made worse. The Asienkorps was halted in its tracks by the sheer difficulty of moving on, and the troops were still in Constantinople two months later.[36]

Falkenhayn was at the Gaza front on 9 and 10 September, and what he saw along the Turkish line convinced him that Palestine must be given the priority which Jamal had always insisted on, and the concept of a great pre-emptive strike was apparently shelved. Back in Constantinople he persuaded Enver to postpone the concentration on Baghdad, but this produced a major political problem for Enver. It would be quite impossible for him simply to transfer the whole of the new Seventh Army, the Turkish component of the Yildirim force, to Jamal's command, for this would give Jamal far too much power, and Enver had little doubt that Jamal would use it first of all to consolidate his own position and increase his political influence in the Ottoman system. Enver therefore bent his devious mind to the destruction of Jamal, who was summoned urgently to Constantinople from his German visit to find that his absence had been used to undermine his power. He retained command of his own Fourth Army, but had Palestine excised from his area of responsibility, which was now restricted to Syria and the lands across the Jordan. Command of the war in Palestine went to Falkenhayn; the troops already in Palestine were now constituted as the Eighth Army, under the command of von Kressenstein (now raised to the rank of general). Jamal retained the Fourth Army, but its purpose was now no more than as a logistical support for the Palestine troops – and for Medina, where a Turkish force was under a desultory siege by the Arabs. All this took time to arrange, and the command system had to be reorganized before the troops gathered at Aleppo could be sent south. So it was not until October that the Seventh Army's divisions could begin to move southwards from the Aleppo concentration area towards Palestine.[37] All this was very disruptive of Turkish preparations. Their forces in the line in Palestine were scarcely reinforced at all, while the Seventh Army slowly gathered 400 miles to the north.

The British forces meanwhile were mainly present by July, with only the Irish Division still to arrive. For the troops in position a regular rotation in the line was instituted, with a period of rest by the shore, and vigorous and detailed training. Sea bathing at Deir el-Belah was popular, but gas-training was not. However, the purposefulness of all this training was convincing, and so the original gingering-up by the new commander-in-chief was reinforced.

The knowledge that no forward movement would take place until September at the earliest allowed this programme to be organized. Battalions were pulled out of the line and given an extended period of rest, combined with a certain amount of preliminary training. An area on the shore became known as 'Regent's Park'. It was 'here and there clad in verdure; palms and junipers, and one or two trees which clustered round the well, gave the otherwise arid sandy waste its name';[38] this was the recollection of the colonel of the 8th Scottish Rifles. An East Anglian officer's memory suggests how basic had become many of the comforts the soldiers looked to: 'Nights of unbroken sleep, no stand-to, and unlimited bathing made the break a thoroughly enjoyable one'.[39] In the midst of rest there came work 'training in company and platoon work including practice in attack, preliminary musketry, and specialist training for Lewis gunners, bombers, signallers and so on'.[40]

There was even leave, and again the simplicity of the pleasures for those who could get to Cairo is remarkable: 'clean linen, lashing of beer, motors, clubs, books, new clothes, Shepheard's grill – how good they seemed after that seven months away from civilization!'.[41] At the same time, the high incidence of venereal disease in the army rather implies that many in the army had more basic pleasures.[42]

When the heat of the summer began to wane, more serious training was undertaken. This comprised a series of exercises designed to prepare the individual soldiers and their units for the planned attack. Two basic requirements were the ability to march accurately at night, and to go for long periods on little or no water. The anonymous historian of the 23rd London Regiment provides the best description of the training for both of these. Essentially, the first was achieved by practice:

Starting with simple exercises the training was worked up until every officer and most NCOs were capable of leading their commands anywhere on the darkest night. Concentration marches of many miles were practiced, each company marching to a common pin-point of the map from a different point of the compass. All officers and senior NCOs would then be fallen out and the men told to find their way home by sections. They got lost and were out in the desert all night, but they learnt to find their way. Deployment and advances on a wide front in columns of platoons were practiced until the battalion could disperse into the darkness and finish up on its appointed frontage on a line three miles distant from the start. And this on a tract of desert as featureless as the open sea.

Water training was also an unpleasant but very necessary accomplishment which had to be acquired. If left to his own devices in the desert a man will easily consume two gallons of water per day. [but] when we got on the move our daily ration was to be two pints, if we were lucky enough to get it! And so we cut down their water, when there was plenty to be had. A morning's training would be started with filled waterbottles, which had to be shown intact upon the return to camp ... They gradually found out that they were as comfortable on the shorter rations as on the larger, for if indeed once one starts to drink under desert conditions, no amount of water is enough to quench one's thirst.[43]

Elaborate timetables were drawn up to train the men in every military art they might require. Colonel Findlay of the 8th Scottish Rifles published one of these timetables which he used in his battalion. An hour of bayonet fighting, physical drills, firing and loading, or bomb throwing (dummy and live), was followed by breakfast, then an hour's close order drill and deployment. Then came two lectures on such things as gas drill, messaging, regimental *esprit de corps*, and attack formation. In the afternoon there was drill, route marching, and so on. All these alternated between lectures (no more than half an hour per lecture), and physical activities (an hour and more on these).[44]

These techniques were put into practice in the line by means of frequent patrols, reconnaissance and raids. The increase in the quantity of artillery was made more potent by having the gunners work as hard as everyone else at their particular skills. The Welsh Division historian quotes Captain Barton on the method:

As for the artillery, batteries became expert in 'test support'. 'It was a daily occurrence for an infantry officer to appear, suddenly, at our observation post, thrust paper into the gunner officer's hand on which was written a map co-ordinate, and murmur 'test support'. The round was supposed to reach the point indicated within a minute. Really it was amazing how this little device speeded up the machine, and all hands thoroughly enjoyed it'.[45]

The water training was extended to the animals, which, like the men, were put on a reducing ration so that they could all operate on as little water as possible. For the men, washing was restricted – but not shaving – and only tea-making was excepted from the strict ration. These restrictions eased the pressure on the pipeline supplies, and on the camel trains which carried forward the fanatis of water. But their main effect and purpose was to enable the horses and the men to go much longer without water than the Turks expected.

Allenby had been given a clear objective – Jerusalem – both by the Prime Minister in their meeting, confirmed by the War Cabinet in mid-August. As the autumn approached, and with it the cooler weather in Palestine, Sir William Robertson clearly apprehended a possible victory by Allenby, and feared that this would drain more troops into the sideshow by prolonging the campaign further into Palestine. Early in October he made a final effort, knowing that Allenby planned to attack soon. After an argument with Lloyd George in the War Policy Committee, Robertson sent two parallel messages to Allenby. In the official message he relayed the official line, an instruction that Allenby was to engage and defeat the Turks in battle. In the parallel, private, message he made it clear that he hoped that Allenby would be very limited in his fight, and asked that he send his estimate of the requirements he had for a further campaign into Palestine, after the breaking of the Gaza–Beersheba line. He emphasized that the Turks could be reinforced by German forces, claiming that two German divisions were 'preparing for the East', and that this force might be increased. In fact he had information that it might be doubled.[46]

Allenby, carefully stating the maximum possible forces he would face, and assuming the Turkish formations to be at full strength, replied that he would need thirteen more divisions in addition to the ten he already had, to hold the Jerusalem line when he reached it.[47] This was the sort of reply Robertson had wanted, though it is difficult to believe that Allenby was serious. He must have known it was absurd to ask for so much. But it was, as he must also have known, all hypothetical, and that Robertson was conducting his own bureaucratic campaign to persuade the War Cabinet not to send any more troops to Palestine, and at the same time to persuade Allenby to make do with what he already had.[48]

The implication of Robertson's letters was that Allenby should settle for a small victory, which would allow Lloyd George and the War Cabinet some political kudos, but would emphasize the uselessness of continuing the Palestinian offensive. Robertson would then be able to withdraw some of Allenby's troops for France, since Allenby's victory would have solved his water problem (by gaining access to Palestinian sources) and would have so blunted Turkish military power in the area that no further offensive actions need be anticipated.

This was asking for the most extraordinary restraint on Allenby's part. He was in command of a large army, with the prospect of battle before him. His whole life was a preparation for the coming conflict, his entire professional expertise was engaged in preparing for it. He could, under no circumstances, be expected to do anything less than attempt to win a complete victory. Robertson must have known this, even as he wrote his dissuading letter. No soldier would be content with a minor victory when he could gain a great one, a victory which would make his name, and one which his peers would respect him for. All this was quite separate from the official instructions, and from Lloyd George's plea in June for Jerusalem. Allenby would inevitably try to crush the enemy, in accordance with these official instructions. It was what he was trained to do.

Allenby was tolerably well informed about the Turks' difficulties and dispositions, and will have scarcely credited Robertson's reports of vastly increased enemy forces. What concerned him particularly was the situation on his immediate front. For information on this he relied partly on reconnaissance by aircraft, but also on his intelligence service's varied sources of information. This was another area which he had shaken up. He had inherited a very able intelligence chief ('Chief Political Officer') in Brigadier-General Gilbert Clayton; a new deputy intelligence chief, Colonel Richard Meinertzhagen, had been transferred from East Africa, and was now put in place at Deir el-Belah. There was a useful network of spies in Palestine, including a group of Jews who had settled there before the war. They had contacted Jewish officers in the Ottoman army, who provided information, and a German Jewish doctor stationed at el-Affuleh, the railway junction in the Vale of Jezreel through which all the reinforcements from the north must come. This was, however, a hazardous source of information, and Allenby instituted a regular aerial reconnaissance of south Palestine once he had received better aircraft which could face down the German Halberstadts that had been dominant for the last few months. The photographs from the reconnaissance were used to produce improved maps of the land they were about to invade, as well as to chart the positions of the various enemy forces. Meinertzhagen's department began to produce regular maps of the dispositions of both forces.[49]

Meinertzhagen was also in control of the counter-intelligence system. The British troops were convinced that the Arabs they found all around them, both the Bedouin and the people of the villages, were spies in the Turkish cause. Some certainly were, though most probably just tried to keep out of the way; they were always ready to steal whatever supplies the army did not guard well enough. When a British night raid set out, the Bedouin lit fires as a warning, which the British assumed were directed at the Turks. It was more likely they were simply warning other Bedouin, including their own families.[50]

This applied to both armies, and the attitude of Turkish officers was exactly the same as that of the British. Fateh Rikvi, Jamal Pasha's private secretary, commented later: 'they would steal horses from the British lines and sell them to us, and then they would steal them from us and sell them back to the British.'[51] Whether this was actually true is perhaps unlikely, but it illustrates the military attitude. The Bedouin were clearly, sensibly, standing aside in order to profit, knowing full well they would still be there when they armies had gone away.

There is no doubt that the Bedouin were great looters, liable to murder any Allied troops found in the desert, and to dismantle crashed aircraft, having killed and stripped the pilots. Nogales Bey had regularly to ride out to try to rescue downed British pilots. On the other hand, the Arabs also knew that such men, if caught alive, would fetch a good price. The Turks paid £50 for each pilot handed over, and even when pilots offered double than that to be conducted back to the Allied lines, the Arabs often regarded £50 in the hand worth more than £100 as a promise. Thus the Arabs' attitude was essentially neutral: the Ottomans had been their nominal rulers for so long – four centuries – that they were the known devils: the war was a temporary condition, from which they wished only to profit. If they had information which could be sold, they would sell it.[52]

Rumours spread through the British army that there were master spies wandering about, usually in disguise, a disguise which they could change in the instant. This was no more than the usual paranoia of wartime, but Meinertzhagen did catch a couple of Arabs and extracted from them the name of their Ottoman paymaster, an Arab merchant who lived in Beersheba. He sent this man a letter of thanks and a supply of money by the hand of an Arab whom he knew would talk when caught, and who would certainly be caught. The merchant was executed by the Turks.[53] But Meinertzhagen was unable to get much in the way of intelligence on the Turkish front-line area: information about Turkish units had to come from prisoners snatched in trench raids and by patrols, and from deserters. Early in October the Turks broke up, amid hideous scenes of torture, the Jewish network in central Palestine. Like the Turkish command decision to concentrate the Yildirim force on Palestine, which was made in that same month, however, this came too late to be effective.[54]

One source of Allenby's and Clayton's information was T. E. Lawrence, whom Allenby met in July, just as he was writing his first appreciation for the War Office. Lawrence was in high favour at the time, having just organized the capture of Akaba, which allowed the opening of land communications with the Arabs.[55] The two men had a long talk, and each was apparently intrigued by the other. Both were cultured men, in their different ways, and Lawrence could and did provide useful information about the Arab Revolt. He had recently been on a long journey into Syria, and could report on the political opinions of important men in Palestine and Syria, notably on their disaffection for the Turks and their likely support for the British. Allenby, so Lawrence claimed, was uncertain if Lawrence was a charlatan (an issue not finally settled even yet), but he did agree to provide him with arms and support, and Lawrence proved to be capable of providing information in return. It was more an alliance than a question of the issuing of orders by the general.[56] But the Arab Revolt was never more than a marginal matter for the British High Command, much more useful in political terms than military. Allenby never relied upon the Arabs in any of his operations, understanding full well their limitations in organization, armament, and motivation.

Allenby's request for extra aircraft was prompted by an appreciation of their utility in war. It was very largely met, and by the time the attack on the Gaza–Beersheba line was made, there were four squadrons based close behind the front line, two each at Deir el-Belah and Weli Sheikh Nuran, a total of over sixty aircraft. The whole was organized as the Palestine Brigade of the Royal Flying Corps, commanded by Brigadier-General W. G. H. Salmond. The main work before the attack began was in reconnaissance and photography, with the aim of producing maps for the army's use. Artillery spotting was to be a major task during the battle, and radio stations were multiplied for that purpose. The greater number of aircraft available made it possible to train for air co-operation with infantry and cavalry as well.[57]

Then there was bombing. A raid on the German aerodrome at Ramleh was combined with a seaplane raid on the Turkish store depot at Tul Karm. A more controversial raid was mounted not long afterwards, on 26 June, on the Turkish camp on the Mount of Olives outside Jerusalem. Colonel Meinertzhagen, for one, was outraged that his side should drop bombs from the air anywhere near the Holy City; it was also unsuccessful: most of the bombs missed and five of the eight aircraft on the raid were lost.[58]

It was not until the arrival of the Bristol fighters in September that the balance of power in the air swung to the British, when, as the historian of Ottoman aviation noted, from late September 'large formations of British aircraft prevented German reconnaissance'.[59] Until then it was relatively easy for the German aircraft to carry out their own bombing raids on the huge British camp. The raids were as hated by the men on the ground as always, but occasionally they could see the lighter side. General Chetwode's headquarters was raided, and later he told what happened:

> A less tragic attack took place at the same time on Eastern Force Headquarters, and as was usual though hard to explain, was watched by troops with the greatest amusement. The following day General Chetwode told how he was debating in his mind whether he should have a second glass of port when an agitated bugler put his head in the tent and said: 'They're 'ere, sir!' and how, in the general *sauve qui peut* for the dugout, he was ruthlessly elbowed out of the way by his staff and the mess waiters.[60]

Allenby planned to make his ground attack in September, before the arrival of the rains expected in October, which would reduce the unmetalled roads to mud and fill the dry wadis with water. But he was subject to delays which were similar to those which afflicted the Turks, though his were less inhibiting. The new divisions he was receiving took longer to arrive than anticipated: the Irish Division did not reach Egypt until September, and was somewhat debilitated by Macedonian malaria: the new 75th Division was only fully constituted even later, in October, with the arrival of British battalions from India. He received a prod from the War Cabinet in September, giving him the formal target of achieving a position on the line Jaffa to Jerusalem after his attack, and suggesting that diplomacy might then take over to remove Turkey from the war.[61]

The British plan of attack had been refined and developed during the previous months. Chetwode's original idea of inserting a mounted force between Beersheba and Abu Hureyra had been abandoned. It was replaced by an attack aimed at capturing Beersheba first. The Turks were understood, by means of an intercepted telegram, to have judged Allenby by his Western Front experience, and expected a short bombardment on the Gaza entrenchments, followed by an infantry assault.[62] This therefore was suggested to the Turks. The Beersheba assault would be preceded by an increasing artillery bombardment of the Gaza positions by the guns of XXI Corps and by a naval detachment offshore. XXI Corps' three divisions had the bulk of the army's artillery for this purpose. The Desert Mounted Corps (three mounted divisions) and XX Corps (four infantry divisions) were to assault and capture Beersheba several days after the bombardment of Gaza had begun. Two divisions, the Yeomanry Mounted Division and the Irish Division, were to provide a link between the two assaults, their units being spread thinly between the two major forces, which were at either end of the line, and so containing all the Turkish forces in their redoubts along the road. Once Beersheba had been captured, and its water supply secured and assured, an assault would then be mounted on the seaward section of the Gaza defences, which by that time was to have been subjected to a long bombardment. After that, the Beersheba forces would move to attack the eastern parts of the Turkish position at Tell esh-Sheria and Abu Hureyra, the infantry of XX Corps flanked on the north by the horsemen of the Desert Mounted Corps. Once those positions had been taken the Yeomanry and Irish Divisions would exploit northwards to establish a flank position at Tell el-Nejile, which was believed to be the eastern end of the Turkish reserve line: seizing it would therefore enable that line to be turned.[63]

The general concept was thus no longer a relatively simple thrust to break the Turkish line and then a wide swing into the Turkish rear areas. Instead there were to be a succession of blows: the Gaza bombardment, the Beersheba attack, the Gaza attack, the assault on the Turkish reserve position at Tell esh-Sheria, an exploitation behind that as far north as Nejile. The object was clearly to keep the Turks unbalanced. The Gaza bombardment was followed by a serious assault, as the Turks expected, which was intended to keep them convinced that the Beersheba attacks and its following moves was still a deception. If Tell esh-Sheria and Tell en-Nejile could be taken, with their water supplies, the mounted forces might be able to exploit right across to the sea, enclosing the whole Turkish army.

There were also deceptions and distractions built into the plan. Lawrence was to mount an attack by his Arab followers into the trans-Jordanian lands, in order to cut a vital railway bridge over the Yarmuk River. (Allenby refused a French request to attach a French liaison officer to Lawrence's force.)[64] And a second subversive group was to be moved north on the Palestinian side, under Lieutenant-Colonel Stewart Newcombe, in their attempt to raise the Arabs on that side. This group was to include a high proportion of officers and NCOs, and to carry a large supply of weapons in order to be able to arm and organize the potential recruits.[65] And, on a wavelength the Turks were known to listen to, messages implying preparations for a landing from the sea were to go out.[66] All this in the name of deceiving the Turkish command and confusing their reaction when the main attack came.

This was, so it seems, the general intention, though the army orders were somewhat vague on the timing of each phase except the first. But the really intelligent part of the plan was its inherent flexibility. If any one of the attacks failed, there were others which could take up the emphasis. The lack of such a set of alternatives had been what had doomed the first and second battles. Allenby had thus drawn the lesson of the Turkish ability to fight defensively, and had in effect built into the plan the possibility of being unsuccessful in any single part. The succession of blows also gave his own forces breaks in which they could reorganize and recover; he also so arranged his attacks and his forces that each part of the plan produced an overwhelming British force to fight a much smaller Turkish force. He retained under his hand sufficient resources to be able to exploit any particular successes, and he had some idea of where these opportunities might arise. The capture of Beersheba had the appearance of an early necessity, to build British morale, though exploitation at that end of the line was surely also possible. He knew that this would be only the preliminary to further fighting, for the Turkish reserve position at Tell esh-Sheria was even stronger than Beersheba. As far back as July he had written to Robertson: 'Beersheba is fortified; but I don't think they could stand there, if attacked. Their main line of defence turns its left back to Tell esh-Sheria.'[67]

It was necessary that the Beersheba plan be concealed from the Turks until the assault went in. A series of deceptions was set up. At more or less regular intervals cavalry demonstrations were made in strength against Beersheba, under cover of which staff officers examined the ground and the approaches to the town. At the same time apparent preparations were made for a landing from the sea to the north of Gaza, by badly concealed naval reconnaissance, and by giving special training to a selected group of soldiers initially from the Middlesex Regiment, which was then expanded to selected men from the whole of the division. They were all expert swimmers, and all were given training which emphasized amphibious warfare. They were told nothing of the overall intentions (because it was not intended that they be used for a landing) but were allowed to speculate; such speculations leaked to the other side, notably the idea that the raid was contemplated on a Turkish coastal battery.[68]

Another deception was to suggest that Cyprus was being organized as a base. The Turkish High Command was certainly nervous about a possible landing in the north. 'Information pointed to such an event and the 12 Corps with headquarters at Adana was very weak. It was realized that any attempt to seriously damage the single line of the railway near the Amanus and Taurus mountains, or between these two ranges, would seriously affect the transport services of Yildirim.' A number of German naval guns and an anti-aircraft battery were moved into the area, and aerial reconnaissance of Cyprus were ordered from a new naval air station at Mersin.[69] As it happens, it was just at this time that the French proposed a project for a landing on the Syrian coast, based on Cyprus. It was vague in the extreme, and would clearly require mainly British forces, particularly shipping. It was sunk without trace by Admiral Jellicoe, the First Sea Lord, as Robertson had expected.[70]

The aerial surveillance of Cyprus by the Turks quickly revealed the truth:

> Large dummy dumps had been constructed in Cyprus to make the Ottoman Army Command believe that the attack would be made behind the lines in Lebanon and French navy aircraft launched an attack on Beirut. On the 17th of October this deception was revealed by a four hour reconnaissance performed over the island by two AEGs from FA 302 which had started out from Silifke in southern Turkey.[71]

By that time, of course, the Turks had spent much time and expended considerable resources in defending Cilicia against a non-existent threat. No doubt it would have been useful to the British had the pretence of the attack being continued longer, but they could consider it a successful subterfuge, even so.

An even more successful deception, simpler and playing to Turkish assumptions, was perpetrated by Colonel Meinertzhagen. In a stratagem which became famous, Meinertzhagen allowed himself to be ambushed while apparently on reconnaissance near Beersheba, and dropped his rifle, his notebook, and some letters and money as he made his escape, supposedly wounded. The documents were seized by the Turks. Later, to reinforce the ruse, an Australian patrol was sent out to look for the lost notebooks; during the search the officer in charge apparently carelessly threw away a copy of his orders to that effect, which he had used to wrap his sandwiches. This, of course, relied on the enemy's understanding of the peculiar Australian attitude to discipline and 'bumf'.

The Turkish reception of the documents is described by Colonel Hussein Husni, Chief of Staff of the Seventh Army:

> In the middle of October a pocket book was picked up which had been dropped by an enemy motor car which had hurriedly retired in front of our patrols. The important document belonged to Major Meinertzhagen, an English liaison officer on the Sinai Front. It was taken straight to von Kress who closely examined it.

The trick was so far successful that work on the Beersheba trenches was observed to stop and increased work was simultaneously observed at Gaza. Yet the Turks were never sure of the authenticity of the pocket book:

> Till the end everyone but von Kress and Falkenhayn wondered if this pocket book was a trap or not. If we could know that it was genuine then we had the enemy's plans. But how could we prove its authenticity? Besides Meinertzhagen is not an English name. Though Kress thought the papers may have been intentionally dropped he was inclined to believe in their genuineness.[72]

Von Kressenstein's reaction is very much that of a man who wants to have his interpretation of British intentions confirmed. Of equal value, perhaps, was the confusion and argument the episode sowed within the Turkish staff.

The naval deception was reinforced by badly enciphered wireless messages which the Turks were known to be able to read. The arrival of the better aircraft, Bristol F2B fighters, restricted the ability of the German planes to carry out reconnaissance of their own. It was made known that Allenby would be away from his GHQ between 29 October and November on a visit to Suez, and, of course, the enemy was expected to understand that no attack could be launched in the general's leave-time.[73]

Most of these deceptions worked largely because they played on known Turkish-German ideas, both about the British and Australians troops and about Allenby. The fear of a naval landing had been in Turkish minds since before First Gaza, and Germans had long had exaggerated ideas of British interest in such moves. The strong development of the British fortifications before Gaza seemed to presage an attack from that direction, as did the concentration of infantry and artillery before the city – the mounted troops were kept well back, at Shellal and other places near the Wadi Ghazze.

The British preparations took a long time, but by late October they were judged to be just about complete. The Irish division had arrived, the guns and ammunition were assembled, dominance of the air established. On the other side, the role of the Yildirim army was finally decided, and the Seventh Army had begun to move south from Aleppo. Some divisions were also sent to Mesopotamia, and others retained in the north as a general reserve. The command headquarters moved south first. Von Kressenstein now commanded the Eighth Army at Gaza and along the Beersheba road as far as the Hureyra Redoubt; the Seventh Army was commanded at this point by General Mustafa Kemal Pasha, and held Tell esh-Sheria and Beersheba,[74] the whole under the command of Marshal von Falkenhayn, whose headquarters were at Jerusalem. Reserves were arriving, and at the end of the month a division had arrived just behind Sheria, and another was arriving further north.[75] Mustafa Kemal, however, had been a vigorous opponent of serving under German command, and resigned from the command of Seventh Army at the beginning of October; he was replaced by Major-General Fevzi Pasha. As Colonel Husni Hussein remarks, the army 'had three commanders before even starting its work'[76] – and Fevzi Pasha took a long time to arrive.

Allenby's plan went into rather more detail about the preparations and movements before the battle than about the follow-up after victory. 'Zero day' was to be preceded by four days of bombardment at Gaza particularly. At last on 22 October the army orders were issued. The date for the Beersheba attack was fixed for the 31st, so the bombardment would begin on the 27th. Corps orders appeared on the 26th, by which time various preliminary moves had already been made; now the movement of the Desert Mounted Corps could begin.

CHAPTER 6

The Third Attempt at Gaza

The bombardment of the city of Gaza and its fortifications was on a greater scale than anything yet seen in this campaign. The divisional artilleries of all three infantry divisions, plus the corps artillery, were all involved, primarily with the aim of suppressing the Turkish guns. 68 heavy guns were used, each with a lavish provision of ammunition, half of them assigned to the 'bombardment' group, and half to the counter-battery groups – though the first task for all the guns was the destruction of the enemy artillery.[1] In addition, naval ships joined in on the 29th, from the British cruiser *Grafton*, the French *Requin* once more, five monitors, seven destroyers (two British, five French), and two river gunboats with some smaller craft. The naval gunfire was here particularly useful, since the ships' guns could reach closer to the Turkish base areas about the Wadi el-Hesi, north of the city. The Turkish railhead at Beit Hanun could be bombarded by the land-based guns, but Deir Sneid, a mile or so to the north, could only be reached by the naval guns. The huge 14-inch guns of the monitor *Raglan* were targeted on the station at Deir Sneid, then on the ammunition depot, and finally at the road bridge over the wadi to the north, all of which were hit before the spotter seaplane was chased away by one of the German Halberstadts.[2]

This bombardment was the continual background to events in the area for five days (and nights) before any serious attack on the city was mounted. It was in part designed to destroy the enemy positions around the city, but also to hide (by its sheer noise) and distract attention from, the movement of forces from the base area towards the east for the attack on Beersheba.

For over a week the two corps which were to be used in the attack on Beersheba, the Desert Mounted Corps and the XX Corps, were gradually shifted eastwards, slowly, steadily, deceptively, secretly. Their old camps at Rafa and towards the Wadi Ghazze were left standing and lit at night, and the troops themselves moved only at night, and then lay still and hidden by day. Any German aircraft which managed to reach the British lines were forced to fly high to avoid the attentions of the British planes. These precautions, designed to hide the cavalry movements, were only partly successful. There were not enough efficient British aircraft to prevent all German aerial reconnaissance. The abandonment of several camps in the rear was quickly detected, but the size of the movement to the east was not. The Turks realized by 23 October 'that a great attack was soon to take place'.[3]

The Turkish fortifications at Beersheba were essentially unfinished. Trenches were prepared around the west and south of the town, but there were few to the east and the north.[4] The Turks expected any attacks to come from the defended directions, because there were no adequate water sources to the south and east. Von Kressenstein had visited Beersheba on 15 October and had commented that 'Owing to the shortage of water ... it is impossible that large mounted forces will operate from the east of Beersheba.'[5]

Beersheba was a small town, situated on the north bank of the Wadi es-Saba, which flowed east–west at that point. It was a major route centre for the area, with five roads radiating in all directions, and several tracks as well. These communications had been enhanced by one of Meissner's narrow-gauge railways, for which the town was now the effective terminus. The town lay also on the boundary of the Judaean hills and the plain. Its wadi, as the term implies, was normally dry. Its importance, both civilian and military, lay not only in the routes it controlled, but also in its numerous wells, reputedly of considerable capacity. It was for this reason that the Turks decided to hold it, despite considerable doubts. It was also the reason Allenby wanted to capture it.

The Turks had fortified the town, but only in accordance with their pre-conceived ideas of its vulnerability. It had been surrounded by a trench system close to the built-up area, and another line had been begun about 3 miles further out, but only to the east, between the railway line and the Wadi es-Saba, was it fully developed. South of the wadi, and south and south-east of the town, the trench line was discontinuous. The result was that the approach from the south-east was defended only poorly; that from the north not at all. To the north-east several hills, including the Tell es-Saba, the beginning of the Judaean hills, were formidable obstacles and could be occupied and defended if necessary.

The British plan of attack was for the infantry first of all to advance cautiously towards the Turkish lines south-west of the town, and for the infantry to seize these lines by a rapid attack. The flanks were to be covered by the cavalry. The divisions involved were the Yeomanry and the London. The 7th Mounted Brigade was on their right flank; the left was to be guarded by the Imperial Camel Corps Brigade with two infantry battalions of the Welsh

Division, a force referred to as 'Smith's Group'. These forces were directed at the relatively well-fortified sector to the west and south of the town, which was defended by the Turkish 27th Division and two regiments, all infantry.

Behind this activity, which to the Turks seemed to be no more than an extension of the British fixed defences – or so it was hoped – two divisions of the Desert Mounted Corps would move eastwards, out of sight and out of range of the Turkish troops. They had to develop water supplies as they went along, first at Khalasa, then at Asluj, both in the Wadi es Saba, but 15 miles or so from Beersheba. The Irish Division covered the completion of the construction of the railway as far as Karm, which again looked to the Turks as though it was being laid to service the new defence line.[6]

The apparent extension of the British line brought a reaction from the Turks which almost revealed to them the real scheme. The main force of the Welsh Division took up a line 7 or 8 miles west of Beersheba, and small detachments were sent forward to occupy a number of small hills, including two known as Hill 630 and Hill 720 (from their heights marked on the maps). These were occupied by two battalions of the 8th Mounted Brigade, of the 1st and 3rd County of London Yeomanry. This minor covering movement, essentially an extended flank guard for the main attack, collided with a Turkish reconnaissance force, which mounted a powerful attack to recover both hills. The Welsh Division headquarters was some distance away, and took little notice of the sounds of battle, for it was assumed that the Turks were simply being menacing. But both hills were recaptured, and the troop on Hill 720 was annihilated, while the 3rd on 630 had only a few survivors. The rescuing force, the Royal Welch Fusiliers and the Herefordshire Light Infantry from the Welsh Division, seemed for a short time to be about to fall into a premature battle with the victorious Turks. Confusion reigned on the British side, and the Turks shelled a crowded target. When the Fusiliers and the Herefords finally began their attack, however, the Turks retired. Despite the evidence before them of a major British movement under way, the Turks did not alter their preconceived idea that Gaza was the main British target. The Welsh Division's movement was written off as establishing a flank guard, or perhaps a normal rotation of units, or a gigantic deception: there were many possible explanations.[7]

By the night of 30 October, the fourth night of the bombardment of Gaza, these movements had placed a semi-circle of British troops round the western and south-western parts of the Beersheba defences. Smith's Group faced the Turkish trenches north of the Wadi es-Saba as far as the old Turkish railway; the London and Yeomanry Divisions – almost 24,000 men with nearly 100 guns – faced the main Turkish defensive position between the Wadi es-Saba and the Khalasa road. In front of this huge force was one Turkish division, the 27th, with fewer than 2,500 men. Well over half of these were Arabs, who were thought to be distinctly less than enthusiastic about fighting for the Ottoman Empire and the Committee of Union and Progress than were the Turkish soldiers from Anatolia who made up most other divisions. This did not prevent them fighting hard, however.[8]

The other half of the Allied line was cavalry, 11,000 men and horses. The Anzac Division had reached Asluj, and behind them came the Australian

6 *The ruins of Gaza.* Gaza city was only a mile or so from the British lines for much of 1917. It was the base from which the Turks conducted their defence. Inevitably it was badly battered. The city was evacuated by the Turks as the prospect of a full-scale British assault approached, though not all the inhabitants actually left. Once that was done, of course, there were no British inhibitions about firing at the city, and it emerged from the ordeal comprehensively wrecked. The city-scape which resulted is reminiscent of the wreckage inflicted on Belgian and northern French towns along the line of fighting on the Western front. (Crown Copyright: Imperial War Museum Q 12865)

Mounted Division, at Khalasa. The 7th Mounted Brigade was to act as a link between the infantry facing the Turkish defences and the cavalry to the east. There were thus two infantry and two cavalry divisions immediately available for the assault, facing a garrison of one small Turkish infantry division, two detached infantry regiments, and the Third Cavalry Division: 24,000 foot and 10,000 horse against about 3,500 foot and 1,000 horse.

The problem was, of course, that much of this small defence force was entrenched, in some cases behind wire entanglements, and all the men and horses of the attacking force needed water within the day. The Turks knew this full well, for this had been what had won them the earlier battles at Gaza. All they had to do was to hold out long enough for thirst to defeat the attackers. They were in holes in the ground, often behind wire, with good fields of fire, looking out over open ground. This was the reason Allenby had concentrated such an overwhelming force. The earlier defeats made the new general more than anxious to succeed; for the sake of his troops' self-belief, success had become absolutely necessary.

During the night of 30 October the attacking divisions moved into the positions from which they were to assault the town. This involved much marching. The infantry divisions had to march a good 8 miles, in the dark, over new ground, on a hot and dusty night without wind, yet they reached their positions, a mile and a half from the Turkish lines, by 3 a.m., and without being detected. Their training had thus already produced results. The hour set for the attack was 4 a.m., so the infantry had the chance of an hour's rest. The approach march had been a model of its kind. Later accounts are unanimous that no obstacles remained (though one Royal Horse Artillery battery did not receive the orders to move.)⁹ The infantry assault was to be directly at the Turkish trenches, but the cavalry were to use their mobility to avoid an initial assault. The Anzac Division was to march round to the east of the town, to seize a group of hills to the north and east, Tell es-Saba and Bir es-Sqati in particular; the Australian Division would follow on taking up a position east of the town. The result would be that the town would be surrounded on three sides. Like the infantry movements, the cavalry approach was to be accomplished in one night. To do this the cavalry divisions had to march up to 30 miles in darkness. The way had been well enough prospected so that they reached their objectives in time, and with only a brush with a single Ottoman patrol. The detachment of seventy camel-men commanded by Lieutenant-Colonel Newcombe was sent north to harass any Turkish troops who might move down the road from Hebron, and to attempt to raise the rebellion in the Turkish rear.

This road cut through wadis and wound through hills, and so it could be easily blocked by a small force.

(It may be noted here that this was fundamentally different from the concept in Chetwode's 'Notes', written in June. Instead of punching through between Beersheba and the Hureyra Redoubt, leaving Beersheba alone, Allenby seemed to be intent on seizing Beersheba first, and then exploiting to cut across the rear areas of the Turkish forces. No doubt he had realized the danger of himself being taken in the flank and rear by the Turks from Beersheba – whose forces in the town included part of the 3rd Cavalry Division. Also, Allenby's plan did not work: the expedients he used when this became clear show that he had thought the whole battle through much more thoroughly than Chetwode's ideas perhaps suggested had been done.)

On the Gaza front the artillery bombardment continued for several days, reaching a peak during this night and the morning of 31 October. The noise helped to hide the clink and clatter and thud of movement further east. There is no doubt that the Turks in Beersheba were taken fully by surprise when they were attacked that morning, but they nonetheless fought well and with determination.

The infantry began the assault at 4 a.m. on 31 October. A hill, '1070', half a mile in front of the lines was the first objective, since it unsighted the British artillery, and was held by a Turkish detachment which could enfilade the British infantry attack. It also held an artillery observation post, whose construction and camouflaging had been observed by British aircraft for several days. This hill was bombarded fiercely from just before 6 a.m., but soon there was so much dust that the guns had to stop to let it settle so that they could again see what they were shooting at. After a resumption, the hill was easily taken by 181 Brigade from the London Division. The covered hole for the artillery observation post was found to contain only the decapitated body of an Austrian officer.[10] The infantry had been moving steadily forward while this was going on, and with the capture of the hill the British artillery moved forward to it and fired at the main Turkish trench line, with the aim of cutting up the wire. The approach to the attack was through difficult country, a desert of small, irregular hills, stony and dusty. One brigade deviated from its assigned line, and the gap had to be filled by support companies – that is, the plan was a flexible one.[11] The supporting artillery, shooting over the heads of their infantry colleagues, was also shooting into the rising sun. This had also been foreseen, and every tenth man in the foot soldiers had a biscuit tin lid on his back, which showed their positions and enabled the artillery to miss them. The historian of the gunners noted that every Turkish machine-gun had been 'completely ruined', but only one of them had actually been hit, and that by a dud British shell; the rest had been damaged mainly by splinters.[12]

Soon after noon the wire was judged to have been cut sufficiently, and the infantry went in. There was a delay while the guns were moved up and registered their new targets, and this left the infantry somewhat exposed, though the broken nature of the ground was now helpful in giving cover. Even so casualties were taken, for the Turkish machine guns were well served. The British artillery beat down these guns and the Turkish artillery, but not before there had been substantial losses. The last crest of the hills 'was traversed with a hail of lead and a line of dead all shot through the head that marked this limit of the advance testify alike to the determination of the attack and to the accuracy of the Turk shooting'.[13]

Even though their wire had not actually been cut very well, after the loss of hill 1070 and the bombardment all morning, in the end the Turks in the trenches did not stand to meet the attack of two full British divisions. By early afternoon the trenches had been taken. No more than 400 Turks were captured, a clear sign that most had left the lines before the assault went in. The Yeomanry and London Divisions moved forward to take up a new line within the Turkish perimeter, facing the lines close to the town. They had reached this position by soon after 1 p.m.

The halt to the attack was attributed by Colonel Hussein Husni to 'losses and exhaustion', but he also admitted that the attack had drawn towards it two more Turkish battalions of the 67th and 2nd Regiments. The defenders in the trenches were regarded as having been annihilated, but there were plenty of fugitives, and they were eventually rounded up and re-embodied. The British casualties were about 1,150, which may well be about the same as the Turks.[15]

This broke the main Turkish defence line. It is an interesting case of the power of the defence, and the difficulty of attacking such positions. To minimize casualties attackers had to approach well spread out, which meant that the defence might well outnumber the attackers at the crucial point, that is, in the trenches. The trench line was a comparatively small place, and could be manned by, in this case, fewer than 2,000 men; the attackers might in theory comprise two whole divisions, but the assault force amounted to no more than nine battalions out of a possible eighteen. Any more men would present too large a target. This had been the case also in the earlier Gaza battles, and the answer was artillery to batter down the main defences, the machine guns, and the hostile artillery, and then to send in successive waves of infantry.

While Hill 1070 had been briefly holding up the infantry, the cavalry were being impeded by two rather more formidable hills. The Anzac Division reached its designated position by about 8.30 a.m. after an all-night march. Its objectives were then two hills: Tell es-Saba, at the confluence of two wadis 3 miles east of Beersheba, and Bir es-Sqati, 3 miles further to the north-east; the former in particular was a strongpoint held by tough troops well entrenched and well armed: 'Tel el Saba was seen to be strongly held by the enemy with several machine guns, which were placed in stone huts and sangars and were thus well protected from our fire from all quarters.'[15]

The 2nd Australian Light Horse Brigade attacked Bir es-Sqati. It escaped serious casualties in its advance by riding in 'artillery order' – widely spread, and moving at speed – to within rifle range of the hill. There the troops dismounted and made a more or less conventional infantry assault. The tell was taken by about 1 p.m., just before the successful infantry assault on the western trenches, but resistance was then encountered a little further on.[16]

Tell es-Saba was much more troublesome, having steeper sides and being equipped with well-sited machine-guns. It was also closer to the town, which meant it was more important to the defence and could be reinforced the more easily. The New Zealand Mounted Brigade, covered by artillery fire which was co-ordinated directly between the regimental and battery commanders, advanced in infantry style, by troops. Assisted by an attack by the Australian 3rd Light Horse Regiment along the Wadi es-Saba on their left, the Auckland Regiment finally attacked with the bayonet and overran the hill. But it took until 3 p.m. before the place was captured.[17]

These mounted divisions had marched 30 miles all through the night, and had now put in difficult attacks all morning and well into the afternoon. Between them the Yeomanry and London divisions and the Anzac Division had accomplished their tasks; the town was enclosed on three sides, and its defences seized to east and west. But the town had to be taken that day, or, according to the current practice, the horses would have to be withdrawn to water, and the troops would have to rest fairly soon. The Australians at Bir es-Sqati had found some water in some small wadis, but that would not last long. The town's wells were deemed essential. The resistance at Tell es-Saba in particular had prevented any later movement by the Anzac Division from that direction into the town.

The reaction of the Turkish commander in the town, Colonel Ismet Bey, who commanded the Turkish Third Corps under General Fevzi Pasha, the recently arrived commander of the Seventh Army, had been limited by his lack of troops. He had three regiments of infantry and two of cavalry, plus some horse artillery. He believed at first that he was facing an attack by one infantry and one cavalry division; his 4,400 troops and the guns were regarded as 'sufficient' to make a successful defence against this force. It was not until 10 a.m. that the attackers on Tell es-Saba were identified as two cavalry divisions, though Ismet had been able to put a battalion on the tell in time to form the strong defence the New Zealanders faced. The infantry attack from the east could not be stopped, even by sending in his last reserve of infantry. Ismet reported the situation to von Kressenstein, who was in overall command until Fevzi Pasha took over. Von Kressenstein, who believed that the attacking cavalry amounted to only two brigades, replied, 'Beersheba will be held; the battle will be contained.' But by 4 p.m. it was clear to Ismet that the battle had in fact been lost.[18]

General Chauvel, the commander of the Desert Mounted Corps, whose task it was to capture the town, had now only two brigades in reserve from the Australian Division, the 4th Australian Light Horse and the British 5th Mounted Brigade, positioned to the south-east of the town at a distance of 4 and 6 miles respectively. These were now the only troops available with which to assault the town. The rest of Chauvel's forces were fully occupied in holding the positions they had taken, or in recovering from their exertions.

The task of the infantry on the west had been just to take the trenches; they had been ordered not to approach the town, since their speed was slow enough to give the Turks time to destroy the wells. They also faced another line of fortifications, which were placed south of the town close to the buildings.

A mounted attack across open ground, over a distance of 4 miles, against trenches which, while not wired, were of unknown strength, size, position, width, and number, and held by an unknown number and quality of troops, was against all the rules. In this situation Chauvel reacted as he and Chetwode had reacted before, at Magdhaba, at Rafa, and at First Gaza. He put the condition of his horses before the completion of the task he had been set. He referred back to Allenby, who was at the headquarters of the XX Corps with Chetwode, and asked permission to withdraw.[19] Had he been allowed to do so the whole plan of battle would have fallen apart. He was, in many ways, quite correct: the horses had been without water for twenty-four hours, and they should be watered, so the rules said. But obedience to the 'rules' had lost Gaza twice.

It is worth noting that the plan for the capture of Beersheba had not gone well. The infantry attack had been held up by the need to take hill 1070 first; the attack on Tell es-Saba had not succeeded until 3 p.m. These forces were unable to move on into the town: the infantry because they were too slow and would give the Turks time to initiate their sabotage; the Anzac forces because they were disorganized after their capture of the hill and needed time to recover. So it was not until about 4 p.m. that this became clear to Chauvel and Allenby. According to the original plan, the Australian Mounted Division had been intended either to attack Beersheba or to turn north to assist the Anzac Division, so it was not until Tell es-Saba was captured that they could be used. No cavalryman would have planned a cavalry attack on the town and its trenches, so what followed Chauvel's request to withdraw was therefore very much an improvisation.

In answer to Chauvel's request, Allenby intervened with decisive effect. He gave Chauvel a peremptory order: 'The Chief orders you to capture Beersheba today, in order to secure water and prisoners.'[20] Allenby had obviously studied the events at Magdhaba, Rafa, and First Gaza, and clearly understood that the generals had been the men who had lost First Gaza, and had shown in the earlier cases that they were excessively tender towards the cavalry.

Chauvel now took the risk of ordering a mounted charge on the fortified town. He had the commanders of the 4th Light Horse Brigade and the 5th Mounted Brigade with him, Brigadier-Generals W. Grant and P. D. Fitzgerald, as well as the divisional commander, Major-General H. W. Hodgson. Grant had also brought the colonels of his regiments with him. Both Grant and Fitzgerald, having been told the problem, wanted to make the attack, which, given the short time involved, had to be a cavalry charge – that is, a mounted ride directly at the Turk's positions, rather than a ride towards them, then an attack on foot. The British regiments had actually been trained for such work, and were armed with the appropriate weapon, the sword. The Australians, on the other hand, had had only a minimum of instruction in a cavalry charge – though they had certainly had some – but were reckless and improvisatory. Prompted by Hodgson – 'Put Grant at it' – Chauvel gave the job to Grant and the Australians.[21]

The English regiments would have made an excellent charge, but they would have taken a longish time to organize, being steadier but slower; the brigade was also 2 or 3 miles further from the town than the Australian brigade. The Australians, steadfastly ignoring the rules all through their service, were just the men for such a wild and unlikely charge. (There was also no doubt a certain Australian national feeling involved: Chauvel, as his letters home show, was sensitive to the feeling back home that the Australians were not receiving enough credit for their work. And so far in the battle the Australians had been used only at Bir es-Sqati, an unimportant conquest not even noticed by the Turkish commanders.) Grant swiftly plotted the process. The 4th Light Horse Regiment would lead, the 12th would assist, but would have a special responsibility to guard the right flank, where there was a line of trenches, against machine gun fire from that area. The artillery of 'A' Battery of the Honourable Artillery Company and the Nottinghamshire Battery of the Royal Horse Artillery, were alerted.[22]

The meeting at which Chauvel ordered the cavalry attack took place about 4.30 p.m. The telephone call to Allenby had been about half an hour earlier. At that time Ismet Bey had begun ordering the evacuation of his forces from the town, and the demolition of the buildings and the water supply. The two commanders therefore both identified that moment, about 4 p.m., as the time at which the Turks were clearly beaten, and one last attack by the British forces would take the town. Since Chauvel, and through him Allenby, had a usable reserve and Ismet Bey did not, the town would fall to the next attack. Saving it and its water supply from destruction was the only objective left. It seems clear that it was Allenby, some distance away at Chetwode's headquarters, and not Chauvel, much closer to the fighting, who recognized the moment.

Colonel Ismet ordered the evacuation of the town at about 4 p.m. The 48th Regiment had been stationed south of the town, was not engaged at that time, and was withdrawn first, followed by the 67th and 81st Regiments, who faced the British infantry on the west.[23] So just when Brigadier-General Grant was organizing for the cavalry attack, the Turkish forces which he would have faced within a mile or two of the start were being withdrawn; the way was opened, all unwittingly, for the Australian charge.[24]

For the Turks remaining in the trenches near the town who were left as a rearguard at the wadi, the prospect was anything but enticing. They already knew that the hill strongpoints to the north-east had been taken, and by cavalry; they already knew that the strongest trench lines on their right had been assaulted with complete success by the British infantry; they knew that the town behind them was due for demolition if they were beaten, which would cut off their retreat, and they probably knew that their fellow soldiers were withdrawing; they had in fact no real hope of surviving the day, except as prisoners. It simply seems to have made them the more determined.

The men in the trenches had thus no support to flank or rear, other than some artillery. And now they could see the beginnings of a cavalry charge, the approach of perhaps 2,000 horsemen, riding directly at the weakest point of the Turkish defences, the stronger elements of which had been demolished. The Australians increased their speed to a gallop, accompanied by artillery and machine-gun fire, throwing up a great obscuring dust cloud, out of which came the thunder of nearly 10,000 hooves. The wonder is that any of the Turks stayed in their poor trenches to fight it out. But they did. Their early shots, rifle and artillery, caused some casualties, but the charge was too rapid for them to adjust their rifle sights,[25] It was not a time in which clear, deliberate thinking was at all easy, and most of their later shots went over the heads of the approaching cavalry. The same happened to their protective artillery, shooting from out of the town behind them. The Turkish machine-guns on the Australian left flank were rapidly silenced by the British artillery, the Notts Battery of the Royal Field Artillery finding the range within two shots, and then by the concentrated fire of the two battalions' machine-guns.[26]

The first line of the Australians put their horses to the trenches when they reached them and overleapt them; the next line stopped to fight it out with the Turks in their holes in the ground. (This is perhaps formalizing the situation too much; after a ride of 4 miles, these lines were ragged and intermixed; but some men certainly leapt over, and some certainly stopped.)[27] The fighting was now hand to hand. Many of the Australians had taken out their bayonets during the charge and now used them at close quarters, or swung their rifles as clubs. The Turks responded with a similar berserk fury, and some went on fighting even after the Australians thought they had surrendered. The fighting became very nasty in places.[28]

The main aim had been to capture the town intact. This is where the lack of Australian military discipline was all to the good, for some of them went careering right on into the town, with the result that the German engineers there were not given enough time to blow the charges they had laid in the houses and in the wells. Some were blown, but most of the demolitions were prevented, notably when two Australian troopers interrupted a German officer systematically blowing up installations through a switchboard.[29] The regiment's commanding officer, Major M. Bourchier, rallied some of his men to go on to occupy the town.[30] From further back, Grant sent in his third regiment, the 11th, to occupy the town and form a defensive line on the north. They found that the remaining Turkish infantrymen were in the act of withdrawing northwards, and their irruption on to the scene in the dusk – the whole charge took place in the diminishing light of early evening – completely disorganized the retreat.[31] About 1,000 prisoners were taken to add to the 100 or so captured by the infantry in the western trenches. But plenty of Turks escaped into the gathering darkness, and a day later 1,250 of the men who had been at Beersheba were mustered at Tell esh-Sheria. The Turkish commander's

> [h]eadquarters were on the point of moving [when] the enemy cavalry, profiting by the breach in the eastern force entered Beersheba and were seen approaching headquarters' former residence. The Commander, with one or two officers, escaped on foot, attached themselves to a body of about twenty infantrymen and escaped by beating off the enemy. He first went to the 81st Regiment and then succeeded in gaining control of his command again.[32]

The fighting elsewhere continued for some time. The Yeomanry Division had been harassed by sniper fire from the Turkish positions north of their conquest and north of the Wadi Saba. Moving notably slowly and cautiously, the division's troops did not clear the last of the Turkish snipers from that area until well into the night.[33] Then there was the task of collecting the prisoners, finding the wounded, burying the dead. The casualties among all the attackers were over 1,400, though the mounted divisions had suffered only lightly.[34] Nearly 2,000 Turks were prisoners, and almost half that number were killed or wounded. A good half of the Turkish forces had escaped, and the Third Cavalry Division had not even been seriously engaged. The British and Australian casualties were overwhelmingly caused because they were the attackers, out in the open, seen to be shot at. Most casualties were British infantry.

This success was notable above all for that terrific cavalry charge. It was an achievement which those who took part in did not easily appreciate. Sergeant H. Langtip described it in his diary very simply:

> We rode all night to get the right around Beersheba, 32 miles in all. It is 9:30 a.m. and we are all standing to. Our horses ready to go into the line to attack within the next few minutes. It was a terrible ride in heavy dust all the way. The horses have still got the saddles on and I don't know when they will get them off to. The attack started at 4:30 p.m. and within half an hour the first trenches were cleared and then they never stopped till they got Beersheba. Our casualties were fairly light considering the ground was as level as a table. Nine o'clock we are camped in the town with outposts out. The Turks blew up the station and engine, set fire to the ammunition and stores. Thousands of prisoners.[35]

Others merely noted it in a single sentence: 'We charged and took it,'[36] or even

7 *Beersheba Water*. The capture of Beersheba was conducted as a rapid surprise operation in order to prevent the Turks from destroying the wells in the town, which were deemed to be an essential for future operations. In fact, several of the wells were badly damaged during the town's capture, and even at full production the water supply was never really adequate to the demands placed on it. The photograph shows one of the damaged wells. The sturdy construction, stone-lined and wide, is medieval or perhaps even ancient work, the donkey-driven wheel at the well-head was the old reliable but slow method, suitable for the demands of the townspeople and the passing caravans, but not for armies. The German engineers installed pumps (seen at the bottom of the picture), pipes, and metal ladders. The destruction concentrated on the machinery, which could be replaced fairly easily. (Crown Copyright: Imperial War Museum Q 13167)

not at all.[37] The commanders were more appreciative, but there is no doubt that the episode has grown in the telling, so that in some Australian accounts it becomes the war-winning victory. In fact, until the Beersheba charge it had been the New Zealanders who had been the prime exponents of this sort of mounted infantry warfare, and it had been, and continued to be, the British infantry who did most of the fighting. At Beersheba, for instance, it was the victorious attack by the two British infantry divisions and the capture of Tell es-Saba by the New Zealanders which were the keys to the conquest of the town by sucking all the Turkish reserves away from the centre, and thus convincing Colonel Ismet to order evacuation, so leaving the approach used by the 4th Light Horse virtually unguarded.

It has to be said also that the charge was directed at an enemy who was in the act of withdrawing. The numbers of men in the trenches cannot have been large. Only two or three machine guns, on the flanks, were encountered, and were suppressed at once. The charge therefore was not a particularly dangerous exercise, though the men involved did not know that at the time.

The charge also had a deplorable effect on the other cavalry regiments in the campaign, who all wanted to have a charge of their own, and even on some of the Australians, who asked to be armed with swords. The Australians were in fact more than lucky in their target, a weakly held line manned by few troops without wire, and without much support. They were extremely well supported by excellent artillery work: when Turkish machine-guns opened up on the charging horsemen, the Notts Battery put them out of action with its second shot, and another machine gun was overrun by an Australian sergeant.[38] But this type of charge was not a practice to be recommended to other cavalry in the age of machine warfare. A pair of tanks supported by artillery would have done the job much more easily. This does not detract from the bravery of the men, of course, but it does emphasize the appalling choices facing a commander of such troops. While one can scarcely blame Chauvel for flinching at the decision, all the more credit is due to Allenby for insisting, and to Grant for appreciating at once what sort of action was required.

It turned out that the damage the German engineers had managed to do to the wells at Beersheba was relatively slight, though the town was widely booby-trapped and had to be occupied very cautiously. Colonel Husni commented that the preparations for demolition had not been very thorough.[39] However, the capacity of the wells was sufficiently reduced by the destruction and by the recent dry weather to make it impossible to water all the horses of the two divisions. This had been the purpose of the whole exercise: to seize the wells and so enable the mounted soldiers to move on to envelop the Turkish rear. Now this proved to be impossible. The problem was made worse because a *khamsin*, a hot, dry, and dusty wind from the desert, blew for the next two or three days, increasing demand, yet making work more difficult than usual.[40] Many of the horses were watered at pools which had formed after a recent thunderstorm, but this was a source which would soon vanish. Meanwhile the Turkish 3rd Cavalry Division was facing the Anzac Division, and remained a menacing presence on the flank of any possible enveloping movement. The Turkish forces were collected at Tell esh-Sheria and then placed to reinforce the cavalry line, so that the Turkish line remained continuous, bent back slightly at Abu Hureyra, but still continuous.[41]

Thus the projected attacks of the second phase turned out to be impossible on the Beersheba flank. The town itself had been taken, and a fragment of the Turkish army had been defeated. The one Turkish division that was present had fought well, but had only been damaged in the process. The overall Turkish position was not even seriously threatened. The fortifications of Gaza were still intact, though battered by the long bombardment. All the fortified positions along the line of the Beersheba road were still held, while others had been partly prepared as fall-back positions in the Turkish rear. And in the hilly, wadi-seamed country to the east of the Turkish railway, there was the unharmed 3rd Cavalry Division. The prediction of Allenby in July that the main fighting would be at Tell es-Sheria had been very acute.

The net result was that the main British effort was now to be directed at Gaza, so the Turkish assumption that the threat to Beersheba was not the main effort turned out to be correct, if only for a time. The forces at the eastern end of the British line were unable to move forward for lack of water, and because the Turkish resistance had not been broken at Beersheba as had been hoped. The troops there were told to recommence their attacks on 3 or 4 November, assuming that the water supplies could be organized.

So the next attack was made at Gaza. This is said, in most accounts, to be a continuation of the bombardment, which itself was an attempt to pin down the Turkish forces in the city, and leave the way clear for the next attack in the east. But the plans for Gaza turn out to be much more ambitious than that. Attention was to be concentrated on the seaward end of the defences, with the aim of breaking through the whole defence line between the city and the coast.[42] This was in part a result of the fighting in the area by Money's Detachment in April, when it was seen that the sand-dunes were not as difficult fighting territory as expected – and the Turkish trenches in such an area were liable to be destroyed fairly easily. Subsequent attacks – raids – had confirmed that. As usual there was a preliminary object, the capture of an advanced Turkish position on Umbrella Hill, a fortified system thrust forward as a salient in front of the cactus-hedged gardens. From there the Turks could enfilade any attack to either side. Once that was done the main attack was to assault the Turkish trenches and posts and redoubts between Umbrella Hill and the sea. These curved round the town so that the advance would move into a steadily narrowing avenue, exposed to flanking fire from the right; but the thinnest defences were at the seaward end, and once they were taken, the whole Gaza position could be outflanked. For an assault which is said to have been no more than a distraction, this was to be an unusually powerful blow. In fact, of course, it was no longer a distraction, and had probably never been one, but was intended to pierce the whole Turkish line and permit exploitation into the country beyond the city. It was designed as a battle-winning attack.[43]

The Turks had greatly increased the power and depth of their defences over the past six months since their victory in April in the second battle. The original object of the earlier British attacks, the complex of defences centred on Ali el-Muntar, was now even more formidable, and the two earlier failures had persuaded the British planners that it was best to avoid them. But the new object was not much less daunting a prospect. Over the 2 miles or so of distance between Umbrella Hill and the coast, there were three groups of trenches complex enough to be regarded as redoubts, called el-Arish, Rafa, and Cricket by the British, and these were connected by a series of trench lines several layers thick, and backed by other trenches and strongpoints. To add to the difficulties, these positions were on firm ground for the most part, whereas the approach the British had to use was over the sand-dunes, where the going was unpleasantly slow and heavy, and very tiring.

The attack was entrusted to the East Anglian Division, with one brigade and the artillery from the Lowland Division attached. Some misdirection was built into the plan as well, with a raid on Outpost Hill, to the east of Umbrella Hill, the day before the main attack. The idea was that the attack on Umbrella Hill would be regarded by the Turks as yet another of these raids, which had been a constant activity for the previous month and more. These attacks were to be carried out by the 75th Division, now fully equipped and recovered in health. To the east of that division, in the area about Sheikh Abbas, was another new unit, called the Composite Force, which included the French and Italian contingents, a West Indian battalion, and the 25th Indian Infantry Brigade, a force amounting almost to a full division in total. It was planned that this force should move forward threateningly towards the Atawine Redoubt, as if making yet another attack, though in the event this move was cancelled.

The Gurkhas of the 75th Division duly raided Outpost Hill in the early hours of 1 November, suffering 25 casualties but accounting for over forty Turks with their rifles and kukris.[44] This was the sixth night of the heavy and increasing bombardment by the guns of the artillery and by the ships off shore, an even heavier concentration of fire on a small area than had been put in on the first day of the battle of the Somme.[45] During the rest of the day the bombardment went on, and in the evening the Turks were allowed to see what appeared to be the beginnings of the embarkation of a landing force at Deir el-Belah; occasional lights and constantly moving boats all through the night maintained the illusion – the embarkees had in fact been dragooned men of the Egyptian Labour Corps, who were then disembarked, no doubt to their own great relief, after dark.[46]

The attack was to take place in four stages, with the possibility of a fifth if all went well. The first stage was the capture of Umbrella Hill. A full battalion and an extra company, all Scottish Rifles, were committed against a garrison assumed to be about 350 strong – odds of about three to one. They were, in fact, spotted as they assembled, but the attack went in on time, behind a creeping barrage, with remarkably few casualties, though they suffered from Turkish artillery retaliation afterwards. To foster the deception that this was only another big raid, like the one the night before on Outpost Hill, there was then a gap of several hours before the main attack went in, with a diminution of the artillery bombardment during that time.[47] The Turks were successfully gulled, and their own artillery fire slackened off. And yet they were not wholly unprepared when, at 3 a.m., a short ten-minute bombardment heralded the full assault; Turkish artillery and machine-gun fire replied at once.

Two and a half brigades were used in the second part of the attack. Two Essex battalions of 161 Brigade, nearest the coast, had a long approach march. Close to the shore the Sixth Battalion captured two posts and then went on to take the Cricket Redoubt with the aid of a tank, which had earlier destroyed much of the Turkish wire. Inland, however, the Fifth Battalion became somewhat confused in the featureless sand-dune landscape exploding with shells into dust, noise, smoke and flying sand, and the barrage had lifted several minutes before the infantry reached the Turkish trenches. They captured the trenches, but took heavy casualties in the process. As a result the battalion was not strong enough to continue the attack:[48] 'The second line [of Turkish trenches] lay on the low ground and those detailed for its capture – what was left of them – gallantly carried on and occupied it; but none of them ever got back.'

The company which should have attacked the Zowaiid Trench, to the right of the Rafa Redoubt, had actually attacked the redoubt itself, while the other company did the opposite; opinion differs on who made the initial mistake. The result was that the redoubt was captured, as was the Zowaiid Trench, but the further objectives towards the city could not be taken. This meant that the Turks still controlled a series of trenches and positions uncomfortably close to the coast, so that the passage along the coast through the sand-dunes remained very narrow. This would have its effect later.

The attack by the battalions of 163 Brigade was even more confused. The objectives here were Burj Trench (to the right of Zowaiid Trench) and part of the el-Arish Redoubt. The Norfolks were damaged by the Turkish bombardment even as they set off at 3 a.m. They then found they had to do more than planned, because Zowaiid had not been taken, and so did not accomplish all their objectives, though they did capture the first Turkish trench line. To their right the Hampshires took Triangle Trench by mistake and also Burj Trench successfully, but their misdirection left the Norfolks with extra work to do, which proved to be too much. The el-Arish Redoubt, a formidable network of trenches, was attacked by the Suffolks of 163 Brigade along with a company of the Norfolks and, from the other side, the Royal Scots and a company of Scottish Rifles from 156 Brigade. They all arrived at the trenches in the wake of the creeping barrage and captured the whole position with minimum casualties, though the fighting had been hand-to-hand at times. Along with the attack on Umbrella Hill, this was the most accomplished of all the attacks that day.[49]

This second phase was thus only three-quarters successful. The resistance of the Turks had been tenacious. Colonel Gibbons of the 1/5th Essex had found that they came out of the trenches to avoid the bombardment, and met their attackers in front of their line, fighting with bayonets; hand to hand fighting in the trenches was common, and every line of trenches had to be taken. Casualties were heavy among the assaulting troops, and they had not always reached all their objectives. It is unusual to find any historian admit this, but F. Loraine Petre in his history in the Norfolk Regiment does so: 'The brigade had fallen considerably short of maintaining its objectives, the result due to the darkness and confusion.'[50] These failed objectives were strongpoints called Crested Rock and Gibraltar, and an area called Island Wood, which between them allowed the Turks still to dominate the captured area. The 161st Brigade had in fact been asked to do more here than it was capable of.

The third phase of the attack was intended to be an expansion of the area taken in the second phase, but 161 Brigade's loss of direction and heavy casualties meant that they could not be attained. The fourth phase, however, was to be the exploitation along the coast by 162nd Brigade, and this could go ahead. The brigade was to go past the lines established by the 161st Brigade in its capture of Rafa Redoubt, and seize some well-spaced trenches as far as a Muslim shrine on the shore called Sheikh Hasan. At that point the British would have got through the whole of the Turkish defences along the shore, except for one more line of discontinuous positions to the north of the city.

162 Brigade, Londoners and East Midlanders, had mixed fortunes. The battalions close to the coast managed with little loss, though they had to take a strongpoint called Gun Hill at the point of the bayonet. Inland, however, the failure of 161 Brigade's attack on the Rafa Redoubt pulled the 10th London Battalion into the fighting there, and they suffered badly when they became separated from their barrage. Nevertheless the proclaimed farthest object of the attack, Sheikh Hasan, was reached by 6 a.m. The whole attack, from the opening bombardment to the capture of the final target, had taken just three hours.

This was the objective as laid down in XXI Corps orders before the battle began, and if it was intended by this attack to fix Turkish attention on Gaza and to imply that another attack would come on the untaken trenches it may be considered a success. But what happened next shows that General Allenby had rather more in mind than Bulfin's Corps orders had made out.

A company of the 4th Northamptonshires, part of the 162nd Brigade, moved out from Sheikh Hasan to break through the final Turkish defences, which consisted of a series of short trenches three-quarters of a mile beyond that point. They seized one of these, designated Lion Trench, thus finally breaching the whole system of trenches around Gaza. Behind them, other troops of the battalion cleared the wire from the beach, though in the event it might have been better to push them forward to take more of the Turks' trenches. The way was thus opened to let the Imperial Service Cavalry Brigade ride through.

This was the Indian brigade which consisted of the three regiments of lancers from Indian princely states, Jodhpur, Mysore, and Hyderabad, a total of about 1,500 horsemen. The brigade had previously been used as part of the Canal defence force and then as lines of communications troops, and had not so far been attached to any of the front-line divisions; therefore, to both armies they were seen as second-rate troops, an understandable mistake, but a mistake nonetheless. The brigade's appearance in the attack would thus be a major surprise, and only Allenby had the authority to so employ it. It was a unit which was under his immediate control, but the commander was one of those who had attended the regular briefings at General Bulfin's headquarters. He was thus close by when the breakthrough came.

This was yet another deception practiced by Allenby on the enemy and, as it turns out, also on subsequent historians, few of whom seem to have noticed this episode. The military historians have been bewitched by the idea that the plan as laid out in an advance actually worked. But it did not. Nor was it the case that the plan as written down was necessarily that which was carried out. Instead the plan actually laid out a series of preliminary attacks whose success would allow further attacks to be mounted. It scarcely mattered where the breakthrough happened, so long one took place. If it had been possible to exploit the Beersheba victory, the troops were there to do so. It had not been possible. The attack on Gaza was another opportunity, and the Imperial Service Brigade was there to exploit it, if possible.[51]

This appearance, for the first time, of the Imperial Service Brigade explains the whole purpose of this Gaza attack. The pattern of the fighting now makes sense. The attack along the coast was intended to punch right through the Turkish defences where they were at their weakest, while the attacks on the redoubts and trenches from Umbrella Hill round to the coast were to push back the Turkish line and establish flank guards. If a mere attention-getting distraction was required, this was unusually definitive. Why open up the whole Turkish position unless that opening was to be used? In fact, of course, it was to be used, and the exploitation was to be by the Indian cavalry, which was to ride right through the sand-dunes and break into the rear of the Turks' Gaza position. This was to be complemented by a new attack in the Beersheba sector, which was supposed to take place on 3 or 4 November. With this brigade, and perhaps others, rampaging about their lines of communications, the whole Gaza garrison, pinned in front by three British infantry divisions, would be isolated.

Before the cavalry brigade could enter the fray, however, the Northamptonshires at Lion Trench were attacked by freshly arrived Turkish troops, who were in sufficient numbers and were so persistent as to force them to retreat. They were too far advanced to be given good artillery support, and no more infantry support was available either. Later attempts to recover control of the forward trenches were also defeated. The battalion suffered over 200 casualties.[52]

The Turkish force was two regiments of the 7th Division, which had been

kept back at Deir Sneid, the Turkish railhead, in expectation of the non-existent British landing from the sea. The Turkish command had finally realized at
dawn that this was not going to happen, for they could see only two trawlers
offshore at that time, and by then the major attack was clearly taking place
at the city. So those regiments, perhaps 2,000 men, were sent to reinforce
the Gaza garrison. They arrived just after the 162nd Brigade had consolidated
its hold on Sheikh Hasan, and not long after the capture of Lion Trench, but
before the Imperial Service Cavalry Brigade could arrive to exploit the breakthrough. The Turks' advance guard drove back the Northamptonshires, and
the main body then advanced in formation to mount a counter-attack, with
the intention of driving the British back along the coast. They were marching,
in the very best military tradition, to the sound of the guns.[53]

This movement had in fact been anticipated by the British artillery staff,
and a barrage had been organized by the XXI Corps heavy artillery just in
case – yet another indication that the breakthrough had been intended for
exploitation. As the Turks advanced towards the British positions, the barrage
struck them, breaking up the attack and causing them, so the British believed,
heavy losses.[54] The Northamptonshires prepared another attempt to take Lion
Trench, but this was later cancelled, and the battalion was used in an attack on
Yunis Trench, to the right of the Northamptonshires and Sheikh Hasan, and
which lay uncomfortably close to the British positions, with the aim of widen-
ing the gap in the Turkish fortifications.

This change marked the effective abandonment of the attempt to break out
with the cavalry, all the more so when the Northamptonshires failed to hold on
to Yunis Trench once they had taken it. A large Turkish force – presumably the
reordered survivors of the artillery-scattered regiments – made an attempt to
retake Sheikh Hasan from a position where they were out of sight of the British
artillery spotters. They were seen, however, from the ships offshore, and were
caught in another barrage, this time of even larger naval shells from the monitors and the destroyers stationed there. So, in a sense, the naval outflanking
move had happened after all.[55]

Both the British attacks, at Beersheba and at Gaza, had failed to defeat the
Turks so vehemently as to lever them out of their fortifications. The official
British historian, Captain Cyril Falls, expressed the result in a contorted way,
saying that the Gaza attack 'had not reached all its objectives, but had fulfilled
the Commander in Chief's object'.[56] This can only be interpreted to mean that
the historian recognized the essential failure, but was unwilling to accept it
or express it. An estimate that the Gaza operations were a success may be

accepted only if the attempted breakout is ignored. On the Turkish side von Kressenstein later described the results as 'a repulse' for the attackers, which is equally unconvincing.[57] But the lack of success for the British meant that they had to prepare for a Turkish counter-attack and to work out their own next moves.

CHAPTER 7

The Turkish Lines Broken

T HE day after the capture of Beersheba, 1 November, as the East Anglian Division was readying itself for its attempt to break through the lines at Gaza, the Turkish Seventh Army command, at Hebron, counted its men, appealed for help, and began moving its under-strength units into position to meet the next attack. The presence of a British force on the Hebron road at Dhaheriye gave concern. This was Newcombe's Force. Colonel Newcombe was aiming to rouse the Arabs of the Judaean Hills on the pattern of the revolt in Arabia, but they were cautious. The Turks brought a force of German motor-men south from Bethlehem, and added two companies of Turkish infantry to them. Newcombe was almost surrounded and, when the Turks attacked on the 2nd, he surrendered. Colonel Husni recorded the events and the 'bag':

> Lieutenant Avilokh directed his two Turkish [companies] to such good purpose that the enemy could offer no resistance and were immediately surrounded and captured to a man. In this fight we captured an Egyptian [*sic*] colonel of the General Staff, a captain, three lieutenants, 16 NCOs, 6 men, 30 Arabs, 93 camels, two heavy machine guns, 10 Lewis guns, many rifles, maps, ammunition, cash and important papers. Our losses were 5 killed and 10 wounded, the enemy's 10 killed and 20 wounded.[1]

The overweighting with officers and NCOs was the result of the aim of the expedition; the rank and file would be the Arabs.

The net result of this Turkish success was to block the Hebron road to any further British exploitation; but it also stretched the Turkish forces very thinly, as Colonel Husni reported:

> [T]he line was very weak. Two regiments and two batteries (2,000 rifles and eight guns) defended a front of 22 to 23 kilometres, that is less than one rifle per 10 metres. This was in fact the weakest part of the line. The Eighth Army was on its right on a 20 kilometre front with five divisions. Moreover all its reserves were behind the right flank. In fact Tell al Sharia was the key to our front.[2]

General Allenby had set the date for the next attack in the east for 3 or 4 November. On the 3rd the Welsh Division, which had scarcely been used in the fight for the town, moved north to take up positions about 5 miles from Beersheba. The target for the next attack was Tell esh-Sheria and the Welsh Division was to be the flank guard for that attack.

The men had a very hard time. For a start the land was different from what they had become used to, stony hills rather than sand desert. By now the *khamsin* was blowing and they found no water at all; for lack of water they sent all their animals back to Beersheba, where the wells were less capacious than expected. One officer described the conditions:

> Hard days these. Very little water, never enough for a wash; bully beef and biscuits unvaried, no mails, officers' kits only 30 pounds and often miles behind, dust and heat. We wore tin hats, and the intense heat of the sun on them made our heads feel like poached eggs.[3]

They had the Imperial Camel Corps on their right and still further east the Anzac Mounted Division and the 7th Mounted Brigade moved out of Beersheba as well, part going along the Hebron road, and part due north towards the prominent hill Tell el-Khuweilfe. This was to be their target for the next week.

The Welsh Division reached the westerly position it was aiming for just before a party of Turks, but other Turks beat the horsemen to Tell el-Khuweilfe. Another target had been Abu Khuff (Abu Hof to the Turks), but that had been occupied by the Turks for some days as a half-way point between Tell esh-Sheria and Dhaheriye. By the end of the day a line had been established, lying more or less east-west, well to the north of Beersheba, but Tell el-Khuweilfe stood before the British forces as a formidable barrier.[4]

Behind that line came other British forces, also moving out of Beersheba. The Irish Division, as little used so far as the Welsh, crossed the Wadi es-Saba and swung west to face a powerful Turkish work called the Khawukah/Rushdi system, which lay a little north of the Gaza–Beersheba road east of the old Hureyra Redoubt and connected that position with Tell esh-Sheria. Then the Yeomanry (infantry) Division came up to take over the rest of the Welsh Division line, while the Welsh Division shifted eastwards to confront Tell el-Khuweilfe directly. Behind them came the Yeomanry Mounted Division, again used only a little so far. And between the Yeomanry infantry and the Irish Divisions came the London Division. Meanwhile the Turks, amid considerable administrative confusion, brought forward only their 19th Division, newly arrived from the north, as part of the Yildirim army. It was put in the line at el-Khuweilfe. The other recently arrived division, the 24th, still incomplete, was brought forward as well. By this time also the 7th Division had been drawn into the fighting at Gaza. There were now no Turkish reserves left. The Anzac Division and the Australian Mounted Division were meanwhile pulled back as far as Karm to rest and water after their exertions in the capture of the town.[5]

The Turks were convinced that another wide sweep around their left flank was intended and they had troops blocking the Hebron road and more troops beyond the road to the east. They bitterly contested the Welsh Division's assault on Tell el-Khuweilfe on the assumption that this was part of a British plan to invade the Judaean hills by way of the Hebron road.[6] The target Allenby had set was in fact another breakthrough attempt, this time to capture Tell esh-Sheria, which was a major Turkish administrative and logistics centre, on the railway – a place which had to be taken if the whole Turkish line from Gaza to Khawukah and Rushdi was to be outflanked and surrounded. Instead of pushing at the handle end of the door, on the Hebron road, his attack would be at the hinge.

The Turks had developed an incomplete and discontinuous line of strongpoints south of Tell esh-Sheria, stretching for about 4 miles east of the railway. Across the railway to the west was the formidable Khawukah-Rushdi system of trenches. Both were the initial objects of the British attack, the strongpoints by the Yeomanry Division, the system by the London Division and part of the Irish. General Allenby had given this task to Chetwode on 4 November, but, thanks in part to the *khamsin* and the shortage of water, XX Corps troops were not in position until early on the 6th.[7]

There were thus several days between the initial advance north and the attack. In that time the Turkish high command repeatedly attempted to organize counters to the British success. But Falkenhayn was at Aleppo until 4 November, and did not reach Jerusalem until the 6th, so his orders tended to be out of date when they arrived (having gone through a translation process of some complexity).[8] Nevertheless the German and Turkish commanders did their best to comply with Falkenhayn's order to counter-attack. Close to the sea the British troops in the most advanced positions at Sheikh Hasan could hear the Turks in the nearest trench – the Yunis Trench – digging away mightily during the night of 2 November, and working at fortifying Turtle Hill, above and behind that position, as well. Early in the morning of 4 November, the Essex battalion of the East Anglian Division attacked the Yunis Trench and captured it briefly, but a rapid counter-attack by the Turks pushed them out again. There were to be no advances by either side along this part of the front without very heavy casualties. The front here had solidified.[9]

The Turkish 54th Division, which occupied the line from the outskirts of the city to the Atawine Redoubt, appeared to mount an attack on the Allied Composite Force holding Sheikh Abbas. The attack was not seriously pressed, being driven off by rifle and machine-gun fire, and was only a strong patrol designed to locate and identify the British forces.[10]

The main source of Turkish anxiety remained the Hebron road. The Welsh Division's repeated attacks on Tell el-Khuweilfe seemed to be an attempt to break the Turkish line so as to permit a major cavalry attack north along the road. The presence of mounted troops at Beersheba and along the road for a short distance seemed to confirm this. This obsession may also be in part a result of the location of Seventh Army headquarters at Hebron itself. General Fevzi Pasha had assumed command soon after the loss of Beersheba, but he had great difficulty in wresting control of all his units in the Khuweilfe area (which the Turks referred to as Abu Hof) from von Kressenstein of the Eighth Army. The result was contradictory orders and confusion in the front line, while from the vantage point of Hebron the British attacks seemed to be directed northwards. The evidence from Colonel Husni is that Seventh Army was not aware of the extent of the British concentration against Tell esh-Sheria until the attack went in, and the Eighth Army was, from its own headquarters at Huj, more concerned with events at Gaza.[11] That is, the Welsh Division's attacks at Khuweilfe and those at Gaza succeeded in attracting all the Turks' attention.

The Turks' new defensive line in front of Tell esh-Sheria was scarcely strong enough to withstand an early assault. Nor, as a result of the Army headquarters' concentration elsewhere, was it well manned. The main work, the Khawu-kah system, extended no further east than the railway line, but beyond that point there were only isolated strongpoints, in fairly obvious locations. This was partly because the fortifications of Beersheba had been intended to cover that flank, and partly it was because the land there rose into the foothills of southern Judaea, where fewer strongpoints were needed to block an invader's progress. Perhaps more important than either of these considerations, there was also the problem of the Turks' chronic manpower shortage; their priority had been the main defensive line.

Neither Turkish army had any reserves left by 4 November, and the expedient was resorted to of secretly withdrawing some of the troops from the central part of the line, which had not been attacked, or even threatened, as yet; they were taken from the 26th Division, from Khirbet Sihan, and from the Hureyra Redoubt. The reserve thus formed, no more than 1,000 men or so, was concentrated at Khirbet Zuheilika, a central position from which it could be moved to any part of the front which came under serious threat, and was referred to as the Zuheilika Group.[12]

Falkenhayn travelled by rail and road to Jerusalem, receiving updates on the situation on the way. When he reached Jerusalem, late on 5 November, he gave permission to von Kressenstein to withdraw the heavy guns from Gaza to a reserve line at Wadi Hesi, 7 miles north of the city. This movement began during the night, and was partly a precaution to avoid the guns' being captured, and partly to prevent a possible landing at the mouth of the wadi.[13] But it is obvious that von Kressenstein and Falkenhayn had now admitted the probability of the loss of the city, that is, Eighth Army (von Kressenstein) expected a further attack at Gaza, just as Seventh Army, concentrating on the fighting at el-Khuweilfe/Abu Hof, was still thinking of an attack towards Hebron.

The British intention, however, was to break this line in the centre, and

8 *A bivouac on the coast.* A bivouac of the Suffolk Regiment (74th Yeomanry Division) on the Palestinian coast during the pursuit north from Gaza in November 1917. The white bell-tents are the company headquarters, and each company is established in a separate location. Apart from that, tents are located and set up to individual preferences. The haphazard arrangement of the tents, and their dark colour, makes the camp very like a Bedouin encampment. Whenever the regiment moved, these tents had to be struck and packed, and an officer went ahead to locate the next day's camp. Each regiment carried a large supply train with it. Often carts were acquired for carrying the heavy equipment. (Crown Copyright: Imperial War Museum Q 12863)

then strike towards the coast. This was a variation on the original plan which had called for a coastwards turn further north, at Tell en-Nejile. Chetwode had marshalled his forces with skill and had produced a dense attacking force of four infantry divisions and one cavalry division against three weak Turkish divisions, say 40,000 infantry and 5,000 cavalry against considerably less than 10,000 Turkish infantry. This was the same sort of proportion which had been laid on against Beersheba, and a much heavier preponderance than in the Gaza infantry attacks. The main strike by this powerful infantry force was to be directed at the Turkish defence works south of Tell esh-Sheria. The Turks were again caught off-balance, because of their preoccupations with Gaza and the Hebron road.

The plan was that the Welsh Division would take care of Tell el-Khuweilfe. It did not greatly matter if they actually captured the position or not; their attack had to prevent the Turkish 19th Division from interfering in matters further west. The Yeomanry Mounted Division was to guard the immediate left flank of the Welsh and the right flank of the Yeomanry (infantry) Division. This was to strike westwards against the strong points east of the railway. The Yeomanry Mounted was thus available for a cavalry exploitation, if that became possible, but its first task was to occupy the gap between the Welsh and Yeomanry Divisions as it expanded.

The British infantry divisions had been brought to such positions that they were able to attack the Turks in flank. The Yeomanry Division was to take the several strongpoints east of the railway, which had to be done before the Irish and London Divisions could tackle the more extensive systems to the west of the railway, because they overlooked the approach the London Division had to take. The Yeomanry would take the Turks' positions serially in flank, moving almost due west. Then the London Division would attack the Khawukah lines. All this was preliminary to an attack on Tell esh-Sheria itself, which was north of the Turkish defences. So three stages were planned: first, the capture of the strongpoints by the Yeomanry Division; second, the conquest of the redoubts by the Irish and London Divisions; and third, a turn north by the Yeomanry and London Divisions in order to take Tell esh-Sheria.

It was only after these attacks had succeeded that the real exploitation could begin. This was to be by the rested Australian and Anzac Mounted Divisions of the Desert Mounted Corps. They would come through Tell esh-Sheria to attack north-west towards Huj, the Turkish Eighth Army headquarters, and from there it was intended that they should reach the coast and so cut off the Gaza garrison from the rear. The infantry would have the less pleasant task of finishing off the old Turkish infantry redoubts along the Gaza–Beersheba road, starting with the Rushdi system and going on to capture the Hureyra Redoubt. No doubt the planners hoped that these last measures might not actually be necessary. For one of the expectations was surely that this breakthrough would so demoralize the Turkish troops that they would give up. But the Turks did not do so, usually. The relatively small number of prisoners at both Beersheba and Gaza had already shown that. They tended to go on fighting until they were killed or overrun. Just like the British, in fact.

The attack had been urged forward by Allenby as early as 4 November, but Chetwode had been unable to organize it until the 6th. Water, of course, was a major problem, and it was not until the 4th that the wells at Beersheba were producing to their full capacity. The attack on Beersheba from the east had meant that reserve stocks of ammunition had now to be moved across the town to the rear of the attacking formations, which themselves had to be moved into place: once there, they had to reconnoitre their fronts and their objectives. Allenby had his finger on the pulse all through. Chetwode's arguments about the unreadiness of his troops were put forward at a conference on the 5th, and accepted. At the same time the commander of the Welsh Division, Major-General Mott, who had succeeded to the command just before Second Gaza, made a vigorous presentation of the case for an attack on Tell el-Khuweilfe. Chetwode was uncertain, so Allenby went across to see Mott, heard his argument, and gave him permission to attack. Allenby will have had his own reasons for permitting the attack, which were not necessarily those of Mott, and he permitted the attack to be made only because it fitted in with his overall intentions, or, as Mott put it, as quoted by the division's historian, 'he wanted to avoid any possibility of the Turks retreating on the whole front before his general scheme was launched'.[14]

The final plans were only settled during the 5th, and orders were changed. Major-General Girdwood, the commander of the Yeomanry Division, did not receive the new orders until late afternoon, and the troops had to move into their starting positions during the night. Nevertheless they were mostly in place by 3.30 a.m., though in one case the relieving battalion of the Yeomanry Mounted Division on the right did not arrive until 5 a.m. The original orders had envisaged a preliminary attack on an isolated strongpoint close to the British front, called by them v 46, but the change made it impossible to carry this out; this was just as well, since the attack was to be made without a preliminary barrage, and an early seizure of this advanced post would have alerted the Turks in the main positions.

The ground was gently rolling and bare, with no cover available. The Turkish trenches were dug into the forward edges of the undulations, all with uninterrupted fields of fire. There was no wire, but lots of machine-guns and field artillery.[15] v 46 was quickly seized at dawn by the Sussex Yeomanry, but then the 229th Brigade discovered the existence of an unexpected circular strongpoint between it and the main Turkish line, and the same battalion had to pound this into submission with some energy. The troops advanced by platoons, and overwhelmed the strong point, 'by a steady and accurate rifle and Lewis gun fire, backed by a constant stream of rifle bombs and hand grenades'. They finally went in to finish the work with the bayonet. Thirty Turks died, and seventy became prisoners. The Sussex men were only half that number.[16]

As ever in such attacks, it was the first fighting which was the hardest, but once these first strongpoints were reduced, the advance went quickly. The three brigades of the Yeomanry Division, men who had originally joined up as horsemen, proved that as infantry they could move almost as fast as on horseback. The troops had to move quickly, at the double, and despite stopping for breathers they soon outran their supporting artillery. They had a mile to go, and were shelled for the second half-mile – speed was thus their salvation. When they reached their objectives, the Turkish infantry fought hard. The Fife and Forfar Battalion achieved its goal, and then had to help the West Somerset Yeomanry, who were held up at a house surrounded by a cactus hedge. Again the Turks resisted fiercely, but the Yeomanry were victorious.[17]

These attacks by the Yeomanry Division were frequently made without the support of the artillery, because of their speed of advance. But they had the compensating advantage that the British attack was against the Turkish flank, and so each post was tackled singly. The later, that is, the more westerly, Turkish positions fell much more quickly, where some of the Turks fled before they could be attacked.

The real danger to the attackers was that they would themselves be taken in flank, from the north. During the Yeomanry Division's attack there were several attempts to interfere with it by troops advancing out of Tell esh-Sheria, and others from the 27th Division, which faced the Yeomanry Mounted Division to the east. In one case a Turkish artillery battery arrived in plain view and had to be attacked by infantry and machine-gunners of the Sussex Yeomanry before it could be driven off.[18]

It is clear that the Turks did not have the manpower available to make a serious attempt to take on the attackers, and what attempts were made were largely uncoordinated and individual efforts. The whole attack by the Yeomanry infantrymen was thus immensely successful. Having started at dawn, the division had captured the whole of the Turkish trenches east of the railway by about 1.30 p.m.[19]

The attacks by the London and Irish Divisions on the Rushdi position could begin only when the Yeomanry men had succeeded and thus eliminated the threat to their flank. In preparation they moved forward to their starting positions, which allowed their artillery to begin a systematic attempt to break up the wire protecting the Turkish trenches; this threat also served to pin down the men in those trenches and prevent them from going to the assistance of those in the lines being attacked by the Yeomanry Division. The artillery thus had time not only to break up the wire, but also to bombard the first trench line to some effect.

A near-contemporary description of the system which the London division was to attack is in the *London Scottish Regimental Gazette*:

> At first sight it looked an even stiffer proposition than the Beersheba one. Aeroplane photos showed that the Rushdi and Kauwukah trenches were deep, well sited, and even more elaborate than was the case at Beersheba. They consisted of a fire trench, a control trench roughly parallel to it, and numerous communication trenches. Machine-gun positions seemed to be everywhere, and the flank was covered by series of detached positions on the hilltops to the east, finishing away in the very difficult terrain in the neighbourhood of the Beersheba–Hebron road.[20]

The gunners of the Royal Field Artillery of the London Division had to get closer to the enemy than usual and became uncomfortably visible in order to ensure that at least some of the wire in the Turks' trenches was cut. The trenches here, in the Khawukah system, were more developed, continuous and well wired, and a much more formidable proposition than the separated strongpoints tackled by the Yeomanry Division. Two trenches parallel to the railway faced the London Division, but, once through them, the whole position would be open, since the other positions and trenches faced generally south: after the initial breakthrough they could be taken in flank. The early artillery bombardment did not seriously damage the Turkish wire and two Royal Field Artillery batteries were sent forward to fire at much closer range. The infantry watched with interest as they arrived and began to fire, for to have guns in front of them was a most unusual experience. And, of course, the Turkish gunners now concentrated on their counterparts.

In front of the ridge, in full view of the enemy, the two batteries continued to pour fire on the Turkish entanglements. They were paying for their gallantry, and many wounded artillery officers and men crawled back over the ridge to receive medical attention at the advanced dressing station ... Only a few men finally remained with the guns, and under the command of a corporal ... they continued to successfully carry out the cutting of the wire.[21]

The account of the infantry attack by the 13th London, 'The Kensingtons', is one in which the tactics developed in training were vindicated. It is worth quoting at length, for it was what every attack against the Turkish trenches must have been like, at least in intention:

The colonel's whistle was in his mouth; the shrill blast was followed by his 'Kensingtons – Advance!' and with his walking stick waving high in the air, he was up the bank in front, leading the Battalion forward. As one man the lines of Kensingtons were up and over too; and so were the Westminsters on their left, and the Civil Service in the rear, until the whole plain was suddenly alive with trim-looking lines of khaki figures, moving forward with the precision of the parade ground. It was a never-to-be-forgotten sight, and, apart from the columns of smoke caused by the bursting shells (the Turkish artillery was now in final, frantic activity) and the spurts of dust kicked up by the bullets, might easily have been taking place on Salisbury Plain. As they went over, a rousing cheer broke out all along the ranks, but soon every man was saving his breath for the grim business of reaching that line of trenches in front. It seemed a long way off.

Immediately in front and running parallel with the trenches was a cutting carrying the narrow gauge supply railway, which was an unsuspected obstacle. A machine gun post here maintained a murderous fire across the Kensingtons' line of advance and for some moments checked progress, but when it became evident that nothing could stop them being overwhelmed by that line of bayonets, the machine gunners waved the white handkerchief and surrendered. Over the cutting and on again, the first wave was then held up by wire, which was incompletely cut by the artillery. From a view earlier on it had seemed to the advancing troops that nothing could have survived our artillery preparation, at least in the matter of wire, but here was unfortunate proof that much of it was little damaged. Hand cutters were quickly in action, and but a few moments sufficed to clear several gaps, but slight as was the check, it resulted in many casualties. Very few yards now separated the first and second waves from the Turkish fire trench, in which two machine guns were in action at almost point blank range. The crew of one of these were guilty of a despicable action for which they paid the just penalty. They waved a white rag, and on being approached by a group of Kensingtons treacherously opened fire again causing several casualties before they were shot down.

The Turks obviously pinned their faith to their wire and machine guns, and, when both these failed, put up very little fight against cold steel.[22]

On the Londoners' left the Irish Division did similar work in their half of the system. Two British infantry divisions were therefore attacking a trench system which was being defended by no more than a single Turkish regiment. It is hardly surprising that it was successful, but it was also an intelligent concentration of manpower. The marshalling of this overwhelming British force is one of the best achievements in the whole battle.

Once the initial assault was successful and the Londoners and the Irishmen were in amongst the Turkish lines, the rest of the Khawukah position crumbled quickly. As with the strongpoints taken earlier, it also was being attacked from an unexpected direction, for it had been built to resist attack from the south, not the east. By 2.30 the two divisions had reached their objectives for the day, which were the whole of the Khawukah trenches and part of the Rushdi system. In fact they were able to go further, for the Turks evidently decided it was not worth holding on to only part of the Rushdi system, and evacuated all of it, the troops taking refuge in the Hureyra Redoubt further west. This would thicken the defences there, for it was from that area that men had been taken for the Zuheilika Group, the small Turkish reserve.

The plan was that the London Division would now turn north and mount an attack towards Tell esh-Sheria, with the Yeomanry Division on its right, while the Irish Division held the conquered trench systems, thus protecting the flank of the northward attack. But the earlier operations, though speedy, had taken longer than intended, and time had to be taken to sort out the mixed-up battalions and evacuate the wounded. By the time all this had been done it was dusk. The 20th London Battalion reached a position close to the station, and reinforcements went forward to assault the town, but their approach was stopped by the machine-gun fire of the Zuheilika group, which had arrived a little earlier, between the time of the arrival of the 20th and that of the reinforcements. It was now dark, and Brigadier-General McNeill of the 230th Brigade (Yeomanry Division) found he could not contact the London Division, whose forces had now halted and gone to ground. He decided not to cross the Wadi esh-Sheria, which ran east–west through the town, until he was certain that his troops were in contact with the London Division on his left. So he kept all his men south of the wadi for the time being.[23]

The Turks were almost spent by this time. They had been driven from two of their strongest positions, and the loss of Tell esh-Sheria would break open their whole line. Their last reserve, the thousand-strong Zuheilika Group, was brought forward to mount a defence of the town, its railway, and its stores. While the London Division rested south of the wadi, the Turks and north of it were reinforced. In the town the Turks fired the ammunition dump, and the glare from the explosions and the flames lit up the attacking troops, while the Turkish machine-gunners were well hidden. Under this cover the Turks withdrew from the town during the night, but only for a short distance: they had not yet given up the fight for the place.[24]

The wisdom of Allenby's agreement to Brigadier-General Mott's request that Tell el-Khuweilfe should be attacked by the Welsh Division as part of the flank guard for the main assault was proved by events there during that same day. Mott allocated four battalions to the attack with two more in reserve, and they were up against perhaps the best of the Turkish divisions, the 19th, which was well experienced in European warfare, for it had come from Galicia. Mott had also allocated all the divisional artillery and more to the bombardment, and the machine-gunners were concentrated to provide the most effective covering fire for the infantry assault.

All this preparation was to no avail. There was a mist in the morning which disorganized the initial attack so that the Herefordshire Light Infantry on the right veered to their left, and moved across the front of the hill instead of going right over it: they were machine-gunned unmercifully by the Turks on the hill, who took them in flank.[25] The artillery barrage did allow the rest of the infantry, two battalions of the Royal Welch Fusiliers and one of the Sussex Regiment, to overrun the hill. On the other side, they were at once counter-attacked by the Turks from three converging directions and driven back. They were then thoroughly disordered by the British artillery, which did not know how far they had got and shelled them by mistake. The division's reserve, another battalion of the Royal Welch Fusiliers, and one of the Imperial Camel Brigade, was called in at once, and this was still only dawn.[26]

The fighting was very confused already, and only became more so. The Cameliers fought their own individual battle on a pair of ridges to the north of the tell. They were joined there by some of the surviving Herefords and the whole group was in part rescued by an Australian machine-gun company which turned up unexpectedly.[27] All this was on the right of the line; on the left, the objective, part of the lower section of the Khuweilfe ridge, had been achieved with some ease, but the troops there were fiercely counter-attacked, which temporarily drove the fusiliers back. Another battalion was brought up as reserve, Middlesex men this time. A further distraction was supposed to be provided by the 158th Brigade launching an attack on a position west of the main part of the tell, but their guns had been taken to help the main assault, and they could make no progress without artillery support. At the end of the day the British were in little better case than at the beginning, established precariously on part of the Khuweilfe ridge, but secure nowhere, having suffered close to 1,000 casualties.[28]

In the sense that they were attempting a conquest, the British had suffered a bloody defeat, and the prospects for the next day were unenticing in the extreme. But the conquest of Tell el-Khuweilfe was only part of the purpose of this attack. Its main purpose in the overall scheme in Allenby's mind was to pin the 19th Division in place. Under attack by a larger British force, that division, a particularly strong formation, was quite unable to send any help to the crumbling Turkish positions in front of Tell esh-Sheria.

In addition the New Zealand Mounted Brigade, of the Anzac Division, was stationed on the Hebron road north of Beersheba. It was half immobilized by lack of water, but to the Turkish command (in Hebron) it looked like a threat. They kept forces in positions to the east of the road as defence, none of which, like the 19th Division, were therefore unavailable to assist at the decisive point, which was Tell esh-Sheria.

This subtlety may not, however, have been appreciated by Major-General Mott, for his attack went further than was required. He used a very large force in the attack on the tell, the capture of which was not actually necessary in the larger scheme. He then committed his own reserves, and another battalion, involved another brigade on his left, and spent a good deal of the day appealing for more reinforcements from the Desert Mounted Corps. These last were not forthcoming. Mott, fixated on Tell el-Khuweilfe, gave a convincing impression that this was a major British enterprise, but it was in fact a sideshow.

During 6 November, therefore, the Turks successfully defeated an attack on the eastern end of their line at Khuweilfe, but at the western end, Gaza, they had begun to move out of the city to establish a new line of defence to the north at the Wadi Hesi. But in the centre that second line of defence had almost been breached. The front held by the 16th division was almost broken, and only Tell esh-Sheria, with its exploding ammunition dump, blocked the British advance.

Allenby ordered attacks for the next day on the left of the line at Gaza, where the 75th Division was to attack Outpost Hill again, and exploit further on if it could. The East Anglian Division was to push forward once again along the coastal area to open the way by taking Yunis and Rafa trenches. On the right the Welsh Division was to mount another attack on Tell el-Khuweilfe, though after its exertions on the 6th this would take some time to arrange. The Anzac and Australian Mounted Divisions were ordered up from Beersheba to wait behind the front in the centre in order to exploit the expected break-through, and the Imperial Service Cavalry Brigade was alerted to exploit at Gaza.[29]

The orders for this exploitation went out from Desert Mounted Corps head-quarters to all the units involved at a quarter to midnight on the 6th.[30] Fifteen minutes later orders went out from the Yildirim headquarters at Jerusalem to the Turkish Eighth Army to gather a reserve at Zuheilika. Meanwhile the army was to prepare a retirement line running from Wadi el-Hesi to Huj to Zuhei-lika – 'if possible one division' – this was a new reserve, the original Zuheilika force having been committed already.[31] The Seventh Army meanwhile deter-mined to stand fast on the line it held, centred still at Tell el-Khuweilfe, Abu Hof and at Dhaheriye on the Hebron road.[32]

The difference between the reactions of Allenby and Falkenhayn to the situation was due to the different information they had. Allenby was close to the line, moving between the several headquarters, available for instant deci-sions, and amenable to argument, as General Mott had found, and as Chet-wode knew. Falkenhayn was issuing orders from Jerusalem, wholly dependent on the meagre information delivered to him by his two army commanders, neither of whom were close to the fighting. The result was that Allenby's orders had relevance to the actual situation, while Falkenhayn's were liable to be contradicted or pre-empted by von Kressenstein and Fevzi Pasha. So von Kressenstein began his retreat on the night of the 5th/6th, and continued the next night; Fevzi Pasha, on the other hand, ordered his men to hold their posi-tions. The Zuheilika Group, not more than 1,000 men, was pushed forwards into Tell esh-Sheria, where the ammunition dump's explosions were lighting up the area, in order to reinforce the troops of the 16th Division, who were still there.

On the morning of the 7th the Irish Division moved against the Hureyra Redoubt, 'a huge mound wonderfully well fortified'.[33] This had been a post relatively easily defended in the second battle when it had been threatened from the south by the Anzac Division. It was now still well defended, but the loss of the Khawukah and Rushdi Systems had surely undermined Turkish resolution. 'To reach its objective the 10th (Irish) Division had to cross a perfectly flat open plain, which was swept from end to end by the fire of enemy guns of all calibres and by machine guns and rifles.'[34]

The Royal Irish Rifles and the Royal Irish Fusiliers led the attack, supported by the 6th Inniskilling Fusiliers in support. It was another fight using machine guns, trench mortars, and with overwhelming numbers on the British side. The system was taken quickly, along with a considerable quantity of stores, two guns, and the field kitchen, which still held hot food when captured – no doubt this lasted only a short time once the Irishman had found it.[35]

At the same time as the Hureyra Redoubt was taken the London Division and part of the Yeomanry Division set about the capture of Tell esh-Sheria. But when they reached it they discovered that the Zuheilika Group, together with the remnants of the 16th Division, had taken up a strong position on the north side of the wadi which ran through the town. The Turkish troops of the group were more or less fresh, having had a fairly easy time in the trenches and now a couple of days' rest in reserve. They were also well equipped with machine-guns, which were as well sited as usual. As the Londoners reached the wadi they discovered that it was being swept most unpleasantly by these machine-guns, and that the Turkish artillery was ranged in on the crossing points.[36]

The Londoners of the two brigades employed (the 180th and the 181st) had moved forward very cautiously, without artillery support. This was all new territory, and not until they reached the wadi did anyone on the British side know what opposition, if any, they would face. So when the wadi was reached on both sides of the town, the attack had to be organized. On the left, two battalions of 180 Brigade attacked without artillery and in silence, coming to grips with the Turks in their trenches on the north side. On the right, two battalions of 181 Brigade had a harder task, facing serious machine-gun fire and some artillery. The commander of the 22nd London Battalion, Lieutenant-Colonel A. D. Borton, won the Victoria Cross by leading the capture of a Turkish gun which was holding up the whole attack and then by marching up and down in the open ignoring the Turkish fire until his men were steady enough to make the final charge. Both brigades were successful in their attacks on the wadi, and drove the Turks out of the town and away to the north. On the right, beyond the town, the Yeomanry Division at last now crossed the wadi and linked up with the Londoners.[37]

This was as hard a fight as any in the whole battle. The Turks had placed the group of machine guns on top of the tell, a huge mound which dominated the whole area, and the fresh Zuheilika group intervened. They resisted the Londoners' attack with skill and determination throughout the day. The survivors retreated beyond the town and were still able to mount counter-attacks later. An attempt by the 4th Light Horse Brigade under Brigadier-General Grant to pass through the infantry was thwarted by the Turks' resistance.[38] It was, therefore, not until the next morning, 8 November, that the mounted troops of the Anzac Division were able to begin to ride through the gap in the Turkish lines opened for them by the infantry.

By this time the British at Gaza had appreciated that the city was in the process of being evacuated. The troops holding Umbrella Hill were the first to realize, as early as 9.30 p.m., that the evacuation was under way. 75th Division's raid on Outpost Hill went in at 1 a.m. and found the trenches empty. The men moved forward cautiously, but found no more than the occasional sniper to oppose them, and they reached and took control of Ali el-Muntar soon after dawn. On the north the assault planned for dawn was superseded by patrols when the silence in the enemy trenches gave the game away. The road north of the city, which had been used by the evacuees, was finally cut in the morning. Too late. By that time the city was deserted.[39]

German and Turkish organization had been successful in this work, and von Kressenstein paid generous tribute to the commander of the Turkish 22 Corps in the city, Colonel Refet Bey, for his skill in conducting such a difficult operation. It is clear that the British had no idea during the evacuation that it was taking place, despite their closeness to the Turkish positions and the ubiquity of their air patrols. It was, nevertheless, a defeat for the Turks and their German assistants, and a triumph for Allenby's generalship. He was the organizer of this victory, who had pushed for the diverging attacks which left the centre of the Turkish line so weakened that it could be broken through in a single day's fighting. In fact, in the vital place the line was unmanned. The cavalry of the Desert Mounted Corps broke through the line at about the same time as the infantry of the East Anglian Division had cut the road north out of Gaza.

CHAPTER 8

The Drive North

T HE successful and secret withdrawal of the Gaza garrison spoilt Allenby's plans for the total destruction of the Turkish army there. It was now not possible to trap the garrison inside the city: the Turks would be able to fight on somewhere else in Palestine. The basic reason for the Turks' success had been the resistance of the Turkish 19th Division at Tell el-Khuweilfe. This had been intended to block any British movement along the Hebron road, but it had also had the effect of deflecting the main British advance. The breakthrough at Tell esh-Sheria led to an exploitation towards the coast, whereas the original intention had been to strike for the coast from 10 miles further north, from Tell en-Nejile. It was the necessary concentration of the Welsh Division, the Camel Brigade, the Yeomanry Mounted Division, and the New Zealanders against the 19th Division which compelled that diversion. By striking for the coast from Tell esh-Sheria, the British forces were unable to attack the Turkish troops who were retreating northwards. From Tell en-Nejile it would have been more likely to succeed in cutting their retreat. As it was, the Turks lived to fight again, several times.

It also changed the nature of the next fortnight's operations. The intention had been to cut across behind the Turks and so encircle most of their forces. But their escape northwards meant that the operation had now become a pursuit, with the British straining to catch up with the fast-retreating Turks, and the Turks attempting at first just to get away and then to establish a defensible position at which they could block any further British advance. It was also a logistical problem, for the Turks were falling back on their supplies, whereas the British were moving away from theirs. The eventual result had to be another stalemate, with the Turks recovering and the British exhausted. It was another severe test of Allenby's generalship.

Allenby ordered a pursuit through the breaks in the Turkish line at Gaza and Tell esh-Sheria and at the same time ordered those gaps to be widened. Falkenhayn and von Kressenstein, on the other hand, ordered active rearguards into operation, though this proved very difficult to organize. The next days, after the breakthrough on 7 November, were therefore a period of fluid warfare, as the British attempted to capture and destroy the defeated Turkish forces, and as those forces scrambled to recover their balance and link together. The British had the advantage of numbers and mobility in the form of their large mounted forces; even so the Turks retreated at speed.

Gaza city was taken over during 7 November: first the old enemy positions on Umbrella Hill, Outpost Hill, and eventually Ali el-Muntar itself by units of the 75th Division; then on the coastal side, the trenches north of Sheikh Hasan – Lion, Tiger, Dog – were occupied by the Northamptonshires once more, and patrols were sent as far as the road leading to the north.[1] Other patrols looked into the city to seek out any stay-behind resisters.

The city, evacuated long since by Jamal Pasha and bombarded for far too long, was wrecked. Very few of the inhabitants had remained, and the temporary soldier occupation was over. The place was littered with shells and shell casings, most buildings were ruined, and collapsed trenches seamed the approaches. But the defences were still formidable. Most of the wood in the city – doors, rafters, planks – had been taken to build the strongpoints and redoubts; most of the wire, despite the bombardment, was still there, uncut, several days later.[2] Three weeks later Sergeant James Scott of the RAMC found the city 'deserted, many houses are wrecked, dead donkeys lying in the streets'.[3]

It has been suggested that the effectiveness of the bombardment had made it probable that the city could have been taken by cavalry.[4] The complete untenability of Ali el-Muntar was noted in December by Sir Ronald Storrs,[5] but Ali el-Muntar was only the final target; to reach it there were trenches, wire (mostly uncut), cactus hedges, and the tenacious Turkish infantry to get through. To imagine that cavalry could have taken the place is plainly ludicrous.

The city was clearly abandoned by the enemy and the British accepted this early on the morning of the 7th. The occupation was swiftly arranged, and the pursuit organized. Two cavalry units were available to General Bulfin of XXI Corps: the Imperial Service Cavalry Brigade, which was some miles away, and the Corps Cavalry Regiment, a group of three yeomanry squadrons, from Glasgow, Hertford, and Lancashire, which had apparently been left without a parent organization when the Yeomanry Division was formed. Despite the long march and the need to water their horses the Imperial Service Brigade went through the city by early afternoon; the Cavalry Regiment had preceded them and had moved north between the road and the sea in the wake of the Northamptonshires; the Imperial Service Brigade moved parallel to this, along the road. Both units met some opposition. The Cavalry Regiment was fired at from the village of Beit Lahi, about five miles north of the city. They quickly took the place. The Imperial Service Brigade was similarly fired at from the village of Beit Hanun. These were both outliers of the new Turkish defence line which was somewhat to the north, using the Wadi el-Hesi as its forward obstacle.[6]

The 157th Brigade of the Lowland Division passed through the men of the East Anglian Division, who were occupying the city. They marched along the coast with the two cavalry units on their right and crossed the wadi near its mouth. This was accomplished in the afternoon of the 7th, and after dark the 5th Highland Light Infantry succeeded in capturing the only Turkish position in the immediate area, a fortified dune called Ras Abu Ameire.[7] Next day the 155th Brigade, battalions of Royal Scots Fusiliers and King's Own Scottish Borderers, crossed the wadi and passed behind the Highland Light Infantry to extend their line northwards. This brought almost the whole brigade into an area of sand-dunes bounded by the coast on the left and a ridge, called by the mapmakers 'Sausage Ridge', behind which the road and railway ran. The brigade was to attack this ridge. They were facing the Turkish 7th Division, which had intervened successfully a week before to prevent the capture of the city. Its units lined the ridge, with a clear field of fire before them. A detachment had been placed to the north, near the old city of Askelon. Brigadier-General Pollock-M'Call inspected the position during the morning of the 8th, and did not like it at all; he was ordered to mount the attack nevertheless.[8]

At Tell esh-Sheria the break in the Turkish line was to be exploited by the Desert Mounted Corps. But this force was able to gather no more than half its brigades at the time. Nominally it contained three cavalry divisions, the Anzac, Australian, and Yeomanry Mounted Divisions, each with three brigades (each of three regiments) plus the 7th Mounted Brigade – ten brigades in all; but the Yeomanry Mounted was still part of the detachment at Khuweilfe which included the Welsh Division and the Imperial Camel Brigade. This was now under the command of Major-General G. de S. Barrow, the commander of the Yeomanry Mounted Division, and was occupied in watching the dangerous 19th Division. The New Zealand Mounted Brigade from the Anzac Division was a couple of miles north of Beersheba along the Hebron road, and the 3rd Light Horse Brigade (part of the Australian Mounted) was waiting to be relieved of its duties in patrolling in front of the Turkish redoubts, which were still occupied. General Chauvel therefore had only five brigades available, and each of them was somewhat under strength after the recent fighting. There were probably fewer than 8,000 horsemen available, instead of the supposed full strength of 17,000.[9]

This force was formidable enough, in all conscience, if it could be applied at the right place. General Chauvel's orders were for an exploitation north and then north-east, past Tell esh-Sheria and then by way of Huj to the coast, with the object of cutting off the troops which were even then retreating from Gaza and those which were still in the redoubts.[10] He did not know, at the time he issued these orders, that Gaza was being evacuated, but the orders would probably not have been different if he had known, since the object remained to capture the whole Turkish army, or as much of it as possible, and the direction of the mounted march would be the same in any case.

Between them, therefore, the Desert Mounted Corps and XXI Corps were being directed as two jaws of a pincer, the first north-east from Tell esh-Sheria, the other north-west from Gaza. But both corps had shed units on their way,

9 *Landing stores.* The supply problems of both armies were enormous. The Turks resolved the issue by keeping their troops short of everything – food, clothes, boots, medicines – except perhaps ammunition. The British tackled the problem with the energy of a sea-going industrial society, building a railway through the desert, a pipeline to carry Nile water to Palestine, and carrying as much as possible by sea. A new port was organised at Deir el-Belah, but further up the coast in Palestine the only method of supply by sea was by transferring goods into surf-boats offshore. Some Pacific islanders were recruited for this work, but most of it, and indeed most of the portaging, was done by Egyptians recruited into the Egyptian Labour Corps. Without these men the British forces would have had much more to do than just the fighting. (Crown Copyright: Imperial War Museum Q 12761)

and were to be faced by Turkish forces who clearly understood well enough that their task was to hold open the jaws of the pincer until their comrades could escape.

The two mounted divisions available at Tell esh-Sheria – the Australian and the Anzac – moved off in sequence, though this had not been the intention. The Anzac Division found no opposition in front of it for several miles and successfully captured the station at Ameidat, taking 400 surprised prisoners and a great quantity of stores.[11] The Australian Division ran into the left wing of the force which had been pushed out of Tell esh-Sheria, partly the Zuheilika Group and partly the remnants of the 16th Division, under the command of Colonel Ali Fuad Bey. They were well dug in and carefully positioned at the top of a ridge the approach to which was a long bare slope. In such a position they were more than a match for the Australian light horsemen. It took much of the rest of the day for this to become clear and for the infantry of the London Division to come to the Australians' assistance and then clear the Turks out of the way. By then it was pitch dark, and movement was no longer possible.[12] The danger of a mounted charge against such a position was demonstrated to a troop of the 11th Light Horse, who leapt over the first line of Turkish trenches only to be annihilated by the next.[13] The Anzacs had also run into opposition. From Ameidat they had sent out patrols north along the railway towards Tell en-Nejile, and north-east in the direction of Huj. Both patrols encountered opposition after a mile or so, which slowed them down, and then a determined Turkish rearguard at Tell Abu Dilakh, only 2 miles from Ameidat, delayed them for the rest of the day.[14]

The breakthrough was thus only partial, and the Turks had swiftly and efficiently organized interim defensive lines. Both the mounted attacks had been blocked by the machine-guns of the defenders, who, as it turned out, were part of the forces which had occupied the Beersheba road redoubts. From the Turkish point of view, therefore, these defensive actions at the ridge of Tell Abu Dilakh and outside Tell esh-Sheria, plus the Wadi el-Hesi line, were holding back the British attack in order that the troops from the redoubts could escape. And this they were doing successfully.

And yet the British, even as they bumped up against these defensive positions, had broken the near-continuous Turkish line which had existed until a couple of days before. The Turkish retirement positions were only rudimentary, and there were gaps between them, which it was the role of the mounted infantry to find and use. The Turkish defences were by no means capable of delaying the retirement for long; their main object had been to prevent their retreat becoming a rout. The explosion of the ammunition dump at Tell esh-Sheria, on the night of 6 November, was repeated at Beit Hanun, just north of Gaza, on the 7th. Both were clear evidence of the Turkish retreat.

The Turks therefore had gained most of another day (the 7th) for their retreating troops to move further north. They had destroyed the remaining stores at the depot at Deir Sneid, as earlier at Tell esh-Sheria, which suggested that the new defensive line at the Wadi el-Hesi was only a delaying tactic, but the longer the Turks delayed the British pursuit, the more likely it was that the weary and defeated Turkish divisions would be able to get far enough away to be able to stop, dig in properly, and get some rest, before the main part of the British forces arrived. As ever, the British found the water problem one of the greatest drags on their progress, and the Turkish rearguards were, of course, sited in such a way as to deny them water supplies.

The first tasks for the British on the next morning, 8 November, were therefore to remove the stubborn rearguards at Sausage Ridge and Tell Abu Dilakh. The second proved easier than the first. The Turks at Tell Abu Dilakh did not stand before the horsemen but conducted a steady fighting retreat, covering their vulnerable infantry and supply convoys with artillery and, above all, by the use of vigorous and well-placed machine-guns. The historians of the 13th London Regiment ('The Kensingtons') comment that the British troops 'began admiringly to appreciate the ability of the Turks to extricate themselves from seemingly hopeless positions'.[14] The Australian Division could do little more than prod them along. Even that stopped when a select force from the Gaza garrison, made up of the 53rd Division with reinforcements from the fittest men from other units, marched across their front and covered the retreat of the troops who had been their quarry for two days. One of the Australian brigades, meanwhile, rode northwards along the railway and captured Tell en-Nejile at last, and then moved across country towards Wadi Jemmame, with its vital water supplies.[16]

At Gaza on that same morning, the 8th, patrols sent out by the Composite Force at Sheikh Abbas discovered that the old redoubts along the road were only very lightly held. Once again the Turks had evacuated a powerful position during the night without those who were supposedly watching it noticing anything. These Turkish forces were substantial parts of the 54th and 26th Divisions, and it was in part to cover their retreat through the narrowing gap between the two British exploiting forces that the stand of the 53rd Division against the Australian Mounted Division had been made. This discovery freed more of the Allied troops for the pursuit, but it took all day for them to start moving.[17] Meanwhile the horsemen of the Desert Mounted Corps could see the long columns of troops marching north, but were quite unable to get past the machine-gun screen.

The British generals, Bulfin and Chetwode, were well informed about the positions of their forces, largely, of course, because those who were actually in contact with the enemy were relatively few in number. On the Turkish side, however, the position was unclear. Eighth Army was in the best case, since it was retreating towards its headquarters, and von Kressenstein and Colonel Refet Bey were close to their troops. For Seventh Army, however, information was poor and fragmentary. Partly this was due to the preceding confusion over command in the Tell esh-Sheria region, but mainly it was because the units were on the move. The 19th Division, which so stoutly blocked the Welsh Division at Tell el-Khuweilfe, was under good control and was now steadily retiring northwards. Between the two armies was the group commanded by Colonel Ali Fuad Bey, the troops originally pushed out of Beersheba and now driven out of Tell esh-Sheria as well. On the morning of the 8th Colonel Hussein Husni, the assistant Chief of Staff of Yildirim, was sent to look for Ali Fuad's forces, finding them north of Tell esh-Sheria, but without any contact with either Seventh or Eighth Army.[18]

It was in these confused circumstances that aircraft were all the more useful. The former German predominance in the air had given way to British supremacy, thanks to the arrival of the Bristol fighters, which represented the next stage in the evolution of military aircraft. Only six had been sent out, but they were enough to transfer dominance. They were not sufficient to prevent the German planes' activity, and the troops at Beersheba always remembered constant German bombing during that battle, but for the first time British aircraft were able to shoot down Germans, and to carry out detailed aerial reconnaissance.

In the new situation after the breakthrough the Royal Flying Corps had two functions: reconnaissance and harassment. Reconnaissance was particularly aimed at locating any positions at which the Turks might make a stand. Regular photographic flights by the Australian squadron based at Weli Sheikh Nuran (near Shellal on the Wadi Ghazze) allowed the production of new maps at great speed on a daily basis. The maps, once drawn, were photographed, and copies sent to corps and army headquarters close by.[19] The knowledge thus available at these headquarters, however, does not seem to have prevented the troops on the ground from regularly bumping unexpectedly into enemy obstacles, and other surprises were to occur.

- What is the significance of the book to the field?
- Is the writing clear and free of jargon?
- Is the book worth buying? Reading? By whom?

4. TONE: Scholarly disputation is best handled in a courteous manner. Criticism, both positive and negative, must be substantiated. Personal attacks on the author, as opposed to strong disagreement with the book, are always inappropriate and will not be published.

5. FOOTNOTES: DO NOT USE. Indicate exact pagination for direct quotes as in the following example: "The military genius of Napoleon is best demonstrated in his capacity for situational flexibility" (p. 323). If it is necessary to translate a foreign-language quotation, include the original on a separate sheet.

6. NAMES: Give the full names of persons you mention in the review.

7. MINOR ERRORS: Unless errors of fact, typography, or spelling and grammar detract in a major way from the quality of the book, it is hoped that the limited number of words in the review can best be expended more profitably in other ways.

GENERAL INSTRUCTIONS TO BOOK REVIEWERS FOR THE

JOURNAL OF MILITARY HISTORY

Book reviews constitute one of the most valuable components of *The Journal of Military History*. It is the policy of the journal to publish book reviews substantially as they are received from reviewers. Therefore, we ask that you read and conform to the following guidelines and to those set forth in the accompanying letter.

1. DEADLINES: While deadlines may be irksome, they are of utmost importance to the smooth functioning of the *Journal*. We implore you to honor the due date as specified on the accompanying letter.

2. LENGTH OF REVIEW: Because of space limitations, we ask that you not exceed the word limitation as specified in the accompanying letter unless specifically authorized to do so by the Editor. Use of fewer words is perfectly acceptable.

3. APPRAISAL: Keep the scholarly interests of the reading audience in mind as you write the review.

   - Does the author clearly state goals and achieve them?
   - What are the goals?
   - Is the work sound scholarship?

Signature

More actively, the Royal Flying Corps had formed a special group, called 'B' Flight, ten aircraft based at Weli Sheikh Nuran, whose purpose was to bomb and machine-gun the retreating Turkish forces. On 7 November aircraft reported Turkish concentrations at el-Mejdel and Beit Duras, north of the Wadi el-Hesi, which had been assumed to be the first Turkish fall-back line. These troops were then attacked by all the planes which could be spared. Next day a new German air base at Irak el-Menshiya, again well north of the supposed Wadi el-Hesi line, was attacked and seriously damaged by the bombs.[20] The railway station there was also damaged by another attack. The result was to drive the German air base back to et-Tine, which was therefore bombed in turn on the 9th; at least ten German planes were claimed to be destroyed in one way or another in these raids, thereby further enhancing the British air superiority.[21]

Encouraging though all this air activity was to the British on the ground, the Turkish rearguards were nevertheless very difficult to shift. On 8 November the two brigades of the Lowland Division which were in action fought all day to dislodge the Turks from Sausage Ridge. Bedevilled by poor maps, which understated the distance they would have to move, and periodically threatened by the regiment of Turks to their north at Askelon, the first attack did not go in until early afternoon, and then four successive frontal assaults all failed. The Scots had to approach in plain view over rising ground for nearly 3 miles, then climb a steep slope, all in the open and under fire. Breathless, hot, and weary, they then faced the well-dug-in Turks, who were armed to the teeth with bombs collected from the stores of a bombing school nearby, and who were unusually willing to fight it out with the bayonet on the crest of the ridge. The regiment posted at Askelon also intervened at awkward moments. It was only in the evening, as dark was falling, that the 6th Battalion Highland Light Infantry, from a position south of the wadi, took the Turkish positions in flank and, collecting the remnants of earlier attackers who had taken refuge on that side, they rolled up part of the defences.[22]

By that time the Turks' stand had done its job. They had covered the forces retreating from Gaza and the redoubts for two full days. Not only that, but the defenders themselves made their escape with some panache. From the top of the ridge, once they had gained it, the Scots could see a force of 1,000 men marching off along the road to the north. They were out of their reach, marching in full regulation formation as though under no pressure at all.[23] Why the Turkish position could not have been taken in flank from the start is not explained. The two brigades suffered 400 casualties in this unimaginative action. The fighting was often hand-to-hand, bayonet and bomb, and the Scots took very few prisoners once they believed that some of their wounded comrades had been bayoneted to death.

The British accounts of this fight all assume that it had been the Turks' aim to hold this line in this same sense as they had held Gaza – as a permanent defensive position. This does not seem to be correct. The position, like that at Tell Abu Dilakh, was not suitable for long-term tenancy, and could be easily outflanked on both north and south (only a single regiment was placed to the north). It was clearly only a holding action. Von Kressenstein restrained the Turkish commander, Refet Bey, from mounting a counter-attack, and meanwhile removed his Army headquarters all the way to et-Tine. The purpose of the defence of Sausage Ridge had been as a rearguard; with some imagination the British could have outflanked it, and saved their several hundred killed and wounded.[24]

The vast majority of the Turks from the positions along the Gaza–Beersheba road, from Gaza city to the Atawine Redoubt, had by now escaped north, beyond the Wadi el-Hesi, thanks in part to the stubborn rearguards at Sausage Ridge and Tell Abu Dilakh. The two prongs of the British pursuit finally met on the evening of the 8th. The Imperial Service Brigade had to fight hard at Beit Hanun; while they were doing so they were joined by the 12th Australian Light Horse Regiment, which formed the left flank of the Australian Mounted Division from the east. These troops had advanced south of Huj almost to the coast that day.[25] On their right flank, to the north, their colleagues of the Anzac Division had taken Wadi Jemmame with its much-needed water supply, and two of the British regiments in the Australian Division, the Warwickshire Yeomanry and the Worcestershire Yeomanry, had undertaken a famous and costly charge at a rearguard of Austrian gunners and Turkish infantry to capture the guns at a position about a mile south of Huj. This was in its way as remarkable a performance as that of the Australians themselves at Beersheba, against as steady a force. The horsemen had been led by a cleverly circuitous and sheltered route towards the target, but had then had to charge across a gully, under constant fire. Their killing was done by the sword, and their task was accomplished, but they suffered almost 50 per cent casualties, for behind the guns they were attacking there were 'six machine guns and 300 Turkish infantry.'[26] This charge badly reduced the usefulness of both regiments for the near future. Not only that, but the withdrawing troops who were being protected by that Austro-Turkish flank guard, got away for lack of any troops available to follow up the charge, and the Yeomanry had to ask for help from the Australians to resist a Turkish counter-attack.[27] By the end of the day the British advance had reached and captured Huj, though the water supplies there had been destroyed. Orders were given for the pursuit to be pushed forward next day to the next possible line for a Turkish defensive stand, the Nahr Suqreir.

On the Turkish side, these events were of little importance, since it seemed that their troops were retiring in some order, protected against serious attack, and fairly well ahead of their pursuers. The Seventh Army was in good condition, had retired 10 miles or so without interference, and was being prepared to launch a counter-attack. The Eighth Army, on the coastal sector, was still retreating as quickly as possible, and had been ordered to form a new defence line along the north side of the valley of the Nahr Suqreir, more than 25 miles from Gaza.[28]

Giving orders to an army is one thing, but getting movement from a weary, transportless, and suddenly unbalanced army is another. General Allenby ordered that the Yeomanry Mounted Division, off on the right with Barrow's force in front of Tell el-Khuweilfe, should be transferred back to the Desert Mounted Corps, which was now more than 20 miles away on the coastal plain. But Barrow had begun to use the division to harass the Turks on his front, who were now beginning their own slow retreat northwards. The division had to break off its action and gather itself before it could begin its march northwestwards. It only reached Huj in the afternoon of the 9th.[29] The Australian Mounted Division spent all that day searching for water, becoming widely spread out in the process, and thus useless for any offensive action. Only the Anzac Division and the 7th Mounted Brigade – a total force of only three brigades, all somewhat worn by now – were really capable of forward movement on the 9th.

Along the coast the Lowland Division could move only one of its brigades northwards, the 156th, the one which had not been used in the previous day's action at Sausage Ridge. Orders had been given for the 75th Division to move north, but it had first to disentangle itself from the old British line below Gaza and then start marching north through the city. The Imperial Service Brigade could not be supplied with food, and had to be withdrawn from Beit Hanun. The East Anglian Division was similarly immobilized, having given up its transport to the Lowland Division. The Irish Division had to be pulled back to the railhead at Karm to be fed, and the London Division could not move further forward than Huj for lack of food and transport. Over in the east, the retreat of the Turkish 19th Division from Tell el-Khuweilfe freed the Welsh Division, but it was merely pulled back to Beersheba for the moment.[30] In other words, the British had already run up against their basic problem: lack of supplies and transport, and the Turks were making good their retreat.

The only brigade of the Lowland Division which could move, the 156th, Royal Scots and Scottish Rifles, did make some progress. Askelon was found to be deserted by the Turks, and a small party pushed on to the big village of el-Mejdel, 16 miles from Gaza, which again was found abandoned, though substantial stores and some precious water supplies were secured.[31] There was clearly to be no attempt by the Turks to make a stand anywhere in this area, and so far as the Lowland Division was concerned the Turks had broken free of the pursuit. The staunch defence of Sausage Ridge had done its work very well.

On 9 November, therefore, the Turks seemed to have very largely escaped from their pursuers for the present, but the strain on everyone was enormous. This nervousness was present right down the line of command, but it was among those in the rear areas that its effects were most pronounced. On that day, when the British had got no further than Askelon and el-Mejdel, a memorable panic engulfed the Turks at et-Tine station. Rumours of a cavalry breakthrough, the absence of hard information, British bombing, a confusion of refugees, and explosions from a bombed ammunition depot, all combined to set off a great *sauve qui peut*. Von Kressenstein claimed that some men did not stop until they reached Damascus – which would, if true, have been a tribute to the local transport system – though most of them recovered fairly quickly. But the disruption of formations in the wake of the panic prevented an earlier solidification of the Turkish resistance.[32]

In fact, the British had not managed to get many of their troops into the line. The Anzac Division, which by now had only two brigades of Australian Light Horse in action, with the 5th Mounted Brigade in reserve, thrust a raiding party well to the north from its camp at Jemmame. For 5 miles no Turks were encountered at all, but at Huleikat bread still hot from the field ovens was found (and eaten), so the forward troops were presumably at that time not far behind the Turkish rearguard. Nevertheless the only Turks the cavalrymen discovered were exhausted fugitives, dying and dead animals, and broken wagons. Nearly 3 miles further on at Qauqaba a column of fugitives was captured. After a break in the early afternoon the 2nd Australian Light Horse Brigade marched on, capturing another exhausted refugee column between Suafir and Qastine. This was as far as they could go, for it was clear that Qastine was strongly held and the mixed band of Australians and their Turkish prisoners was shelled indiscriminately by guns in Qastine. The advanced troops were therefore pulled back to Suafir for their night bivouac, capturing more Turks on the way. Meanwhile others of the division had been given el-Mejdel by the small party of Scots from 156 Brigade which had captured it.[33] Sergeant Harder of the 1st Australian Light Horse described el-Mejdel as the 'a big village, very filthy'. He commented that they were 'supposed to reach a village 15 miles further on that night, but after some 5 miles struck a strong Turkish position', which stopped them.[34]

The Turks had very largely got away, despite the brief panic at et-Tine and the vigorous pursuit by the Anzac brigades. The lack of serious opposition to that advance by the Australians until some way north of the el-Mejdel was a sign that the main bulk of the Turkish fighting troops had escaped. The rearguards which had blocked progress by both the Desert Mounted Corps and the Lowland Division on 7 and 8 November had allowed all the rest to get clear and had themselves then moved off, presumably during the night of the 8th/9th. The pathetic captures by the Australians were the final sick and dying remnants of the retreating forces, and the apparently well-served artillery at Qastine and Sergeant Harder's 'strong position' showed that the Turks really were prepared to stand at the Nahr Suqreir.

The next day, 10 November, confirmed it. The Lowland Division had orders to move forward along the road to Ashdod, just south of the Nahr Suqreir, and occupy that place. The Desert Mounted Corps found that the Anzac horses had ridden themselves out on the previous day, but that the Australian Mounted Division had now recovered somewhat. The Yeomanry Mounted Division, having watered its horses, was ordered to march across the rear of these two and take up position between the Anzacs and the Lowland Division, to form a powerful concentration in the plain facing north. Now all these mounted divisions faced the new Turkish defence line, backed by two of the infantry divisions, the Lowland and the 75th, which came up for Gaza; the only cavalry absentees, the New Zealand Brigade and the Imperial Camel Brigade, were on their way from Beersheba.[35]

A radio message had been intercepted on 9 November from Falkenhayn, now in Jerusalem, ordering an attack from the Hebron area by the Seventh Army against the British right.[36] This was an obvious move, given the long and sparsely guarded British flank which faced the hills, and the Seventh Army was still well organized and not seriously damaged. Allenby ordered the Imperial Camel Brigade to bivouac near Tell en-Nejile as a precaution, and alerted the London Division at Huj, just in case. The Welsh Division was close to the

Hebron road and was capable of intervention, if needed. In the event the British decided that virtually nothing actually happened, but the Seventh Army did shift across from the Hebron road to establish a new centre at Beit Jibrin, close to their right flank. No actual attack transpired on the 10th.[37]

When the Australian horsemen advanced north to take up their positions beside the Anzacs they found no opponents to fight, but they did discover that the Turks were digging in furiously along a line from Sommeil south-east to Zeita, east of the railway line. And when the 157th Brigade of the Lowland Division reached Ashdod, it was discovered that the town was under bombardment from across the Nahr Suqreir. The Scots crossed the river to remove this nuisance, and had a difficult time of it. They had already marched 15 miles that day to get to the Turkish line, in a *khamsin* which was blowing out of season – three divisions had already been issued with winter clothing – and now they were asked to attack in the dark. The Turks were fully prepared, having sited their machine-guns with just such an eventuality as a night attack in mind. The brigade found itself in as nasty a fight as it had endured at Sausage Ridge.[38]

10 *The result of a cavalry charge.* One result of any action is casualties. At el-Maghar on 13 November the charge of the Buckinghamshire Yeomanry captured the ridge (off the photograph to the right), but the slaughter of horses was considerable. The open nature of the ground explains how they could be caught by Turkish machine-gun fire, but also shows how it would have been even more suicidal for infantry, moving at walking pace, to attempt an attack. Given that the fighting had to take place, a cavalry charge, covering the ground much faster than the infantry, was the quickest and cheapest means of defeating the Turks. The photograph was taken only after the human casualties had been removed. (Crown Copyright: Imperial War Museum Q 61497)

Turkish resistance was clearly stiffening all along their chosen defence line. When all these reports could be collated at headquarters it could be seen that the new Turkish position lay from the mouth of the Nahr Suqreir to Beit Jibrin, north of the river, a line about 20 miles long (shorter than the Gaza–Beersheba line) anchored on the sea to the west and the hills to the east. Their troops had very competently executed an extremely difficult retreat, and had now managed to establish themselves on their chosen line of defence with a day or so's respite. The 3rd Division had fought hard against the Lowlanders in the dark, and the Australians beyond the railway had also found that they faced a prepared defence.[39]

The British forces had now moved 25 miles north from Gaza along the coast, but the new line where they were halted ran almost north–south from the mouth of the Nahr Suqreir to Tell el-Khuweilfe and Beersheba. Little effort had been made to fight in the hills, where a defence was easier to organize; the easier terrain along the coast had allowed the horsemen to advance. Falkenhayn had seen the chance to attack the long flank, but it had not been possible to mount such an attack so far.

The British supply situation was now very difficult. Three of their divisions, the Irish, the London, and the East Anglian, were now held well to the rear so that transport and supplies could be concentrated on the troops at the fighting front. Similarly the Welsh Division had been retained south of Tell el-Khuweilfe, partly for supply reasons – it had given up its transport – and partly as a standing threat to the Turks at the Hebron road. It was thus a more equal contest at the fighting line in terms of numbers and supplies than the overall force numbers on either side would suggest.

The Turks had lost a good deal of equipment in the retreat, though their casualties in soldiers had not been crippling. They had frequently had considerable difficulty in holding on to their artillery, which the British were always keen to capture or immobilize. Yet they were falling back on their supply bases, and the new defence line was admirably sited for this purpose. It lay more or less parallel to, and 10 miles or so in front of, the railway from Jaffa to Jerusalem, and from which a branch line led south to et-Tine. Roads led towards the new line along the coast, towards Hebron, and also to et-Tine. If the chosen line at the Nahr Suqreir could be stabilized and held, their supplies and reinforcements could be brought forward efficiently – they had removed all locomotives and rolling stock from the lines to Gaza and Beersheba during the retreat. The British, who could not use these narrow gauge railways, though they were well equipped with motor transport, would then be in even greater supply difficulties. The Turks had the advantage of troops whose general food and clothing requirements were much less than those of the British soldiers. And the rains were due, which would reduce the roads to quagmires. The Turkish line was well chosen.

Allenby pushed at it. The difficulties of supply became secondary. The enthusiasm of the soldiers, epitomized by the Scots' long march and night fight across the Nahr Suqreir on the 10th, was something to be used. And speed was essential. The toughness of the Turkish soldiers was legendary, and once they had been able to dig for any length of time, they would be very difficult to shift. The British had been very impressed by the strength of the redoubts along the Gaza–Beersheba road: they had no wish to face another series of such strongpoints on the new Turkish line. So if the British wished to continue their offensive actions, they had to do so quickly, before the Turkish positions became too strong. The line the Turks had chosen to stand on was to some extent protected by the Nahr Suqreir in front; their left flank now rested in the hills of Judaea and their right on the coast. The difficulty of working round the flank of this new line might be even greater than at Beersheba.

The Turkish problem was disorganization. Great crowds of men had converged on the stations of the Jerusalem railway, at et-Tine, el-Affulleh, Ramleh, and Wadi es-Sarar – this last was called by the British 'Junction Station', where the track from the south joined the Jaffa–Jerusalem line. These men had to be stopped from fleeing further north, sorted out into their units, and then sent back to the front. After the panic at et-Tine on the 9th this was done by some excellent Turkish and German staff work during the 10th and 11th, but the Turkish Eighth Army, holding the front on the Turkish right roughly from the railway to the sea, was still in no condition to fight seriously on the 12th.[40] The front there, in other words, which the Lowland Division and the Anzacs had encountered on the 9th, was no more than a thin crust of positioned troops, with some artillery, but with little or no depth and no reserves, yet.

The other Turkish army, on the other hand, the Seventh, was in a much better case. This was the force which held the line from the railway south of et-Tine to Beit Jibrin. Its formations had not been seriously damaged during the retreat, partly because they had moved more slowly, and partly because they had not been harassed to any serious degree by the British, though the men were very tired. It was this army, comprising four divisions, which Falkenhayn determined to use in a pre-emptive counter-attack, so as to give the Eighth Army more time to recover and settle into its new positions. He could clearly see that the British had put their main strength down on the coastal plain, which was where the two infantry divisions which had been brought forward were located, while the force facing the Seventh Army was no more than the one mounted division, the Australian.

Allenby was the one man who could energize the weary British formations at the front. The troops' spirits were clearly high, and if they could be resupplied and rested, if only briefly, he could expect them to respond. He pushed General Bulfin of XXI Corps to thicken up his front-line force in the plain by moving forward more infantry brigades, and Bulfin gave the Lowland Division the task of a preparatory attack across the Nahr Suqreir. This was to capture the village of Burqa and a nearby hill, called Brown Hill, which gave a wide field of view from which to observe and to direct artillery fire. The Royal Scots and the Scottish Rifles had little difficulty in taking the village, but the single battalion of Royal Scots who were sent against Brown Hill had a much more difficult task. The battalion was very much under strength, and though the men managed to reach the top of the hill in their attack, with very few men left they were swiftly thrown off again by a Turkish counter-attack. The quality of the British army as it now was, however, was shown by the next development. Brigadier-General H. J. Huddleston of the 232nd Brigade (75th Division) was not far off, saw what was happening, and got permission to send his Gurkha battalion to the Royal Scots' assistance. The survivors of the Royal Scots cheered the Gurkhas' arrival and joined in the new attack, very late in the day by now, and the Hindu Gurkhas and the Presbyterian Scots drove the Muslim Turks off the hill, which was crowned by a cairn older than any of their faiths.[41]

This attack confirmed to the Turkish command that the next main British attack would come in the plain. It also showed that their thin line would be quite unable to resist that attack with any hope of success. A battalion of the light horse of the Anzac Mounted Division pushed across the Nahr Suqreir to enlarge the small bridgehead acquired the previous day just north of Ashdod. There could be no point in these attacks unless it was to prepare the way for greater ones in the near future.

At the same time as the attacks on Burqa and Brown Hill the Turks had put in, rather unexpectedly, their major counter-attack on the British right. The Seventh Army brought four divisions to attack the Australian Mounted Division, which had become very spread out in its advance. It had been probing forward from its base around Sommeil to discover the strength of the Turks on its front, and had found that there were none. The troops rode through several villages, first Barqousa and Balin, and then forward to Tell es-Safi and el-Qastine, without finding any enemy soldiers at all. By noon the division was spread over a large area on a front on the north of at least 6 miles, and on the east almost as much. Unknown to any of them, to the north there were the 54th, the 53rd, the 16th, and the 26th Turkish Divisions, all approaching, and to the east were the 3rd Cavalry and the 19th Divisions, stationary but waiting and ready.

The Turks did not outnumber the men of the Australian division by anything like so much as is implied by this catalogue of formations. Whereas the Australian Division's three brigades had between them perhaps 4,000 men, together with a battery of the Honourable Artillery Company, each of the Turkish divisions was probably less than 2,000 strong. Further, the Turks' plan was to hold the 3rd Cavalry and 19th Divisions back until the Australian line began to crumble, so the Australians were subject to attack by no more than about 5,000 Turks, but the Turkish artillery was of greater power, range, and weight than the Honourable Artillery Company could produce. On the other hand, the Turkish soldiers were extremely tired after much marching about, and both sides noticed their weariness and lethargy in the attack.

The most advanced Australian cavalrymen were hastily withdrawn when the size of the Turkish attack became clear. Tell es-Safi was thus rapidly lost, and the Turks first came up against serious opposition when they approached Balin. Two of the yeomanry regiments of the 5th Mounted Brigade, the Gloucestershires and Warwickshires, were now driven back steadily from position to position, first out of Balin, then out of Barqousa. They were reinforced by the Worcester Yeomanry, and, as they fell back, came to be flanked by the 4th and 3rd Australian Brigades. Luckily for them, the Turkish advance was so slow that darkness fell before the 3rd Cavalry Division could be used, and the 19th Division was left unused at Beit Jibrin. By the end of the day the Australian Mounted Division had been driven back to its starting point, and the Turks had made a start on developing a major flank attack against the whole British army. Persistence here could bring the Turks out into the coastal plain in the rear of the advanced forces further north.[42]

The actions of 12 November, therefore, threatened to swing the whole battlefield around. The Turkish attack out of the hills against the British right flank, combined with the beginning of the British attack against the Turkish right in the plain, were pressing on opposite flanks. Most crucially, however, the Turkish attack had not compelled any rearrangement of the British forces, whose concentration in the plain was now accomplished.

Falkenhayn's reaction to the British attacks on his right in the plain on 12

November was first to halt the Seventh Army's attack and then to take away from it the 16th Division plus one regiment. This was, in fact, what he had hoped the British would have to do in the face of the Seventh Army's attack. That he himself had to do it, and not Allenby, was a clear demonstration of the British numerical superiority, which was in turn the basic reason for the British victory. Ali Fuad Bey, in command of the Seventh Army attack, could therefore mount no more attacks. The Turks were spread so thinly that the 16th Division was needed to face the British attack he expected next day in the north. Sure enough it came, from two infantry divisions and two cavalry divisions.

Near the coast the Yeomanry Mounted Division was acting as flank guard to the Lowland Division; next to the Scots was the 75th Division, which was in turn flanked by the Australian Mounted Division. Allenby had thus produced the classic formation of infantry in the centre and cavalry on the flanks; Hannibal and Alexander and Cromwell would have been proud. Further, these formations were sufficiently well acquainted with each other by now to be able to co-operate readily, and after their advances and victories in the past two weeks, all were aggressively minded, even though they were still often all too prepared to obey their orders to the letter rather than in the spirit.

The infantry forces were directed towards Junction Station, the capture of which would seriously impede Turkish communications, and might disrupt the whole Turkish front. Three Turkish divisions barred the way. The 3rd (infantry) on the north, and on the east the 7th and the 54th. Each of these was fairly well established in cactus-hedged villages converted into strongpoints, and the 7th Division in particular held the main natural obstacle on the line, a ridge rising about 100 feet above the plain in front of it, occupied by the villages of el-Maghar and Qatra. This ridge lay directly in front of the Lowland Division. It continued southwards, where the village of el-Mesmiye was held by the 54th Division. This formation had been part of the Turkish counter-attack on the 12th, and had, with the rest of the Turkish forces, withdrawn during the night. It now held a strong position astride the main Gaza road, and to its east the 26th Division held the strong position of Tell es-Safi. The British plan was for the 75th Division to drive up the road at least as far as el-Mesmiye, while the Lowland Division would attack the villages to the north on the main part of the ridge. They would then pause to allow the artillery to come up, and to give the troops a rest, and then move on to Junction Station.

The situation for the British attack was in fact dangerous. If the Turks at the el-Maghar ridge stopped the advance of the Lowland Division, the 75th would have to stop as well or risk being taken in both flanks since their position would then form a huge salient. The Turkish 3rd Division blocked the northern exit from the plain at the villages of el-Qubeibe and Zenuqa, its line linking the flank of the 54th Division and the sand-dunes. If the division held its ground, the northernmost British forces would be boxed in. It was to be attacked by the horsemen of the 8th Mounted Brigade of the Yeomanry Mounted Division, which was probably not strong enough to capture the villages. The British attack, therefore, had to succeed at the el-Maghar-Qatra Ridge, or it would fail everywhere.

For the Turks, the el-Maghar-Qatra position was the hinge of their whole front. If the British broke through, the Eighth and Seventh Armies could well be separated – and, of course, the Junction station at Wadi Sarar would be lost. In a sense, however, this was the lesser consequence. The two armies had been separated more or less ever since the British breakthrough at Tell esh-Sheria and had in many ways fought separate fights. Their further separation would not be disastrous, since it was clear to all that the ultimate British aim was to take Jerusalem, in which case the Eighth Army would threaten its flank; if, however, the British attacked the Eighth Army, the Seventh would be positioned similarly.

The Lowland Division was, in fact, stopped dead in its tracks at the el-Maghar ridge. The battalions of the 156th Brigade which were sent to the attack, Royal Scots Fusiliers and King's Own Scottish Borderers, were severely under strength after fighting several battles on the way north, especially at Sausage Ridge and Brown Hill. Their targets, the two villages of el-Maghar and Qatra, on the ridge top, were each surrounded by gardens and cultivation, and protected by cactus hedges – like two miniature Gazas. The Scots battalions came forward as far as a wadi at the foot of the ridge and there they stuck, unable to get any further forward in the face of accurate machine-gun fire and artillery from the Turks holding the village and the ridge.[43]

To the Scots' right the 75th Division's two attacking brigades, the 232nd and the 233rd, men from the English South West – Somerset, Devon, Hampshire, Wiltshire – brigaded with the Gurkhas who had helped the Royal Scots at Brown Hill, took the undefended villages of el-Qastine and Tell et-Turmus. At the double village of el-Mesmiye, on a lower and southward extension of the ridge upon which Qatna and el-Maghar were situated, the Turks fought back. As elsewhere, there were cactus hedges and houses and trees to hide the defenders, who were well supplied with machine-guns and determined gunners. There was also firing from the 75th's own right flank, which should have been covered by the 4th Australian Light Horse Brigade, who were themselves blocked by the Turks further back. It was necessary to mount a special attack to clear this flank, and even then the third brigade of the division, the 234th, had to come up to help out. One company of the 58th Vaughan's Rifles, an Indian Frontier Force regiment, suffered badly when it bumped into a Turkish force which itself was about to mount an attack on the flank of the 233rd Brigade. The Rifles attacked at once and so spoiled the Turks' intentions, but at the cost of heavy casualties. The remainder was rescued by the 11th Australian Light Horse, arriving at last, who took the Turks themselves in flank and drove them off. All this took all day, el-Mesmiye being finally captured as the light failed.[44]

The Lowland Division at el-Maghar and Qatra were also rescued from its predicament by the unexpected arrival of mounted troops. The Yeomanry Mounted Division's first task was to capture Yibna, a large village or small town near the inland edge of the sand-dunes, and then to attack both north and east against the Turkish 3rd Division and the right wing of the 7th. The 8th Mounted Brigade (three London Yeomanry regiments) took Yibna, and was then sent to conduct the attack northward against el-Qubeibe and Zernuqa. The 6th Mounted Brigade (yeomanry from Berkshire, Buckingham, and Dorset) was directed against el-Maghar, apparently without realizing that it was already being attacked by the Lowlanders. The third brigade, the 22nd Mounted (yeomanry from Lincoln, Stafford, and the East Riding of Yorkshire), was sent between its colleagues towards Aqir, a village lying a couple of miles behind the Maghar ridge, but without any specific order to go farther than the ridge.

The 6th Mounted assembled over 2 miles from the ridge they had to attack, north of the place at which the Scots were stuck. They advanced and took cover from the Turkish machine-gun fire in a wadi, and then charged over more or less open ground. They cantered for the first part of the charge, then moved up to a gallop when the Turkish gunners found their range. This brought them quickly to the ridge, which most of them managed to ride up. The sight of their approach, swords flashing, horses snorting, men yelling, was too much for most of the defenders, who broke and fled down the eastern slope. Perhaps the decisive moment came when a fox started up before the Buckinghamshire horsemen, who responded with the English rural tribal cries of 'tally-ho' and 'view-halloo' – noises likely enough to frighten anyone not used to such vocal barbarisms. As so often in this campaign, it was the speed of the horses which preserved the lives of most of the men, and many of the horses themselves as well. But once at the top of the ridge, the horses were blown, and no pursuit other than by machine-gun fire was possible.

This charge had given the Scots their chance. The Turks in el-Maghar had turned their fire away from the Scottish infantry on to the English horsemen to the north when the charge began. At that time the Scots' brigade commander, Brigadier-General Pollock-M'Call, was up with the forward troops of the two battalions of the King's Own Scottish Borderers, who were stuck below the ridge. When he saw what was happening the brigadier seized the moment. Waving a rifle, he stood up and led his Scotsmen in a charge of their own up the hill. No doubt more than amazed at the sight of a brigadier not only in the front line but carrying a rifle, and running as well, the soldiers followed, compelled by his example. Meanwhile the Berkshire Yeomanry had been sent along the top of the ridge from the north to take the village. The two British forces met there, each claiming to have captured the village, though the Berkshires graciously handed over their prisoners to the infantry. This capture in turn permitted the Royal Scots Fusiliers to work their way forward into the Qatra gardens, and soon that village was more or less taken, though there were stubborn groups of Turks who went on fighting for some time after that.[45]

The long distance the British troops had to advance before coming into contact with the Turkish defences, and then the stubborn fight the Turks made at el-Maghar and Qatra meant that the day had almost ended when the Turkish line was broken. Qatra was finally cleared about the same time as el-Mesmiye fell to the 75th Division. The land in front of them was unknown; a case in point is that when the Royal Scots Fusiliers came in sight of Qatra they saw beside the Arab village a small group of European-style houses and a neatly laid-out area of orchards and gardens. From al-Maghar and the ridge north of the village another of these communities could also be seen, and before it the Arab village of Aqir. These were the first of many such settlements which the troops would reach and capture in the next few days. They were Zionist settlements, largely peopled by Jews from eastern Europe, but financed from Britain and the United States. The limitations of the mapmaking of the Royal Flying Corps are suggested by the fact that none of those settlements was anticipated by anyone in the army, despite their regularity of plan, and the red tile roofs of many of their buildings, which contrasted with the less planned, earth-coloured Arab villages. Similarly the defects of the intelligence acquired by Meinertzhagen's people is astonishing: many of his spies in Palestine were Jews, yet these Jewish settlements were not included in the information collected.

From the ridge north of el-Maghar could be seen the retreat of masses of Turkish troops in considerable disorder. Major J. F. M. Robinson of the East Riding Yeomanry, part of the 22nd Mounted Brigade, took half a squadron (about fifteen men) in a charge across the plain towards Aqir, seized that village, and fired on the still-retiring Turks. A full squadron charged across on his right towards the Jewish settlement of Ekron, south-east of Aqir, but was itself fired on by what appeared to be a strong force stationed in that village. Major Robinson tried to induce more troops to come down from the ridge to his support, but they either would not or could not. Under fire by what seemed to be a substantial force in Ekron, well in advance of any support, and ignored by the other British troops within sight, the major decided he was too exposed to a counter-attack and withdrew. The Turkish force in Ekron was in fact the very last troops available to the commander of the whole Turkish corps, Colonel Refet Bey. He had organized his headquarters people, cooks and officers, guards and staff captains and messengers, as an improvised defence force, and himself commanded, riding back and forth most impressively on a white horse, attracting ineffective British fire.[46] What a day, when a British brigadier leads a charge and a Turkish corps commander commands a platoon.

The enterprise of Major Robinson was in stark contrast to the complete failure of the rest of 22 Mounted Brigade to exploit their victory. Apart from the Staffordshire Yeomanry squadron and half a squadron of the East Riding Yeomanry none of the cavalry moved off the ridge they had captured. The Berkshire Yeomanry, of course, were sent to clear the village of el-Maghar, and the other regiments had suffered casualties, and their horses were tired after their long charge. Plenty of excuses can be made and reasons found for their inactivity – dark was approaching, their orders had specified a pause at the ridge – but Robinson's men and horses had done as much as everyone else and could still operate. For all the rest to simply sit on the ridge and watch as the fleeing Turks got away is an example of the extraordinary lack of enterprise too often seen. This was a tendency among all too many of the British units. They did what their orders said, and no more. Sometimes this produced the heroic fight-to-the-death mentality of the troops on Hills 720 and 630 before the Beersheba battle, but it also produced excessive constraint and even timidity in attacks. Partly it came about because they had only been given outline orders – 22 Mounted Brigade had not even been informed of the activities of the infantry close by in attacking the same ridge – and any co-operation was purely accidental and *ad hoc*. The cavalry simply did not know what else was going on, which is certainly a good excuse for doing only what one is told. But to ignore the fleeing Turks was surely, at the least, unintelligent and unimaginative. It was, however, all of a piece with the general conduct of the whole pursuit since Beersheba and Gaza: once again, the British forces had defeated the Turks in a straight fight, and, once again, the Turks had escaped to regroup.

On the other wing of the Yeomanry Mounted Division to the north, the advance against the Turkish 3rd Division was barely resisted. The two villages of el-Qubeibe and Zernuqa were occupied by the Middlesex Yeomanry of 6th Mounted Brigade, who had been held up well short of them for the whole of the 13th.[47] They were followed up by the Imperial Camel Brigade, who guarded 6th Mounted's northern flank. Behind these forces, two brigades of the Anzac Mounted Division, the 1st Australian Light Horse and the New Zealand Brigades, moved along to fill the gap between the Cameliers and the sea. The charge of the 6th Mounted Brigade eastwards at the el-Maghar ridge had left the northern flank open; Allenby's dispositions therefore took account of the envisaged result; the Australians and New Zealanders had moved forward 15 miles to this new position during the day.

By midnight, therefore, the British front had thrust out to the north and the east, everywhere successfully, but only at the el-Maghar-Qatra ridge had it been seriously opposed.[48] The defeat of the Turkish forces there meant that the way was now open to capture Junction Station. The more advanced Turkish positions were now all too vulnerable, and et-Tine station was abandoned, and the formidable Turkish forces of the Seventh Army which had attacked the Australians the day before also began to withdraw. This all implied that the Turks were organizing themselves yet another line of defence. And they began the more difficult process of evacuating the Junction station at Wadi es-Sarar.

One officer, Major-General P. C. Palin, in command of 75 Division, saw the opportunity which was presented. He ordered his 234th Brigade to make a night march to the station. Brigadier-General Anley interpreted the very sparse orders he was given liberally at first, and sent on ahead a battalion of Outram's Rifles, another Indian regiment, to establish itself a mile in front of the station as soon as possible. Anley's intention was to take the station during the night by surprise, if possible. This turned out to be eminently possible, though it did not happen.

A Turkish supply column was captured on the march, and an attack by other Turkish troops was beaten off soon after, neither of which were exactly silent operations, yet the Rifles reached their appointed position a mile or so from the station and could see that it was functioning quite normally, all lit up.

The battalion had been given supplementary instructions to cut the railway line north of the station, and a demolition party was marching with them; but the demolition party's mule, carrying their explosives, ran away during the fight with the Turks. Here again lack of imagination and information worked its evil spell. If the station was surprisable, it could be taken, and if it was taken there was no need to cut the line, at least not yet, since by the very fact of capturing the station the line would, for the Turks' purposes, be cut. Yet the battalion spent time searching for the mule, and then the demolition party was unable to get close enough to the railway to blow it because of the large number of Turks near the chosen spot. Time passed, and after all the excitement Anley decided he could not surprise the station after all, so the battalion stayed in its place for the rest of the night – even though the station's lights were on and no formed troops could be detected in the area. At least two full trains left the station during that time.[49]

Perhaps it does not do to criticize too strongly. The troops and their commander had made a night march into unknown country and had had two

11 *Junction Station.* Junction Station was one of the main targets of the British advance during the pursuit north from Gaza and Beersheba. For soldiers from Britain it was an unimpressive place, though as a railway station it was not unlike country stations in Australia or New Zealand. Its importance was that it was the junction of three lines, to Gaza, to Jaffa, to Jerusalem, and by controlling it the British severed the rail connections between the two main Turkish armies. As a bonus the British captured engines and rolling stock, which the Turks had successfully removed from the southern line. The line's narrow gauge meant that the British vehicles could not use the track. (Crown Copyright: Imperial War Museum Q 12711)

encounters with enemy troops. The second encounter had been particularly unnerving, for the Turks came out of the darkness screaming 'Allahu Akbar', and had almost reached the brigade headquarters. Anley's force was now well out in advance of any other British unit, and, while he could see the station, he could not be expected to assume that such an important strategic place would be unguarded. The blazing lights must have looked like a trap. And yet, and yet … Anley's orders had been to 'make for' the station, which surely implied capturing it. It was so important – the main objective of the whole attack by four British divisions – that risks had to be run, nerves steeled, and difficulties surmounted. They were not.

Two Australian armoured cars were sent forward by General Palin next morning. They overtook the Rifles as they probed forwards toward the station in the dawn. The cars, in typical Australian style, drove right into the station, shot up the Turks who were still there, then roved about until the riflemen arrived. It turned out that at least one train full of men had left soon after dawn, and rumour had it that von Kressenstein himself had been one of the passengers.[50] Perhaps it was a good thing that Brigadier-General Anley and an Indian rifle battalion did not come up against a train full of desperate Turks under the personal command of von Kressenstein. But this was the second time in a few hours that a senior Turkish commander might have been captured had a little more in enterprise been shown by British commanders and their men.

The depot at the station was a treasure store of food, petrol, ammunition – and the British had plenty of captured enemy guns for that ammunition – and, most welcome of all, two locomotives and some rolling stock. The British at last were able to get the narrow gauge railway to work for them. There were even supplies of timber, that scarcest of Palestinian commodities, with which to fire the locomotives, and the machine shops were in full working order. A full hospital – full of wounded, doctors, and nurses – was also captured. But the station was still within range of the Turkish artillery, so the troops of 234 Brigade fired up the locomotives and drove them out of the station to get them out of range. But an Australian demolition party with the 7th Mounted Brigade, sent to blow up to the railway bridge north of the station, carried out its task even after the station had been taken – lack of communication and imagination once more.[51]

When daylight permitted, the rest of the British forces moved forward. Only at two places was there any serious opposition. In the north the New Zealand Brigade moved north out of el-Qubeibe and met a determined resistance from the Turkish 3rd Division, by now no more than 1,500 strong. They fought the New Zealanders for most of the day in the lands and orchards of another of the Jewish settlements, Nes Ziyona (whose Arab name was Ayn Kara). To the east the New Zealanders' comrades of the 1st Australian Light Horse Brigade were at the same time being entertained at another Jewish settlement, Rehovoth, which they had been surprised to find on the site of what their maps showed as Khirbet ('ruins of') Deiran. In the end the Turks facing the New Zealanders broke off the fight and withdrew to the north.[52]

The significance of these Turkish actions at Junction Station and at Nes Ziyona was that, once again, they were retreating in order to construct a new defence line, and the 3rd Division was acting as an active rearguard. This was clearly successful, and the Anzac Division made only minor progress during the 15th. Next day the New Zealanders found no one to oppose their advance, and they rode into Jaffa in the morning, to an enthusiastic welcome from the inhabitants, who had either avoided Jamal's evacuation order or had returned.

The other resistance was encountered at another ridge, called the Abu Shushe ridge, east of and parallel to the railway line. This rose higher than the el-Maghar-Qatra-Mesmiye ridge, and guarded the road from Jaffa towards Jerusalem. Behind it could be seen the main range of the Judaean Hills, and this ridge was the last before the hills proper. It was held by the 16th Division of the Seventh Army, formerly from the Australians' front, which had been able to take up that position during the 13th and 14th. During the 14th, after the capture of the station and the New Zealanders action at Nes Ziyona, the British merely advanced across the railway to line up before this new obstacle.

The British formation even now remained the classic one of the infantry force protected on both wings by cavalry, for the Australians had been brought forward to a position south of Junction Station, and the Yeomanry Mounted Division was still on the left, about Ne'ane on the railway. Between them were the Lowland and 75th Divisions, as before. To the north, beyond the Yeomanry Mounted Division, the New Zealanders and the 1st Australian Light Horse of the Anzac Division pursued the retreating Turks of the 3rd Division northwards during the day, capturing first a weary supply column which had no fight left in it, and then Ramleh and Lydda, both on the main railway line. But it was clear that the main forces of the Turkish Eighth Army in the north had escaped, again.[53]

The Abu Shushe ridge was another formidable obstacle, even worse than the el-Maghar ridge, steep-sided and boulder-strewn. It was also the point at which the Turks must stand if they were to have any hope of holding a continuous front line, for it sheltered the only remaining line of communication connecting their forces at Jerusalem and the Eighth Army the coastal plain. Without Abu Shushe these two forces would be separated by 40 miles of inhospitable hill country. Similarly, the British had to take the ridge if they were to have the luxury of deciding which of the Turkish armies they were to concentrate on next.

The attack on the ridge was made by the same formation which had taken the el-Maghar ridge two days before, the Berkshire and Buckinghamshire and Dorset Yeomanries of 6 Mounted Brigade, supported by the brigade artillery. It was a splendid mounted attack, coming at the Turks from three directions, rushing from point to point, taking cover, breathing the horses, always covered with great expertise by both machine-guns and artillery. The Turks were beginning to shake even before the final charge was put in, and that charge finally unnerved them to flight. But then the same thing happened as after the capture of el-Maghar. Having gained their stated objectives, the yeomanry stopped, rested, and watched as the Turks fled in disorder down the other side of the ridge, harassed only by the ever-more-distant gunfire. Most of the Turks once again lived to fight another day.[54]

One man who did not was Major Neil Primrose, the younger son of the former Prime Minister Lord Rosebery. He had been a junior minister in the British government, a supporter of Asquith during the Liberal party's break-up, and the Lloyd George *coup* of a year before had sent him into the army as a respite from politics.

The majority of the Turks may have escaped. Nevertheless, the continuous Turkish line was now finally and decisively broken, for the first time since the capture of Tell esh-Sheria. There were now two distinct Turkish armies, which were separated by a considerable length of territory. To the north, taking up a position beyond Jaffa, was the Eighth Army. Von Kressenstein was with this army now that he had escaped from Junction Station. To the east, in front of Jerusalem, was the Seventh Army under Fevzi Pasha. Falkenhayn was still in Jerusalem. He had ordered a general withdrawal on the 14th, which was why the New Zealanders were able to enter Jaffa, but the new Turkish positions were more formidable than any since the Gaza–Beersheba line. Behind them all brooded Jamal Pasha, whose long defence of the Gaza position might now seem to have been rather more successful a proceeding than that of the men who had succeeded him. And the British had finally run out of steam.

CHAPTER 9

The Hills of Judaea

THE surprise with which the British forces in the plain beheld the European-style villages of the Jewish settlers is curious for intelligence reasons, but it was paralleled by another revelation. 'The papers have been full of the wretched inhabitants of Palestine starving of hunger', wrote Trooper Idriess in early December. 'It is certainly not true of the people we have seen so far.'¹ One of the most pleasant aspects of reaching better-watered land was the profusion of fruit available. 'Struck a fine orange orchard that the owner had left so we helped ourselves pretty well', noted Trooper Burchill in his diary, adding, 'also plenty of wine',² and Private Brockie put it in context: 'You can imagine how we eat oranges. For three weeks we had nothing but bully beef and hard biscuits, so the oranges did us a lot of good.'³

Relations with the Jewish inhabitants were generally good. Colonel Olden of the 10th Australian Light Horse, from Western Australia, found himself chatting to a saucy Jewish girl from Perth,⁴ and General Chauvel stayed in a house in Richon which belonged to another Western Australian.⁵ The Arabs, however, were more suspicious. Idriess, still commenting about the misleading newspaper reports, wrote

> they are supposed to welcome us as 'liberators' with open arms and tears of joy. Instead ... they tell us lies to keep us from drawing water from their wells, and for the rest let us know very plainly that we are aliens, and to keep our distance.⁶

The difficulty of making generalizations, however, is illustrated by the different experiences of Gaza and Jaffa. Both had been evacuated by order of Jamal Pasha. Gaza had been bombarded and besieged; Jaffa fell without a fight. Weeks after its capture, Gaza was still deserted; no doubt the former inhabitants had been taken far into the interior. At Jaffa not all the inhabitants seem to have been removed, and considerable numbers had returned even before the city was captured. General Chauvel's New Zealanders took the city on 16 November, and three days later he wrote to his wife that 'all the better class of residents have been deported', but a week later he was writing that 'the inhabitants of Jaffa ... of all shades of colour are streaming back into it from all directions in every sort of conveyance.' He also noted that reports of starvation were wrong. 'Restaurants and cafes of sorts are springing up in towns and villages where they sell to the troops tea and coffee, cakes, honey and oranges, and brown bread can be bought almost anywhere.'[7]

Varied reactions such as these are normal – varied on both sides – and are a sign that for some days the armies stopped fighting, the Turks having broken contact, the British having reached the end of their energy, for the moment. But already the different attitudes to each other prefigure the later developments of social and political relationships between British, Jews, and Arabs.

The British army turned east from Junction Station, and spent the next month fighting an extremely difficult war in the Judaean Hills. The prize was the city of Jerusalem, then as ever a bone of contention. The Ottoman Empire had no wish to lose control of yet another famous city to succeed Baghdad, Cairo, and Mecca. It was an empire which before all else was Islamic; its sultan carried the title of Caliph; it claimed to be waging *jihad* against the infidel invaders of Islam's lands, and the guardianship of holy cities was a responsibility the empire took seriously.

Jerusalem was a holy city only partly because of its Islamic connotations; for Christians it was the place where Jesus Christ and walked and preached and taught; it was also the place to which Jews turned, and which their exiled members had promised each other every year at the Passover feast for 2,000 years: 'Next year in Jerusalem.' It was therefore a place to be coveted, to be quarrelled over, to be fought for. And it was about to be the subject of battle. For as long as historians could discern, this had been the city's role. No one on either side in the war in Palestine expected to fight for the city to be easy.

Not only it was it the subject of armed conflict, but of diplomatic conflict as well. The future control of the city had been a subject of dispute among the Allies since the Ottoman war began. The British had made its conquest a specific war aim, and the Prime Minister had inspired General Allenby to fight for it. The French, and to some extent the Italians, had sent military detachments to Palestine so as to be able to stake their claims to a share of the spoils of the Ottoman Empire; for the French in particular, control of 'Syria', a country they would define as widely as possibly, was a serious ambition. The Italians had no serious hope of participating in a carve up of Palestine, but they had hopes of a share of Anatolia. The French, however, were very keen to establish their 'right' to a presence in Palestine. And yet, even as the battle to break through the Gaza–Beersheba line was in progress early in November, that French ambition had been trumped by a neat British diplomatic trick.

On 2 November the British Foreign Secretary, Arthur Balfour, sent a letter to Baron Rothschild, the most prominent Jew in Britain, a wealthy banker, the head of the British branch of a European-wide family, and an active promoter of Jewish causes. The letter proposed that, if the war was won by the Allies, Palestine would be designated as a national home for the Jewish people.[8] Lord Rothschild was president of the English Zionist Federation, which had

12 *The hills of Judaea.* The hills of Judaea, with their rocky terrain, undulations and overlooking heights, were land admirably suited to defensive tactics, and were improved by well-placed redoubts. The Turks' preparations in this area stopped in its tracks the British attack towards Jerusalem in November 1917. The one British success was at Nebi Samweil, which allowed the British to claim it as a victory, but, since the object was to take Jerusalem, it must be seen as a British defeat. The defensive possibilities of the land are well shown by this photograph, taken after the later Turkish defeat. The irregularities of the land were accentuated, and the redoubts, trenches, and sangars only reinforced the attacker's difficulties. (Crown Copyright: Imperial War Museum Q 12875)

financed some of the Jewish settlements in Palestine which the British troops would view with some surprise two weeks later. The letter from the Foreign Secretary, however, was by no means actuated by a desire to benefit anyone but his own country; it was in fact one of a long sequence of diplomatic measures concerning the future disposal of Ottoman lands.

The letter was a result of another stage in the diplomatic dance in which the Allies had been involved since the war began. It was later lauded as a great humanitarian gesture and condemned as a wicked plot, but the preceding Cabinet discussions about it show that it was the product of hard-headed political calculation. The later consequences were wholly unintended and quite unpredictable. It had been the subject of several discussions in the British Cabinet spread over several months – where the only Jewish minister, Edwin Montagu, argued strongly against it – and between Allied governments. It was argued that such a declaration would encourage support for the Allies in the United States and in Russia, the two countries in the world which had very large Jewish populations. But behind it all was the knowledge that, if Britain promoted such a policy, it would necessarily be up to her to implement it, and this would in turn mean that she would have to exercise political control over Palestine. One aim of the Balfour Declaration was thus to freeze out France (and anyone else) from any post-war presence in Palestine.[9]

This was, of course, only part of the matter. It was actual possession, troops on the ground and administrators in office, which would determine the future of Palestine. The French detachment there was only three battalions, fewer than 3,000 soldiers, of indifferent quality, and they had hardly been used in any of the fighting. The French government had sent a senior general, Bailloud, to command them, to British annoyance,[10] and as the time for a military decision approached, there arrived also Georges Picot, who had negotiated the original Sykes-Picot Agreement in 1916, which laid out a framework for the division of the Ottoman lands. Picot began to agitate for that agreement to be instituted in the form of a joint Franco-British administration of the conquered land.[11] For the moment no decision could be made; the fighting took priority.

There was also another ally with ambitions for Palestine. The Arab rebellion was containing a substantial Turkish force at Medina, and the rebels had captured Akaba in June 1917, which facilitated communications with the British in Egypt and Sinai. As part of Allenby's plan for the Gaza-Beersheba battle, the Arabs from Akaba went on a raid against the Mecca Railway in Transjordan, led by Major T. E. Lawrence. The raid had only minor success,[12] but the mere threat tended to preoccupy still more Turkish troops. The Arab leader, the

Sharif Husayn of Mecca, now calling himself Amir, or King of the Hejaz, had been clear from the start that Palestine and Syria were Arab lands which should be included in his future kingdom.[13]

The stage was set for the next century of conflict, though no one considered this at the time. The people in control in Palestine were the British, by virtue of conquest. Their diplomacy was successful in deflecting French claims, and the agreement with Sharif Husayn had been vague enough to please both parties at that time, and could allow the British government, reinforced by articulate Jewish opinion, to claim temporary control. The declaration of support for the idea of a Jewish National home was not something which many in Palestine took note of at the time. For a start the letter was sent on 2 November, and it was only on the 9th, as the British forces were advancing beyond Ashdod, that it was published in *The Times*; yet another month passed before there was any real public comment on it.[14] Until Jerusalem was taken the whole idea was speculative anyway, just as were any promises to the Sharif Husayn, or any ambitions of the French.

Meanwhile on the ground in Palestine, the fighting relentlessly claimed more lives so that these political ambitions could be realized. One of these was particularly ironic. In the charge of the Royal Buckinghamshire Hussars at el-Maghar Major Evelyn de Rothschild was killed. He was the son of the addressee of the Balfour letter, and he died just as his regiment came in sight of the first of the Zionist colonies which his father had helped finance. Three days later his cousin and his colleague in the same squadron, Major Neil Primrose, the son of the former Prime Minister, was also killed, in the charge to capture Abu Shushe.[15]

The soldiers were those who were most directly affected by the contest, in that they were those in immediate danger, and it does not seem that even Allenby gave much thought to the political problems of the campaign – although by turning east to take Jerusalem he was in fact obeying the Prime Minister's directive as well as responding to the much deeper conditioning of his upbringing and education.

Jerusalem was an attractive target for all its religious and historical connotations, but it is worth wondering if it was not, in the circumstances of 1917, a distraction from the real business of the campaign, which, from the British military point of view, was the defeat and destruction of the Turkish army in Palestine. Suppose Allenby had ignored Jerusalem, left the Seventh Army to hold the city, and concentrated instead on the easier target, the Eighth Army down on the plain. Falkenhayn used the next weeks to reinforce that army, but in the third week of November it was still very weak, and the British had overwhelming numbers of troops facing it. It seems probable that Allenby could have removed the Eighth Army from the board with relative ease, so that the Seventh Army would then itself become an easier target, perhaps by a British move north and east to Nablus to the Jordan Valley, as happened in September the following year. But this sort of continuing exploitation was not possible, partly due to logistical problems – though these were being solved – but mainly because the political imperative was to take Jerusalem. The argument is, of course, merely speculative, but the complete destruction of the Turkish army in Palestine would have been of much greater political effect in late 1917 than it was a year later. It might even have knocked the Ottoman Empire out of the war. The other problem with going through Jerusalem was that it was so wholly predictable a move. Allenby was a cunning commander and did not much like doing predictable things, unless it was as a mask for something unpredictable. Even before Junction Station was taken, the Turkish high command was considering how to deal with the British campaign into the hills of Judaea.

Marshal Falkenhayn had a meeting with Enver Pasha in Jerusalem on the evening of the 13th, just as the el-Maghar-Qatra Ridge was being taken. The future of the campaign was discussed, and it was appreciated that the British would soon move against the city. In view of the shortage of Turkish troops it was also decided to avoid having them locked up there in a siege[16] – the burden of supporting the 22nd division in besieged Medina was a clear warning. It was after this meeting that the two Turkish armies were in effect drawn back: the Eighth north of the Nahr el-Auja, a few miles north of Jaffa, and the Seventh into the Judaean Hills to block the way to Jerusalem. The defence of the city, and command or the Turkish 20th Corps, was given to Ali Fuad Bey, who had done well in the retreat from the south, and was promoted to major-general for his pains. On the 19th Falkenhayn moved his own headquarters north to Nablus, geographically equidistant from the two armies, but also well clear of potential capture in Jerusalem.[17]

General Allenby had no wish to fight anywhere near the holy city. It needed no imagination to guess the reaction in Britain to British shells landing near the Holy Sepulchre; Colonel Meinertzhagen had expressed outrage – perhaps only privately – at the news of British bombs falling on the Mount of Olives, even though that was the site of the German-Turkish headquarters.[18] Militarily the city could best be captured by causing its garrison to leave. Given the situation of the two enemy forces, there were only two ways out for the

Turks – north or east. North would take the Turks along the road which ran along the top of the plateau, towards Nablus; east would take them down into the Jordan valley and across the river near Jericho, if they could make it. The easier of these routes was to the north, which was also the only way by which the Turkish forces would retain the ability to fight on for any part of Palestine; going east would take them into Transjordan and leave the Eighth Army to be driven out by overwhelming British strength.

Allenby therefore ordered that no fighting should take place within 6 miles of the city, and he directed that the attack should aim to cut the northern road at Ramallah and Bire, twin villages on either side of the road, 10 miles north of the city.[19] This actually made good military sense, for if he could cut the road there the Turks would be surrounded on three sides, for the Welsh Division blocked the route south. The problem was that the way from the coastal plain to Ramallah-Bire was extremely difficult, virtually unmapped, and very easy to defend.

In theory Allenby had the advantage of interior lines, his forces being now situated between the two Turkish armies, so he could have switched his strength from one front to the other, taking each army separately. In practice the difficulties of such movements in the conditions of the primitive Palestinian road and rail system were prohibitive. Furthermore, the Turkish Seventh Army was in a notoriously good position. The Judaean Hills had frequently been held by armies against attack from the plain in the past, and in a contest between the occupants of those hills and forces in the plain, the hillmen had usually won: the Israelites had beaten the Philistines, the Maccabees the Greeks, the early Crusaders the Muslims, and later the Muslims had beaten the coastal Crusaders, all from a base in the Judaean Hills, which the Turks now held, and attacking into the coastal plain, or defending against an attack from that direction.

Allenby had anticipated the problem and had thought it through already. He was a careful and knowledgeable student of previous campaigns in Palestine and was able to identify places where Biblical fights had taken place, and to profit from the knowledge. The Bible and George Adam Smith's *Historical Geography of the Holy Land* were constantly to his hand. The particular English involvement in the Third Crusade was another aspect, for Richard Coeur-de-Lion had fought all along the southern Palestinian coast which Allenby had just conquered, and Crusader castles could often be identified. It was constantly in British minds as they fought to reach Jerusalem that Coeur de Lion had come to within sight of the city, but had failed to capture it. Allenby knew full well the difficulties of a campaign from out of the plain up into the hills, and the strong position which the hillmen held.

He must also have been tempted to continue the pressure on the Eighth Army to the north. This was the weaker of the two Turkish armies, and for the present it was isolated, for it would take several days to bring troops in to reinforce it, either from the north, or from Jerusalem. Eliminating the Eighth Army might well persuade the Seventh to withdraw northwards without fighting, in fear of having its northward communications cut by a British thrust across through Nablus to the Jordan. To be set against this notion was the known predilection of Falkenhayn and the Turks for flank attacks – as at the first battles of Gaza and a few days before at Tell es-Safi – and the probable extension of British supply lines northwards to breaking point. There were thus good military reasons for avoiding such a move, though a swift knockout blow northwards, taking two or three days, might have been possible. Yet Allenby, even if he thought of it, clearly dismissed the idea. There was the instruction of the Prime Minister; there was the military instinct to attack the strongest opposing force in the knowledge that its destruction would likely cause the rest to flee; but above all there was surely the ideological imperative to be known as the captor of Jerusalem.

Allenby was also under contradictory pressures from London. On the one hand, there had been his interview with Lloyd George, whose insistence on the need for a victory – in particular a victory in Palestine and the capture of Jerusalem, before the end of the year – still had great force. The War Cabinet, on the other hand, was worried by the danger that he would become too deeply committed to a long campaign in Palestine, and had warned him, in a message on 11 November, not to extend himself too far, knowing that some of his troops might have to be withdrawn for service in France next spring.[20] The Bolshevik seizure of power in Russia had taken place while the third Gaza battle was being fought, and on 9 November copies of the 'Decree of Peace' were sent to the troops. A week later the Bolshevik Foreign Minister, Leon Trotsky, circulated a plea to all the powers at war, asking for peace be made, and on the 19th he called for an armistice on all fronts. No notice was taken of these messages because the extent of Bolshevik control was unclear, and in fact they were mainly designed to appeal to the Russians, as the Bolsheviks set themselves up as the party of peace. It was obvious to all observers that the country was collapsing into disorder, and if that continued the Germans and Austrians (and Turks) would soon be able to bring their forces from the Eastern Front to the other fronts. On 1 December the Bolsheviks sent a commission through the lines to conclude an armistice. A fortnight later the armistice came into force, though the subsequent peace negotiations took longer. By that time it was certain that German troops would be available to reinforce the Western Front in the spring. All this occurred while the British Army in Palestine was winning its victories, and while the next stage in the fighting, for Jerusalem, was going on. The War Cabinet's warning was timely, though Allenby paid no heed.

A strong guard, mainly cavalry of the Anzac Division plus the Imperial Camel Brigade and the 7th Mounted Brigade, was placed to face the Turks in the north, with the Nahr el-Auja between the two armies. The East Anglian division and the Australian Mounted Division were further back, near Junction Station.[21] The Yeomanry Mounted Division, the Lowland Division, and 75th Division were to put in the attack against the Turks in the hills.[22] But to succeed, rather greater British forces had to be available in order to relieve and reinforce the assault troops when necessary. It was thus time to begin to move forward the troops left behind near Gaza, and the London Division began marching north on the 19th. Yet the matter was urgent, so the attack would have to be made by the troops who were on the spot.

The Turks were pushed off the Abu Shushe Ridge on 16 November, but they had already been a retreating for two full days, and the action there was unimportant for them.[23] In effect they had broken all contact with the British forces and, because of Allenby's determination to concentrate on the capture of Jerusalem, they were given several more days during which to rest, sort themselves out, and prepare for the next attack. Falkenhayn began moving troops out of Jerusalem to reinforce the Eighth Army at the Nahr el-Auja, and troops south of Jerusalem were to be withdrawn and placed north of the city, leaving only the very weak 27th Division as a guard for Bethlehem – there was still no sign of any British move northwards through Hebron. This brought the 3rd Cavalry Division north of the city as the right guard for the Jerusalem defences. The 19th Division, still a particularly strong formation, having had virtually no fighting since it stopped the Welsh Division at Tell el-Khuweilfe, was sent on a long march north to Nablus and then south again to fill the gap between the two Turkish armies; it was thus out of the line for days.[24] But the net result was that by the time the British had climbed into the hills the Turks had a defence prepared at Jerusalem, and had begun to repair the damage done to the Eighth Army. And Falkenhayn was plotting his riposte.

The troops at Jerusalem constructed new defences, using the hills and villages to the west of the city to establish themselves in a series of redoubts and strongpoints with good fields of view and fire down into every line of approach the British must use. This was not difficult, for the number of routes they could use was very limited.

Jerusalem stands about 2,700 feet above sea level at the summit of the hills, which take the form of a long narrow plateau lying north–south. To the east the land drops steeply down into the rift valley which contains the Dead Sea and the Valley of the Jordan River. To the west, from which the British Army had to approach, the slope is less steep, but it is seamed by valleys formed by streams flowing westwards towards the Mediterranean. Between the steep valleys spurs of the plateau project westwards. Each spur was the site for one or more villages; the routes into the hills follow the valleys. The defenders held the plateau and the villages.

The main road runs north and south from Jerusalem: south to Hebron and Beersheba, north to Nablus. The main route west was the old Roman road to Jaffa; it keeps to the plateau for a time, then dips down a moderately gentle slope to the plain. The railway followed the Wadi es-Sarar to approach the city on a more southerly course. Along all these routes were a series of villages, often on hilltops, which could be easily defended. In particular there was a string of these places west of the Nablus road, on the projecting spurs – el-Qastal, Beit Surik, Nebi Samweil, Biddu, Beit Izza, el-Jib, Beitunye, Ramallah, el-Bire on the road itself – which would feature in the coming campaign. It was in these places that the Turks would make their stand.

The dominating situation of the Turks is suggested, if inadvertently, by a brief comment by a visitor to Nebi Samweil, a village and shrine about 8 miles north-west of Jerusalem, on a commanding height, at about 2,950 feet. It is not clear when the visit took place, but since the book was published in 1918 it seems likely it was before the war. The author, the Rev. J. E. Wright, describes the extensive views:

> As you stand in the village, on the roof of one of the houses which clus-ter round the summit, and look over the rolling hills to the south-west, stretching below you to the Philistine country, and the sea ... you can see up to Ebal and Gerizim (30 miles away) ... the barren hills of Hebron to the south, ... and on the west, the inevitable mountains of Moab. Such a conspicuous hill, so central and with such an extensive view, is very naturally named in the old Testament Mizpah ('watch tower'). From its position, it has of necessity occupied an important place in history. The

Crusaders called it Mons Gaudii. It was their first camp in sight of the sacred city which they had come to recapture.[25]

Allenby used three divisions in his attack. Each was given a target place to reach and a different route to go by. On the left, the Yeomanry Mounted Division was given the task of cutting the Nablus road at Ramallah and el-Bire; to its right, the Lowland Division was to march as far as Beit Liqya, along a minor road which led eventually to Jerusalem; to the south the 75th Division was to march along the main Jaffa–Jerusalem road, with its first target the village of Qaryat el-Inab; both Beit Liqya and Qaryat el-Inab were at the start of the hills but not in them. To the south again the flank of the 75th was to be guarded by the 5th Mounted Brigade which would follow the railway line along the valley of the Wadi Sikke.

This was worked out by reference to old maps which had been made decades before by the Palestine Exploration Fund, an archaeological society whose interests and priority had been with conditions 2,000 years before. The roads marked on it, usually as 'Roman road', turned out to be tracks only, and even the one metalled road was unfit for the traffic it had to bear. These were routes which had rarely seen a motor car, and had been formed over thousands of years by the passage of nothing heavier than a laden horse or camel or a loaded wagon; they had not been paved for 1,500 years. To expect them to bear the burden of a full British division, its artillery, supply wagons, horses, and camels, without giving way, was to be excessively optimistic.

And it rained. For the first time in the whole campaign the British forces had to cope with the element their homeland knew so well. This was a heavy, continuous downpour which began just as the infantry were beginning the climb into the hills. The 'roads' turned out to be tracks, which the rain and the thousands of feet of the troops and their animals quickly reduced to quagmires. It was difficult to advance, and difficult to get supplies up to the forward troops; those troops were thus cold and wet and hungry. The Turks defended hills and villages here and there. None of these defences at the start of the British advance were very serious; all were rearguard actions, but all of them took time to overcome and the closer to the main road the British came, the tougher the resistance they faced.

General Bulfin of the XXI Corps, in overall command of the assault, had planned to cut the Nablus road on the second day. The infantry invasion of the hills began early on the 19th, though the Yeomanry Mounted Division started out the day before. All three divisions advanced easily as far as the foothills, and then found that their routes were nothing like as comfortable as expected. The Yeomanry Division, hoping to trap the Turkish garrison of Jerusalem by severing the road, had to leave their Royal Field Artillery battery behind, though the 'Bing Boys' – the Hong Kong and Singapore Mountain Battery – kept up with them; all other wheeled transport was soon sent back to the plain. Thus lightened, part of the 8th Mounted Brigade got to within 7 or 8 miles of el-Bire, and the 22nd Mounted was a little behind, on the first day. The horsemen found they were in a new country of steep terraced slopes and loose stones, which was rough, very uncomfortable to walk on, for both men and horses.[26]

The Lowland Division found the same difficulty in moving forward its wheeled transport, and it also had to leave its attached horse artillery behind. As intended, two of its brigades, the 156th and the 157th, reached as far as Beit Liqya by dark, but supplies were short, the men had no shelter, and they were still dressed in the summer uniforms which they had worn in heat of the desert.

The 75th Division was the only one of the three to face any serious armed

13 *Field artillery on the move.* The Somerset Battery of the Royal Horse Artillery, part of the Anzac Division, is shown on the march in the foothills of Judaea in November 1917. The enormous quantity of material and animals required for a mobile army in Palestine was one of its major problems. The fodder and water required for the horses was always a major restriction on operations. The photograph shows just one battery; the whole division had at least

opposition. The Turks had placed small parties on several of the hills flanking the route – the division was following the main Roman road, which followed the easiest gradients – and each of these parties had to be dealt with. The whole division was expert at this sort of fighting, all battalions having operated on the Indian frontier. The 58th Vaughan Rifles, an Indian frontier regiment, succeeded in each case with little loss, backed up by the battalion of the Dorsetshire Regiment. But each operation took time, and by nightfall the division was a couple of miles short of its target position.[27] By that time the Yeomanry Division's brigades had passed through Beit Ur et-Tahta and 22nd Brigade had struggled on as far as Ain Arik, about 4 (direct) miles from el-Bire; but the 8th Brigade was still a couple of miles further back.

Despite the conditions, the three divisions had mainly achieved the targets set the previous day. 75th Division was a little behind, but by only a short distance. Opposition had been minimal, but what there was had been responsible for 75th Division's shortfall. The real problem was that the British, having seen a movement of Turkish troops northwards along the Nablus road, had assumed that this was a withdrawal. That is, they were not expecting serious

5,000 horses for its soldiers, more for other batteries, and had to be supplied by several thousands of camels, their herdsmen, and, later, mules and donkeys as well. And men, of course. To make such a force move at all was a major achievement in itself; to make it fight and win battles verges on the miraculous. (Crown Copyright: Imperial War Museum Q 12706)

resistance. In fact the movement was part of Falkenhayn's redeployment of troops from the Seventh Army to bolster the Eighth. The Turks were actually simply waiting for the British to struggle up to within range before fighting.

The Turkish rearguards spun out the British attack for three days, standing to fight briefly at a series of hills and passes before fleetly withdrawing. On the Yeomanry Division section, on the 20th, 22nd Brigade pushed forward against Ain Arik and reached a hill ominously called el-Muntar, about 3 miles short of el-Bire, but only in the strength of two squadrons of the Staffordshire Yeomanry.[28] The 8th Brigade attacked a spur only a mile or so from Ramallah, known as the Zeitun ridge, from the tomb of a sheikh on its western tip. This spur, with a flattish narrow surface, projected out westwards, flanked by steep slopes into the neighbouring valleys, 1,000 feet deep. The Berkshire Yeomanry climbed up to the plateau, but there found that they could make no further progress; they clung to the positions they had reached during the night, but next morning they were shelled, outflanked, and attacked from two sides. They fell back down the slope and were withdrawn to their starting point, two hamlets in the valley east of the ridge called Beit Ur el-Foqa and Beit Ur el-Tahta.[29]

The divisional commander, General Barrow, who was close to the fighting all through, is unstinting in his praise of his men, but it is clear from his account that the Turks had simply to sit in their positions and fire to block any advance: 'the whole attack was brought to a standstill by a very superior rifle and machine-gun fire.'[30] He might also have mentioned artillery, for the British forces, for the first time, had to attack without the guns preparing the way – the Hong Kong and Singapore Mountain Battery had only light guns – whereas the Turks had the whole area surveyed, and the likely targets registered. There was also, to everyone's chagrin, a German-piloted British aircraft which flew over to drop smoke bombs as artillery markers.[31]

To the south-west the Lowland Division's task for the 20th was to act as a link between the Yeomanry Mounted and the 75th, who were both directed to attack Ramallah-el-Bire on converging lines. This required the capture of the hamlet of Beit Duqqu, 4 miles east of their previous day's position, an attack assigned to the 157th Brigade. It was first necessary to capture another village, Beit Anan, which was quickly accomplished by a combination of forces, and Beit Duqqu fell soon after to the Highland Light Infantry. But the Turkish defenders were very stubborn, and one isolated group in a strong situation held out all day, while another was able to enfilade the Scots' position from another hill nearby; then the next village, el-Qubeibe, was also a source of

Turkish fire. In the end, these Turks all slipped away during the night.[32] The 75th Division pushed forward equally slowly, and on that day only managed to reach and take Qaryat el-Inab, which had been the division's objective for the day before; the 232nd Brigade only managed to do this because it was reinforced by two battalions sent forward by the 233rd. The division's last objective, the hill overlooking Qaryat el-Inab, was taken in rain and mist by the joint exertions of no fewer than three battalions.[33]

All three divisions, after two days of exhausting climbing in the rain and cold without food supplies, had now come up against the real Turkish defences. None of the objectives laid down for the 18th had yet been reached, and the problems were multiplying. The roads had disintegrated under the strain, becoming long hollows of mud. The necessary supplies were not getting through – on the night of the 20th the 75th Division was down to eating its iron rations. Behind the line reached by the advanced troops of the Lowland Division, the troops of one of its brigades had been diverted to assist a Royal Engineers Field Company to rebuild the road.[34]

The supply problem had hampered the attack into the hills from the start. Allenby had wanted to use the Australian Mounted Division in the hills, and to bring forward the three infantry divisions which were still near Gaza. It was not possible to supply such a large force, however, and the infantry had to wait until the Turkish railway was working, and until the British railway from Egypt had been brought forward to link with it. They were of different gauges, however, and all goods had to be transhipped. The extension of the railway to Gaza was accomplished by 28 November, but until then a constant convoy of motor vehicles linked the two railheads, necessitating two transhipments. Some supplies were landed at the mouth of the Wadi el-Hesi, and later at the mouth of the Nahr Suqreir, but this work had to be done through the surf, and took time and effort. (West African and Rarotongan labourers, being experts at this, were recruited.) Jaffa was a port-city, but it was too close to the front line, and too exposed to submarine and air attack, to be used yet.[35]

Until these bottlenecks were relieved, supplies to the front-line troops would be limited, and therefore the number of troops who could be put in that line was also limited. Even then, the difficulties of moving supplies along the miserable trackways from the plain into the hills made it very difficult to keep the soldiers already there in action. Once the supply system began working, however, the numbers of soldiers were still constrained by the geography of the battlefield. The tracks were so narrow that troops were moving up in single file. The hills were to be attacked by battalions, or by brigades at the most. The valleys and hilltops were so narrow and restricted that it was physically impossible to get larger numbers into action. The fighting for the next two weeks revolved around contests for hills, villages, observation points.

The British advance had driven deep into the hills, but it had not yet had any real opposition until the 21st. It was on that day that all three divisions came up against the prepared Turkish defences. Indeed, the Yeomanry Mounted Division had done so to a degree the previous day. They were now given three new main objectives: the village of Beitunye for the Yeomanry, the village of Beit Izza for the Lowland Division, and Nebi Samweil, mosque, village, and shrine, for the 75th. All these objectives were well short of the original objectives of the 18th. None of these places was central to the Turkish defences of Jerusalem, but all were well defended since they were forward of the Nablus road: if any of them fell, the road would be endangered. The Turks were thus defending their means of retreat from the city.

The Yeomanry tried again to take control of the long narrow plateau of Sheikh Abu ez-Zeitun, aiming to capture the village of Beitunye, a couple of miles along the ridge-top. The 6th Brigade and the 8th Brigade sent battalion after battalion into and around the plateau, all without success. The Turks held the easternmost hillock, on which Beitunye stood, against all attacks. The third brigade, the 22nd, was sent northabout, to take Beitunye from the flank, but also failed, halted by well-served Turkish artillery firing into their flank from Ramallah. The Turks put in a well-timed counter-attack from the southern flank in the afternoon, and compelled the retreat of successive battalions. The whole division was thereupon ordered back as far as Beit Ur el-Foqa and Beit Ur et-Tahta, a retreat of more than 4 miles, to its starting point. For the next two days the division did not move, immobilized by shortages of food, clothing, and ammunition, by the need to care for its horses, by its own casualties, and by the lack of any artillery support. It had begun this fight under strength, with only about 1,200 riflemen available; it was now reduced to no more than 800.[36] In other words, this part of the British attack had been defeated.

The next division to the south, the Lowland, sent the 6th Battalion of the Highland Light Infantry forward to take the village garrison of Beit Izza, which lay on the flank of the 75th Division occupying a hill from which they could have enfiladed any attack by that division. It was not strongly held, but any further advance by the Lowlanders depended on the capture of other villages, notably the high point of Nebi Samweil.[37] The British forces, preoccupied with bringing supplies up difficult tracks and along steep and narrow wadis, made no further movement.

On that same day, the 75th sent 232 Brigade (by now only two battalions) along the main Jerusalem road to take el-Qastal, more as a diversion than as a serious threat to the city, which was only 4 miles further on. Thus the strict orders to keep 6 miles from the city were ignored. With the several hills and villages held by the Turks, and only providing support to its neighbours, such injunctions had to be dispensed with; the 4th Somerset Light Infantry were left at el-Qastal as a flank guard. The main part of the division was sent up a track north-east of Qaryat el-Inab to take Biddu, the village on the western end of another plateau spur. This could only be done because the Lowland Division had already taken el-Qubeibe and Beit Izza. This capture was accomplished quickly by the 4th Dorsetshires, which then moved on eastwards to establish a defence line while the rest of the division laboriously climbed the track. A company of the Hampshires occupied another village to the south, Beit Surik. Combined with the Lowland Division's occupation of Beit Izza to the north, this brought the division out of the wadis and on to the plateau. Their transport, however, was still struggling along the narrow deliquescent tracks, and before them, both the 75th and the Lowlanders, was a bare, nearly flat land, with no cover, where the Turks had established yet another part of their interlocking defences.

In front of the position which the Dorsetshires had taken up was the hill of Nebi Samweil, a mosque and village built around the shrine of the prophet Samuel. It was the highest point for miles around, a good 200 feet higher at its summit than any other hill. It provided, for whoever held it, an unmatchable observation point, as the Rev. J. E. Wright had noted, and as such it was coveted by both sides. It took all day to assemble most of the 75th Division's battalions around Biddu, on the western end of the spur, 2 miles from the mosque, so it was not until dark was falling that two battalions, 123rd Outram's Rifles and the Duke of Cornwall's Light Infantry were sent through the Dorsetshires to the attack. They were followed by two more battalions, the 5th Hampshires and the 3/3rd Gurkhas, as they arrived soon after. The attack was immediately successful, with relatively light casualties, but the Turks, evidently surprised, made no serious effort to hold the village.

So easy a capture of such a position requires an explanation, and it would seem to be the result of the time of day. For having taken the Turks' trenches – 'shallow, miserable trenches' – the Cornishmen saw a Turkish regiment marching towards them. No doubt this was the relief which the evicted Turks had been expecting to arrive after sunset, and they had been surprised in the act of preparing to leave.

The Cornishmen assumed that the approaching Turks were intending to surrender, so an officer and a dozen men went out to accept it. The Turks, on the other hand, assumed that it was the British who were surrendering. After a stand-off for some time, which must have been amusing only in retrospect, the British nonchalantly slid back to their trenches, and the Turks turned about and marched off, harassed by the now militant Cornish rifleman.[38]

This turned out to be the furthest British advance. The four battalions at Nebi Samweil were subjected to sustained counter-attack for the next two days, suffering heavy casualties, but holding on to the position, sometimes only by throwing stones at their attackers, as the Gurkhas had to do on one occasion, and at one point reduced to a single machine-gun manned by a single officer.[39] They were supposed to be reinforced on the 22nd by battalions from the Lowland Division, but if they were to get to Nebi Samweil it seemed necessary first to capture el-Jib, another fortified village a mile or so north of Nebi Samweil. But to get to el-Jib it was first necessary to conquer a small hill before it, and that could not be done without British artillery support. This fight used up the battalions of the Lowland Division who were supposed to reinforce the 75th in Nebi Samweil. It was only after dark on the 22nd that it was possible for two battalions of the Scottish Rifles to reach the mosque.[40]

Next day the 75th Division sent two battalions, Gurkhas and Somersets, in another attempt to capture el-Jib, and then, when these troops became stuck, the Devon Battalion to help. All three got to within a mile of the village, but could make no further progress in the face of a well-situated Turkish defence, consisting mainly of machine-guns firing from north and south as well as from the village.[41] In the afternoon some useful artillery at last reached Biddu, but by then it was clear that the infantry would have to be withdrawn, and this was done during the night.

It was clear that the whole Turkish defence needed to be attacked, or at least preoccupied, for any further advance to take place, for to capture the Turkish positions one by one would cost far too many casualties. The defensive system was so well laid out that an attack on any one point drew fire from several directions; only by forcing each position to concentrate on its own defence could any of them be seriously threatened. Therefore, on the next day, 24 November, 75th Division would attack el-Jib, the Yeomanry Mounted Division (which had by now sent back its horses to the plain as being useless in the hills) would make a demonstration in the northern sector, and the Lowland Division would operate at Nebi Samweil. Further, General Allenby ordered an attack in the plain, where the East Anglian Division would attack across the

Nahr el-Auja in an attempt to persuade the Turkish high command that a new offensive was being made there.[42]

The only attack which succeeded was the crossing of the Auja, which had been the diversion. The Royal Scots were stopped dead in their attempts to clear the cottages and enclosures of Nebi Samweil village, but gave no ground, though at very high cost;[43] the Highland Light Infantry, who were intended to exploit the British success, were sucked into the Nebi Samweil fighting;[44] the attack towards el-Jib by the Royal Scots Fusiliers and the King's Own Scottish Borderers did not even reach as far as the Somersets, Gurkhas, and Devons had done the day before.[45] That evening Allenby, persuaded by Bulfin, called off the attack all along the front in the hills.[46]

There has been a good deal of British obfuscation over this battle. It is described as the 'battle of Nebi Samweil' by the 'Battles Nomenclature Committee', and since that village had been captured and held against the immediate Turkish counter-attacks, this permits it to be regarded as a victory. In reality it was a very expensive defeat. Three British divisions – two infantry and one mounted – had attacked positions held by three under-strength Turkish divisions and had succeeded at only one point. In every other attack, on Sheikh Abu ez-Zeitun, on el-Jib, and out of the salient of Nebi Samweil, their attacks had been comprehensively defeated. Their cumulative casualties came to well over 2,000 men. Further, to describe the fight as between three divisions on each side is misleading, since the Turkish divisions were only about the strength of a British brigade. The British divisions were certainly under strength even when the fight started, but they must have outnumbered the Turks by a factor of at least three to one. It is notable that the Official History scarcely mentions Turkish casualties. This is because, first, there were few, and second, the failure to conquer any of the Turkish-held positions meant that no body-count could be made. Even estimates are absent. When an army counts its own casualties and ignores those of its enemy, this is a clear indication of its defeat. The Turks had won a most convincing defensive victory.

While these attacks were failing, the other divisions were moving north. The London Division, now based at the foot of the hills, sent one brigade forward in preparation for taking over the front held by the 75th. The Yeomanry (infantry) Division was about to begin its march north from Gaza. In the north already were the East Anglian Division and the Anzac Division facing the Eighth Army across the Nahr el-Auja. From these two divisions the New Zealand and the 161st Brigades were to make the crossing of the Auja with the intention of hinting to the Turks that another offensive in the plain was in the offing, and hoping to distract the Turkish command in the hills.

The New Zealanders, first the Canterbury Regiment, then the Wellington Regiment, rode across the bar of the river and cleared the north bank. Inland the 2nd Light Horse Brigade and the Auckland Regiment made a demonstration to distract the defenders (a diversion within a diversion), and two battalions of the Essex Regiment were sent across to establish a firmer defence. The village of Sheikh Muwannis, 2 miles inland, was taken without a fight, and so was the hill of Khirbet Hadra, a couple of miles further on. The whole bridgehead was, however, only a mile deep, and was served only by a pontoon bridge at Jerishe, where the Essex men had crossed.

The problem with an operation designed as a diversion is that no one involved is committed to it. So when, before dawn next day, the Turks replied with heavy shell fire on Khirbet Hadra, the whole position collapsed almost at once. By 8 a.m. Hadra was abandoned, and not long after Muwannis was attacked, and at once it was also abandoned. Before noon the New Zealanders and the Essex men were all back on the south bank of the river, having suffered over 200 casualties. The Turks' casualties were double that, but they were the attackers and had won another victory.[47]

This marked the end of the fighting for several days. The British were exhausted, cold, wet, and hungry, and had been beaten. The attacking divisions in the hills could do no more, and new divisions were coming forward to take their places. In the plain, no more diversions were planned, and in the hills, a new plan was required. Meanwhile, true to type, Marshal Falkenhayn wanted a counter-attack to be made.

All the time, while the fighting had been going on to the north of Jerusalem, Turkish forces were being rearranged. The British in the hills were fighting the 3rd Cavalry Division and the 24th and 53rd Infantry Divisions. The formidable 19th Division had meanwhile been sent on a march northwards with the intention of using it to reinforce the Eighth Army, and a new formation, 20th Division, was moving south out of Syria, also to bolster the forces near the coast. The 20th did arrive in the plain, but the 19th, having marched through Nablus and as far west as Tulkarm, was redirected southeastwards.[48] For Falkenhayn had detected a gap in the British line.

Here was irony. The British had successfully forced the two Turkish armies apart in order to attack them one at a time. In doing so they had left themselves vulnerable to a Turkish counter directed at the gap which had opened up between their own forces. This gap lay between the left flank of the Yeomanry

Mounted Division at Beit Ur et-Tahta and the right flank of the East Anglian Division near Shilta, a distance of about 5 miles. It was made the more threatening by the weak condition of the Yeomanry Mounted, which, with only 800 riflemen, was covering a front of about 3 miles. And the East Anglian Division was also spread thinly.

The 75th Division was gradually relieved by the arrival of the London Division between 24 and 27 November, and the Lowland Division was also pulled out of the line, its position also being taken over by the Londoners. Both relieved divisions were seriously below strength by this time, while the London Division was not, so the change from two divisions to one in the line was not a serious reduction in manpower. But the Yeomanry Mounted Division stayed on its hills for the moment, the intention being to relieve it with the Australian Mounted Division, which had originally been intended to take part in the attack several days before. Meanwhile the 7th Mounted Brigade, which had been under Desert Mounted Corps' direct orders, was moved towards the gap in the line between the East Anglians and the Yeomanry Mounted.[49]

These various movements, British and Turkish, took time. The Turks, whose reinforcements had not been fighting recently, were ready first, and sent in a wide series of assaults aimed mainly at cutting the British lines of communication and supply. The first came at 2:30 a.m. on the 27th, directed on the 19th London at Nebi Samweil, and about the same time on the Yeomanry Mounted Division's outposts at the Zeitun plateau and nearby hills. In the plain the Turkish 16th Division launched a major attack south along the railway line, aiming at Lydda. The assault on the 6th Mounted Brigade at Sheikh Abu ez-Zeitun alerted General Barrow, and through him, the corps headquarters, to the gap to the west of the Yeomanry Mounted Division's position, and the 7th Mounted was ordered into the hills to reinforce his forces. The troops rode along a difficult track right across the front of the approaching 19th Division, each in ignorance of the other.

That ignorance was dispelled at dawn on the 28th when the newly arrived British brigade was attacked by the newly arrived Turkish division. This was therefore the fourth attack on the British positions. Those in the east, at the Zeitun plateau and Nebi Samweil, would seem to have been aimed at holding the British forces in position, and pushing them back if possible; those to the west, by the 16th Division in the plain and by the 19th Division in the hills, were much more serious, being aimed at cutting the British lines of supply and communication with the forces in the hills. This was a serious attempt to drive the British forces back into the plain, with the intention of destroying at least two of their divisions.

The attack in the plain had been expected, since considerable troop movements had been noted on the previous days. It fell on the 4th Northamptonshire battalion, holding position in and around the German colony village at Wilhelma, on the 10th London Battalion to the south-east at Deir Tuweif, and on the 5th Bedfordshire Battalion at Beit Nebala. To the north-west the Imperial Camel Brigade, at a feature called Bald Hill, was also attacked. The Bedfordshires and the Londoners had little difficulty in defending themselves, but the Cameliers and the Northamptonshires had a more daunting task.

The Northamptonshires were alerted by the previous day's movements, and resisted most competently. The attack came as a series of bombardments and infantry advances, but the Turkish attacks soon stood in isolation, after the Turks had arrived within 400 yards of Wilhelma. The Cameliers were driven off Bald Hill, but this took the Turkish attackers away from those at Wilhelma, thus opening the gap between them. This in theory opened the way for an attack on the Northamptonshires' flank, but the commanding officer, Lieutenant-Colonel J. Brown, put in a counter-attack first. Leaving only a small force in his defences, he sent two platoons to each flank of the Turkish position. (He thereby repeated Hannibal's tactics at Cannae.) These threats compelled the attackers to withdraw. The Cameliers did not retake Bald Hill, but this did push the Turks out of other positions they had captured.[50]

The whole fight was over in a day. That it was conducted under the eyes of the Eighth Army commander, General von Kressenstein, suggests the importance attached to it. But it had been badly managed. The infantry and artillery attacks were not well co-ordinated, the attacks on the eastern British position, the Londoners and the Bedfordshires, were weak, and that on the Cameliers did not achieve much. On the whole the attack looks half-hearted, by weary and unenthusiastic troops.

The attack on Nebi Samweil came in the afternoon, after some shelling in the morning. The British forces were new to the position, the 17th and 19th London Battalions having taken over on the 26th. The Turkish attacks may therefore have been put in to test the new occupants. The fighting went on all afternoon and into the early night, though without the Londoners losing any positions.[51]

Similarly the attacks on the Yeomanry Mounted positions on the Zeitun Ridge have the appearance of a continuation of the former fighting, but this time the Turks were successful.[52] Yet they found the same problem that the

14 *Treating the wounded*. The care of the wounded was one aspect of warfare in which the Great War saw considerable improvement over previous wars. Medical teams kept close to the fighting, and, where possible, clean and airy buildings were requisitioned as temporary hospitals. In the Holy Land there were plenty of churches and monasteries available for such use. The photograph shows the interior of the monastery at Khirbet el-Inab in the valley of the Wadi Sarar just west of Jerusalem. The soldiers are from the Somerset Light Infantry and the Wiltshire Regiment who took the village on the 20 November. It became the main dressing station for men of the 75th and the 52nd Lowland Divisions during the fighting around Nebi Samweil. (Crown Copyright: Imperial War Museum Q 12626)

British had found when attacking the other way: the capture of one position only exposed the captors to attack from other enemy-held positions in the neighbourhood, which commanded their new conquests and left them open to destruction. And attacking hills and fortified villages was very expensive in manpower. Neither side was going to win the fight for Jerusalem in this area any more than at Nebi Samweil.

The attack by the 19th Division on the 7th Mounted Brigade, west of the Yeomanry Mounted, was a different matter altogether. It came a day later, and struck at a point of the line which was effectively unmanned, or had been until that morning. The arrival of the 7th Mounted, which had marched up overnight, and was about to have breakfast, was thus extremely timely. The two regiments of the brigade, plus one from the Yeomanry Mounted – as it happened all three came from the north-east English Midlands, South Notts Hussars, Sherwood Rangers, and Lincolnshire Yeomanry – defended a ridge called Hellabi Ridge. They were driven back for a time, and there was some desperate fighting, with the brigade's horses running loose in the rear and some close action. Among the Sherwood Rangers, every man was fighting, except for ten at headquarters, and among the South Notts Hussars the horse-holders were reduced to one man for ten horses. The pressure eased somewhat in the afternoon, and the troops rallied and recovered their lost ground. The Turks began to outflank the horsemen to the west, but were stopped by the 155th Brigade of the Lowland Division, which until then had been in the act of retiring for a rest, but had responded to a call for help.[53]

The pressure was too much for the Yeomanry Mounted, whose advanced posts, including Sheik Abu ex-Zeitun, had to be given up.[54] The 4th Australian Light Horse Brigade had followed the 7th Mounted into the hills, and arrived to assist the Yeomanry Mounted in time to block a further advance by the Turks. At the other end of the line, beyond the (former) gap, the 5th Norfolks were driven out of Shilta, but Turkish exploitation was again blocked by the arrival of more Scots of the Lowland Division, whose annoyance at being deprived of their period of rest fuelled their fury in attack.[55]

By the end of the 28th the Turkish attacks had all failed, despite having driven back the British forces in several places. The aim had been the breakthrough into the British rear, and in this the attackers had failed. The responses of the British commanders to the attacks had been quick and accurate, and the soldiers had fought furiously, no doubt in the knowledge that a Turkish breakthrough at the gap would be disastrous not only for themselves but also for the rest of the British forces in the hills. The prospect of a Turkish force across the communications of the London and Yeomanry Mounted Divisions was one to chill the heart of any commander. The fighting qualities of the Yeomanry Mounted Division were tested again, but it was the fury of the Lowland Division's soldiers at being denied their rest which is especially remarkable. That division had been badly battered at Nebi Samweil and at el-Jib, every battalion losing substantial numbers of men, but those battalions turned to once more, and drove the Turks back everywhere.

Several fights, from the plain to Nebi Samweil, went on with gradually diminishing intensity for two or three more days, but by the end of 29 November it was clear that they would not succeed. Once again it was the defensive side which had proved the stronger. The Turkish attacks suffered the same sort of casualties as the British at el-Jib, but they could afford them less. By the first days of December the British positions had all been held, and it was time to consider once more how to capture Jerusalem.

CHAPTER 10

Jerusalem for Christmas

THE fighting in the hills was just about finished, for the time being, by 1 December. The Turks held the line before Jerusalem which they had established before the recent battles, but the British were well entrenched close to the city. And during the fighting the British divisions which had been recuperating had been brought forward. The London Division was already in position; the Yeomanry (infantry) Division came up on its left, to relieve the Yeomanry Mounted, a process which greatly strengthened the line since the infantry were much more numerous than the horsemen. The Irish Division had been marching north from Gaza for some days; it was in the line by 1 December, taking over from the improvised defence by the Lowland Division and the 7th Mounted Brigade along the north. The forces which had battered vainly at the Turkish defences for the last fortnight were brought back to the plain for a rest. In the first days of December each side shuffled about, evacuating inhospitable posts, improving the line, and on the British side, thickening up the population of the line to produce a powerful concentration. The Irish and Yeomanry Divisions extended their positions; the London Division contracted. The Welsh Division began to move north from Beersheba along the Hebron road.

The arriving troops had been well rested and had re-equipped with winter clothing, the better to face the wet, cold conditions in the hills. The general supply situation was also much improved – this had been, of course, a precondition for moving the Gaza divisions northwards. The gap between the two railway systems had now been filled by the extension of the Egyptian railway as far as Deir Sneid, north of Gaza, where supplies could be transferred more easily to the Turkish railway. The difference in gauge remained awkward, and the standard-gauge line continued to be extended, being laid beside the narrow-gauge Turkish line, reaching Ashdod by Christmas Day. But the rains, which had so distressed the troops in the hills, were also a problem in the plain, where every stream filled with water, every track collapsed into mud, and the railway was frequently cut by the washing out of its foundations.[1]

Allenby was under some pressure from London, contradictory as usual. The War Cabinet and the Prime Minister wanted him to reach and capture

Jerusalem; but there was also talk of a Turkish collapse. The CIGS stamped on this: 'there is little likelihood, in view of the German mastery of Turkish governmental institutions, of detaching Turkey from her alliance',[2] and he had earlier pointed out that so pervasive was the German presence in Turkey that 'it would seem impossible to prevent news of peace negotiations from reaching German ears'.[3] Robertson warned Allenby to be careful not to get too involved, since he might be required to give up some of his troops next year. Yet he was also told about this time, and certainly before Jerusalem fell, that he was to be reinforced by a new division, the 7th Indian (or 'Meerut') Division, which was to be withdrawn from Mesopotamia, and sent to Palestine.[4] This, of course, was a most pleasant mark of government approval. It was also a clear indication that it was in Palestine that the war against the Ottoman Empire would be fought; the Mesopotamian theatre was no longer to be active.

There was also pressure from the Foreign Office, which was anxious about the actual capture of the city of Jerusalem and the necessary procedures and ceremonies involved. All the officials and generals on the British side were adamant that fighting in the city should be avoided, this being regarded as likely to rebound on British heads. No one else had ever bothered about not fighting in the city, a much besieged and fought-over place, and the Turks had not shown any particular sensitivity over it, and their decision not to fight for it or stand a siege there was based purely on military considerations. Indeed, the history of the city had been largely that of a fortress as well as a sacred site, and its walls are still today a substantial obstacle: one does not wall a city unless it is expected to be under serious threat, or to be a major part of the defence of the country. It was ironic that some men were now openly talking about this campaign being the Last Crusade, when the First Crusade, which had taken the city for Christendom, had perpetrated the most notorious bloodbath of the Middle Ages. That phrase the 'last' crusade, was also rather tempting fate. As it proved, of course, the city remained in Christian – that is, British – hands for no more than thirty years. The First Crusade managed three times that. Both occupations ended in tears, though.[5]

The British government was, of course, concerned about its reputation, and planned a propaganda coup which would help to establish the British 'right' to rule in the city. There is nothing quite so suggestive of sheer power as the conspicuous refraining from exercising and displaying it. The massacres which had disfigured the Crusades were now regarded as being the prerogative of the Turks, whose wartime treatment of the Armenian Christian minority in eastern Anatolia had been close to genocidal. There had also been two examples in Palestine of what could be seen as this typical Turkish behaviour pattern. In March Jamal Pasha had ordered Jaffa to be evacuated, with only farmers to remain in the city. This followed the near loss of Gaza in the first battle and was clearly a pre-emptive move by a very suspicious Turkish governor in the light of the activities of Arab rebels and Jewish spies. It was also a move which should have removed vulnerable civilians from the scene of the next battle. (The contemporary evacuation of Gaza could be explained as a measure to protect the inhabitants.) Protests against the expulsion of Jaffans by both the German and Austrian consuls – Germans had substantial holdings of property in the city – were without effect; on 9 April the city was evacuated. The Jews, 9,000 in number, were largely cared for by German, Austrian, and Jewish charities, but the far greater number of Arabs were simply left to fend for themselves. The Ottoman government did not accept responsibility for feeding the subjects it was depriving of their homes and livelihood. On the other hand, a Jewish account of the expulsion explains that the Jews of the town had to travel at their own expense, while the Arabs were able to get shelter nearby, and were treated 'with conspicuous indulgence'.[6] It is clear that rival historians compete in claiming the greater suffering for their people.

Then on 19 April, ten days after the Jaffa expulsion, Jamal announced that Jerusalem would also be evacuated. This was the day of the second British assault on Gaza, but even the failure of that attack did not immediately change Jamal's intentions. It took a high-level diplomatic protest by the German Foreign Minister, Arthur Zimmermann, to the Ottoman High Command in Constantinople to get the order for the evacuation rescinded. This near-panic reaction is a sign that the German government was as sensitive over Jerusalem as everyone else. The failure to evacuate the city is no doubt part of the background to the joint Turkish-German decision not to fight for it, nor to allow a siege to develop.[7]

In their preparations for the conquest of the city, the British also wanted to present themselves as contrasting with the behaviour of their enemies. What was particularly in mind in the case of Jerusalem was the behaviour of the Kaiser twenty years earlier. On a state visit, he had ridden into the city on a white horse through a section of the city wall which had been demolished especially for him. So both these actions – the horse and the demolition – had to be avoided, as had any hint of violence in the city – for these were the behaviour traits the Allies had particularly affixed to Turkish and German reputations. There was to be no fighting in or near the city, no violation or desecration of any of the religious monuments of any faith, careful respect to the

Muslim inhabitants, and no arrogant 'conquering hero' behaviour by Allenby. It also meant that as many of the Allies as possible were to be accommodated in the ceremony of occupation, yet no Allied flags were to be flown. Triumphalism in the Holy City was to be avoided. Preparations for the resulting anticipated propaganda triumph – Lloyd George's Christmas present – were careful and thorough, and fully worked out well in advance. The proclamation which Allenby was to make had been written in the Foreign Office and sent to him as early as 21 November, and his participating troops had been carefully selected and detailed for the task. Muslim soldiers in the 58th Vaughan's Rifles had been kept out of the earlier fighting so as to be available as guards for the Mosque of Omar. Other units were nominated in advance to play their parts, and no doubt new kit was issued, and much spit and polish indulged in.[8]

As if to emphasize the extreme delicacy of the moment, on 6 December Jamal Pasha, in a speech in Beirut, publicized the arrangements the Allies had made for the future division of Syria-Palestine, notably the Sykes-Picot Agreement for partition and influence.[9] This was the result of the Bolsheviks' revelation of these wartime agreements, but Jamal had his eye particularly on the Arabs. He no doubt knew a good deal about the arrangement Amir Husayn had made with the British; to reveal the duplicitous nature of British arrangements elsewhere would be advantageous to the Turks. It was too late to have any effect on the battle for Jerusalem, and in fact the Arabs did not pay much heed to it yet. Jamal's own reputation had sunk a good deal during the war, and his oppression of Syrians and Palestinians did not help his credibility. For a good part of the Arab population of Syria and Palestine the prospect of an end to Turkish rule might well outweigh any apprehension concerning what would come after.

The failure of Jamal to carry out his stated intention to evacuate Jerusalem presented the British with the first major test of their policy towards the local population. All three of the other towns they had captured, Gaza, Beersheba, and Jaffa, had been evacuated before they arrived, so they could pose as liberators. The evacuees from Jaffa certainly seem to have been glad to be able to return under British rule – but they had been seeping back even earlier. The major part of the population of the conquered area was rural: farmers and agricultural labourers living in villages. The Arabs in their villages seem mostly to have held themselves as aloof as possible, no doubt experiencing the normal suspicion of government to be found amongst all taxpayers; the Jews in their new settlements tended to welcome the conquerors, presuming, no doubt, that their treatment by the British would be better than that by the Turks.

The British conquest had been rapid, and little or no civilian administration had yet been set up. The prospect of having Jerusalem to rule, with its large population of many sects and languages, while at the same time fighting the army of the former rulers, was not attractive. Hence the very delicate approach to the issue, a conciliatory proclamation, the mock-humble ceremony. Of the Arabs – the great majority in all areas – it is probable that most who had any opinions would have supported either Amir Husayn's rebellion or the continuation of Ottoman rule. There is no indication that any of them viewed the prospect of British rule with any pleasure. They had been part of the Ottoman Empire for four centuries; change was not necessarily to be welcomed.

Of course, before any of this became relevant, the city had to be taken. Only then could the attempt be made to calm Arab apprehensions. It was clearly impossible to penetrate the Turkish defences around Nebi Samweil, and the Turkish line from there northwestwards to the mouth of the Nahr el-Auja had now solidified. The only unattempted area was south of Nebi Samweil. Fighting towards the city in this area would mean breaking the British self-imposed rule of no fighting within 6 miles of the city; the rule therefore vanished, and plans were made for a converging advance.

General Chetwode organized two forces: on the one hand, the London and Yeomanry divisions, who would form the main attack from west of the city; and on the other, the Welsh Division, to which was attached the County of London Yeomanry (Westminster Dragoons), a heavy artillery battery, and a light armoured car battery, which was now given instructions to begin to move north along the Hebron road. It was known that the Turks had withdrawn northwards, but just how far they had gone was unclear, for there were active patrols as far south as Hebron. This force was called, for its commander, Mott's Detachment.

The plan was made to take the city from the south and west. Mott's Detachment would close on the city from the south. From the west the main assault was to be made to the south of Nebi Samweil. The two divisions were faced by a fairly well-developed system of redoubts and trenches, which the Turks had built a year earlier and had recently strengthened in anticipation of attack, but had never yet been assaulted. Nebi Samweil was to be the hinge of the movement, with the London and Yeomanry Divisions swinging round between that position and the city, linking on the right with the Welsh Division when it arrived.

This was a fundamentally less ambitious plan than the original conception, which had been to cut the Nablus road north of the city and envelop the

Turkish forces so that they should either surrender or be driven off eastwards towards Jericho and the rift valley. Chetwode's plan aimed only to drive the Turks northwards, or possibly east as well, to capture the city, that is, but not the enemy army. The first plan had envisaged the destruction of that army, the second plan only its defeat.

The plan was explained to commanders in a meeting at Qaryat el-Inab on 3 December. The speed of march of Mott's Detachment was to govern the whole. If the Turks moved to block his force, the other divisions would attack north of the city; if not, the Welsh Division would drive the Turks northwards.[10] The Welsh Division had been stuck at Beersheba for a month, deprived of its transport, which had been taken to assist the other divisions during the supply difficulty, and had been plagued by ill-health as well. It had gathered supplies slowly, and was now capable of movement.[11] On 4 December it began to march up the Hebron road. The absence of opposition was known, because a pair of Australian Light Armoured cars had been driven down the road and through Hebron on 1 December in a vain search for a spy.[12] Yet an absence of Turks on 1 December did not necessarily mean their absence several days later. The Welsh Division advanced with circumspection, leaving one brigade behind to guard the southern part of the road and see to the forwarding of supplies. It appears to have moved slowly, but it had to travel 50 miles as the crow flies on a road which was narrow and poorly made, and needed to haul its own supplies, by a variety of methods – rail, trucks, camels, mules – from Gaza.[13] But Mott's extreme carefulness delayed progress even more.

The two brigades, cavalry battalion, and assorted mechanical groups reached Hebron and passed the town by the 6th, and at that point orders were given 'to go full steam ahead until shot at', without bothering with reconnaissance.[14] General Mott, however, regularly took counsel of his fears, and believed any report by uninformed civilians of the presence ahead of Turkish forces. Chetwode impatiently ordered him onwards.[15]

The advance guard of the detachment, the 7th Cheshires, supported by two of the division's horse batteries, pushed a small Turkish force off the last ridge south of Jerusalem on the morning of the 7th, but could not get much further that day because of rain. Mott thought he had located Turkish defences south of Bethlehem, though there were none to speak of. He was able to make contact with a detachment of the 10th Australian Light Horse to his left, but was well short of his detachment's objectives.[16] Chetwode, still impatient, ordered the London and Yeomanry Divisions, which were now facing the main Jerusalem defences on a narrow front, to make their attacks.

They were facing fairly substantial defences, prepared before the original British attack into the hills but were scarcely touched as the attack moved to the north. They were in the form of a series of redoubts, as in the defences along the Gaza–Beersheba road, in this case sited on the forward slopes of the projecting spurs so as to dominate the approaches, which were always uphill, all on steep slopes. South from Nebi Samweil there were the defences of Beit Iksa, the 'Heart' and 'Liver' Redoubts before Lifta, Deir Yesin, two systems behind Ain Karim, and trench lines of lesser strength strung round the south-western and southern approaches to the city. All these fortifications, spread over a distance of no more than 4 miles, looked out over open slopes and dominated all the valleys. An assault upon them looked to be extremely expensive.

The attack was to be by two brigades from each division, by surprise, and with no artillery preparation. This decision was made all the easier by the almost complete absence of artillery on the British side, by the decision to approach by night and attack at dawn or before, and by well-conducted explorations of the approach routes. Clear stages were laid down, so that salients should not be allowed to develop, as at Nebi Samweil, and to avoid exposing forces with different tasks to attack in flank, though in the event this was not wholly achieved. Strict instructions were given to avoid damaging or desecrating a specific list of sacred buildings.

The Welsh Division's failure to reach its preliminary positions was the main difficulty. Mott's Detachment was still south of Bethlehem on December 7, the night before the main attack was to go in. The detachment's role in the main attack was to guard the right flank of the London Division, for if it was not in position, the Londoners would be held up in their turn. The next morning the vital road junction south of Bethlehem, which the division had to cross to join in the attack, came under extremely accurate shell fire from a Turkish battery near Bethlehem. This paralysed General Mott, for he had been given strict instructions not to endanger the Church of the Nativity in the town, or Rachel's Tomb, a mosque on the road north out of the town. Unable to advance and unable to retaliate, he dithered all morning, until a peremptory order from Chetwode got him moving about noon. When he finally attacked his main objective at Beit Jala at 4 in the afternoon, there was no opposition.[17]

Chetwode's impatience was, in fact, productive. Had the Welsh Division come much closer, the Turks in the trenches may well have been alerted. As it was, the lack of artillery preparation was a successful ruse, and the attacks by the London and Yeomanry Divisions achieved surprise along much of the line.

Four brigades – two in each division – advanced in the night, with the intention of launching their attacks at dawn. Each division was given a set of successive objectives to be reached which were supposed to result in a new front line running directly east from Nebi Samweil, the pivot on which the advance was to swing.

Needless to say, the plan was not carried out. As it happened, two of the attacks succeeded in achieving total surprise, but the others had to fight. And instead of a simultaneous attack at dawn, the assault was a succession of attacks from right to left beginning at 2 a.m. None of the day's objectives was reached.

The rightward attack, by two London battalions, marched off along a tortuous route at 5.15 on the evening of the 7th. The historians of the 13th Battalion, the Kensingtons, described the approach march:

> something like two and a half direct miles had to traversed in silence, the best part of a brigade of men in full equipment moving in single file, accompanied by mules carrying Lewis guns and tools, jumping down a long succession of four-foot terrace walls on the one side and scaling similar obstacles on the other.[18]

What is more, the men were chilled to the bone by a cold drizzle which afflicted them throughout the afternoon of the 7th, and which was alleviated only in part by the forced cheerfulness of General Shea, who arrived on an unexpected visit, during which he cracked jokes and gave away oranges.[19]

The Kensingtons were the leading battalion, and took their first objective, an ancient watch tower south of Ain Karim between 2 and 3 a.m., but it then became obvious that the Turks were alert and had occupied Ain Karim, which had been clear of them earlier. There were fierce and prolonged fights for the battalion's targets, two hills, accompanied by Turkish counter-attacks from the south.

The 13th were in effect fighting two actions, one on each flank. The commanding officer of the London Scottish, coming along behind, realized this and sent his own battalion through between the 13th's flanks to take the main objective, Tumulus Hill. Fighting was generally difficult and confused for both battalions, with much depending on individual initiative, since few men could follow what was happening. The attack on Tumulus Hill was held up by a determined Turkish machine-gun post, until it was destroyed by the action of Corporal C. W. Train, who took it in flank; Train was awarded the Victoria Cross, as much for saving the lives of his comrades as for his bravery. It was a perfect example of one man's actions having a disproportionate effect on the whole attack. Soon after his work the whole Turkish position collapsed.[20]

To the left the 16th London, Queen's Westminsters, of the 179th Brigade, reached and took over the village of Ain Karim by 3.30 a.m., and overwhelmed the Turks in the redoubt to the north less than an hour later. There was much less fighting here than to the south, though a Turkish battery proved dangerous until put out of action by a corporal and a rifleman: Rifleman Smith ended the fight by breaking the neck of the last Turk in the battery. A long series of trenches, extending for three-quarters of a mile from west to east, was occupied by 6.30. This was a crucial success, for this redoubt had been intended to provide flank support to the trenches to the south which the London Scottish had to fight for, and their fight was still going on.[21]

The 180th Brigade, north again, was also divided into two columns, to attack to either side of the village of Deir Yesin. The 19th London (St Pancras) Regiment had a hard time south of the village. They had seized the first position, but they had to fight hard for the village itself. Beyond was a ridge pockmarked by quarries, and held by snipers and machine gunners. It took reinforcements from the 20th, the brigade reserve, and an attack organized by the brigadier himself and involving a full-scale assault to drive the Turks off, finally at bayonet point. This action was sufficiently crucial to the whole attack to be watched by both Generals Chetwode and Shea. The two battalions which struck at the Turkish positions north of the village fared differently. The 17th London attacked the trenches near the village, but could not make much progress until the 19th and 20th had succeeded in their attacks to the south – hence in part the concern of the generals. The 18th London Irish had the task of taking the redoubts to the north, called from their map shapes 'Liver' and 'Heart'. They looked most formidable, but in fact fell very quickly, both coming under control by about 6 a.m.[22]

Fighting continued at Deir Yesin and Ain Karim until nearly 8 a.m., by which time some of the troops had been fighting for six hours. They had achieved the first objectives of the four laid out in the operation order, but had not gained contact on the right with the Welsh Division. But the Turkish defence line had been captured.

To the north the Yeomanry Division had a narrower front to attack, but its objectives were overlooked in part by the Turkish positions in front of Nebi Samweil, and its brigades were much weaker, having had to detach battalions for other work. The 12th Royal Scots Fusiliers moved to seize the group of trenches which lay across the Wadi Hannina from Liver Redoubt. The Turks were apparently asleep, despite all the noise which had emanated from the fighting to the south. The whole position was taken, with over 100 prisoners, in minutes.[23] The 230th Brigade had a much more difficult approach march, ending in a steep rock-strewn slope directly overlooked by the fortified Turkish positions; as a result they were late, being the last to finish their attack. Two battalions, the 10th Buffs and 12th Norfolks, were used, for the Turkish position was over a mile long. Opposition was vigorous for a time, and the two battalions bunched together, leaving a flank open, but by soon after 7 a.m. they had captured the whole trench. The further advance, on the village of Beit Iksa, was very difficult, being enfiladed by machine-gun fire from Nebi Samweil. The village was eventually captured in the afternoon, but there were still untaken Turkish positions to their front when further operations were stopped.[24]

All along the line these two divisions had been a strikingly successful. In several cases their initial objectives had been taken with no trouble and few casualties. But little more than the first objectives of four had been reached before all the attacks were halted, by Chetwode's direct order.[25] The problem was not the resistance to the London and Yeomanry Divisions, but the tardiness of the Welsh Division. Major-General Mott had to be given a direct order – 'Push your attack' – before he would move, being paralysed by artillery fire from positions in and about Bethlehem. He was very reluctant to shell the town in view of the orders to avoid damage to the sacred buildings, and even more loath to order his men to cross the road south of the town, which the Turkish artillery commanded.[26] The order nerved him to move, but by that time Chetwode had had to stop the other divisions, for fear that the Turks south of Jerusalem would take the Londoners in flank. When Mott did send forces forward he found no opposition at all; even the Turkish guns stopped firing about noon.[27]

Then, during the night of the 8th/9th, the Turks, in silence, slipped away from their positions yet again. None of the British knew anything about it until next morning, when some cautious patrolling gradually revealed that the Turks' defences along the whole line were empty, apart from snipers. This was the price paid for the slowness of the Welsh Division on the previous day. Had Mott been more enterprising, the London and Yeomanry Divisions would have been able to advance much further on the 8th, to reach the outskirts of the city all along the line, and cut the Nablus road. There would have been no Turkish positions to reconnoitre so carefully, and the Turkish forces might have been badly damaged, if not destroyed. Instead, the Turks had once more

disengaged successfully and were retreating to new positions with their customary rapidity. The whole process of attacking a well-prepared Turkish army
would therefore have to be done again at another line of fortifications. The
chance to destroy the whole Jerusalem defence force had gone.

The Turks withdrew through the city all night. The city governor, Izzet Bey,
personally destroyed the keys in the telegraph office and had the lines cut, then
requisitioned the only cart left in the city (belonging, until that moment, to the
American consul) and left. Troops in various conditions seeped away all night
and into the morning, seizing food where they could find it, but not delaying
their travels.[28] The suddenness of their withdrawal may have saved the city
from damage, but the Turks tended not to cause damage as they left, except to
militarily valuable places such as bridges.

It took some time to hand the city over to the attackers. Izzet Bey had given
the keys of the city to the mayor, who now came out with a crowd of notables
and the keys in his hand and tried to surrender them to the British forces. He
first chanced upon two wandering cooks of the 20th London Battalion, who
would have nothing to do with him. He then came across two sergeants of the
19th London Battalion, who did not know what to do. He encountered two
artillery majors, who went off to get advice. He then met Lieutenant-Colonel
N. Bayley of the 303rd Brigade Royal Field Artillery, who accepted the keys
and chatted for a while. Then Brigadier-General C. F. Watson of the 180th
Brigade arrived: he calmed the mayor down, for the difficulty of surrendering
the city was making him understandably nervous; the brigadier then went into
the city with Bayley and an escort of ten gunners. Finally Major-General Shea,
commanding the London Division, arrived, and formally accepted the surrender of Jerusalem, having received permission to do so from General Chetwode.[29] When he went into the city, he was greeted by crowds who were wary
but pleased. Some had taken the opportunity to plunder the Turkish army
barracks in the brief interval between the Turks' departure and the posting of
the British guards. The 10th Australian Light Horse was ordered into the city,
and was greeted, like General Shea, with a mixture of suspicion and pleasure.[30] Meanwhile the Turkish forces continued their retreat, gaining time and
distance the while.

The Yeomanry Division's 231st Brigade was greatly relieved to find that the
Turks before Nebi Samweil had gone; its other brigades to the south could
therefore advance to the objective-line which had been laid down some days
before. They found little or no opposition. The London Division, however,
which had further to go and had the task of actually reaching and crossing

15 *Surrender*. The Mayor of Jerusalem (with a walking stick) came out of his city early on 9 December to surrender to the approaching British, who had taken several defensive positions in the previous two days. The Turkish army had withdrawn through the city during the night. (The last troops were still moving out as the mayor tried to surrender.) This photograph shows his second attempt to surrender; the first British troops he met had been two privates who simply ignored him. He then met these two sergeants of the 19th London Regiment: Sedgwick (left) and Hurcombe. It seems they were photographed by a member of the American Protestant mission in the city. (The United States were not at war with the Ottoman Empire.) The mayor then climbed up the British rank structure until a general finally deigned to take responsibility. The mayor took care to have with him some officers as a guarantee of his military credibility. (Crown Copyright: Imperial War Museum Q 13213 B)

the Nablus road, was held up here and there by Turkish rearguards. South of Jerusalem the Welsh Division moved at dawn, and reached the southern walls before 9 a.m., which was about the time the mayor finally met a British soldier willing to accept the keys. The cheers of the people at the Welsh Division's arrival, however, was a clear indication of what had happened.[31]

But the Turks were still retreating along the road east of the city which ran along the Mount of Olives. The Welsh Division had sent forward only an advance guard of the Westminster Dragoons and the 5th Welch Battalion, plus some artillery. They were kept at bay near the city by machine-gunners on the Mount. A second battalion, the 4th Welsh, had been ordered to join them, but was sent by an impossible route. It was after 2 p.m. when the 5th Welch were ordered to capture el-Azariye (Biblical Bethany), which would cut the Turks' escape route; the failure of the 4th Battalion to arrive prevented that operation.[32] By the next day most of the Turks had gone.

While the advance guard of the Welsh Division was groping its way around the city, along the western side and round the north, leaving a guard at the Jaffa gate, the London Division pushed forward across the northern side of the city, and the Yeomanry Division finally escaped out of the Nebi Samweil trenches and both divisions got across the Nablus road. All three divisions took up defensive positions at the line which had been the stated objective of the original attack, forming a line stretching east from Nebi Samweil and then south to the Mount of Olives.

Next day, two squadrons of the 10th Australian Light Horse, made a careful reconnaissance northwards. They came up against Turkish resistance 6 miles north of the city, 5 miles from the British troops in their 'forward' defences, so discovering that the Turks were still close by.[33]

General Allenby came to Jerusalem on December 11, a fortnight before Christmas, two days after the Jewish feast of Hanukah – which was the day of the city's surrender – to make his ceremonial entry. For the Muslims' benefit some predictions had been disinterred (or, perhaps more likely, invented by British propagandists): that an Arabic pronunciation of Allenby as 'el-Nebi' meant 'the Prophet of God', that his name spelt backwards as 'ibn Allah' meant 'the Son of God'; how these blasphemous interpretations were supposed to help is unclear. An old prophecy that only when the waters of the Nile flowed into Palestine would the land be freed of Turkish domination was also trumpeted, and the pipeline from Qantara to Gaza adduced as evidence. This was a good example of twisting to one's own advantage a self-evidently political allegory referring to the Ottoman domination, or perhaps even that of the

Crusaders.[34] Perhaps these stories – if the Muslims ever actually heard them – were some reassurance. Certainly the behaviour of the Mayor in surrendering the city showed that he knew how to behave so as to minimize the risks run by him, his people, and his city.

Allenby's entry had been carefully prepared according to instructions from Britain received well in advance. The studied lack of ceremony was itself ceremonious, but replete with all the necessary symbols. He was welcomed by the city's military governor, Brigadier-General M. W. Borton, providing a strong hint of the iron fist: Borton had already established a clear military control over the city. The velvet glove was Allenby's act of walking into the Holy City, conspicuously avoiding the hole in the wall broken for the Kaiser nearly twenty years before. But the Jaffa gate was no more than 20 yards from the Kaiser's gap, and it was opened especially for the new conqueror; the first time for decades it had been so used. Was it more arrogant to have a gate specially opened, or to have a hole made in the wall? And, of course, being a general and a conqueror, Allenby had a guard of honour.

In fact there were four of them. As he approached the gate – having climbed down from his Rolls-Royce (he didn't have very far to walk) – there were fifty British soldiers, carefully including English, Welsh, Scots, and Irish, to the right, and to the left fifty Australians and New Zealanders, also carefully representative of all their homelands; these men had been selected, and then trained, polished, and primped up for the past three weeks in preparation for this occasion. Inside the gate there were twenty French soldiers to the right and twenty Italians to the left, representatives of the Allies involved in the war against Turkey alongside the British Empire.

Allenby was also accompanied by a flock of officers. His own aides included Lord Dalmeny, the son of the Earl of Rosebery, the former Prime Minister, whose younger brother had died at Abu Shushe. Colonel Wavell represented the War Office. The French and Italian contingent commanders were there, as were their and Allenby's senior staff officers. Also attending was Georges Picot, the French High Commissioner for Syria (still to be conquered), and one of the negotiators of the pact which had laid down the lines on which the lands of the Levant were to be divided between Britain and France. Major T. E. Lawrence was present by special permission of General Allenby, perhaps the nearest to a representative of the Arab Revolt who was available.

All in all, it was a very military occasion, and in view of all the various uniforms present it was perhaps irrelevant that no Allied flags were flown in the city; this again was by previous arrangement by way of the London government.

The city notables at last met the man to whom they had surrendered, and heard a conciliatory proclamation promising continuity and protection, even though the city was now under martial law. Already a guard of Indian Muslim soldiers from the 58th Vaughan's Rifles had been placed on the Haram esh-Sharif, the Muslim Mosque of Omar, and the traditional Muslim guardians of the Temple site were assured that their office would continue. This last was a suggestion from Lloyd George, prompted by Sir Mark Sykes, both of whom had taken a minute interest in all these details. It was, after all, an overwhelmingly Muslim and Arab city which had been conquered, and the majority population had to be conciliated. The proclamation was in six languages, the English, French, and Russian of the Allies, plus Hebrew, Arabic, and Greek, local languages.[32]

As a propaganda gesture all this was very satisfactory and most successful. The practical reassurances might be directed at the local population, but the propaganda was aimed squarely at Christian Europe and America. This was a world in which most ordinary Europeans' historical knowledge was basically anecdotal, comprising a heady mixture of nationalistic and religious stories, and centred on the doings of a series of heroes, usually male, often military. One of the heroes the English learned about at school (and also possibly the Scots, the Irish, and the Welsh) was King Richard Coeur-de-Lion, who had refused to look on the city which he could not conquer; the French recalled the whole Crusading movement as basically their invention and used the Crusader kingdoms as evidence of their claim to dominion in the area; the Italians could console themselves that the movement had been begun by a pope, and sighed for the greatness of ancient Rome, which had ruled here; the Germans remembered the death on crusade of their Emperor Frederick Barbarossa, who, Arthur-like, was not really dead, but only sleeping, to awake when his people needed him most. During his visit 20 years before the Kaiser had presented to the German Hospice a painting of himself and his wife in medieval dress.

Yet in political terms it was military power on the ground which counted.

16 *Allenby in Jerusalem*. Two days after the surrender of Jerusalem, General Allenby visited the city in a carefully prepared display of British power, with the object of promoting a propaganda victory for the Christian world and a reassurance of good treatment for the Muslim world. On instructions from London he walked rather than rode, and the guards for his entrance were provided by men from every nation whose forces were employed in the Allied army in Palestine – even the Italians, who had only 500 men there and had done no fighting. Muslim soldiers guarded the Mosque of Omar. The general's visit was well enough publicized in the city to ensure a good crowd of local spectators of all the local religions, marshalled on the Jaffa Gate, and at all vantage points. The proclamation he made, in six languages, was the foundation for British rule for the next thirty years. But by conciliating all the religious groups, the British largely abdicated much of the responsibility for governing. (Crown Copyright: Imperial War Museum Q 12616)

Allenby, after the proclamation was read out, greeted all the locally important men, including the heads of the local Christian churches. It cannot have escaped their notice that the Allied representatives were thoroughly relegated to supporting roles. On the day of entry into the city, Georges Picot commented that it would now be necessary to set up an administration for the city of Jerusalem, clearly implying the inclusion of a French element in that administration; Allenby stated firmly that it was a military area still, and martial law applied.[35]

At a more basic level, Jerusalem was one of those cities everyone had heard of – the Holy City, the scene of the Crucifixion, the Resurrection, and so on. British officers noticed the cheerfulness, even joy, on soldiers' faces at the knowledge that they had liberated the city from the grip of the Turk: its capture was noted in every contemporary diary, war diary, and letter – 'the news was flashed round', explains the historian of the 10th Australian Light Horse.[36] Probably every soldier in the Allied forces in Palestine visited the city during his service there, and went on one of the conducted tours of the city's sights, guided by the forces' chaplains. After the magic of the name and the excitement of conquest, the reality was inevitably disappointing. Brigadier-General Ryrie, commander of the 2nd Light Horse Brigade in the Anzac Division, noted in a letter on 16 December: 'I have seen men who have been in Jerusalem and they say it is an appallingly dirty place.'[37]

The Arabs who lived there took due note of the forbearance of the Allies after years of Turkish wartime oppression. The arrival of several tens of thousands of soldiers, all eager to visit the city and to buy a souvenir to take home, was a great encouragement to mercantile enthusiasm. The inclusion of Hebrew in the languages of the proclamation was in part a recognition that there was a sizable Jewish population in the city, but it was also a response to the Balfour Declaration of six weeks before, and a gesture to the Jewish colonies who had so generously welcomed the Allied troops as they advanced northwards through the plain. (But the Australians noticed that food and wine produced by the Zionist settlements was freely available in the city shops, and at a lower price than they had been charged by the settlers at the place of production.)[38]

The many languages in use in this city, symbolized by the multilingual proclamation, did suggest a major future problem: it was not going to be possible to conciliate every group. So the unceremonial ceremony was not merely a military occasion, as the plethora of uniforms superficially suggested: it was very conspicuously a political one also. Only one flag, that of the British commander-in-chief, was permitted to be flown – but, of course, that only emphasized the

British predominance. Palestine, the message was, had become a part of the British Empire.

Allenby had produced the city of Jerusalem for the Prime Minister's Christmas after all, though Lloyd George was ill when the time came to announce the capture in the House of Commons. Instead Andrew Bonar Law, the Chancellor of the Exchequer and leader of the Conservative party, made the announcement, which was sandwiched between two other, exceptionally banal items, in the House of Commons style: even so it set off a round of cheers.[39] The newspapers played it up all over the Allied world, where it became less a matter of conciliating the faiths of all religions and more the 'Last Crusade', Christianity recovering its own city from the benighted infidel.[40]

17 *Allenby and the Jerusalemites.* After his ceremonial entry into Jerusalem, and the reading of his conciliatory proclamation, General Allenby and his staff met the leading men of the city and the heads of the several religious groups. The photograph shows them symbolically separated into two groups: the British officers, several of whom show symptoms of a terminal boredom, face the Muslim, Jewish, and Christian religious leaders and the local Turkish notables, all of whom, not surprisingly, seemed to be somewhat apprehensive. The British arrogance is not shared by Allenby, shown leaning forward to greet one man, and attended by a French officer (in kepi) and an Italian (whose chicken-feather headdress is just visible). This symbolic separation remained a reality during the whole of the British rule in the city. (Crown Copyright: Imperial War Museum Q 12619)

The excitement once more revived the extravagant hopes of the removal of the Ottoman Empire from the list of enemies. This time it was Allenby who poured cold water on London's optimism. The rainy season would prevent any further attacks for at least two months, he reported on 14 December. He was asked by the CIGS, at the instance of the War Cabinet, to submit his proposals for two suggested advances: to conquer the rest of Palestine, and to accomplish a drive as far as Aleppo. He replied, on 20 December, when his troops were still fighting in the neighbourhood of Jerusalem, that with his present force he thought he could advance to a line between Haifa and Nazareth – as far as he had already come from Gaza – but that to reach Aleppo he would need sixteen or eighteen divisions. It was, he pointed out with some force, 350 miles to Aleppo from Jerusalem. His preference was to advance, as he said, 'step by step'.[41]

But Arabs did not read the Allied newspapers, and Allenby himself, conscious that his army included a large number of Muslims, both Indian soldiers and Egyptian labourers, disliked talk of a crusade.[42] He might also have mentioned Hindus, Buddhists, and no doubt others. The wide variety of Christians would also pose a problem: every sect had its claim on Jerusalem, and every sect had political backing. No wonder he insisted on maintaining martial law.

And, of course, he was quite right, for the fighting near the city was by no means over. The Turks may have abandoned the city, but they had not gone very far, and rear guards had been left to allow the retreating forces to get away. Firing was heard in the city on the day of the ceremony, and there were precautionary aircraft patrols overhead – which also emphasized Allied power, of course.

The Turks were only a few miles away, as the Australian patrol on the 10th had shown, and any further advance by the British northwards was delayed until the situation to the east of the city was cleared up. The Welsh Division troops at last took el-Azariye/Bethany on the 11th, the day Allenby ceremonially entered the city. That was the last move by either side for some days, and both sides slumped into weary exhaustion. Lawrence says he was told by Allenby that 'the British were marched and fought to a standstill'.[43] There was a tacit break in the fighting by both sides, as though the capture of Jerusalem was clearly recognized by both as having been the object of their exercises for the moment, and it was time for a rest. But the Turks were still too close to Jerusalem, and their proximity and alertness in their latest positions were signs that they had not yet given up on the city.

This was also the case in the plain, where the Turks were still too close to

Jaffa for comfort. They did not bombard the city, rather to the surprise of the British, who cynically assumed it was because there was a lot of property in the city owned by Turks and Germans.[44] The roadstead, although by no means as capacious as the British would have liked, was too exposed to Turkish fire for British tastes, so that the Navy insisted it could not safeguard both the landing place at the mouth of the Wadi Suqreir and Jaffa harbour.[45] Also the Turks were still intermittently active in the area, mounting a battalion-sized attack east of Lydda on 1 December.[46] In fact, both sides made local attacks aimed at improving their lines, or of seizing a tactically important hill. The British brought into the line in early December the two divisions which had fought so hard in the hills, the Lowland and the 75th, after their rest. This gave General Bulfin three infantry divisions facing the Nahr el-Auja, the East Anglians being already there; the Anzac Mounted Division was close behind them. The Turks had improved their defences north of the river since the British raid three weeks earlier, and also held positions south of the river some way inland. The only crossings of the river, a bridge and a mill dam, had been destroyed.

A plan was made: a day-long bombardment of the Turkish positions, then a night crossing of the river. For the crossing pontoons were brought from Egypt and primitive boats on the coracle pattern were made locally: two temporary bridges were prepared by the Royal Engineers.[47] As the time for the attack approached, Major-General Hill, commanding the Lowland Division, suggested abandoning the artillery preparation and trying a surprise silent night crossing. Bulfin agreed, despite the bombardment being his plan, but artillery was not abandoned altogether: a version of the Gaza plan was used, a slow bombardment over several preliminary days, which was intended to keep the Turkish patrols in hiding, and to accustom the enemy to the noise, while allowing the guns to register targets. This bombardment would continue during the crossings.

The preparations were lengthy: the pontoons were ordered up from Egypt as early as 7 December. The artillery had to be moved forward carefully so that the guns would remain hidden in the orchards. The locally made pontoon bridges used barrels requisitioned nearby and wood from dismantled sheds at Jaffa. Careful reconnaissance was made to discover Turkish patrolling habits, and to locate the means of crossing the river.[48] Preliminary attacks were made east of the railway to prepare for the main attack. This finally went in on the night of 24th December.

The initial crossing, about a mile upstream from the mouth of the river, was by a company of the 7th Scottish Rifles in the coracles, in order to establish a bridgehead to cover the building of one of the pontoon bridges and the cross-ing of other troops. It was a clear night, with a half moon, but none of the Turks noticed the activity. The crossing was slow and difficult, and, of course, took longer than intended. By 11 p.m. two full battalions and two other com-panies, 8th Scottish Rifles, 7th Highland Light Infantry, 4th Royal Scots, were across. One company of the HLI went off to capture – by surprise, the Turks being all asleep – the Turkish posts commanding the bar of the river; a second company was to guard the eastward flank, and others fanned out to the north. By midnight, after more troops had crossed the river at the bar and at the first pontoons, the whole of 156 Brigade was on the north bank, and all the nearby Turkish positions had been captured.

At the bar of the river the 6th Highland Light Infantry of 157 Brigade had to cross in 4 feet of water under artillery fire, even though their comrades had control of the northern bank, but by 1.30 a.m. they and the 5th Argyll and Sutherland Highlanders were across and moving north: they took their target, a high point on the coast called Tell er-Ruqta, 2 miles north of their cross-ing point, by 3.30 a.m., with only a little fighting. Further upriver 155 Brigade mounted a demonstration a mile beyond the ruined Hadra bridge, which was also menaced, both of which feints gave distracting cover for the real cross-ing, which was by the 5th King's Own Scottish Borderers, mainly by rafts. The floating bridge they were intending to install proved too heavy to move easily; nevertheless the brigade's target, a series of positions about the commanding mound of Khirbet Hadra, was taken by dawn. All the initial objectives had thus been reached, with minimal casualties. The only real fight was made at a ruined bridge below Khirbet Hadra, but this did not last long.[49]

This was a splendid operation. It was carried out by a division which was under strength after the casualties it had taken in the fighting since the break-ing of the Gaza line and above all in the hills; though it certainly outnumbered the Turks who were its victims. The operation is always seen as a model, com-bining surprise, flexibility in execution, and good preparation, with attainable targets. But what is perhaps the most remarkable thing is the sheer military professionalism of these soldiers, mostly volunteers into the New Army from the industrial towns of western and southern Scotland. In the past two months these men had fought in the desert, in trenches, had conducted open warfare on the plains, fought a hill campaign, and had now mounted an opposed river crossing by night.

To the east the East Anglian Division had mounted some neat attacks on the Turks south of the river on December 21, but next day the Turks pulled back. On the coast they were hurried along by bombing from aircraft and shelling by naval gunfire, but the Auckland Regiment of the Anzac Mounted Division could not pursue because of the muddy ground after the recent rains. In effect, the Turks pulled back several miles once their line was broken at the river. The new line the British now established – by their own choice, for the first time – ran from Arsuf southeastwards to the river at Ferekhijeh, up to 9 miles from Jaffa, which could now thus be regarded as free of the threat of bombardment.[50] Perhaps the Scots of the Lowland Division did not realize it, their history education not being England-centred, but the seaward anchor of their line, Arsuf, was the scene of a victory by Richard Coeur-de-Lion over Saladin; this had been a victory which, like the recent capture of Jerusalem, ensured that the westerners would remain in Palestine some time for the foreseeable future.

Yet there is something lacking in this 'Battle of Jaffa', as it is rather pretentiously called. Highly competent though it was, the object was no more than minor and local, an adjustment of the line, not a serious attempt at conquest. The Turks lost some men and some ground, certainly, but their line was quickly restored. Allenby had a huge superiority of manpower, and knew that he would soon receive another division, the 7th Indian from Mesopotamia. Merely straightening his line, pushing the Turks back from Jaffa, was a peculiarly unambitious ambition. The troops were in high fettle – if any soldiers had the right to be battle-weary, the Lowlanders did, but they had conducted a masterly operation.

We may wonder if, had the British been aware of the change in command in the Turkish Eighth Army, they might not have been more adventurous. General Kress von Kressenstein was superseded by General Javed Pasha early in December.[51] Such a change could only be encouraging to the British. The competence of von Kressenstein had been proved often, and his removal from command could only weaken the Turkish forces in front of them. Even if Javed Pasha proved capable – as he did – the Turkish command was bound to be disrupted for a time.

The same unambitious consideration – to counter the nearness of the Turkish lines – operated to the north of Jerusalem. The Turks had cut loose from their British attackers on 9 December, but over the next fortnight they reshuffled their divisions and brought troops forward again to closer contact, and were reinforced by the arrival of their 1st Division from the north. The British forces were readied so as to push the Turks away again.

The usual lengthy preparations were made, principally to the roads and tracks which were needed as supply lines and for bringing up the guns. The intended date for the attack was 23 December, with successive blows that day, the next, and on the 25th. But, not for the first time in the campaign, the weather turned out to be the decisive influence. Rain damaged the roads, soaked the men, and prevented the attack. Several preliminary moves had already been made, against increasing opposition, and one of these, by the 18th London, failed totally on the 23rd.[52]

The Turks had brought the tough 19th Division back from the hills to block the Nablus road, and the newly arrived 1st Division was put into the line at the Zeitun plateau, which had been so bitterly fought over in the Nebi Samweil battle. This in fact had been the target of the first phase of the planned British attack. By the time the British attack was called off, there were six Turkish divisions in the line facing them north of Jerusalem, not all of them in any great strength – but half that number had stopped the first British attempt to capture Jerusalem. On that day it was finally realized at Chetwode's headquarters, from intercepted radio messages and a number of other intelligence details, that this massing of Turkish strength was for offensive, not defensive, purposes. It is a sign of the growth of confidence in the British command that the Turkish attack was now swiftly incorporated into Chetwode's own offensive plans. The weather had delayed the Turkish attack just as it had that of the British.

On 27 December, therefore, the Turkish attack which came was anticipated and the Turks 'found the enemy completely ready for them'.[53] The 19th Division moved southwards along both sides of the main road against the positions of the London Division. Without preliminary bombardment, the first attacks drove back the Londoners' outposts; then a heavy bombardment came in on their main positions. To the south-east the 26th Division launched a strong attack on the Welsh Division only a mile or so north of the Jericho road. Here the outposts mostly held, but not without a stern fight. Another attack was made on an isolated company of the Middlesex Regiment which was posted in an old monastery at Deir ibn Obeid south-east of Jerusalem. This was carried out by the 7th Cavalry Regiment, and was apparently intended to get across British communications, or perhaps to draw troops away from the main fight to the north. The Middlesex company held out for a day, then got away.[54] The attack was thus along a front of more than 6 miles, and it was known that the 1st Division, facing the junction of the Yeomanry and Irish Divisions further north, was supposed to attack as well.

The Turks' initial objectives were a line of villages about a mile in front of their starting line, including Nebi Samweil. Some of the planned attacks did not actually take place, but it would seem that the plan was a mirror-image of the abandoned British plan – a series of blows, the first by the 19th Division, then by the 26th on the left (against the Welsh Division), and third by the 1st Division on the right. This third attack did not happen because it was anticipated by an attack by the Irish Division and 229 Brigade of the Yeomanry Division against positions held by the Turks. The names familiar from the original British attack recurred, as the Zeitun plateau, Ain Arik, and el-Muntar were all captured during the 27th and 28th.

There was no real chance of surprise in this attack: the Turks were obviously alert, and the approach was over open stony ground and up steep hills, all of which were overlooked by the Turkish positions. But the combination of artillery and infantry was masterly. 229 Brigade captured the Zeitun ridge in the morning and the Irish Division, after some difficult fighting in steep country, kept pace in the north. Next day Chetwode ordered the London and Welsh Divisions to join in, and, with only occasional delays imposed by the usual Turkish rearguards, the whole line was shifted north along the Nablus road to beyond Ramallah and el-Bire. It was clear by the morning of the 28th that most of the Turks were pulling out, but the British advance was still notably cautious and slow. Yet by the end of the day, Jerusalem was out of range of Turkish artillery and in no danger of being lost.[55]

Meanwhile on the Nablus road, the Londoners endured three attacks, then put in a well-timed counter-attack which regained all their lost ground. By dawn on the 27th all the Turkish attacks had stopped on this part of the front. The attacks on the Welsh Division continued after dawn, and captured some hills, but without seriously damaging the line. Hardly any of the British reserves had been required to hold these attacks.

The Turkish attacks had presumably been aimed ultimately at the recapture of Jerusalem, though only their first objectives are known. The British attacks, on the other hand, were essentially local offensives designed to achieve strictly limited objectives. In other words, they were now settling down for the rest of the winter in the hills, as they had already done in the plain.

They could do so with a good deal of satisfaction. The southern half of Palestine had been conquered, including Jerusalem; Jaffa's capture promised to ease the supply difficulties. Above all, the Gaza–Beersheba fortified line had been eliminated, so that the opportunities for further warfare were much more attractive. The British army in Palestine had developed into a well-trained, flexible instrument, capable of all the various tasks likely to be assigned to it.

In political terms, Allenby and Balfour between them had seen off the fairly feeble French attempts to be involved in the administration and control of the conquered land, and soon that administration would be formalized in the Occupied Enemy Territories Administration, from which France could be excluded. The requirements of the British government and its empire were fully served.

CHAPTER 11

Why the British Won

WITH the capture of Jerusalem the immediate task imposed on General Allenby by the Prime Minister had been accomplished. As Allenby told T. E. Lawrence, the achievement left the British Army exhausted; their enemy was similarly finished for the present. It was now winter, and both armies had largely outrun, or lost touch with, their supplies during the previous month. It was wet and cold, and the troops were hungry and weary, and required to be re-equipped; the fighting died down to patrolling, both by air and by land.

This was not the only reason the fighting ended, however, for the crossing of the Auja and the repulse of the Turkish counter-attacks north of Jerusalem both showed that the British forces, if not the Turks, were still capable of forward movement. Allenby suggested that the 'rainy season' was a major hindrance, but the real reason for the halt was the uncertainty as to the next move. That is, it was necessary to elicit a new political directive before the British army could go on to conquer territory to the north, much of which had been assigned diplomatically to the French in the putative post-war division of the spoils.

Allenby had achieved what he had been sent east to do. But in the meantime the war at large had changed. Two Russian revolutions had resulted in the Bolshevik Party's seizing power, and it was clear that in order to keep its grip on that country it was going to have to stop fighting its German and Austrian enemies. By December a truce been agreed, and the Bolsheviks and the Germans were involved in peace talks, though it took another three months to reach agreement. It was clear that the Germans had won their eastern war.

This was exactly what Robertson and Haig had long feared. There was now absolutely no doubt that the Western front in France and Belgium and Italy had become the only fighting front which mattered, with the exception of the submarine war. To every general with the slightest imagination, to every politician in the West who had access to even the most superficial information, it was clear that the spring would bring a massive German offensive on the Western front.

The conquest of the southern half of Palestine in 1917 was, therefore, a

military enterprise which was a self-contained event, separated from the preceding advance across Sinai to Gaza by being under the command of General
Murray and by its relatively small scale, and from the later campaign into Syria
by almost a year and by the nature of the forces employed by General Allenby.
It is worth looking at this particular campaign as a unit before briefly outlining
the rest of the events.

Politically it was Allenby's conquest which set the scene for the future in
this area, with its conflicts between British, Jews, and Arabs. It had been a
possibility that the British would content themselves with expelling the Turks
from Sinai, and then stand on guard at el-Arish, in which case there would
have been no Balfour Declaration and no Mandate. Without physical conquest
it would have been difficult for either Britain or France to claim control of
Syria-Palestine. (Mesopotamia was a different matter.) The necessities of the
Great War, as seen from London, had made Allenby's campaign worth while.
It had been a useful way of encouraging support for the war in Britain, and,
so it was calculated, also in Russia and the United States – hence the Balfour
Declaration. The exigencies of the particular situation in 1917, therefore, were
the driving force. The entry of the United States into the war, and the exit of
Russia from it, meant that the political imperatives had changed.

In military terms two elements of the 1917 campaign stand out. The fighting
qualities of both armies were quite remarkable. The skills of the Lowland Division have been mentioned in connection with the crossing of the Auja and its
other fights, but much the same could be said of all the other British and Imperial forces. The achievements of Australian Light Horse Brigades have been
particularly celebrated (not least by themselves), but many Australians gave
the palm for skill and accomplishment to the New Zealand Brigade. Even so, it
was the British infantry, mainly New Army volunteers or pre-war Territorials,
who did most of the fighting. More than once, as for example at Tell esh-Sheria,
it was the infantry who had to break the enemy position so that the cavalry and
light horse could then go ahead to exploit. This is, of course, the normal military practice, but it is the exuberant cavalry rides which seem most spectacular,
and which get the publicity attention.

It is easy to praise the winners, the men who won battles, conquered lands,
captured cities, and occupied territory, and there is no doubt that the British
and imperial forces deserve the praise given them. But it seems to me that
the Turks were the soldiers who come out of this campaign as the toughest,
most obdurate, and most professional of fighters. They were not without their
victories, of course, notably the first and second battles of Gaza, but also Nebi

Samweil, and later the defeat of the two British raids across the Jordan in spring 1918. However, it was in defeat that the skills of these troops were especially shown.

From Gaza to Jerusalem the Turks were driven back, defeated in every fight large and small, until Nebi Samweil. Yet the army survived, and most of its divisions, however depleted, were still in the fight at Jerusalem and the Auja. For 70 miles the Turks were pushed back, a distance over which most armies would have disintegrated. Yet at the end the they were still capable of counterattacks at both the Auja and north of Jerusalem. If a fighting retreat is the most difficult of military operations, the Turks come through with flying colours. To this we must add the fact that the Turkish army in Palestine was always outnumbered by at least two to one and usually more, that the troops were badly fed, racked by disease, and were commanded by German foreigners whom they cordially, and sometimes not so cordially, detested. Mustafa Kemal's refusal to work with German generals, or exercise command under them, was an attitude shared in some degree by Turks of all ranks. Burdened by all these problems, the Turkish soldiers still managed a successful retreat for 70 miles without losing their military cohesion, and put in repeated counter-attacks on the way. At the end of the two months from the opening of the fighting late in October to the end of the year, the Turks were still fighting hard. The truly admirable people of this campaign were the ordinary Turkish soldiers.

The commanders, being less anonymous, have received the most attention, and most of the praise. Several of the Turkish commanders stand out for their skills, notably Refet Bey and Ismet Bey, the defeated commanders at Gaza and Beersheba respectively. Two of the Germans, von Kressenstein notably and to some extent Falkenhayn as well, emerge with considerable reputations, though it does not seem that Falkenhayn enhanced a reputation in Palestine which was already burnished by the Romanian campaign. On the British side it is Allenby who dominates. Some of the corps and division commanders, notably Shea of the London Division, and to some degree Chetwode, deserve praise, but without Allenby's direction they would not be of much interest.

Allenby, it bears repeating, took over a defeated and glum army, retrained it, and used it to defeat a formidable and victorious foe. He did have some extra troops over those Murray had used, but not so many that they made a decisive difference. It was his method of using them – his planning – which was his distinguishing characteristic. Murray's forces at the first and second battles of Gaza outnumbered the enemy, but his plan (or Dobell's) did not permit his numbers to be used effectively, because the attacks were directed at very narrow fronts, so allowing the enemy to concentrate and fight on his own terms, and leaving large numbers of British troops unused. By attacking at several points, by replacing his fighting units after relatively short periods and so giving the weary soldiers rest, and above all by concentrating overwhelming numbers at small points on the front, Allenby was able to force the weary Turks into errors and to defeat. (It may be noted also, that this, in strategic terms, was what Lloyd George advocated in pushing for a campaign to

18 *Turkish prisoners.* Once the actual fighting was over, relations between Turkish and British soldiers tended to be relatively friendly. The Turks were pleased to find their food supply much improved, as was the medical attention they received. The captured British, on the other hand, found they were treated by the Turks in the way the Turks treated their own soldiers. As a result most captured Turks survived, while many British prisoners died. In the photograph the Scottish officer is supervising the Turkish prisoners being removed from Junction Station late in November 1917, using captured Turkish trucks. Note that the same train is also carrying British (or perhaps Australian) soldiers. The British troops are still in their summer, that is, desert, dress. Note that not a single British soldier in the picture is armed. (Crown Copyright: Imperial War Museum Q 12714)

eliminate the Ottoman Empire, and what Germany was doing in 1917 in removing Russia, and to an extent Italy, from the list of its active enemies; Allenby's grand tactics were thus only a smaller version of grand strategy.) Note also the achievements of the Lowland Division as an example once more. It had been fought to a standstill in the Judaean Hills in late November; but then after only a few days' rest it was capable of the masterly battle campaign across the Auja; meanwhile the London and Yeomanry Divisions, previously rested, were able to take up the work in the hills. So the British superiority in numbers at last told, and this was the result of Allenby's methods.

It is a curious characteristic of military men that they like to insist that their plans were carried out successfully, and without change. This is something which can be discerned as early as 1917 in the Palestine area, in reports by Colonel Wavell to the War Office, and he said it again in his lecture, in his book on the campaign, and in his biography of Allenby, published in 1940. Field Marshal Montgomery was, notoriously, another who was insistent on the success of his plans in detail. In fact, of course, the most admirable quality in generalship is adaptability, the willingness and ability to adjust to new conditions as they arise. For even the best prepared plans go wrong – it is the one certain thing about them. It is always necessary to improvise in the middle of a battle, and superior generalship shows that quality by the speed and success of the general's adaptations.

Allenby possessed this quality of adaptability. He quickly discovered the real strength of the Turkish position at Gaza–Beersheba, which was the fortifications of the city and the prepared position at Tell esh-Sheria, and planned accordingly. So he was able to bring three British infantry divisions to attack the Turkish lines south of Tell esh-Sheria from the flank. He was a master of misdirection and deceit in his battles, producing unexpected concentrations, making threats which were discerned as feints and then attacking there anyway – as at the city of Gaza – employing distractions (the Cyprus 'base', Lawrence's raid on the Yarmuk bridges) – and lies and feints all around, hiding some units from view (both from the enemy and even from some historians) so as to bring them into play at the crucial moment – as the two cavalry units at Gaza were intended to be used. And he was quite capable of cancelling attacks if they were not going to be worth making.

He attacked at the enemy's weak points, as along the shore at Gaza, from the flank at Sheria, and eventually in the hills south of Nebi Samweil. The contrast with Murray and Dobell is stark: they repeatedly flung their troops at the strongest enemy positions. Allenby thereby minimized casualties, where his predecessors had maximized them. But Allenby's corps and division commanders tended to go blindly at the enemy when left to themselves – Mott at Tell el-Khuweilfe, Chetwode at Rafa, Bulfin at the Zeitun plateau; it takes considerable willpower to bypass the enemy's strongest positions. One may take it as highly probable that if a subtle manoeuvre took place in the Palestine campaign, Allenby's fingerprints can be detected.

The result of the Palestine campaign was the first military defeat for the Central Powers which led to a substantial loss of territory. This, of course, had already happened to the Allies, in the German conquest of large areas of Belgium and northern France, of Russia and Romania, and the Italian loss of much of the North East after Caporetto. But the victory at Gaza–Beersheba, and again to some degree in the Judaean hills, was different. It was the defeat of an entrenched army, composed of experienced and successful troops, who were well served by modern weapons (artillery and machine-guns and aircraft) by an army which had to approach over open ground. It was, that is, a Western Front-type of battle. So not only was the defeat a damaging psychological blow against the Central Powers, but it also pointed the way to their eventual defeat in France. The defence based on trenches, artillery, redoubts, and other fortifications, could not in the end prevail over repeated attacks – if the attacker was willing to accept the necessary casualties.

The victory at Jerusalem was greeted with jubilation among the allies, as is only to be expected. Lloyd George seized the moment and told Allenby that it was the resolve of the War Cabinet in London to drive the Ottoman Empire out of the war as soon as possible. He was asked for his troop requirements to achieve this, and gave them, but he also pointed out that an advance any time soon was out of the question for logistical reasons.

Allenby developed plans to invade across the Jordan River, in order to clear his inland flank and break the Turks' railway supply route along the Hejaz Railway. First it was necessary to reach the river itself; in February the British descended into the valley and took Jericho, establishing the forward line at the River Auja, about 5 miles north of the town. The British flank was now properly guarded, lying as it did along the Dead Sea and the southern end of the River Jordan. Once again, of course, these were biblical names to conjure with in the West. There was a good deal of disappointment, however, at the small size of the river, though the dirt and squalor of Jericho no longer came as a surprise.

In March and April Allenby organized major attacks across the Jordan in order to establish control over the high plateaux to its east , and in particular of Amman, the Turkish headquarters in the area. The capture of this place, a railway centre, would sever the Turkish supply line to the garrisons along the line as far as Medina. Two attempts were made, in March and late in April; both failed. These failures led to a realization that close co-operation with the Arab forces was going to be next to impossible, for the various tribal groups would scarcely co-operate with each other, never mind the British, and giving orders to any of them was pointless, since they would simply ignore them. It also turned out that it was extremely difficult to move at any speed along the poor roads beyond the river. The Turks proved perfectly capable of reacting swiftly to the attacks, even defeating with some loss an Australian force, and although the British managed to reach Amman they could not hold it. Twice the British forces crossed the river; and twice they were driven back to their crossing point.

These attacks were later described as raids, thus apparently reducing their significance, though no doubt had they been successful battle names would have been awarded, and Allenby certainly intended them to inflict severe losses of men and territory on the Turks. They did heighten Turkish awareness of the possibility of major attacks in the area, but on the British side the idea was now discounted. The difficulty of the terrain, not to mention the tough Turkish response and the difficulty of co-operating with the Arabs, meant that the British planners' attention returned to Palestine, and in particular to the lowlands. Allenby did keep a force in the Jordan Valley all through the summer, however, an unprecedented accomplishment, and they convinced the Turkish command that another attack across the river was likely.

The great German attack in the West came in March 1918, coincidentally beginning on the same day as the first raid towards Amman. Immediately Allenby was ordered to give up many of his tried and trained troops. Two divisions, the Lowland and the Yeomanry, went in April, even before the second raid beyond the Jordan, and a total of another nine cavalry and 23 infantry battalions, plus artillery and machine-gun companies, were also sent later in the month. In their place Allenby received mainly Indian troops, from France, from Mesopotamia, and from India. Eventually he would have a large army, but not as large as that with which he had conquered southern Palestine, and the troops in many cases were not acclimatized and were barely trained. Certainly by May his army had completely changed in composition and was not fit in any way to fight the Turks and Germans in front of them. Only one of his divisions, the London, remained intact. The Indian and British troops were otherwise organized in the same way as Indian Army divisions, with one British and three Indian battalions per brigade. But Allenby did keep his Australian and New Zealand brigades, and he pushed two British West Indian regiments into the line, where they fought particularly well.

Allenby was therefore simultaneously deprived of many of his best troops and suffered two serious defeats. He was, in other words, set back to the situation he faced when he took over the Egyptian Expeditionary Force in the summer of 1917. He had a disorganized army, many parts of which were effectively untrained for the fighting they would have to do. And the Amman raids might even be seen as the equivalent of the first two battles of Gaza – defeats. By the summer he was faced with having to attack the Turkish line, which had in the meantime once again solidified.

But Allenby, unlike Dobell and Murray, had a great victory under his belt, and had been quite truthful in his reports – and he also had the support of the Prime Minister. So he was able to set to work to train up his new army and to develop a new attack plan. The summer of 1918 was therefore spent in training, planning, and organizing for the next offensive, just as that of 1917.

All this disruption meant that it was impossible for the British forces to launch any serious attacks during the summer. On the enemy side, by contrast, the Turks were looking to take advantage of the Russian collapse and began to move forward in the Caucasus. The Young Turk government was Turkish nationalist in its policy, with the result that, as the fighting fronts in Palestine and Mesopotamia became inactive in the first months of 1918, Turkish attention switched to other areas where their advance might meet with local support: the Ottoman government had largely written off the Arab lands, but still had no wish to face military defeat there.

Allenby's new plan was much more extensive than that before Gaza. The aim was not just to break through the Turkish line but to destroy the whole Turkish army in Palestine. To do this it was necessary to move large British forces through the Turkish line very rapidly and to have them penetrate deep into the Turkish rear areas, so that those Turkish troops who were not killed in the attacks should be captured later. Their headquarters were to be captured or paralysed, and none of the rear forces was to be given the time to organize, or even improvise, defensive positions. The fighting in southern Palestine in 1917 had shown that the Turks had a great capability for recovery, that they were able to retreat quickly and effectively to use the land to form defensive positions. This was not to be permitted this time.

By all accounts it was Allenby personally who devised the plan of campaign. General Smuts had made a suggestion for an attack in February, wholly conventional, which met with War Office approval; even Allenby's first plan was not much better, being distinctly limited in scope. He proposed a fairly modest, conventional attack which would have involved an advance of about 20 miles north along the coastal plain, from the start line at the Nahr el-Auja to about Tulkarm, and then a turn east more or less along the railway line towards Nablus. After some time he changed his mind, and instead produced a much more adventurous idea for a much larger infantry breakthrough followed by a much greater cavalry exploitation. It was a classic military formulation, but on a much greater scale than anyone else had so far envisaged. It was a mark of the confidence he had in his army that he could propose it. This time the exploitation was designed to extend in the first day or two for nearly 50 miles.

Allenby, in planning this way, was playing to his own major strength, and taking advantage of a particular Turkish deficiency. The Turks had over 100,000 men in their armies between Damascus and the front line, but they had only 32,000 in the line itself, and of these only about 20,000 were in that part of the line between the coast and the Jordan; and just about all the Turkish cavalry was stationed to the east, beyond the Jordan River. This was the arm in which Allenby's army was overwhelmingly strong. He could put double the number of infantry into the line, he had a superiority in artillery, but above all he had 12,000 men in his cavalry forces as compared with the Turks' 2,000. His plan was designed to capitalize on this superiority, and it was this which produced his new victory.

(Note that both armies were now substantially smaller than at any other time during which Allenby had been in command. He was to fight the coming battle with an army of eighteenth-century size; one which was smaller than either of the armies at Waterloo, for example. Because of this it was an army much easier for a general to control in battle than was usual in the Great War: this was another of the reasons for his victory, for he was a much better general than any of his enemies.)

Deception was the key to the plan. A great fuss was made in requisitioning a Jerusalem hotel, which implied that a major headquarters was being set up there, suggesting an attack along the Nablus road, or across the Jordan. Advantage was taken of the fact that Turkish spies could penetrate into Palestine relatively easily, but they were given the chance to discover only certain things. The Australians, whom the Turks rightly feared, were placed in the Jordan Valley, once again implying a likely attack eastwards across the Jordan. A Turkish spoiling attack by two German regiments and two Turkish divisions was made into the valley in July; the Australian First Brigade had the satisfaction of completely trouncing this; they were particularly pleased to find that they were by far better fighters than the vaunted Germans; as a result German prestige on the Turkish side subsided.

These various deceptions were designed to obscure the fact that the main assault was actually to be in the plain by the coast. Carefully and secretly Allenby concentrated four full infantry divisions, almost four hundred guns, and three cavalry divisions into a front of less than 20 miles, where they faced only two (small) Turkish infantry divisions. The infantry divisions were to punch a wide hole in the Turkish line so that three cavalry divisions could ride through and cut the Turkish rear communications and so surround the whole Turkish army.

The planned cavalry exploitation was the real surprise. The targets were now, first of all, Tulkarm; then el-Affuleh, a major railway junction; then Samakh, the Jordan crossing just south of the Sea of Galilee; and then Deraa, well to the east of the Jordan. This last was much too far for the forces in Palestine to reach, so it was allocated to the Arab guerrilla forces, but it was intended that the cavalry force in the Jordan Valley – 'Chaytor's Force' – would reach the town as soon as possible.

It nearly went wrong. An Indian sergeant deserted to the Turks on the night before the assault was due to go in. It came as no real surprise to the Turks that the assault was coming, and the sergeant could only give a date, not the plan as a whole. But some Turkish commanders were already apprehensive, and wished to pull their troops back several miles, so that an assault would have to cross an empty space before reaching the Turkish lines, and so lose tactical surprise. The Turkish commander, General Liman von Sanders, decided that it was too late to pull back. He was probably right, since if he had moved he would abandon what seemed to be good defences, and his army would have been caught disorganized and defeated in the open even more quickly than it was.

Allenby's overall plan also involved several other attacks in succession at different points of the line, designed in part to reinforce the impressions provided by the deceptions, but also to gain specific objects and positions. Chaytor's Force in the Jordan Valley manoeuvred and patrolled threateningly; that facing Nablus under Chetwode put in an attack the day before the main assault, to attract Turkish attention. To the east, beyond the river, the Arabs made attacks on the railway even earlier. Then, after all this activity inland, the main attack was made near the coast.

This took place on the night of 18/19 September. The attack was instantly successful, and the Turkish front was destroyed by noon. The cavalry moved though the gap. By afternoon the forward troops were in Tulkarm. To the east General Chetwode developed his attack towards Nablus, utilizing the fact that parts of the line were fairly thinly held, and avoiding the obvious route along the road by developing a pincer movement using two divisions. Virtually the whole Turkish line from the coast of the River Jordan collapsed. From then on it was a matter of preventing any units from making a stand, and exploiting the initiative ruthlessly.

General von Sanders was nearly captured at his general headquarters at Nazareth by the British cavalry on the 20th, which was an advance of 50 miles in two days. The bridge across the Jordan at Samakh, at the southern end of the Sea of Galilee, was taken in a set-piece assault on the 25th. Chaytor's Force, a comprehensively mixed force, crossed the Jordan and took Amman that same day. To the east the Arabs harassed all the Turkish forces round Deraa and cut the railway line repeatedly. By the 26th every Turkish unit was in headlong retreat.

The destruction of the Turkish forces was almost total, and from now on political objectives tended to take centre stage. Allenby gave orders on the 26th that Damascus was the next target for capture. The Arabs particularly wished to be able to capture the city themselves, which was seen as the likely future capital of an Arab state encompassing Syria and Palestine, Mesopotamia, and Arabia. There is some dispute about who got there first, but it seems likely that the Australian Mounted Division passed through the city before the Arabs arrived. But the two forces had different objectives. The Arabs wanted the city for itself. The Australians wanted to get through it to ensure that the road further north was not blocked, and to cut off the retreat of Turkish troops in the city. Local notables in the city seized on the confusion of the moment to raise the Arab flags. But the future of the city still remained for political negotiation.

Beyond Damascus there are three routes northwards. One is along the Lebanese coast through Beirut and on to Lattakia; one inland route lies along the desert edge east of the Antilebanon Mountains, to Homs; between, there is the long, narrow Beqaa Valley. This was all territory which the French claimed as part of their spoils of war. A token contingent with Allenby's army, two regiments (one of Armenian infantry, the other Algerian) had been sent to Palestine expressly so that the French should have a military presence when the Allied army reached Syria, and French warships sailed into Beirut harbour before the 7th Meerut Division could reach it by land from the south. All along the coast the French asserted control. And so the three Allied armies took on increasingly political roles.

The pursuit along the inland route through the Beqaa Valley went on day after day, largely by the British 5th Cavalry Division, which included British Yeomanry and Indian cavalry regiments, and an armoured car column. They were paced on the east by an Arab force which moved as quickly along the desert-edge route. The further north they all went, the more difficult it was to keep the troops supplied, and the smaller the Allied contingent became. Turkish rearguard actions tried to halt the advance here and there, but demoralization was almost complete. Before Aleppo, which was said to be strongly held, the Arab force joined up with the British cavalry. The Turkish commander in Aleppo refused a British summons to surrender; the Arabs went into the city and drove the Turkish garrison out. Aleppo was taken on 26 October. At this point it was later calculated that the British had captured 75,000 prisoners, over three hundred guns, and the equipment of three Turkish armies.

The armistice negotiations on the island of Mudros in the Aegean had already started. The Allied army at Salonica had already knocked Bulgaria out of the war, so cutting the Turkish communications with Germany, and preventing any further supplies getting through. In Syria, however, the Allied advance had now at last run out of steam. The Turks, on the other hand, were beginning to recover. In particular, one of their commanders, Mustafa Kemal, had scraped together a small but worthwhile force, and had taken up a defensible position at Maritain, not far north-west of Aleppo. The British cavalry from the city probed northwards and was smartly repulsed. Once again the Turkish power of recovery is astonishing. Three-quarters of the Turkish forces in Syria had been captured; still more had been killed; yet under a tough and resolute commander they turned and fought back effectively. The Turkish force, as it happened, then continued its retreat, but had the war gone on much longer it seems likely that a major Turkish counter-attack could have been mounted, and might well have driven back the Allied armies, by this time much weakened by influenza and spread out all too thinly from Gaza to Aleppo. They could well have been driven a long way south.

Just in time the armistice negotiations ended, on 31 October. The armies stood where they were, and the Ottoman Empire in effect resigned itself to the loss of Syria, Palestine, and Mesopotamia. Needless to say, the Allies almost immediately quarrelled amongst themselves over who should control the conquered lands.

Composition of the Egyptian Expeditionary Force

Listed here are the units involved in the Palestine campaign. The British also had large forces in Egypt, which provided the necessary logistic and administrative support for the army in the field, and held down Egypt itself.

⁂ MARCH–APRIL 1917: FIRST AND SECOND BATTLES OF GAZA

GENERAL HEADQUARTERS
Commander-in Chief: General Sir Archibald Murray
Chief of Staff: Major General Sir A. Lynden-Bell

EASTERN FORCE
General Officer Commanding: Lieutenant-General Sir Charles Dobell
Imperial Camel Brigade: 3 battalions
Hong Kong and Singapore Camel Battery
Imperial Service Cavalry Brigade: Mysore Lancers; Hyderabad Lancers; Jodhpur Lancers; Kathiawar Signal Troop
52 (Lowland) Division (Major-General W. E. B. Smith)
155 Brigade: 1/4 and 1/5 Royal Scots Fusiliers; 1/4 and 1/5 King's Own Scottish Borderers
156 Brigade: 1/4 and 1/7 Royal Scots; 1/7 and 1/8 Scottish Rifles
157 Brigade: 1/5, 1/6 and 1/7 Highland Light Infantry; 1/5 Argyll and Sutherland Highlanders
Divisional Troops: Royal Glasgow Yeomanry; 261, 262 and 263 Brigades, Royal Field Artillery
1 Dismounted Brigade: 1/1, 1/3 Scottish Horse; 1/1 Ayr Yeomanry; 1/1 Lanark Yeomanry

54 (East Anglian) Division (Major-General S. W. Hare)

   161 Brigade: 1/4, 1/5, 1/6 and 1/7 Essex Regiment

   162 Brigade: 1/5 Bedfordshire Regiment; 1/4 Northamptonshire Regiment; 1/10 and 1/11 London Regiments

   163 Brigade: 1/4 and 1/5 Norfolk Regiment; 1/5 Suffolk Regiment; 1/8 Hampshire Regiment

74 (Yeomanry) Division (Major-General E. S. Girdwood)

   229 Brigade: 16 Devonshire Regiment; 12 Somerset Light Infantry; 14 Royal Highlanders; 12 Royal Scots Fusiliers

DESERT COLUMN (Lieutenant-General Sir Philip Chetwode)

Australian and New Zealand Mounted Division (Major-General Sir Harry Chauvel)

   1 Australian Light Horse Brigade: 1, 2 and 3 Light Horse Regiments

   2 Australian Light Horse Brigade: 5, 6 and 7 Light Horse Regiments

   New Zealand Mounted Rifle Brigade: Auckland, Canterbury and Wellington Mounted Rifle Regiments

   22 Mounted Brigade: 1/1 Lincolnshire Yeomanry; 1/1 Staffordshire Yeomanry; 1/1 East Riding Yeomanry

   Divisional Troops: Leicester, Somerset, Inverness and Ayr Batteries, Royal Field Artillery

Imperial Mounted Division (Major-General H. W. Hodgson)

   3 Australian Light Horse Brigade: 8, 9 and 10 Light Horse Regiments

   4 Australian Light Horse Brigade: 4, 11 and 12 Light Horse Regiments

   5 Mounted Brigade: 1/1 Warwickshire Yeomanry; 1/1 Gloucestershire Yeomanry; 1/1 Worcestershire Yeomanry

   6 Mounted Brigade: 1/1 Buckinghamshire Yeomanry; 1/1 Berkshire Yeomanry; 1/1 Dorsetshire Yeomanry

   Divisional Troops: Notts and Berks Batteries Royal Horse Artillery

53 (Welsh) Division (Major-General A. G. Dallas)

   158 Brigade: 1/5, 1/6 and 1/7 Royal Welch Fusiliers; 1/1 Herefordshire Regiment

   159 Brigade: 1/4 and 1/7 Cheshire Regiment; 1/4 and 1/5 Welch Regiment

   160 Brigade: 1/4 Royal Sussex Regiment; 2/4 Royal West Surrey Regiment; 2/4 Royal West Kent Regiment; 2/10 Middlesex Regiment

   Divisional Troops: 1/1 Hertfordshire Yeomanry; 265, 266 and 267 Brigade Royal Field Artillery

⁂ JUNE–DECEMBER 1917
THIRD BATTLE OF GAZA TO THE CAPTURE OF JERUSALEM

GENERAL HEADQUARTERS

Commander-in-Chief: General Sir Edmund Allenby

Chief of Staff: Major-General Sir A. Lynden-Bell (until September); Major General L. J. Bols (from September)

DESERT MOUNTED CORPS (Lieutenant-General Sir Harry Chauvel)

Australian and New Zealand Mounted Division (Major-General E. Chaytor)

1 and 2 Australian Light Horse and *New Zealand Mounted Brigades* (as above)

XVIII Brigade Royal Horse Artillery (Inverness, Ayr and Somerset Batteries)

Australian Mounted Division (Major-General H. W. Hodgson)

3 and 4 Australian Light Horse and *5 Mounted Brigades* (as above)

XIX Brigade Royal Horse Artillery: Notts Battery Royal Horse Artillery, and A & B Batteries Honourable Artillery Company

Yeomanry Mounted Division (Major General G. de S. Barrow)

6, 8 and 22 Mounted Brigades (as above)

XX Brigade Royal Horse Artillery (Berks, Hants and Leicester Batteries)

Attached: Hong Kong and Singapore Mountain Battery; 7 Mounted Brigade; Imperial Camel Corps Brigade

XX CORPS (Lieutenant-General Sir Philip Chetwode)

53 (Welsh) Division (Major-General S. F. Mott) (as above)

60 (London) Division (Major-General J. Shea)

179 Brigade: 2/13, 2/14, 2/15 and 2/16 London Regiments

180 Brigade: 2/17, 2/18, 2/19 and 2/20 London Regiments

181 Brigade: 2/21, 2/22, 2/23 and 2/24 London Regiments; 301, 302 and 303 Brigade Royal Field Artillery

74 (Yeomanry) Division (Major-General E. S. Girdwood)

229 Brigade (as above)

230 Brigade: 10 East Kent Regiment; 16 Sussex Regiment; 15 Suffolk Regiment; 12 Norfolk Regiment

231 Brigade: 10 Shropshire Light Infantry; 24 Royal Welch Fusiliers; 24 Welch Regiment; 25 Royal Welch Fusiliers; XLIV, 117 and 268 Brigades, Royal Field Artillery

Corps Troops: 1/2 County of London Yeomanry; XCVI Heavy Artillery Group
Attached:

10 (Irish) Division (Major-General J. R. Longley)

29 Brigade: 6 Royal Irish Rifles; 5 Connaught Rangers; 1 and 6 Leinster
Regiment

30 Brigade: 1 Royal Irish Regiment; 6 Royal Munster Fusiliers; 6 and 7
Royal Dublin Fusiliers

31 Brigade: 5 and 6 Royal Inniskilling Fusiliers; 2 and 5 Royal Irish Fusiliers

XXI CORPS (Lieutenant-General E. S. Bulfin)

52 (Lowland) Division (Major-General J. Hill) (as above)

54 (East Anglian) Division (Major-General S. Hare) (as above)

75 Division (Major-General P. C. Palin)

232 Brigade: 1/5 Devonshire Regiment; 2/5 Hampshire Regiment;
2/4 Somerset Light Infantry; 2/3 Gurkhas

233 Brigade: 1/5 Somerset Light Infantry; 1/4 Wiltshire Regiment;
2/4 Hampshire Regiment; 3/3 Gurkhas

234 Brigade: 1/4 Duke of Cornwall's Light Infantry; 2/4 Dorsetshire
Regiment; 123 Outram's Rifles; 58 Vaughan's Rifles; XXXVII,
172 Brigades, Royal Field Artillery; 1 South African Field Artillery
Brigade

Corps Troops: Composite Regiment (1 squadron each of Royal Glasgow
Yeomanry, Duke of Lancaster's Yeomanry, Hertfordshire Yeomanry);
XCVII, C and 102 Heavy Artillery Groups

GHQ TROOPS

Palestine Brigade Royal Flying Corps: 11, 14 and 113 Squadrons Royal
Flying Corps; 67 Squadron Australian Flying Corps; VIII and IX
Mountain Brigades Royal Field Artillery

Maps

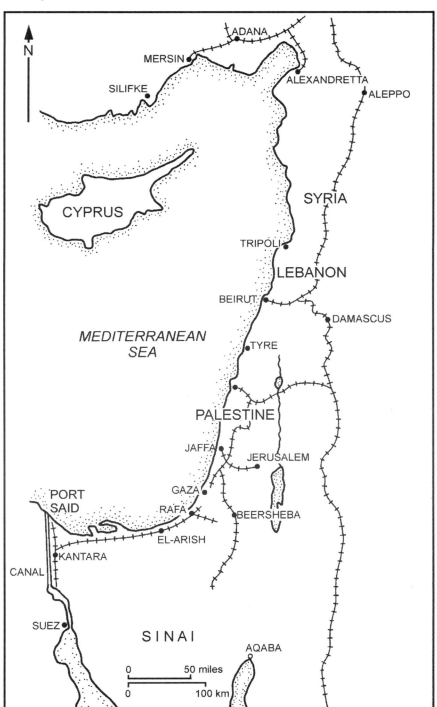

MAP 1 Syria-Palestine, 1917

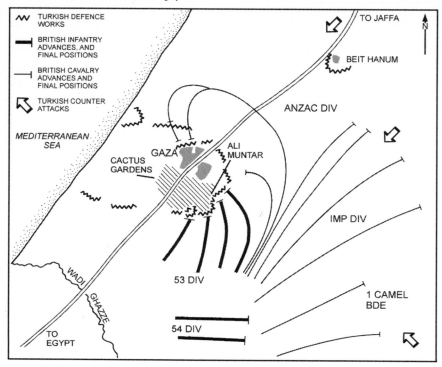

MAP 2 First Gaza

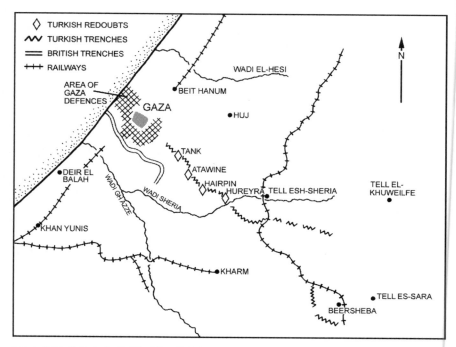

MAP 3 Gaza–Beersheba fortified line, October 1917

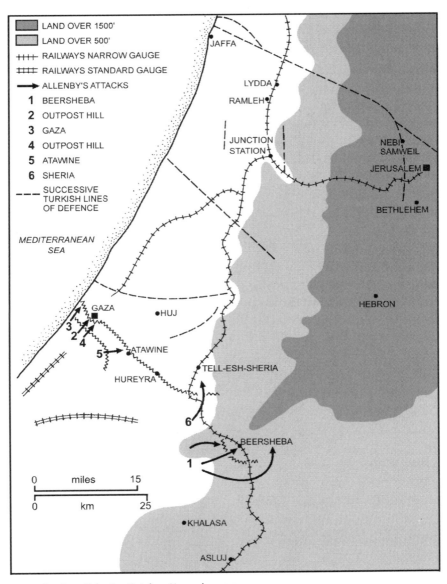

LAND OVER 1500'
LAND OVER 500'
┼┼┼┼ RAILWAYS NARROW GAUGE
Ⲓ┼Ⲓ┼Ⲓ RAILWAYS STANDARD GAUGE
➤ ALLENBY'S ATTACKS
1 BEERSHEBA
2 OUTPOST HILL
3 GAZA
4 OUTPOST HILL
5 ATAWNE
6 SHERIA
─ ─ ─ SUCCESSIVE
TURKISH LINES
OF DEFENCE

MEDITERRANEAN
SEA

JAFFA

LYDDA
RAMLEH

JUNCTION
STATION

NEBI
SAMWEIL

JERUSALEM

BETHLEHEM

HEBRON

GAZA
•HUJ

ATAWINE

TELL-ESH-SHERIA

HUREYRA

6

BEERSHEBA

1

0   miles   15
0   km   25

•KHALASA

ASLUJ•

MAP 4 Southern Palestine October–November 1917

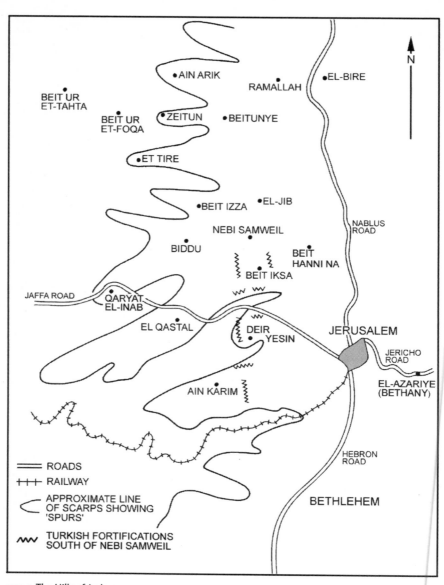

N

BEIT UR
ET-TAHTA

AIN ARIK

RAMALLAH

EL-BIRE

ZEITUN

BEIT UR
ET-FOQA

BEITUNYE

ET TIRE

BEIT IZZA

EL-JIB

NEBI SAMWEIL

NABLUS
ROAD

BIDDU

BEIT
HANNI NA

BEIT IKSA

JAFFA ROAD

QARYAT
EL-INAB

EL QASTAL

DEIR
YESIN

JERUSALEM

JERICHO
ROAD

EL-AZARIYE
(BETHANY)

AIN KARIM

HEBRON
ROAD

BETHLEHEM

ROADS

RAILWAY

APPROXIMATE LINE
OF SCARPS SHOWING
'SPURS'

TURKISH FORTIFICATIONS
SOUTH OF NEBI SAMWEIL

MAP 5 The Hills of Judaea

Notes

Abbreviations

ANZ – Archives New Zealand, Wellington

AWM – Australian War Museum, Canberra

IWM – Imperial War Museum, London

New DNB – New Dictionary of National Biography

NZNL – New Zealand National Library, Wellington

Off. Hist. – Official History of the War: Sir G. MacMunn and C. Falls, *Military Operations, Egypt and Palestine*, vol. 1 (London, 1928); C. Falls, *Military Operations, Egypt and Palestine*, vol. 2 (2 volumes in 3) (London, 1930)

TNA – The National Archives, Kew, London

Yildirim – Hussein Husni Amir Bey, *Yilderim*, trans. Captain C. Channer (typescript in IWM)

Prologue: To the Border of Palestine

1 An excellent map of the dispositions is in C. G. Powles (ed.), *The History of the Canterbury Mounted Rifles, 1914–1919* (Auckland, 1928), entitled 'Action at Rafa, 9 January 1917'; another is in *Off. Hist.*, vol. 1, opposite 263.

2 Reported as a rumour by I. L. Idriess, *The Desert Column* (Sydney, 1932); C. G. Nicol, *The Story of Two Campaigns: Official War History of the Auckland Mounted Rifles Regiment, 1914–1919* (Auckland, 1921), only remarks on crossing the line.

3 *Off. Hist.*, 1.266.

4 Powles, *History of the Canterbury Mounted Rifles*, 133; *Off. Hist.*, 1.266, reports 45 only.

5 A. B. Moore, *The Mounted Riflemen in Sinai and Palestine* (Auckland, 1920), 57.

6 Nicol, *Story of Two Campaigns*, 130; Powles, *History of the Canterbury Mounted Rifles*, 134.

7 The reserves of ammunition had been left at Sheikh Zowaiid, several miles away, in order to speed the overnight advance.

8 *Off. Hist.*, 1.271, n.1.

9 *Off. Hist.*, 1.267, n.

10 C. G. Powles, *The New Zealanders in Sinai and Palestine*, The Official History of New Zealand's Effort in the Great War, vol. 3 (Auckland, 1923), 77–8.

11 J. H. Luxford, *With the Machine Gunners in France and Palestine: Official History of the New Zealand Machine Gun Corps* (Auckland, 1923), 195.

12 *Off. Hist.*, 1.268; these orders were prepared by General Chauvel's staff.

13 *Off. Hist.*, 1.258; A. J. Hill, *Chauvel of the Light Horse: A Biography of General Sir Harry Chauvel* (Melbourne, 1978).

14 Nicol, *Story of Two Campaigns*, 132, and Powles, *History of the Canterbury Mounted Rifles*, 135, both report this withdrawal, but it is not mentioned by 'C' [Lord Cobham], *The Yeomanry Cavalry of Worcestershire, 1914–1922* (Stourbridge, 1926), in his account of the fight. Most units in this attack withdrew or regrouped at one time or another, and this may have been what the New Zealanders saw; alternatively, the withdrawal may have been expunged from memory.

15 ANZ, WA 42/1, Wellington MR War Diary; 43/1, Canterbury MR War Diary.

16 Powles, *History of the Canterbury Mounted Rifles*, 135.

17 Powles, *History of the Canterbury Mounted Rifles*, 135–6; Moore, *Mounted Riflemen*, 59; Nicol, *Story of Two Campaigns*, 132; *Off. Hist.*, 1.268.

18 *Off. Hist.*, 1.268–9.

19 *Off. Hist.*, 1.269.

20 *Off. Hist.*, 1.269; N. C. Smith, *The Third Australian Light Horse Regiment, 1914–1918* (Melbourne, 1993), 50–1.

21 *Off. Hist.*, 1.270.

22 *Off. Hist.*, 1, Order of Battle, apps. 2 and 3.

23 Moore, *Mounted Riflemen*, 57–8.

24 Powles, *History of the Canterbury Mounted Rifles*, 136.

Chapter 1: The Decision to Invade Palestine

1 For accounts of the imperialist process see J. Marlowe, *Spoiling the Egyptians* (London, 1974), and D. S. Landes, *Bankers and Pashas: International Finance and Economic Imperialism in Egypt* (New York, 1958). For accounts of British rule see Earl of Cromer, *Modern Egypt*, 2 vols. (London, 1908), and Afaf Lutfi al-Sayyid, *Egypt and Cromer: A Study in Anglo-Egyptian Relations* (London, 1968).

2 A more detailed description of all this is P. G. Elgood, *Egypt and the Army* (London, 1924), chs. 1–6.

3 *Off. Hist.*, vol. 1, chs. 7–9.

4 Much discussed since; the negotiations were extremely tricky on both sides: E. Kedourie, *In the Anglo-Arab Labyrinth: The MacMahon–Husayn Correspondence and its Interpreters, 1914–1939* (Cambridge, 1976); cf. D. Fromkin, *The Peace to End All Peace: Creating the Modern Middle East, 1914–1922* (London, 1989), ch. 3.

5 *Off. Hist.*, 1.221.

6 An interesting description of the live-and-let-live situation in the Aden interior is in H. O. Lock, *History of the Fourth Battalion, History of the Dorsetshire Regiment, 1914–1919* (Dorchester, 1932).

7 F. J. Moberly, *The Campaign in Mesopotamia*, 4 vols., History of the Great War (London, 1923–7).

8 Murray to Robertson, 15 February 1916, printed in *Off. Hist.*, 1.170–4.

9 *Off. Hist.*, vol. 1, chs. 10, 11 and 14.

10 *Off. Hist.*, 1.251–3.

11 D. R. Woodward (ed.), *The Military Correspondence of Field Marshal Sir William Robertson, Chief of the Imperial General Staff, December 1915 – February 1918*, Army Records Society (London, 1989), no. 17, Robertson to Murray, 15 March 1916.

12 Woodward, *Military Correspondence of Field Marshal Sir William Robertson*, no. 44, Robertson to Murray, 1 August 1916.

13 *Off. Hist.*, 1.243–4.

14 All accounts of life in Sinai remark on these features.

15 'A British general', was the characterization of Corporal A. S. Metcalfe of the 1st Light Horse: AWM, 1 DRL 497, Metcalfe to 'Harry', January 1917.

16 Woodward, *Military Correspondence of Field Marshal Sir William Robertson*, no. 103, Robertson to Murray, 10 January 1917.

17 See the contrast between Robertson's letters to Murray of 12 December 1916 and 10 January 1917: Woodward, *Military Correspondence of Field Marshal Sir William Robertson*, nos. 93 and 103.

18 *Off. Hist.*, 1.272–3.

19 *Off. Hist.*, 1.15–16.

20 The following section is based on the Order of Battle as set out in the *Off. Hist.*, vol. 1, apps. 2 and 3.

Chapter 2: Defeat at Gaza

1 E. E. Ramsaur, *The Young Turks: Prelude to the Revolution of 1908* (New York, 1957), 100–1.

2 Both men published their memoirs: Djemal Pasha, *Memories of a Turkish Statesman* (London, 1922); F. Kress von Kressenstein, 'Zwischen Kaukasus und Sinai', *Jahrbuch des Bandes der Asienkampfer* (1921 and 1922), summarized very fully in the *RUSI Journal* 6 (1922), 503–13, as 'The Campaign in Palestine from the Enemy's Side'.

3 *Off. Hist.*, 1.276–7.

4 *Off. Hist.*, 1.280.

5 *Off. Hist.*, 1.276–7.

6 *Off. Hist.*, 1.280.

7 W. Raleigh and H. A. Jones, *The War in the Air*, vol. 5, The Official History of the War (Oxford, 1935), 203.

8 Raleigh and Jones, *War in the Air*, 204–5.

9 Raleigh and Jones, *War in the Air*, 205.

10 *Off. Hist.*, 1.271–2, 279.

11 *Off. Hist.*, 1.297.
12 Raleigh and Jones, *War in the Air*, 210, an appreciation of the success of the German air reconnaissance.
13 Printed in *Off. Hist.*, 1.413, app. 8.
14 Printed in *Off. Hist.*, 1.415, app. 9.
15 The operation order is in *Off. Hist.*, vol. 1. apps. 8 and 9.
16 Idriess, *Desert Column*, 186–7. The diaries are in the AWM, reference 1 DRL 0973; they differ slightly from the printed version.
17 J. D. Richardson, *History of the 7th Light Horse Regiment, AIF* (Sydney, [1923]), 41.
18 AWM 2 DRL 817, Letters of Signalman R. H. Chandler, letter dated 1 April 1917.
19 AWM 1 DRL 0032, Account of Lt-Col C. H. Anderson, p. 9.
20 C. H. D. Ward, *History of the 53rd (Welsh) Division, 1914–1918* (Cardiff, 1927), 79, quoting a contemporary account.
21 O. Teichman, *Diary of a Yeomanry MO* (London, 1921), 119–20.
22 Ward, *History of the 53rd (Welsh) Division*, 76–81; A. Crookenden, *The History of the Cheshire Regiment in the Great War* (Chester, [1938]), 183.
23 *Off. Hist.*, 1.321.
24 *Off. Hist.*, 1.321.
25 Ward, *History of the 53rd (Welsh) Division*, 81–5 and 89–90; G. A. Parfitt (ed.), *Historical Records of the Herefordshire Light Infantry and its Predecessors* (Hereford, 1982), 95–6.
26 T. Gibbons, *With the 1/5th Essex in the East* (Colchester, 1921), 68.
27 Chetwode's annoyance is described most vividly by Ward, *History of the 53rd (Welsh) Division*, 78; the account in *Off. Hist.*, 1.297–8, is much more decorous.
28 ANZ WA 42/1, Wellington MR War Diary, WA 42/1, 26 March 1917.
29 NZNL, MS Paper 4312/4, Diary of Harold Judge, 26 March 1917.
30 Richardson, *History of the 7th Light Horse Regiment*, 42.
31 P. K. Kemp, *The Staffordshire Yeomanry, QORR, in the First and Second World Wars* (Aldershot, 1953), 28.
32 Powles, *History of the Canterbury Mounted Rifles*, 148.
33 'C' [Cobham], *Yeomanry Cavalry of Worcestershire*, 89.
34 AWM, PRO 1577, Letters of Lieutenant W. A. McConnan, 31 March 1917.
35 Sir F. Fox, *The History of the Royal Gloucestershire Hussars Yeomanry, 1898–1922* (Southampton, 1923), 128–30.
36 Gibbons, *With the 1/5th Essex in the East*, 70.
37 *Off. Hist.*, 1.307.
38 *Off. Hist.*, 1.311–12.
39 *Off. Hist.*, 1.309–10.
40 Gibbons, *With the 1/5th Essex in the East*, 71–2.
41 *Off. Hist.*, 1.312–13.
42 *Off. Hist.*, 1.302.

Chapter 3: Defeated Again

1   The telegrams are printed in *Off. Hist.*, 1.322–5.

2   This is the burden of Roberton's telegram of 2 April 1917 (*Off. Hist.*, 1.324–5).

3   Thus the British have the dubious distinction of having introduced both chemical and tank warfare to the Middle East.

4   Raleigh and Jones, *War in the Air*, 214–15 (numbers quoted from 209n); AWM MSS 0862, O. Nikolajsen, 'Ottoman aviation, 1911–1919'.

5   *Off. Hist.*, 1.331; L. von Sanders, *Five Years in Turkey* (Annapolis, MD, 1928), 166.

6   *Off. Hist.*, 1.331.

7   *Off. Hist.*, 1.358–62, and table on 367.

8   *Off. Hist.*, 1.330n.

9   'C' [Cobham], *Yeomanry Cavalry of Worcestershire*, 96.

10   *Off. Hist.*, 1.332–4.

11   S. Gillon, *The KOSB in the Great War* (London, 1930), 263–4.

12   *Off. Hist.*, 1.3401.

13   W. S. Brown, *War Record of the 4th Battalion, King's Own Scottish Borderers and Lothian and Border Horse* (Galashiels, 1930), 97; R. R. Thompson, *The Fifty-Second (Lowland) Division, 1914–1918* (Glasgow, 1923), 324.

14   Brown, *War Record of the 4th Battalion, King's Own Scottish Borderers*, 98, quoting Second Lieutenant Broomfield.

15   Gillon, *The KOSB in the Great War*, 265.

16   Brown, *War Record of the 4th Battalion, King's Own Scottish Borderers*, 100–1.

17   According to Thompson, *Fifty-Second (Lowland) Division*, casualties in each brigade were: 155 Brigade 1025; 156 Brigade 511; 157 Brigade 337; Artillery 12. 155 Brigade began the day with a strength of 2,500 men. The KOSB suffered 13 officers and 47 other ranks killed, 8 officers and 226 other ranks wounded, and 1 officer and 54 other ranks missing, a total of 347 casualties.

   One of the officers killed was Lieutenant Charlie Law, the second son of Andrew Bonar Law, leader of the Conservative Party, Chancellor of the Exchequer and *de facto* Deputy Prime Minister. The death was unconfirmed for many months. The Chancellor's eldest son was killed in France later in the year (R. Blake, *The Unknown Prime Minister: The Life and Time of Andrew Bonar Law, 1858–1923* (London, 1955), 354–6).

18   J. Buchan, *The History of the Royal Scots Fusiliers, 1676–1918* (London, [1925]), 397.

19   *Off. Hist.*, 1.342–3.

20   Ward, *History of the 53rd (Welsh) Division*, 105–6.

21   Mott was a substantive major, and now a temporary Major-General.

22   *Off. Hist.*, 1.343.

23   Ward, *History of the 53rd (Welsh) Division*, 106–7; he spends longer on this detail than on all the rest of the assault.

24   The division suffered 584 casualties, a quarter of those in the Lowland Division, and a sixth of those of the East Anglian (*Off. Hist.*, 1.348).

25 Raleigh and Jones, *War in the Air*, 217.

26 [Anon.], *The Northamptonshire Regiment, 1914–1918* (Aldershot, [1932]), 333.

27 *Off. Hist.*, 1.338–9.

28 G. F. and E. M. Langley, *Sand, Sweat and Camels: The Australian Companies of the Imperial Camel Corps*, paperback edn (Sydney, 1995), 90–1.

29 F. L. Petre, *The History of the Norfolk Regiment, 1685–1918*, vol. 2: *1914–1918* (Norwich, [1926]), 145–6.

30 *Off. Hist.*, 1.339.

31 E. W. Hammond, *History of the 11th Light Horse Regiment, Fourth Light Horse Brigade, Australian Imperial Forces, War 1914–1919* (Brisbane, 1942), 69–70.

32 AWM MSS 0862, Nikolajsen, 'Ottoman aviation'.

33 Raleigh and Jones, *War in the Air*, 217.

34 Hammond, *History of the 11th Light Horse Regiment*, 71.

35 IWM 86.51.1, Account of Driver T. B. Marshall, 12.

36 Idriess, *Desert Column*, 207.

37 NZNL, MS Papers 43/12/4, Diary of Harold Judge, [19] April 1917.

38 L. Broinowski, *Tasmania's War Record, 1914–1918* (Hobart, 1921), 146–7.

39 Richardson, *History of the 7th Light Horse Regiment*, 47.

40 R. de Nogales, *Four Years beneath the Crescent*, trans. M. Lee (London, 1926), 345. Nogales's account is a good deal more personal, romantic, and vague than those of the Australian regiment-historians, but enough similarities are visible to show they are dealing with the same events.

41 J. W. Wintringham, *With the Lincolnshire Yeomanry in Egypt and Palestine, 1914–1918* (Grimsby, 1979), 60.

42 *Off. Hist.*, 1.347.

43 *Off. Hist.*, 1.347; this was Brigadier-General Hare's doing (cf. n. 29 above).

44 *Off. Hist.*, 1.347–8.

45 Raleigh and Jones, *War in the Air*, 217–18.

46 *Off. Hist.*, 1.318.

47 *Off. Hist.*, 1.350.

Chapter 4: The Wider Context

1 Hammond, *History of the 11th Light Horse Regiment*, 70.

2 *Off. Hist.*, 1.348–9, makes no attempt to analyse the causes other than pointing to the strength of the Turkish positions and the quality of the Turkish soldiers. It also makes the curious comment that it 'has none of the interest of the first battle', a purely theoretical, academic judgement which all too easily ignores the actual events.

3 *Off. Hist.*, 1.347–8.

4 See, for example, the account by E. W. Gladstone, *The Shropshire Yeomanry*,

MDCCXCV–MCMXLX: The Story of a Volunteer Cavalry Regiment (Manchester, 1953), 219.

5 J. Ewing, *The Royal Scots, 1914–1919* (Edinburgh, 1925), vol. 2, 102.

6 *Off. Hist.*, 1.352–3.

7 Nogales, *Four Years beneath the Crescent*, 346–8.

8 NZNL, MS Papers 6565–1, 'Brockie's Chronicles' (the recollections of Walter Box Brockie, 4th King's Own Scottish Borderers); Brockie survived the Gaza hospital, and was sent as a prisoner of war to Damascus and Aleppo.

9 C. Ponsonby, *West Kent (QO) Yeomanry and 10th (Yeomanry) Batt., The Buffs, 1914–1919* (London, 1920), 44.

10 *Off. Hist.*, 1.351.

11 AWM PR 00535, Papers of Sir Harry Chauvel, Letters to his wife, 26 April 1917.

12 For an account, cf. L. L. Robson, *The First AIF: A Study of its Recruitment, 1914–1918* (Melbourne, 1982). To one from Britain the local war memorials in Australian towns and villages are at first sight bemusing: they have huge lists of names. In Britain only the dead are so commemorated, and so the Australian casualties seem staggering. It is only when one knows of the conscription crisis that one realizes that the names are those of men who *enlisted*, and that the dead are marked out, usually with crosses. Clearly the memorials were erected by those who volunteered. But to have such a memorial visible to every man as a reminder of the divisive nature of the politics of war was to be a poisonous legacy for the next twenty years.

13 AWM PR 00535, Papers of Sir Harry Chauvel, letters to his wife, 12 May 1917.

14 TNA WO 106/721, Robertson to War Cabinet, 23 April 1917.

15 *New DNB*, Sir Archibald Murray.

16 For a clear discussion of these battles see R. Neillands, *The Great War Generals on the Western Front, 1914–1918* (London, 1998), 325–62.

17 E. Kedourie, *England and the Middle East: The Destruction of the Ottoman Empire, 1914–21* (Hassocks, Sussex, 1978), ch. 2; Fromkin, *The Peace to End All Peace*, part 3.

18 M. Kent, *Oil and Empire: British Policy and Mesopotamian Oil, 1900–1920* (London, 1976); Fromkin, *Peace to End All Peace*. These agreements have been the subject of much discussion and feature in almost every book concerning the War and the Middle East.

19 See the maps reproduced in J. Fisher, *Curzon and British Imperialism in the Middle East, 1916–1919* (London, 1999).

20 Fromkin, *The Peace to End All Peace*, ch. 23; Kedourie, *In the Anglo-Arab Labyrinth*.

21 Printed in Fisher, *Curzon and British Imperialism*, app. 3, 305–6.

22 See the account in *Off. Hist.*, 1.225–41.

23 C. M. Andrew and A. G. Kanya-Forstner, *France Overseas: The Climax of French Imperial Expansion, 1914–1924* (Stanford, CA, 1981), 110–13.

24 *Off. Hist.*, 1.358.

25 Raleigh and Jones, *War in the Air*.

26 Y. Sheffy, *British Military Intelligence in the Palestine Campaign, 1914–1918* (London, 1998), 69–73.

27 This mosaic is now on display at the AWM.

28 *Off. Hist.*, 1.356; Sheffy, *British Military Intelligence in the Palestine Campaign*, 263–6.

29 W. P. Pink, 'Meissner Pasha and the construction of railways in Palestine and neighbouring countries', in *Ottoman Palestine, 1800–1914: Studies in Economic and Social History*, ed. G. G. Gilbar (London, 1990), 179–218.

30 Y. Sheffy, 'The origins of the British breakthrough into South Palestine: the ANZAC Raid on the Ottoman Railway, 1917', *Journal of Strategic Studies* 22 (1999): 124–47.

31 Pink, 'Meissner Pasha and the construction of railways in Palestine'.

32 Nogales, *Four Years beneath the Crescent*, 318–26; this raid is not mentioned in *Off. Hist.*

33 Raleigh and Jones, *War in the Air*, 218.

34 *Off. Hist.*, 1.358–60 and 2.1.19–21.

35 Raleigh and Jones, *War in the Air*, 218 n.

36 Sanders, *Five Years in Turkey*, 174.

37 G. H. Bourne, *The History of the 2nd Light Horse Regiment, Australian Imperial Force, August 1914 – April 1918* (Tamworth, NSW, [1926]), 45; the same raid is discussed by Broinowski, *Tasmania's War Record*, 148, who describes the 'two regiments' as 'two squadrons' – a much more likely force.

38 Several of these are detailed in Sanders, *Five Years in Turkey*, 175–7.

39 Sheffy, *British Military Intelligence in the Palestine Campaign*, 153.

40 He ended his life attempting to put these ideas into practice by rousing the Turks of Central Asia against the Bolsheviks who were intent on reconquering the area; cf. P. Hopkirk, *Setting the East Ablaze* (Oxford, 1984), 154–71.

41 I. Orga, *Phoenix Ascendant: The Rise of Modern Turkey* (London, 1958), 59–60; Djemal Pasha, *Memories of a Turkish Statesman*, 183–5; *Off. Hist.*, 2.1.4–7.

42 Fromkin, *The Peace to end All Peace*, 214–15; P. G. Weber, *Eagles on the Crescent: Germany, Austria, and the Diplomacy of the Turkish Alliance, 1914–1918* (Ithaca, NY, 1970), 107–8 and 153–4.

43 Djemal, *Memories of a Turkish Statesman*, 183–4.

44 Kedourie, *England and the Middle East*, 62–4.

45 E. D. Akarli, *The Long Peace: Ottoman Lebanon, 1861–1920* (London, 1993), 133–74, D. R. Divine, *Politics and Society in Ottoman Palestine: The Arab Struggle for Survival and Power* (Boulder, CO, 1994), 169–90.

46 C. E. Dawn, *From Ottomanism to Arabism: Essays on the Origins of Arab Nationalism* (Urbana, IL, 1973), ch. 6, an article originally published in the *Middle East Journal*, 1962.

47 Dawn, *From Ottomanism to Arabism*, chs. 5 and 6; R. Khalidi, 'Arab nationalism in Syria, the formative years, 1908–1914', in *Nationalism in a Non-national State: The Dissolution of the Ottoman Empire*, ed. W. W. Haddadd and W. Ochsenwald (Columbus, OH, 1977), 207–37; cf. also for a personal and anecdotal view, G. Lewis, 'An Ottoman officer in Palestine, 1914–1918', in *Palestine in the Late Ottoman Period: Political, Social and Economic Transformation*, ed. D. Kushner (Jerusalem, 1985), 402–15.

48 Divine, *Politics and Society in Ottoman Palestine*, 178.

49 A. Aaronsohn, *With the Turks in Palestine* (London, 1917); this is a highly coloured and possibly exaggerated account; Aaronsohn was a British agent, and his book appeared during the war, clearly aimed at rousing sympathy in Britain and the United States. For a Turkish view, see Lewis, 'An Ottoman officer in Palestine'.

50 TNA WO 106/1514, report by Director of Military Intelligence, 8 August 1917.

51 Sheffy, *British Military Intelligence in the Palestine Campaign, passim.*

52 *Off. Hist.*, 1.354–5.

53 Cf. M. Hughes, *Allenby and British Strategy in the Middle East, 1917–1919* (London, 1999), 53–4.

54 E. Wyrall, *The History of the Duke of Cornwall's Light Infantry, 1914–1919* (London, 1932), 340.

55 *Off. Hist.*, 1.358.

56 Robertson to Murray, 12 May 1917, quoted by Sheffy, 'The origins of the British breakthrough into South Palestine', 136.

57 *Off. Hist.*, 1.363–4; Powles, *New Zealanders in Sinai and Palestine*, 110–14; H. S. Gullett, *The Australian Imperial Force in Sinai and Palestine*, The Official History of Australia in the War of 1914–1918, vol. 7: (Sydney, 1937); Sheffy, 'The origins of the British breakthrough into South Palestine', 139–41.

58 Sheffy, 'The origins of the British breakthrough into South Palestine', 141, referring to the Turkish official history.

59 'C' [Cobham], *Yeomanry Cavalry of Worcestershire*, 107.

60 Pink, 'Meissner Pasha and the construction of railways in Palestine'.

61 IWM, Chetwode papers, Chetwode to Lynden-Bell, 24 May 1917.

Chapter 5: The Allenby Effect

1 TNA WO 106/721, Robertson to War Cabinet, 23 April 1917.

2 J. C. Smuts, *Memoirs*, quoted by D. Lloyd George, *War Memoirs*, vol. 4 (London, 1935), 1832.

3 Woodward, *Military Correspondence of Field Marshal Sir William Robertson*, no 142, Robertson to Admiral Jellicoe, 11 May 1917.

4 Lloyd George, *War Memoirs*, vol. 4, 1830–3.

5   L. James, *Imperial Warrior: The Life and Times of Field Marshal Viscount Allenby* (London, 1993), 106.

6   James, *Imperial Warrior*, 104–5; this antagonism is glossed over in Sir A. P. Wavell, *Allenby, a Study in Greatness: The Biography of Field-Marshall Viscount Allenby of Megiddo and Felixtowe*, vol. 1 (London, 1940), 193.

7   Wavell, *Allenby*, vol. 1, 185.

8   Lloyd George, *War Memoirs*, vol. 4, 1835; James, *Imperial Warrior*, 111–14; Wavell, *Allenby*, vol. 1, 198, points out that the Prime Minister was only one of three men who claimed to have given Allenby a copy of this book.

9   Wavell, *Allenby*, vol. 1, *passim*.

10   Lloyd George, *War Memoirs*, vol. 4, 1835; TNA CAB 23/3, War Cabinet, 5 June 1917.

11   TNA WO 106/1513, Robertson to War Cabinet, 14 July 1917.

12   Wavell, *Allenby*, vol. 1, 198.

13   *New DNB*, Viscount Allenby.

14   Wavell, *Allenby*, vol. 1, 186–7.

15   Hughes, *Allenby and British Strategy in the Middle East*, 17, quoting Shea's oral testimony in IWM.

16   Wavell, *Allenby*, vol.1, 198.

17   James, *Imperial Warrior*, 114–17.

18   IWM 86/43/2, Diary of Captain C. J. Ratcliff, 10 July 1917.

19   NZNL MS Papers 6565–1, Diary of Harold Judge, [4] July 1917.

20   Wavell, *Allenby*, vol. 1, 197.

21   Wavell, *Allenby*, vol. 1, 187.

22   G. Inchbald, *Camels and Others* (London, 1968), 66–7. (It has to be said that I can find no other description of this event in other accounts of the Camel Brigade, or biographies of Allenby; was the author elaborating?).

23   Wavell, *Allenby*, vol. 1, 187.

24   Wavell, *Allenby*, vol. 1, 197.

25   A nice account is by A. B. 'Banjo' Paterson, *Happy Dispatches* (Sydney, 1935); Paterson, by then a major, was also in Egypt in 1917, stationed at Qantara on the Canal.

26   James, *Imperial Warrior*, 116.

27   A. T. Q. Stewart, *The Ulster Crisis* (London, 1967), 168–72, for a brief account.

28   *New DNB*, Sir Philip Chetwode; James, *Imperial Warrior*, 51–4.

29   IWM, Chetwode Papers; the document is printed in full in W. C. Garsia, *A Key to Victory: A Study in War Planning* (London, 1940), app. C, and summarized in *Off. Hist.*, 2.1.7–14.

30   TNA, WO 106/721, Allenby to Robertson, 12 July 1917, summarized in *Off. Hist.*, 2.1.14–16.

31   A. P. Wavell (ed.), *Other Men's Flowers: An Anthology of Poetry* (Harmondsworth, 1960), 336; James, *Imperial Warrior*, 126–8.

32 Lloyd George, *War Memoirs*, vol.4, 1836.

33 TNA WO 106/718, 123–30, Wavell to Director of Military Operations.

34 Sanders, *Five Years in Turkey*, 178–81; *Off. Hist.*, 2.1.4–7 and 42–3.

35 Djemal, *Memories of a Turkish Statesman*, 183–5.

36 *Off. Hist.*, 2.1.42–3.

37 Djemal, *Memories of a Turkish Statesman*, 192–3; Orga, *Phoenix Ascendant*, 60–3; Nogales, *Four Years beneath the Crescent*, 386–7.

38 J. M. Findlay, *With the 8th Scottish Rifles, 1914–1919* (London, 1926), 104.

39 C. C. R. Murphy, *History of the Suffolk Regiment, 1914–1927* (London, 1928), 208.

40 Gladstone, *The Shropshire Yeomanry*, 220.

41 Ward, *History of the 53rd (Welsh) Division*, 115.

42 James, *Imperial Warrior*, 123.

43 R. J. H. Shaw (ed.), *The 23rd London Regiment, 1798–1919* (London, 1936), 110–11.

44 Findlay, *With the 8th Scottish Rifles*, 103.

45 Ward, *History of the 53rd (Welsh) Division*, 116.

46 Woodward, *Military Correspondence of Field Marshal Sir William Robertson*, no 174, Robertson to Allenby, 5 October 1917.

47 TNA WO 106/313, Allenby to Robertson, 9 October 1917.

48 Falls in *Off. Hist.*, 2.1.26–7 assumed that the reinforcements were actually intended to be sent, but that the scheme was then abandoned; D. R. Woodward, *Field Marshal Sir William Robertson, Chief of the Imperial General Staff in the Great War* (Westport, CT, 1998), 161–2, emphasized the private nature of much of the correspondence, and that Robertson's bureaucratic campaign in London was self–defeating since the War Cabinet gradually lost confidence in his argument. How much of this Allenby appreciated is unclear – probably he knew full well what was going on – but it is obvious his estimate of an extra thirteen divisions was never going to be met, and he knew it. James, *Imperial Warrior*, ignores this matter.

49 Sheffy, *British Military Intelligence in the Palestine Campaign*, 269–73; R. Meinertzhagen, *Army Diary, 1899–1926* (London, 1960), 224–5; H. V. F. Winstone, *The Illicit Adventure: The Story of Political and Military Intelligence in the Middle East from 1898 to 1926* (London, 1982); A. Engle, *The NILI Spies* (London, 1959). It is important not to overestimate the contribution of the Jewish agents: they were just one of several sources of information available to the British.

50 An example is in 'C' [Cobham], *Yeomanry Cavalry*, 109–10.

51 Lewis, 'An Ottoman officer in Palestine'.

52 Nogales, *Four Years beneath the Crescent*, 351–3.

53 Meinertzhagen, *Army Diary*, 216.

54 Engle, *The NILI Spies*.

55 *Off. Hist.*, 2.1.239–41; T. E. Lawrence, *Seven Pillars of Wisdom: A Triumph*, 5th edn (London, 1976), book 4, esp. 234–8.

56 Lawrence, *Seven Pillars of Wisdom*, 258–62; Wavell, *Allenby*, vol. 1, 193.

57 Raleigh and Jones, *War in the Air*, 225–35.

58 Meinertzhagen, *Army Diary*, 214–15; Raleigh and Jones, *War in the Air*, 232–3.

59 Ward, *History of the 53rd (Welsh) Division*, 114.

60 AWM MSS 0862, Nikolajsen, 'Ottoman aviation', 185.

61 TNA WO 33/935, 8317; James, *Imperial Warrior*, 132.

62 Quoted in James, *Imperial Warrior*, 131.

63 The orders are printed as app. 7 in *Off. Hist.*, 2.2.676–80; the orders for the three corps follow at 680–90.

64 James, *Imperial Warrior*, 132.

65 James, *Imperial Warrior*, 131; neither Lawrence's nor Newcombe's intentions are included in the discussion of the plan of attack in *Off. Hist.*, 2.1.25–7.

66 A. Wavell, *The Palestine Campaigns* (London, 1930), 107.

67 TNA WO 106/718, 193, Allenby to Robertson, 26 July 1917.

68 R. W. H. W. Williams Wynn and H. N. Stable, *Historical Records of the Montgomeryshire Yeomanry*, vol. 2 (Oswestry, 1926).

69 *Yildirim*, part 1, ch. 4.

70 AWM MSS 0862, Nikolajsen, 'Ottoman aviation', 185.

71 TNA WO 106/155, correspondence regarding a project for a landing.

72 *Yildirim*, part 1, ch. 4.

73 *Off. Hist.*, 2.1.30–2; Meinertzhagen, *Army Diary*, 222–4 and 283–6.

74 E. J. Erickson, *Ordered to Die: A History of the Ottoman Army in the First World War* (Westport, CT, 2001), 171.

75 Erickson, *Ordered to Die*, 172.

76 *Yildirim*, part 1, chap. 4.

Chapter 6: The Third Attempt at Gaza

1 *Off. Hist.*, 2.1.64–5.

2 *Off. Hist.*, 2.1.65–6; H. Newbolt, *Naval Operations*, vol. 5, History of the Great War (London, 1931), 77–9.

3 *Yildirim*, part 2, ch. 1, 2nd page.

4 Sketch 3 in *Off. Hist.*, 2.1., app., p. 51.

5 *Yildirim*, part 3, ch. 1 and part 2, ch. 4: 'From Beersheba towards the desert there was no water to be found sufficient for the needs of an army.' This was always in Turkish and German minds, and they regularly dismissed the possibility of a large attack on Beersheba from the desert side for that reason.

6 The orders are printed in *Off. Hist.*, 2.2.680–5.

7 Ward, *History of the 53rd (Welsh) Division*, 120–1; *Off. Hist.*, 2.1.38–9; *Yildirim*, part 2, ch. 3, 7th page.

8 *Off. Hist.*, 2.1.42, quoting numbers from Turkish sources.

9 A. D. Thorburn, *Amateur Gunners: The Adventures of an Amateur Soldier in*

France, Salonica and Palestine in the Royal Field Artillary (Liverpool, [1934]), 78–9.

10 *Off. Hist.*, 2.1.51 n.

11 C. H. D. Ward, *History of the 74th (Yeomanry) Division in Syria and France* (London, 1922), 88.

12 Thorburn, *Amateur Gunners*, 79–80.

13 Williams Wynn and Stable, *Historical Records of the Montgomeryshire Yeomanry*, 74.

14 *Off. Hist.*, 2.1.48–52; *Yildirim*, part 3, ch. 1, 7th page.

15 Broinowski, *Tasmania's War Record*, 151.

16 Richardson, *History of the 7th Light Horse Regiment*, 56–7.

17 Moore, *Mounted Riflemen*, 85–7; Broinowski, *Tasmania's War Record*, 151–2; J. H. Luxford, *With the Machine Gunners in France and Palestine: Official History of the New Zealand Machine Gun Corps* (Auckland, 1921), 205–26.

18 *Yildirim*, part 3, ch. 1, 8th page.

19 *Off. Hist.*, 2.1.57; a more colourful account is in James, *Imperial Warrior*, 134.

20 Wavell, *Allenby*, vol. 1, 211; cf. James, *Imperial Warrior*, 134.

21 The most detailed account of these events and of the charge is by N. C. Smith, *Men of Beersheba: A History of the 4th Light Horse Regiment, 1914–1919* (Gardendale, Vic., 1993), 118–32, full of detail but somewhat exaggerating its importance; another is by Hammond, *History of the 11th Light Horse Regiment*, 80–3; one would much prefer an account closer to the events, and one unaffected by hindsight. Hammond's account is quoted extensively by G. W. Nutting, *History of the Fourth Light Horse Brigade, Australian Imperial Forces, War 1914–1918*, ed. E. W. Hammond (Brisbane, 1953).

22 G. G. Walker, *The Honourable Artillery Company in the Great War, 1914–1919* (London, 1930), 135–6.

23 *Yildirim*, part 3, ch. 1, 8th–9th pages.

24 There is a problem of timing involved in all this. Grant, in his subsequent report (WO 95/4472, app. 6) says that his brigade began to move soon after '1600' hours. The DMC war diary says the brigade 'galloped Beersheba defences' at '1730', and entered Beersheba at '1800'. At '1805' it records that 'orders [were] received and issued to the effect that Beersheba had to be captured during the night 31st/1st November' – orders which could only have come from Allenby. And at '1610' the diary had recorded small parties of Turks being seen to leave Beersheba northwesterly. Some of these timings – '1610', '1805' – are sufficiently precise to be accepted; others are clearly rounded, and were probably estimated later. But it seems clear that Grant will have known that Beersheba was being abandoned when he received his orders; it would be likely that this knowledge spread through his troops, for he had brought a lot of his officers with him to the meeting with Hodgson and Chauvel.

25 Wavell, *The Palestine Campaigns*, 123.

26 Smith, *Men of Beersheba*, 122.

27 Smith, *Men of Beersheba*, 123–4.

28 Smith, *Men of Beersheba*, 124–5, suggests that it was the death of a popular lieutenant, Ben Meredith, which angered the Australian troopers; in fact, they were probably just fighting mad. According to the various accounts quoted by Smith (124–7), the death of Meredith was caused by three different men, which suggests that its cause was really unknown.

29 Smith, *Men of Beersheba*, 129.

30 Smith, *Men of Beersheba*, 126–7.

31 *Off. Hist.*, 2.1.59.

32 *Yildirim*, part 3, ch. 1, 9th page.

33 *Off. Hist.*, 2.1.50–1.

34 *Off. Hist.*, 2.1.52 and 60.

35 AWM PR 00053, Diary of Sargeant H. Langtip, 31 October.

36 AWM PR 91/053, Diary of Trooper S. Broome, 31 October.

37 AWM PR 00613, Diary of Trooper W. E. Smyth, written up on 26 April 1918, an entry covering the whole of the previous year: the elapsed time will have given perspective to the events at Beersheba.

38 *Off. Hist.*, 2.1.59.

39 *Yildirim*, part 3, ch. 1, 9th page.

40 TNA, WO 161/65, Report of Water Supply to the Army, 1914–1918, 49–51.

41 *Advance* – [Anon.], *A Brief Record of the Advance of the Egyptian Expeditionary Force* (London, 1919), plate 7 (situation at 2/11/17).

42 I have argued this in my article 'Subtlety, misdirection and deceit: Allenby's grand tactics at Third Gaza', *Royal United Services Institute Journal* 140 (1995): 58–62, though I have changed my views somewhat since then. I still reject the interpretation imposed by the early historians, Wavell, Bowman-Manifold, and Falls.

43 *Off. Hist.*, 2.2, apps. 7 and 11 (XXI Corps orders).

44 *Off. Hist.*, 2.1.67.

45 So claimed Falls, *Off. Hist.*, 2.1.65, n.2. Yet von Kressenstein commented that the bombardment had less effect than the British expected – that was the case on the Somme as well, of course. The resistance of the Turks, and their alertness on the night of the attack suggest that von Kressenstein was correct.

46 *Off. Hist.*, 2.1.66; Newbolt, *Naval Operations*, vol. 5, 79.

47 *Off. Hist.*, 2.1.6–68; Findlay, *With the 8th Scottish Rifles*, 106–7.

48 Gibbons, *With the 1/5th Essex in the East*, 96–8.

49 Petre, *The History of the Norfolk Regiment*, vol. 2, 150–1; C. T. Atkinson, *The Hampshire Regiment*, vol. 2: *1914–1919* (Glasgow, 1952), 296–8; Murphy, *The History of the Suffolk Regiment*, 209–10.

50 The XXI Corps war diary records that 'under GHQ instructions ISC Brigade

moved to vicinity Tell el Jemmi' during 4 November (TNA W 95/4479). 'GHQ instructions' came, of course, from Allenby.

51 Petre, *The History of the Norfolk Regiment*, vol. 2, 151.

52 [Anon], *The Northamptonshire Regiment*, 335.

53 *Yildirim*, part 3, ch. 3, 11th page.

54 *Off. Hist.*, 2.1.73; this is no actually noticed in *Yildirim*.

55 *Off. Hist.*, 2.1.73.

56 *Off. Hist.*, 2.1.74.

57 *Yildirim*, part 3, ch. 3, 9th page.

Chapter 7: The Turkish Lines Broken

1 *Yildirim*, part 3, ch. 3, 9th page; the 'Egyptian colonel' was, of course, Newcombe.

2 *Yildirim*, part 3, ch. 3, 22nd page.

3 Ward, *History of the 53rd (Welsh) Division*, 128, quoting Captain Le Fleming.

4 Ward, *History of the 53rd (Welsh) Division*, 126.

5 Dispositions shown in [Anon.], *A Brief Record of the Advance of the Egyptian Expeditionary Force*, plate 7.

6 *Off. Hist.*, 2.1.73; Ward, *History of the 53rd (Welsh) Division*, 128–31.

7 *Off. Hist.*, 2.1.88.

8 *Yildirim*, part 3, ch. 1, 19th page, and, for the translation problem, 17th page.

9 *Off. Hist.*, 2.1.73–4.

10 *Off. Hist.*, 2.1.74; not mentioned in *Yildirim*.

11 *Yildirim*, part 3, ch. 3, 8th to 21st pages.

12 *Off. Hist.*, 2.1.106.

13 *Yildirim*, part 3, ch. 3, 21st and 22nd pages.

14 *Off. Hist.*, 2.1, 88–9; Ward, *History of the 53rd (Welsh) Division*, 131–3.

15 R. C. Boyle, *A Record of the West Somerset Yeomanry, 1914–1919* (London, [1922]), 112–13.

16 H. I. P. Edwards, *The Sussex Yeomanry and 16th (Sussex Yeomanry) Battalion, Royal Sussex Regiment, 1914–1919* (London, [1921]), 102.

17 W. S. Brownlie, *The Proud Trooper: The History of the Ayrshire (Earl of Carrick's Own) Yeomanry from its Raising in the Eighteenth Century till 1964* (London, 1964), 298.

18 Edwards, *Sussex Yeomanry*, 105.

19 Ward, *History of the 74th (Yeomanry) Division*, 97–101.

20 J. H. Lindsay, *The London Scottish in the Great War* (London, 1925), 278, quoting an edition of the *Gazette* of July 1918.

21 [Anon], *The Prince of Wales' Own Civil Service Rifles* (London, 1921), 301–2.

22 O. F. Bailey and H. M. Hollier, *'The Kensingtons', 13th London Regiment* ([London, 1936]), 293–5; this was published for the Old Comrades Association, the two authors having been sergeants in the regiment.

23 *Yildirim*, Part 3, Ch. 3, 16th page; P. H. Dalbiac, *History of the 60th Division (2/2nd London Division)* (London, 1927), 127–9.

24 Dalbiac, *History of the 60th Division*, 129.

25 Parfitt, *Historical Records of the Herefordshire Light Infantry*, 103–4.

26 Ward, *History of the 53rd (Welsh) Division*, 133–5.

27 Langley, *Sand, Sweat and Camels*, paperback edn, 101–2.

28 *Off. Hist.*, 2.1.104–5.

29 *Off. Hist.*, 2.1.74–5, 107, 111.

30 *Off. Hist.*, 2.2, app. 13, Desert Mounted Corps orders.

31 *Yildirim*, part 3, ch. 3, 25th page.

32 *Yildirim*, part 3, ch. 3, 26th page.

33 W. Trimble, *The Story of the 6th Service Battalion of the Inniskilling Fusiliers* (Enniskillen, [1919]), 33.

34 R. M. P. Preston, *The Desert Mounted Corps: An Account of the Cavalry Operations in Palestine and Syria, 1917–1918* (London, 1921), 43.

35 M. Cunliffe, *The Royal Irish Fusiliers, 1793–1950* (Oxford, 1952), 336.

36 Shaw, *The 23rd London Regiment*, 120–1.

37 *Off. Hist.*, 2.1.108–9.

38 Dalbiac, *History of the 60th Division*, 130.

39 *Off. Hist.*, 2.1.74–6.

Chapter 8: The Drive North

1 *Off. Hist.*, 2.1.75.

2 A good description is in R. Coldicott, *London Men in Palestine, and How they Marched to Jerusalem* (London, 1919), 37–40; *Off. Hist.*, 2.1.75.

3 AWM 3 DRL 6595, Diary of Sargeant L. S. Harder, 9 November 1917.

4 Hughes, *Allenby and British Strategy in the Middle East*, 49–50.

5 R. Storrs, *Orientations* (London, 1937), 290.

6 *Off. Hist.*, 2.1.130.

7 [Anon.], *The Fifth Battalion, Highland Light Infantry*, 169–71.

8 *Off. Hist.*, 2.1.132–3.

9 Dispositions are shown in [Anon.], *A Brief Record of the Advance of the Egyptian Expeditionary Force*, plate 9.

10 *Off. Hist.*, 2.2.693, Desert Mounted Corps operation order 6 November.

11 L. C. Wilson and H. Wetherell, *History of the Fifth Light Horse Regiment, Australian Imperial Force, 1914–1919* (Sydney, 1926), 129; Richardson, *History of the 7th Light Horse Regiment*, 60–61.

12 Preston, *The Desert Mounted Corps*, 45.

13 Hammond, *History of the 11th Light Horse Regiment*, 87–93; Dalbiac, *History of the 60th Division*, 132.

14 *Off. Hist.*, 2.1.113–14.

15 Bailey and Hollier, '*The Kensingtons*', 299–300.

16 Richardson, *History of the 7th Light Horse Regiment*, 61–2, is the only regimental history among the Australians to say much on this; others breeze through the day as though nothing more had happened than a comfortable ride through the countryside.

17 *Off. Hist.*, 2.1.137.

18 *Yildirim*, part 3, ch. 4, 2nd–4th pages.

19 Raleigh and Jones, *War in the Air*, 240–1.

20 AWM MSS 0862, Nikolajsen 'Ottoman aviation', 187, however, reports the destruction of one aircraft, and damage to four others. It was normal for patrols to overestimate the success of their raids.

21 Raleigh and Jones, *War in the Air*, 241–3.

22 *Off. Hist.*, 2.1.129–32; [Anon.], *The Fifth Battalion, Highland Light Infantry*, 172–5; Gillon, *The KOSB in the Great War*, 272–3.

23 *Off. Hist.*, 2.1.137.

24 *Off. Hist.*, 2.1.141 (reporting von Kressenstein's account, which is ignored in the main text).

25 *Off. Hist.*, 2.1.119.

26 IWM 84/55/1A, letter of Lieutenant A. C. Alan-Williams, 14 November 1917, written in hospital in Alexandria.

27 *Off. Hist.*, 2.1, 119–24; H. A. Adderley, *The Warwickshire Yeomanry in the Great War* (Warwick, [1922]), 123–30; 'C' [Cobham], *Yeomanry Cavalry of Worcestershire*, 128–33; cf. also Teichman, *Diary of a Yeomanry MO*, 182–6; Marquess of Anglesey, *A History of the British Cavalry, 1816–1919*, vol. 5: *1914–1919, Egypt, Palestine, and Syria* (London, 1994), 180–2.

28 *Yildirim*, part 3, ch. 4.

29 *Off. Hist.*, 2.1.127.

30 Dispositions in [Anon.], *A Brief Record of the Advance of the Egyptian Expeditionary Force*, plate 11.

31 Ewing, *Royal Scots*, vol. 2, 520.

32 *Off. Hist.*, 2.1.141, quoting von Kressenstein's account.

33 G. L. Berrie, *Under Furred Hats* (Sydney, 1919), 113–14; Broinowski, *Tasmania's War Record*, 152–3; Richardson, *History of the 7th Light Horse Regiment*, 62–3.

34 AWM 3 DRL 6595, Diary of Sergeant L. S. Harder, 9 November.

35 *Off. Hist.*, 2.1.142–4.

36 Wavell, *The Palestine Campaigns*, 150.

37 *Off. Hist.*, 2.1.140.

38 *Off. Hist.*, 2.1.144–5; the regimental histories scarcely mention this fight.

39 The line is marked in [Anon.], *A Brief Record of the Advance of the Egyptian Expeditionary Force*, plate 12, as 'rearguards' (10 November), and on plate 13 as a 'freshly dug and incomplete' line (11 November).

40 *Yildirim*, quoted in *Off. Hist.*, 2.1.155.

41 *Off. Hist.*, 2.1.152–4; Ewing, *Royal Scots*, 520–5 (Major Ewing himself commanded in this action); Findlay, *With the 8th Scottish Rifles*, 114–16. Also involved were some yeomanry who scouted the position and guarded the right flank of the Royal Scots, and a troop of Australian Light Horse who joined in for the fun of it and were nearly shot by the Cameronians in mistake for Turks.

42 Adderley, *Warwickshire Yeomanry in the Great War*, 144; 'C' [Cobham], *Yeomanry Cavalry of Worcestershire*, 140–3; Fox, *History of the Royal Gloucestershire Hussars Yeomanry*, 178–81; Walker, *Honourable Artillery Company in the Great War*, 226–9; Hammond, *History of the 11th Light Horse Regiment*, 95–6; T. M. Darley, *With the Ninth Light Horse in the Great War* (Adelaide, 1924), 106–7; Nutting, *History of the Fourth Light Horse Brigade*, 33.

43 Gillon, *The KOSB in the Great War*, 274–5; Brown, *War Record of the 4th Battalion, King's Own Scottish Borderers*, 105–6.

44 H. O. Lock, *History of the Fifth Battalion*, History of the Dorsetshire Regiment, 1914–1919 (Dorchester, 1932), 89; C. T. Atkinson (comp.), *The Devonshire Regiment, 1914–1918* (Exeter and London, 1926), 299–300; G. Blick, *The 1/4th Battalion, The Wiltshire Regiment, 1914–1919* (Frome, 1933), 77–9. None of the British regimental histories have anything to say about the 58th Rifles' exploit, which is in *Off. Hist.*, 2.1.161–2.

45 Brown, *War Record of the 4th Battalion, King's Own Scottish Borderers*, 106; Gillon, *The KOSB in the Great War*, 275–7; J. C. Swann, *The Citizen Soldiers of Buckinghamshire, 1795–1926* (Aylesbury, 1930), 69–71. The divisional commanders arranged between them that the cavalry would attack to assist the Scots, but even as they were discussing the arrangements, the Buckinghamshire Yeomanry put in its attack: *Off. Hist.*, 2.1.166; Sir G. de S. Barrow, *The Fire of Life* (London, [1942]), 168–9; Anglesey, *History of the British Cavalry*, vol. 5, 191–8.

46 *Off. Hist.*, 2.1.170–1; Kemp, *The Staffordshire Yeomanry*, 49–50.

47 C. Stonham and B. Freeman, *Historical Records of the Middlesex Yeomanry, 1797–1927*, ed. J. S. Judd (Chelsea, 1930), 180.

48 Dispositions on 13 November are shown in [Anon.], *A Brief Record of the Advance of the Egyptian Expeditionary Force*, plate 14.

49 *Off. Hist.*, 2.1.162–3.

50 *Off. Hist.*, 2.1.163.

51 *Off. Hist.*, 2.1.164 and 174.

52 Moore, *Mounted Riflemen*, 88–90; Nicol, *Story of Two Campaigns*, 162–6; Luxford, *With the Machine Gunners in France and Palestine*, 208–11; *Off. Hist.*, 2.1.176–8.

53 Moore, *Mounted Riflemen*, 94–5.

54 C. W. Thompson, *Records of the Dorset Yeomanry (Queen's Own), 1914–1919* (Sherborne, 1921), 87–9; Swann, *Citizen Soldiers of Buckinghamshire*, 71–2.

Chapter 9: The Hills of Judaea

1 AWM 1DRL 0373, Notebooks of Trooper I. L. Idriess, vol. 8, 16 November 1917. This was rewritten for publication, rather altering the sense, in *Desert Column*, 278.

2 AWM PRO 0991, Diary of Trooper W. R. Burchill, 14 November 1917.

3 NZNL, MS Papers, 6565 – 1, 'Brockie's Chronicles'.

4 A. C. N. Olden, *Westralian Cavalry in the War: The Story of the 10th Light Horse Regiment AIF in the Great War, 1914–1918* (Melbourne 1921), 183–7.

5 AWM PRO 0535, Chauvel to his wife, 17 November 1917.

6 AWM 1 DRL 0373, Notebook of Idriess, vol. 8; cf. Idriess, *Desert Column*, 278–9.

7 AWM PRO 0535, Chauvel to his wife, 19 and 26 November 1917.

8 L. Stein, *The Balfour Declaration* (London, 1961); the letter is published frequently, as for example in C. H Sykes, *Cross Roads to Israel* (London, 1965), 11, and summarized in every book on the modern Middle East.

9 Fromkin, *The Peace to End All Peace*, chs. 33 and 34; E. Monroe, *Britain's Moment in the Middle East, 1914–1956* (London, 1963), ch. 1.

10 Andrew and Kanya-Forstner, *France Overseas*, 151. General Bailloud was tactful; he was also unwilling to allow such doubtful troops to be put into the front line; privately the British did not like the look of the French and were brutally contemptuous of the Italians.

11 Andrew and Kanya-Forstner, *France Overseas*, 152–3.

12 Lawrence, *Seven Pillars of Wisdom*, book 6.

13 I. Friedman, *The Question of Palestine, 1914–1918: British–Jewish–Arab Relations* (London, 1973), ch. 6.

14 Fromkin, *The Peace to End All Peace*, 297–9.

15 Swann, *Citizen Soldiers of Buckinghamshire*, 70–2; neither of these is mentioned in S. Schama, *Two Rothschilds and the Land of Israel* (London, 1978), which seems extraordinary.

16 *Off. Hist.*, 2.1.183.

17 C. Falls, 'Falkenhayn in Syria', *Edinburgh Review* 250 (1929), 284.

18 Meinertzhagen, *Army Diary*, 214–15.

19 XXI Corps order no. 14, 18 November 1917, published in *Off. Hist.*, 2.2.696–7 (app. 6).

20 Noted by Wavell, *Allenby*, vol. 1, 223, though, having been sent on 11 November, it had no special relevance to the attack towards Jerusalem.

21 Dispositions shown in [Anon.], *A Brief Record of the Advance of the Egyptian Expeditionary Force*, plate 17.

22 XXI Corps order no. 14 (note 19).

23 *Off. Hist.*, 2.1.183, noting the absence of comment in *Yildirim*.

24 *Off. Hist.*, 2.1.154–5, 182–3, 217, based on *Yildirim*.

25 J. E. Wright, *Round about Jerusalem: Letters from the Holy Land* (London, 1918), 127–8.

26 A good description is S. F. Hatton, *The Yarn of a Yeoman* (London, [1930]), 183–5.
27 Lock, *History of the Fourth Battalion*, 95.
28 Kemp, *The Staffordshire Yeomanry*, 53–5.
29 Barrow, *Fire of Life*, 173–7.
30 Barrow, *Fire of Life*, 17.
31 Kemp, *The Staffordshire Yeomanry*, 54.
32 [Anon.], *The Fifth Battalion, Highland Light Infantry*.
33 *Off. Hist.*, 2.1.193–4.
34 Thompson, *Fifty-Second (Lowland) Division*, 439.
35 *Off. Hist.*, 2.1.184–5; G. E. Badcock, *A History of the Transport Services of the Egyptian Expeditionary Force, 1916–1917–1918* (London, 1925).
36 *Off. Hist.*, 2.1.199–200; Barrow, *Fire of Life*, 177–8.
37 Thompson, *Fifty-Second (Lowland) Division*, 441.
38 *Off. Hist.*, 2.1.198; Wyrall, *History of the Duke of Cornwall's Light Infantry*, 347–8.
39 Wyrall, *History of the Duke of Cornwall's Light Infantry*, 349–50.
40 Findlay, *With the 8th Scottish Rifles*, 127.
41 Blick, *The 1/4th Battalion, The Wiltshire Regiment*, 82–4; Atkinson, *Devonshire Regiment*, 303–5.
42 *Off. Hist.*, 2.1.208.
43 Ewing, *Royal Scots*, 530–3.
44 [Anon.], *The Fifth Battalion, Highland Light Infantry*, 180–1.
45 Brown, *War Record of the 4th Battalion, King's Own Scottish Borderers*, 111; Gillon, *The KOSB in the Great War*, 279–81.
46 *Off. Hist.*, 2.1.211–12.
47 Nicol, *Story of Two Campaigns*, 168–71; Luxford, *With the Machine Gunners in France and Palestine*, 212–14; Moore, *Mounted Riflemen*, 95–6; Powles, *History of the Canterbury Mounted Rifles*, 179–81; Gibbons, *With the 1/5th Essex in the East*, 109.
48 *Off. Hist.*, 2.1.217.
49 *Off. Hist.*, 2.1.218–19.
50 [Anon.], *The Northamptonshire Regiment*, 336–7; a better account is in *Off. Hist.*, 2.1.221–3.
51 Dalbiac, *History of the 60th Division*, 148–50; F. W. Eames, *The Second Nineteenth: Being the History of the 2/19th London Regiment* (London, 1930), 88–92.
52 Barrow, *Fire of Life*, 180–82.
53 G. Fellows and B. Freeman, *Historical Records of the South Nottinghamshire Hussars Yeomanry, 1794–1924* (Aldershot, 1928), 260–2; H. Tallents, *The Sherwood Rangers Yeomanry in the Great War, 1914–1918* (London, 1926), 126–34; [Anon.], *Through Palestine with the Twentieth Machine Gun Squadron* (London, [1920]), 48–60; Barrow, *Fire of Life*, 182–4.
54 Barrow, *Fire of Life*, 184–5.
55 Thompson, *Fifty-Second (Lowland) Division*, 471.

Chapter 10: Jerusalem for Christmas

1 *Off. Hist.*, 2.1.292.
2 TNA WO 106/722, Appreciation of the Situation in Palestine, 8 April 1918.
3 TNA WO 106/1516, Memorandum on the Situation in Turkey.
4 *Off. Hist.*, 2.1.293.
5 The titles of two books give the flavour though there are several more of the same type: V. Gilbert, *The Romance of the Last Crusade: With Allenby to Jerusalem* (New York, 1923), and C. Sommers, *Temporary Crusaders* (London, 1919); but even three generations of trouble in the 'Holy Land' did not prevent A. Bruce from calling his book *The Last Crusade: The Palestine Campaign in the First World War* (London, 2002). It is doubtful if the ordinary soldiers thought of themselves a crusaders; journalists liked the idea, though.
6 Divine, *Politics and Society in Ottoman Palestine*, 177, quoting Jamal Pasha quoting a Jewish resident of Jaffa.
7 Winstone, *The Illicit Adventure*, 293–4.
8 TNA, WO 33/946, 8583–5, 8693.
9 Kedourie, *England and the Middle East*.
10 *Off. Hist.*, 2.2.698–9 (app. 17), XX Corps Order 17, 5 December 1917.
11 Ward, *History of the 53rd (Welsh) Division*, 144.
12 *Off. Hist.*, 2.1.238–9.
13 *Off. Hist.*, 2.1.239, n. 2.
14 Ward, *History of the 53rd (Welsh) Division*, 148.
15 Ward, *History of the 53rd (Welsh) Division*, 148–51.
16 Ward, *History of the 53rd (Welsh) Division*, 151.
17 *Off. Hist.*, 2.1.250–1; Ward, *History of the 53rd (Welsh) Division*, 152–4, emphasizes the adverse weather conditions.
18 Bailey and Hollier, *The 'Kensingtons'*, 310–12.
19 Bailey and Hollier, *The 'Kensingtons'*, 312.
20 Lindsay, *The London Scottish in the Great War*, 293–6.
21 Dalbiac, *History of the 60th Division*, 156–8.
22 Dalbiac, *History of the 60th Division*, 159.
23 *Off. Hist.*, 2.1.248.
24 Petre, *The History of the Norfolk Regiment*, vol. 2, 316–17.
25 Dalbiac, *History of the 60th Division*, 160.
26 Ward, *History of the 53rd (Welsh) Division*, 152–5, quoting Mott's report; also *Off. Hist.*, 2.1.250–51.
27 Ward, *History of the 53rd (Welsh) Division*, 155–6.
28 *Off. Hist.*, 2.1.254–6; M. Gilbert, *Jerusalem in the Twentieth Century* (London, 1996), 49–51.
29 *Off. Hist.*, 2.1.252–4; Dalbiac, *History of the 60th Division*, 63.
30 Olden, *Westralian Cavalry in the War*, 190–1.
31 Ward, *History of the 53rd (Welsh) Division*, 158.

32 Ward, *History of the 53rd (Welsh) Division*, 158, 160.

33 Ward, *History of the 74th (Yeomanry) Division*, 135–6; Dalbiac, *History of the 60th Division*, 160–2; Olden, *Westralian Cavalry in the War*, 191–2.

34 *Off. Hist.*, 2.1.259–61; Wavell, *Allenby*, vol. 1, 230–3 (quoting Allenby's own account, in a letter to his wife); James, *Imperial Warrior*, 140–2; Gilbert, *Jerusalem in the Twentieth Century*, 54–5; Lawrence, *Seven Pillars of Wisdom*, 358.

35 Wavell, *Allenby*, vol. 1, 236; a more romantic account is in Lawrence, *Seven Pillars of Wisdom*, 360.

36 AWM PR 84/193, letters of Major-General Ryrie, 16 December 1917, written from Esdud (Ashdod).

37 Olden, *Westralian Cavalry in the War*, 189.

38 Olden, *Westralian Cavalry in the War*, 190–1, perhaps reflecting contemporary European perceptions of Jews, insists that the Jewish inhabitants had deliberately hoarded flour so as to be able to sell bread and cakes to the approaching British troops!

39 *Hansard*, 5th series, C(1917), 875.

40 See the press summary in James, *Imperial Warrior*, 143.

41 TNA WO 106/722, Appreciation of the Situation in Palestine, 8 April 1918, and associated correspondence.

42 *Off. Hist.*, 2.1.213.

43 Wavell, *Allenby*, vol. 1, 230 n.

44 Lawrence, *Seven Pillars of Wisdom*, 360.

45 *Off. Hist.*, 2.1.268.

46 *Off. Hist.*, 2.1.265.

47 *Off. Hist.*, 2.1.267–8.

48 Findlay, *With the 8th Scottish Rifles*, 136–7.

49 *Off. Hist.*, 2.1.270–3; Findlay, *With the 8th Scottish Rifles*, 138–9; Thompson, *Fifty-Second (Lowland) Division*, 487–96; Brown, *War Record of the 4th Battalion, King's Own Scottish Borderers*, 113–16; Gillon, *The KOSB in the Great War*, 285–6; [Anon.], *The Fifth Battalion Highland Light Infantry in the War, 1914–1918* (Glasgow, 1921), 189–91.

50 *Off. Hist.*, 2.1.274–5.

51 *Yildirim*, part 4, ch. 5, 3rd page.

52 *Off. Hist.*, 2.1.278; *Yildirim*, part 4, ch.5, 4th page.

53 *Yildirim*, part 4, ch. 5, 6th page.

54 E. Wyrall, *The Die-Hards in the Great War*, vol. 2: *1916–1918* (London, [c.1930]), 321–2.

55 *Off. Hist.*, 2.1.286–90.

Sources and Bibliography

A PARTICULAR difficulty exists with respect to the study of the Great War in Palestine. There are, of course, always difficulties with the study of any event or period in the past, in that the sources are always incomplete, often inaccurate, and invariably present a distorted view of events. All that is normal; historians get used to detecting and coping with such matters. For Palestine in 1917, however, there is a further part of the problem. It is that the story of the campaign has been set in stone from the start, which is Allenby's reports of 1917–18.

He was followed by a set of military historians, men who were usually soldiers first and historians second, who essentially reproduced the interpretation of events which Allenby had promulgated. As early as 1919 Colonel Wavell laid out this interpretation in a lecture; General Bowman-Manifold followed not long after; General Sir George Macmunn and Captain Cyril Falls used it in the *Official History*; a succession of biographers of Allenby, from Savage in 1925 to James in 1993, have scarcely dissented. Only in recent years has the orthodoxy been undermined, by examining military events in the light of politics, a dimension largely ignored by the official histories.

The effect of this orthodoxy has been to dictate to other historians how the campaign is to be described. It becomes particularly the case after the publication of the official histories in Britain, Australia and New Zealand, and it is very noticeable in the regimental histories: those published before, say, 1930 do not necessarily follow the official line; those published since do, even to the extent of quoting extensively from them. This means that the later regimental histories have to be treated with some care, and those which appeared earlier, in the 1920s, need to be examined for divergent accounts of events. Sometimes events turn up which the Official Histories ignore. And of course, this emphasizes the virtue of primary sources, even where, as with official documents, they are of little use otherwise.

The private primary documents, letters, diaries, and so on, present their own difficulties, in that they are intensely personal, and describe events – when they actually do so – in a way which emphasizes the individual experience. And they are episodic, for in a time when the ordinary soldiers were particularly busy, they had no chance to do any writing. There is a curious divergence in these personal documents. The great majority of diaries are little more than cryptic notes (as all diaries seem to be) of appointments, locations, and so on; similarly, the great majority of letters are written to personal acquaintances, family, friends, wives, sweethearts, and are more concerned with those relationships than the experiences of the soldiers. This means that the truly valuable documents are very few, and were composed by men who were self-consciously literate, even literary, in their imaginations. The vast majority of the soldiers in these events are silent.

There is even a clear variation between the different national groups. The most loquacious were the Australians and New Zealanders, whose letters are often full of the excitement of the campaign and of wonder at the experience. The British were more numerous, but less inclined to write in ways which an historian finds useful. No doubt this was in part a class matter: the Australians in particular were strongly middle-class in origin, and were all volunteers, who, by definition, were very interested in expressing their feelings and justifying their experiences. It is also probably a matter of education, in that the British – or, at least, in deference to Scots' sensibilities – the English education system was not designed to foster either imagination or observation skills. Of the other participants – Indian, Turk, Arab, Egyptian, West Indian, and so on – little or nothing remains.

I have attempted in the foregoing account to take note of these matters without burdening the text or the reader with too much historiographical discussion, an historical approach even more dry-as-dust than most. But it seemed worth pointing it out.

Sources

Collections have been examined in the Imperial War Museum, London, the Australian War Museum, Canberra, the New Zealand National Library, the New Zealand Archives, both in Wellington, the National Archives at Kew. Not every document finds its way into the detail of this account, but those which are particularly relevant are referred to in the notes.

Many of the Regimental Histories, and Divisional Histories contain extensive quotations from the primary sources.

Bibliography

[Anon.] *A Brief Record of the Advance of the Egyptian Expeditionary Force.* London, 1919.

—— *Through Palestine with the Twentieth Machine-gun Squadron.* London, [1920].

—— *The Fifth Battalion, Highland Light Infantry in the War, 1914–1918.* Glasgow, 1921.

—— *The History of the Prince of Wales' Own Civil Service Rifles.* London, 1921.

—— *The Northamptonshire Regiment, 1914–1918.* Aldershot, [1932].

—— 'Palestine reminiscences', *The Royal Air Force Quarterly* 5 (1934): 401–17.

—— *A War Record of the 21st London Regiment (1st Surrey Rifles), 1914–1919.* [London, 1927].

Aaronsohn, A. *With the Turks in Palestine.* London, 1917.

Adams, R. F. C. *The Modern Crusaders.* London, 1920.

Adderley, H. A. *The Warwickshire Yeomanry in the Great War.* Warwick, [1922].

Adelson, R. *Mark Sykes: Portrait of an Amateur.* London, 1975.

Ajay, N. 'Political intrigue and suppression in Lebanon during WWI', *International Journal of Middle East Studies* 5 (1974): 140–60.

Akarli, E. D. *The Long Peace: Ottoman Lebanon, 1861–1920.* London, 1993.

al-Sayyid, Afaf Lutfi. *Egypt and Cromer: A Study in Anglo-Egyptian Relations.* London, 1968.

Anderson, M. S. *The Eastern Question, 1774–1923.* London, 1966.

Andrew, C. M., and A. S. Kanya-Forstner. *France Overseas: The Climax of French Imperial Expansion, 1914–1924.* Stanford, CA, 1981.

Anglesey, Marquess of. *A History of the British Cavalry, 1816–1919*, vol. 5: *1914–1919, Egypt, Palestine, and Syria.* London, 1994.

Annabell, N. *Official History of the New Zealand Engineers during the Great War, 1914–1918.* Wanganui, 1927.

Antonius, G. *The Arab Awakening.* London, 1945.

Atkinson, C. T. 'General Liman von Sanders on his experiences in Palestine', *Army Quarterly* 3 (1922): 257–75.

—— *The Queen's Own Royal West Kent Regiment, 1914–1919.* London, 1924.

—— (comp.) *The Devonshire Regiment, 1914–1918.* Exeter and London, 1926.

—— *The Royal Hampshire Regiment*, vol. 2: *1914–1919.* Glasgow, 1952.

Badcock, G. E. *A History of the Transport Services of the Egyptian Expeditionary Force, 1916–1917–1918.* London, 1925.

Bailey, O. F., and H. M. Hollier. 'The Kensingtons', 13th London Regiment. [London, 1936].

Baly, L. *Horseman, Pass By: The Australian Light Horse in World War I.* East Roseville, NSW, 2003.

Barrett, J., and P. E. Deane. *The Australian Medical Corps in Egypt.* London, 1918.

Barrow, Sir G. de S. *Two Cavalry Episodes in the Palestine Campaign, 1917–1918.* London, 1937.

—— *The Fire of Life.* London, [1942].

Benn, W. *In the Side Shows: Observations of a Flyer on Five Fronts.* London, 1919.

Benson, E. F. *Crescent and Iron Cross.* London, 1918.

Berrie, G. L. *Under Furred Hats.* Sydney, 1919.

Blick, G. *The 1/4th Battalion, The Wiltshire Regiment, 1914–1919.* Frome, 1933.

Blackwell, E., and E. C. Axe. *Romford to Beirut, via France, Egypt and Jericho: An Outline of the Record of B Battery, 271st Brigade RFA.* Clacton-on-Sea, 1926.

Blake, R. *The Unknown Prime Minister: The Life and Time of Andrew Bonar Law, 1858–1923.* London, 1955.

Blaser, B. *Kilts Across the Jordan: Being Experiences and Impressions with the Second Battalion 'London Scottish' in Palestine.* London, 1926.

Blaxland, G. *The Buffs.* London, 1972.

—— *The Middlesex Regiment.* London, 1977.

Bluett, A. *With our Army in Palestine.* London, 1919.

Bostock, H. *The Great Ride: A Story of a Trooper in the Third Brigade Scout Troop.* Perth, 1982.

Bott, A. *Eastern Nights and Flights.* London, 1920.

Bourne, G. H. *The History of the 2nd Light Horse Regiment, Australian Imperial Force, August 1914 – April 1918.* Tamworth, NSW, [1926].

Bovis, H. E. *The Jerusalem Question, 1917–1968.* Stanford, CA, 1971.

Bowman-Manifold, M. G. E. *An Outline of the Egyptian and Palestine Campaigns, 1914–1918.* London, 1923.

Box, A. (ed.). *The Best Fellows Anyone Could Wish to Meet …: George Auchterlonie and the 8th Light Horse Regiment, AIF.* Melbourne, 1993.

Boyle, R. C. *A Record of the West Somerset Yeomanry, 1914–1919.* London, [1922].

Bray, N. N. E. *Shifting Sands.* London, 1934.

Bremond, E. *Le Hedjaz dans la Guerre mondiale.* Paris, 1931.

Brereton, J. *Chain Mail: The History of the Duke of Lancaster's Own Yeomanry.* Chippenham, n.d.

Broinowski, L. *Tasmania's War Record, 1914–1918.* Hobart, 1921.

Brown, W. S. *War Record of the 4th Battalion, King's Own Scottish Borderers and Lothian and Border Horse.* Galashiels, 1920.

Brownlie, W. S. *The Proud Trooper: The History of the Ayrshire (Earl of Carrick's Own) Yeomanry from its Raising in the Eighteenth Century till 1964.* London, 1964.

Bruce, A. *The Last Crusade: The Palestine Campaign in the First World War.* London, 2002.

Brugger, S. *Australians and Egypt, 1914–1919.* Melbourne, 1980.

Buchan, J. *The History of the Royal Scots Fusiliers, 1676–1918.* London, [1925].

Bullock, D. *Allenby's War: The Palestine-Arabian Campaign, 1916–1918.* London, 1988.

Burne, A. H. 'Notes on the Palestine campaign', *The Fighting Forces* 9 and 10 (1932–3) (7 sections).

'C' [Lord Cobham] *The Yeomanry Cavalry of Worcestershire, 1914–1922*. Stourbridge, 1926.

Celiker, F. 'Turkey in the First World War', *Revue Internationale d'Histoire Militaire* 46 (1980): 163–203.

Cocker, M. *Richard Meinertzhagen: Soldier, Scientist and Spy*. London, 1989.

Coldicott, R. *London Men in Palestine, and How they Marched to Jerusalem*. London, 1919.

Collins, R. J. *Lord Wavell, 1883–1941: A Military Biography*. London, 1947.

Connell, J. *Wavell: Scholar and Soldier*. London, 1964.

Cook, G. 'Sir Robert Borden, Lloyd George, and British military policy, 1917–1918', *Historical Journal* 14 (1971): 371–95.

Cotterell, P. *The Railways of Palestine and Syria*. Abingdon, 1984.

Cromer, Earl of. *Modern Egypt*, 2 vols. London, 1908.

Crookenden, A. *The History of the Cheshire Regiment in the Great War*. Chester, [c.1938].

Cunliffe, M. *The Royal Irish Fusiliers, 1793–1950*. Oxford, 1952.

Cutlack, F. M. *The Australian Flying Corps in the Western and Eastern Theatres of War, 1914–1918*. St Lucia, Queensland, 1923.

Dalbiac, P. H. *History of the 60th Division (2/2nd London Division)*. London, 1927.

Dane, E. *British Campaigns in the Nearer East, 1914–1918: From the Outbreak of the War with Turkey to the Taking of Jerusalem*. London, 1918.

Darley, T. H. *With the Ninth Light Horse in the Great War*. Adelaide, 1924.

Dawn, C. E. *From Ottomanism to Arabism: Essays on the Origins of Arab Nationalism*. Urbana, IL, 1973.

Divine, D. R. *Politics and Society in Ottoman Palestine: The Arab Struggle for Survival and Power*. Boulder, CO, 1994.

Djemal Pasha. *Memories of a Turkish Statesman*. London, 1922.

Dowson, E. 'Further notes on aeroplane photography in the Near East', *Geographical Journal* 58/5 (1921): 359–70.

Duguid, C. *The Desert Trail*. Adelaide, 1919.

Eames, F. W. *The Second Nineteenth: Being the History of the 2/19th London Regiment*. London, 1930.

Edwards, H. I. P. *The Sussex Yeomanry and 16th (Sussex Yeomanry) Battalion, Royal Sussex Regiment, 1914–1919*. London, [1921].

Elgood, P. G. *Egypt and the Army*. London, 1924.

Elliot, G. F. S. *War History of the 5th Battalion, King's Own Scottish Borderers*. Dumfries, 1928.

Elliott, W., and A. Kinross. 'Maintaining Allenby's armies: a footnote to history', *Royal Army Service Corps Quarterly* 13 (1925): 114–28.

Engle, A. *The NILI Spies*. London, 1959.

Erickson, E. J. *Ordered to Die: A History of the Ottoman Army in the First World War*. Westport, CT, 2001.

Ewing, J. *The Royal Scots, 1914–1919*, 2 vols. Edinburgh, 1925.

Falls, C. 'Falkenhayn in Syria', *Edinburgh Review* 250 (1929): 272–89.

—— *Military Operations, Egypt and Palestine*, vol. 2 (2 volumes in 3). The Official History of the War. London, 1930.

Fellows, G., and B. Freeman. *Historical Records of the South Nottinghamshire Hussars Yeomanry, 1794–1924*. Aldershot, 1928.

Findlay, J. M. *With the 8th Scottish Rifles, 1914–1919*. London, 1926.

Fischer, F. *Germany's Aims in the First World War*. London, 1967.

Fisher, J. *Curzon and British Imperialism in the Middle East, 1916–1919*. London, 1999.

Foster, W. J., J. G. Bourne, and R. Osborne. 'Operations of the mounted troops of the Egyptian Expeditionary Force', *Cavalry Journal* 11 (1921).

Fox, Sir F. *The History of the Royal Gloucestershire Hussars Yeomanry, 1898–1922*. Southampton, 1923.

Freeman, B. *The Yeomanry of Devon*. London, 1927.

French, D. *The Strategy of the Lloyd George Coalition, 1916–1918*. Oxford, 1995.

Friedman, I. *The Question of Palestine, 1914–1918: British–Jewish–Arab Relations*. London, 1973.

—— *Germany, Turkey and Zionism, 1897–1918*. Oxford, 1977.

Fromkin, D. *A Peace to End All Peace: Creating the Modern Middle East, 1914–1922*. London, 1989.

Galbraith, J., and R. Huttenbach. 'Bureaucracies at war: the British in the Middle East in the First World War', in *National and International Politics in the Middle East*, ed. E. Ingram, 102–25. London, 1986.

Gardner, B. *Allenby*. London, 1965.

Garsia, W. C. *A Key to Victory: A Study in War Planning*. London, 1940.

Gibbon, F. *The 42nd (East Lancashire) Division, 1914–1918*. London, 1920.

Gibbons, T. *With the 1/5th Essex in the East*. Colchester, 1921.

Gilbar, G. G. (ed.). *Ottoman Palestine*. London, 1990.

Gilbert, M. *Jerusalem in the Twentieth Century*. London, 1996.

Gilbert, V. *The Romance of the Last Crusade: With Allenby to Jerusalem*. New York, 1923.

Gillon, D. Z. 'Antecedents of the Balfour Declaration', *Middle Eastern Studies* 5 (1969): 131–55.

Gillon, S. *The KOSB in the Great War*. London, 1930.

Gladstone, E. W. *The Shropshire Yeomanry, MDCCXCV–MCMXLX: The Story of a Volunteer Cavalry Regiment*. Manchester, 1953.

Goodsall, R. H. *Palestine Memories, 1917–1918–1925*. Canterbury, 1925.

Grainger, J. D. 'Subtlety, misdirection and deceit: Allenby's grand tactics at Third Gaza', *Royal United Services Institute Journal* 140 (1995): 58–62.

Gullett, H. S. *The Australian Imperial Force in Sinai and Palestine*. The Official History of Australia in the War of 1914–1918, vol. 7: Sydney, 1937.

—— , C. Barrett, and D. Barker. *Australia in Palestine*. Sydney, 1919.

Gwinn, P. *British Strategy and Politics, 1914–1918*. Oxford, 1963.

Haddad, W. W., and W. Ochsenwald (eds.). *Nationalism in a Non-national State: The Dissolution of the Ottoman Empire*. Columbus, OH, 1977.

Halbern, P. *The Naval War in the Mediterranean, 1914–1918*. London, 1987.

Halton, S. F. *The Yarn of a Yeoman*. London, [1930].

Hamilton, A. S. *The City of London Yeomanry (Roughriders)*. London, 1936.

Hamilton, J. *Gallipoli to Gaza: The Desert Poets of World War One*. East Roseville, NSW, 2003.

Hammond, E. W. *History of the 11th Light Horse Regiment, Fourth Light Horse Brigade, Australian Imperial Forces, War 1914–1919*. Brisbane, 1942.

Hamshaw, T. H. 'Geographical reconnaissance by Aeroplane photography, with special reference to the work done on the Palestine front', *Geographical Journal* 55 (1920): 349–76.

Harper, G. (ed.). *Letters from the Battlefields: New Zealand Soldiers Write Home, 1914–1918*. Auckland, 2001.

Hill, A. J. *Chauvel of the Light Horse: A Biography of General Sir Harry Chauvel*. Melbourne, 1978.

Holloway, D. *Hooves, Wheels, and Tracks*. Melbourne, 1990.

Holt, P. M. *Egypt and the Fertile Crescent, 1516–1922*. London, 1966.

Hopkirk, P. *Setting the East Ablaze*. Oxford, 1984.

Hourani, A. *The Emergence of the Modern Middle East*. Berkeley, CA, 1983.

Howard, H. N. *The Partition of Turkey: A Diplomatic History, 1913–1923*. Norman, OK, 1966.

Hughes, C. E. *Above and Beyond Palestine: An Account of the Work of the East Indies and Egypt Seaplane Squadron, 1916–1918*. London, 1930.

Hughes, M. 'General Allenby and the Palestine campaign', *Journal of Strategic Studies* 19 (1996): 59–88.

—— 'Lloyd George, the generals and the Palestine campaign, 1917–1918', *Imperial War Museum Review* 11 (1997): 4–17.

—— *Allenby and British Strategy in the Middle East, 1917–1919*. London, 1999.

Hunt, B., and A. Preston. *War Aims and Strategic Policy in the Great War, 1914–1918*. London, 1977.

Hurewitz, J. C. 'The entente's secret agreements in World War I: loyalty to an obsolescing ethos', in *Palestine in the late Ottoman Period: Political, Social and Economic Transformation*, ed. D. Kushner. Jerusalem, [1986].

Idriess, I. L. *The Desert Column*. North Ryde, NSW, 1985, originally published 1928.

Inchbald, G. *Camels and Others*. London, 1968.

—— *Imperial Camel Corps*. London, 1970.

Ingrams, D. (ed.). *Palestine Papers, 1917–1922: Seeds of Conflict*. London, 1973.

Jabotinsky, V. *The Story of the Jewish Legion*. New York, 1945.

Jaehk, E. *The Rising Crescent*. New York, 1944.

James, L. *Imperial Warrior: The Life and Times of Field Marshal Viscount Allenby*. London, 1993.

Jones, I. 'Beersheba: the Light Horse charge and the making of myths', *Journal of the Australian War Memorial* 2 (1983): 26–37.

—— *The Australian Light Horse*, Australians at War. North Sydney, NSW, 1987.

Jourdain, H. N. F. *The Connaught Rangers*. London, 1928.

Kearsey, A. *The Operations in Egypt and Palestine, August 1914 – June 1917, Illustrating the Field Service Regulations*. Aldershot, 1929.

—— *A Summary of the Egypt and Palestine Campiagns with Details of the 1917–1918 Operations*. Aldershot, 1931.

Kedourie, E. *England and the Middle East: The Destruction of the Ottoman Empire, 1914–21*. London, 1956; reissued Hassocks, Sussex, 1978.

—— *The Chatham House Version and Other Studies*. London, 1970.

—— *In the Anglo-Arab Labyrinth: The MacMahon–Husayn Correspondence and its Interpreters, 1914–1939*. Cambridge, 1976.

Kemp, P. K. *The Staffordshire Yeomanry, QORR, in the First and Second World Wars*. Aldershot, 1953.

Kent, M. *Oil and Empire: British Policy and Mesopotamian Oil, 1900–1920*. London, 1976.

—— (ed.) *The Great Powers and the End of the Ottoman Empire*. London, 1984.

Khalidi, R. 'Arab nationalism in Syria, the formative years, 1908–1914', in *Nationalism in a Non-national State: The Dissolution of the Ottoman Empire*, ed. W. W. Haddadd and W. Ochsenwald, 207–37. Columbus, OH, 1977.

Kinross, Lord. *Ataturk: A Biography of Mustafa Kemal, Father of Modern Turkey*. New York, 1965.

Kirkbride, A. *An Awakening: The Arab Campaign, 1917–1918*. Tavistock, 1971.

Klieman, A. 'Britain's war aims in the Middle East in 1915', *Journal of Contemporary History* 3 (1968): 237–53.

Kress von Kressenstein, F. 'Zwischen Kaukasus und Sinai', *Jahrbuch des Bundes der Asienkampfer* (1921).

—— 'The campaign in Palestine from the enemy's side', *RUSI Journal* 6 (1922): 503–13.

—— *Mit dem Turken zum Suezkanal*. Berlin, 1938.

Kushner, D. (ed.). *Palestine in the Late Ottoman Period: Political, Social and Economic Transformation*. Jerusalem, 1986.

Landes, D. S. *Bankers and Pashas: International Finance and Economic Imperialism in Egypt*. New York, 1958.

Langley, G. F. *Sand, Sweat, and Camels: The Australian Companies of the Imperial Camel Corps*. Kilmore, 1976; paperback edn, Sydney, 1995.

Larcher, P. M. 'La campagne du général de Falkenhayn en Palestine (1917–1918)', *Revue militaire française* n.s. 18 (1925), 28–52, 176–186.

—— *La Guerre Turque dans la Guerre Mondiale*. Paris, 1926.

Lawrence, T. E. *Seven Pillars of Wisdom: A Triumph*, 5th edn. London, 1976.

Lesch, A. M. *Arab Politics in Palestine, 1917–1939: The Frustration of a Nationalist Movement*. Ithaca, NY, 1979.

Lewis, G. 'An Ottoman officer in Palestine, 1914–1918', in *Palestine in the Late Ottoman Period: Political, Social and Economic Transformation*, ed. D. Kushner, 402–15. Jerusalem, 1985.

Lighthall, W. S. 'The Royal Air Force in the Palestine campaign, 1917–1918', *Cross and Cockade Journal* 11 (1970): 169–80.

Lindsay, J. H. *The London Scottish in the Great War*. London, 1925.

Lloyd George, D. *War Memoirs*, vol. 4. London, 1935.

Lock, H. O. *With the British Army in the Holy Land*. London, 1919.

—— *History of the Fourth Battalion, History of the Dorsetshire Regiment, 1914–1919*. Dorchester, 1932.

—— *History of the Fifth Battalion, History of the Dorsetshire Regiment, 1914–1919*. Dorchester, 1932.

Lord, J. *Honor, Empire, the Life and Times of Colonel Richard Meinertzhagen*. New York, 1970.

Luxford, J. H. *With the Machine Gunners in France and Palestine: Official History of the New Zealand Machine Gun Corps*. Auckland, 1923.

McCance, S. *History of the Royal Munster Rifles*. Aldershot, 1927.

Macdonnell, N. 'The British campaign in Palestine', *Transactions of the Canadian Military Institute* 22 (1984): 120–34.

McKale, D. 'Germany and the Arab Question in the First World War', *Middle Eastern Studies* 29 (1993): 236–53.

MacMunn, Sir G., and C. Falls. *Military Operations, Egypt and Palestine*, vol. 1. The Official History of the War. London, 1928.

Macpherson, W., W. P. Herringham, T. R. Elliot and A. Balfour (eds.). *Medical Services*, vol. 1: *Hygiene of the War*. The Official History of the War. London, 1923.

Marlowe, J. *Spoiling the Egyptians*. London, 1974.

Martineau, C. D. *A History of the Royal Sussex Regiment*. Chichester, n.d.

Massey, W. T. *The Desert Campaigns*. London, 1918.

—— *How Jerusalem was Won: Being the Record of Allenby's Campaign in Palestine*. London, 1919.

—— *Allenby's Final Triumph*. London, 1920.

Maurice, Sir F. 'The campaigns in Palestine and Egypt 1914–1918 in relation to the general strategy of the war', *Army Quarterly* 18 (1929): 14–23.

—— *The 16th Foot: A History of the Bedfordshire and Hertfordshire Regiment*. London, 1931.

May, E. *Signal Corporal: The Story of the 2nd London Irish Rifles (2/18th Battalion, London Regiment), 1914–1918*. London, 1972.

Meinertzhagen, R. *Middle East Diary, 1917–1956*. London, 1959.

—— *Army Diary, 1899–1926*. Edinburgh, 1960.

Mejcher, H. 'British Middle East policy, 1917–1921: the inter-departmental level', *Journal of Contemporary History* 8 (1973).

Millett, A. R., and W. Murray. *Military Effectiveness*, vol. 1: *The First World War*. Boston MA, 1988.

Moberly, F. J. *The Campaign in Mesopotamia*, 4 vols., History of the Great War. London, 1923–7.

Monroe, E. *Britain's Moment in the Middle East, 1914–1956*. London, 1963.

Moody, R. H. S. *Historical Records of the Buffs, East Kent Regiment, 1914–1919*. London, 1922.

Moore, A. B. *The Mounted Riflemen in Sinai and Palestine*. Auckland, 1920.

More, J. *With Allenby's Crusaders*. London, 1923.

Murphy, C. C. R. *Soldiers of the Prophet*. London, 1921.

—— *The History of the Suffolk Regiment, 1914–1927*. London, 1928.

Murray, A. *Sir Archibald Murray's Despatches, 1916–1917*. London, 1920.

Neillands, R. *The Great War Generals on the Western Front, 1914–1918*. London, 1998.

Neulen, H. W. *Feldgrau in Jerusalem: Das Levantkorps des kaiserlichen Deutschland*. Munich, 1991.

Nevakivi, J. *Britain, France, and the Arab Middle East, 1914–1920*. London, 1969.

Newbolt, H. *Naval Operations*, vols. 4 and 5, History of the Great War. London, 1928, 1931.

Newell, J. 'Allenby and the Palestine campaign', in *The First World War and British Military History*, ed. B. Bond, 189–226. Oxford, 1991.

—— 'Learning the hard way: Allenby in Egypt and Palestine, 1917–1919', *The Journal of Strategic Studies* 14/3 (1991): 363–87.

Nicol, C. G. *The Story of Two Campaigns: Official War History of the Auckland Mounted Rifles Regiment, 1914–1919*. Auckland, 1921.

Nogales, R. de. *Four Years beneath the Crescent*, trans. M. Lee. London, 1926.

Nutting, G. W. *History of the Fourth Light Horse Brigade, Australian Imperial Forces, War 1914–1918*, ed. E. W. Hammond. Brisbane, 1953.

Ogilvie, D. D. *The Fife and Forfar Yeomanry*. London, 1921.

Olden, A. C. N. *Westralian Cavalry in the War: The Story of the 10th Light Horse Regiment AIF in the Great War, 1914–1918*. Melbourne, 1921.

Olson, W. J. *Britain's Elusive Empire in the Middle East, 1900–1921*. New York and London, 1982.

Orga, I. *Phoenix Ascendant: The Rise of Modern Turkey*. London, 1958.

Parfitt, G. A. (ed.). *Historical Records of the Herefordshire Light Infantry and its Predecessors*. Hereford, 1962.

Paterson, A. B. (Banjo). *Happy Dispatches*. Sydney, 1935.

Petre, F. L. *The History of the Norfolk Regiment, 1685–1918*, vol. 2: *1914–1918*. Norwich, [1926].

Pink, P. W. 'Meissner Pasha and the construction of railways in Palestine and neighbouring countries', in *Ottoman Palestine, 1800–1914: Studies in Economic and Social History*, ed. G. G. Gilbar, 179–218. London, 1990.

Ponsonby, C. *West Kent (QO) Yeomanry and 10th (Yeomanry) Batt., The Buffs, 1914–1919*. London, 1920.

Powles, C. G. *The New Zealanders in Sinai and Palestine*. The Official History of New Zealand's Effort in the Great War, vol. 3. Auckland, 1923.

—— (ed.) *The History of the Canterbury Mounted Rifles, 1914–1919*. Auckland, 1928.

Preston, R. M. P. *The Desert Mounted Corps: An Account of the Cavalry Operations in Palestine and Syria, 1917–1918*. London, 1921.

Pritchard, H. C. *History of the Corps of Royal Engineers*, vol. 5: *Palestine*. Chatham, 1952.

Pugsley, C. *The Anzac Experience: New Zealand, Australia, and Empire in the First World War*. Auckland, 2004.

Raleigh, W., and H. A. Jones. *The War in the Air*, vol. 5. The Official History of the War. Oxford, 1935.

Ramsaur, E. E. *The Young Turks: Prelude to the Revolution of 1908*. New York, 1957.

Reece, R. H. *Night Bombing with the Bedouins*. London, 1919.

Richardson, G. *After Gallipoli*. Hawick, 1992.

Richardson, J. D. *The History of the 7th Light Horse Regiment, AIF* Sydney, [1923].

Robertson, J. *With the Cameliers in Palestine*. Dunedin, 1938.

Robson, L. L. *The First AIF: A Study of its Recruitment, 1914–1918*. Melbourne, 1982.

Rolls, S. C. *Steel Chariots in the Desert*. London, 1937.

Rothwell, V. H. *British War Aims and Peace Diplomacy, 1914–1918*. Oxford, 1971.

Sachar, H. M. *The Emergence of the Middle East, 1914–1924*. New York, 1969.

Sainsbury, J. D. *The Hertfordshire Batteries, Royal Field Artillery*. Welwyn, 1996.

Sandars, M. L., and P. M. Taylor. *British Propaganda during the First World War*. London, 1982.

Sandars, R. *The High Walls of Jerusalem: A History of the Balfour Declaration and the Birth of the British Mandate for Palestine*. New York, 1983.

Sanders, L. von. *Five Years in Turkey*. Annapolis, MD, 1928.

Savage, R. *Allenby of Armageddon: A Record of the Career of Field Marshal Viscount Allenby*. London, 1925.

Schama, S. *Two Rothschilds and the Land of Israel*. London, 1978.

Shaw, R. J. H. (ed.) *The 23rd London Regiment, 1798–1919*. London, 1936.

Shaw, S. J., and E. K. Shaw. *History of the Ottoman Empire and Modern Turkey*, vol. 2: *Reform, Revolution and Republic: The Rise of Modern Turkey*. Cambridge, 1977.

Sheffy, Y. 'Institutionalised deception and perception reinforcement: Allenby's campaign in Palestine', in *Intelligence and Military Operations*, ed. M. Handel. London, 1990.

—— *British Military Intelligence in the Palestine Campaign, 1914–1918*. London, 1998.

—— 'The origins of the British breakthrough into South Palestine: the ANZAC raid on the Ottoman Railway, 1917', *Journal of Strategic Studies* 22 (1999): 124–47.

Simon-Eberhard, M. *Mit dem Asienkorps zur Palestine Front*. Berlin, 1927.

Simpson, C. V. *Maygar's Boys*. Mooroodoc, 1998.

Smith, N. C. *Men of Beersheba: A History of the 4th Light Horse Regiment, 1914–1919*. Gardenvale, Vic, 1993.

—— *The Third Australian Light Horse Regiment, 1914–1918*. Melbourne, 1993.

Sommers, C. *Temporary Crusaders*. London, 1919.

Stanley, W. R. 'Review of the Turkish Asiatic railways to 1918: some political-military considerations', *Journal of Transport History* 7 (1966): 189–203.

Starr, J., and C. Sweeney. *Forward, the History of the 2nd/14th Light Horse (Queensland Mounted Infantry)*. St Lucia, Qld, 1989.

Stein, L. *The Balfour Declaration*. London, 1961.

Steuber, Dr. *Jildirim: deutsche Streiter auf heiligen Boden*. Berlin, 1926.

Stewart, A. T. Q. *The Ulster Crisis*. London, 1967.

Stirling, W. F. *Safety Last*. London, 1953.

Stonham, C., and B. Freeman. *Historical Records of the Middlesex Yeomanry, 1797–1927*, ed. J. S. Judd. Chelsea, 1930.

Storrs, R. *Orientations*. London, 1937.

Sumner, I., and R. Wilson. *Yeomanry of the East Riding*. Beverley, 1993.

Sutherland, L. W. *Aces and Kings*. London, 1920.

Swann, J. C. *The Citizen Soldiers of Buckinghamshire, 1795–1926*. Aylesbury, 1930.

Sykes, C. H. *Cross Roads to Israel*. London, 1973.

Tallents, H. *The Sherwood Rangers Yeomanry in the Great War, 1914–1918*. London, 1926.

Tamplin, J. M. S. *The Lambeth and Southwark Volunteers*. London, 1965.

Tanenbaum, J. K. *France and the Arab Middle East, 1914–1920*. Philadelphia, 1978.

Tauber, E. 'The capture of the NILI spies: the Turkish version', *Intelligence and National Security* 6 (1991): 701–10.

—— *Arab Movements in the First World War*. London, 1993.

Teichman, O. *Diary of a Yeomanry MO*. London, 1921.

Thompson, C. W. *Records of the Dorset Yeomanry (Queen's Own), 1914–1919*. Sherborne, 1921.

Thompson, R. R. *The Fifty-Second (Lowland) Division, 1914–1918*. Glasgow, 1923.

Thorburn, A. D. *Amateur Gunners: The Adventures of an Amateur Soldier in France, Salonica and Palestine in the Royal Field Artillery*. Liverpool, [1934].

Tibawi, A. L. *Anglo-Arab Relations and the Question of Palestine, 1914–1921*. London, 1977.

Trimble, W. *The Story of the 6th Service Battalion of the Royal Inniskilling Fusiliers*. Enniskillen, [1919].

Trumpener, U. 'Liman von Sanders and the German-Ottoman alliance', *Journal of Contemporary History* 1 (1966): 179–82.

—— *Germany and the Ottoman Empire, 1914–1918.* Princeton, NJ, 1968.

—— 'German officers in the Ottoman Empire, 1880–1918', *Jahrbuch des Instituts fur deutsche Geschichte* 1 (1975): 30–43.

—— 'Suez, Baku and Gallipoli: the military dimension of the German–Ottoman coalition, 1914–1918', in *Coalition Warfare: An Uneasy Accord*, ed. K. Neilson and R. A. Prete, 29–51. Waterloo, Ontario, 1983.

Tuchman, B. *Bible and Sword: How the British came to Palestine.* London, 1982.

Usborne, C. V. *Smoke on the Horizon: Mediterranean Fighting, 1914–1918.* London, 1933.

Verey, A., *et al. The Berkshire Yeomanry, 200 Years of Yeoman Service.* Stroud, 1994.

Vernon, P. V. (ed.). *The Royal New South Wales Lancers, 1885–1985.* Parramatta, NSW, 1986.

Verrier, A. (ed.). *Agents of Empire, Anglo-Zionist Intelligence Operations, 1915–1919: Brigadier Walter Gibson, Aaron Aaronsohn and the NILI Ring.* London, 1995.

Walker, G. G. *The Honourable Artillery Company in the Great War, 1914–1919.* London, 1930.

Ward, C. H. D. *History of the 74th (Yeomanry) Division in Syria and Palestine.* London, 1922.

—— *History of the 53th (Welsh) Division, 1914–1918.* Cardiff, 1927.

—— *Regimental Records of the Royal Welch Fusiliers*, vol. 4: *1915–1919: Turkey – Bulgaria – Austria.* London, 1929.

Wasserstein, B. *The British in Palestine: The Mandatory Government and the Arab-Jewish Conflict, 1917–1929.* London, 1978.

Wasti, S. T. 'The defence of Medina, 1916–1919', *Middle Eastern Studies* 27 (1991): 642–53.

Wauchope, A. G. *A History of the Black Watch (Royal Highlanders) in the Great War*, vol. 3: *New Army.* London, 1926.

Wavell, A. P. 'The strategy of the campaigns of the Egyptian Expeditionary Force', *Army Quarterly* 3 (1922): 235–49.

—— *The Palestine Campaigns.* London, 1931.

—— *Allenby, a Study in Greatness: The Biography of Field-Marshall Viscount Allenby of Megiddo and Felixtowe*, vol. 1. London, 1940.

—— *Allenby: Soldier and Statesman.* London, 1946.

—— (ed.), *Other Men's Flowers: An Anthology of Poetry* (Harmondsworth, 1960)

Weber, F. G. *Eagles on the Crescent: Germany, Austria, and the Diplomacy of the Turkish Alliance.* Ithaca, 1970.

Weldon, L. B. *Hard Lying: Eastern Mediterranean, 1914–1919.* London, 1925.

Whitehorne, A. C., and Sir T. O. Marden. *The History of The Welch Regiment.* Cardiff, 1932.

Wilkie, A. H. *Official War History of the Wellington Mounted Rifles, 1914–1919.* Auckland, 1924.

Williams Wynn, R. W. H. W., and H. N. Stable. *The Historical Records of the Montgomeryshire Yeomanry*, vol. 2. Oswestry, 1926.

Wilson, L. C., and H. Wetherell, *History of the Fifth Light Horse Regiment, Australian Imperial Force, 1914–1919*. Sydney, 1926.

Wilson, R. H. *Palestine 1917*, ed. H. D. Millgate. Tunbridge Wells, 1987.

Winstone, H. V. F. *The Illicit Adventure: The Story of Political and Military Intelligence in the Middle East from 1898 to 1926*. London, 1982.

Wintringham, J. W. *With the Lincolnshire Yeomanry in Egypt and Palestine, 1914–1918*. Grimsby, 1979.

Wood, W. de R. *The History of the King's Shropshire Light Infantry in the Great War, 1914–1918*. London, 1925.

Woodward, D. R. *Lloyd George and the Generals*. Newark, NJ, 1983.

—— (ed.) *The Military Correspondence of Field Marshal Sir William Robertson, Chief of the Imperial General Staff, December 1915 – February 1918*. Army Records Society. London, 1989.

—— *Field Marshal Sir William Robertson, Chief of the Imperial General Staff in the Great War*. Westport, CT, 1998.

Wright, J. E. *Round about Jerusalem: Letters from the Holy Land*. London, 1918.

Wylly, H. C. *History of the Queen's Royal Regiment*, vol. 7. Aldershot, [1926].

—— *The Loyal North Lancashire Regiment*, vol. 2. London, 1933.

Wyrall, E. *The Die-Hards in the Great War*, vol. 2: *1916–1919*. London, [c.1930].

—— *The History of the Duke of Cornwall's Light Infantry, 1914–1919*. London, 1932.

Yapp, M. E. *The Making of the Modern Middle East, 1792–1923*. Harlow, 1987.

Young, J. *With the 52nd (Lowland) Division in three Continents*. Edinburgh, 1920.

Zeine, Z. N. *Arab-Turkish Relations and the Emergence of Arab Nationalism*. Beirut, 1958.

—— *The Struggle for Arab Independence: Western Diplomacy and the Rise and Fall of Faisal's Kingdom in Syria, 1914–1920*. Beirut, 1960.

Zurcher, E. J. *The Unionist Factor: The Role of the Committee of Union and Progress in the Turkish National Movement, 1905–1926*. Leiden, 1984.

—— 'Between death and desertion: the experience of the Ottoman soldier in World War I', *Turcica* 28 (1996): 235–58.

Index

(The Arabic article (*el-*, etc.) is ignored in the alphabetical listing.)